Competitive Regionalism
FTA Diffusion in the Pacific Rim

Edited by

Mireya Solís
Associate Professor, School of International Service, American University, USA

Barbara Stallings
William R. Rhodes Research Professor, Brown University, USA

and

Saori N. Katada
Associate Professor, School of International Relations, University of Southern California, USA

First published 2009 by
PALGRAVE MACMILLAN

Palgrave Macmillan in the UK is an imprint of Macmillan Publishers Limited, registered in England, company number 785998, of Houndmills, Basingstoke, Hampshire RG21 6XS.

Palgrave Macmillan in the US is a division of St Martin's Press LLC, 175 Fifth Avenue, New York, NY 10010.

Palgrave Macmillan is the global academic imprint of the above companies and has companies and representatives throughout the world.

Palgrave® and Macmillan® are registered trademarks in the United States, the United Kingdom, Europe and other countries.

ISBN-13: 978-0-230-57778-7   hardback
ISBN-10: 0-230-57778-4   hardback

This book is printed on paper suitable for recycling and made from fully managed and sustained forest sources. Logging, pulping and manufacturing processes are expected to conform to the environmental regulations of the country of origin.

A catalogue record for this book is available from the British Library.

Library of Congress Cataloging-in-Publication Data

Competitive regionalism : FTA diffusion in the Pacific Rim / edited by
    Mireya Solís ... [et al.].
        p. cm. — (International political economy series)
    Includes bibliographical references and index.
    ISBN 978-0-230-57778-7 (alk. paper)
    1. Free trade—Pacific Area. 2. Free trade—East Asia.
        3. Pacific Area—Commerce. 4. East Asia—Commerce. 5. Pacific Area—
        Commercial treaties. 6. East Asia—Commercial treaties.
        I. Solís, Mireya.

    HF2570.7.C66 2009
    382'.71095—dc22   2009013631

10 9 8 7 6 5 4 3 2 1
18 17 16 15 14 13 12 11 10 09

Printed and bound in Great Britain by
CPI Antony Rowe, Chippenham and Eastbourne

Contents

Figures

Tables

Acknowledgments

In carrying out this collaborative project involving participants from around the Pacific Rim, we owe numerous debts of gratitude to several individuals and institutions. Special thanks are owed to Shujiro Urata who played a pivotal role in the grant application process and who generously hosted our second conference at Waseda University in the spring of 2008. We are also extremely grateful to the Center for Global Partnership (CGP) of the Japan Foundation for financing the major portion of this research project. Without the support from CGP, the project would have never taken off, and we very much appreciate the help of its dedicated staff: Tomoki Akazawa, Carolyn Fleisher, and Melanie Standish. We feel extremely fortunate to have received additional financial support from other sources and take this opportunity to thank them all: the Japan–United States Friendship Commission; the Global COE Program-Global Institute for Asian Regional Integration (GIARI) and the Organization for Asian Studies (OAS) of Waseda University; and the Center for International Studies (CIS) at the University of Southern California (USC), as well as several of its other centers: the US–China Institute, the East Asian Studies Center, the Korean Studies Institute, the Marshall Business School, and the School of International Relations. In managing these grants, we benefited from the expertise and competence of Conrad Hohenlohe and Stefanie Drame at American University, and Indira Persad, Brianna Shepard, and Marisela Schaffer at USC.

We were fortunate to hold two international conferences. Both proved to be very productive opportunities for the exchange of ideas and allowed the project to mature intellectually. We first convened in December 2007 in Los Angeles, hosted by the CIS at USC. The Center's Director, James Patrick, was very supportive of our project, and Indira Persad did a splendid job in managing such a complex event. We met again in Tokyo the following spring hosted by Waseda University. We are grateful to Satoshi Amako, the program leader of the Global COE program at GIARI, for the warm welcome he accorded us, and to the following staff of GIARI and OAS for running such a smooth conference: Miki Honda, Masato Kamikubo, Atsuko Maruyama, Shoko Miyano, Yoji Osada, Kaoko Takahashi, and Atsuko Tsuriya.

At these two conferences and panels at the International Studies Association and the American Political Science Association, we benefited from the feedback of a very distinguished group of scholars, whose names are listed in alphabetical order as follows: Maxwell Cameron, Yukiko Fukagawa, Geoffrey Garrett, Stephan Haggard, Axel Huelsemeyer, Ken Jimbo, David Kang, Masahiro Kawai, Long Ke, Akira Kotera, Ellis Krauss, James Lehman,

Edward Lincoln, Noriyuki Mita, Gregory Noble, Jeff Nugent, John Odell, T. J. Pempel, Neantro Saavedra-Rivano, Jeffrey Schott, Richard Stubbs, Keiichi Tsunekawa, Yorizumi Watanabe, Susumu Yamakage, and Ming Wan. While we profited tremendously from their insights, they are in no way responsible for any errors that still remain.

We are also very grateful to the contributors of this edited volume. Their expertise, commitment, and wisdom allowed this project to move to a successful completion. The chapter authors agreed to multiple rounds of revisions displaying a lot of patience and good humor, and it was an honor and pleasure working with them.

We also want to convey our thanks to our diligent research assistants who put many hours of work gathering data, drafting tables, and cleaning up text: Jason Enia, Christina Faegri, Christina Gray, Yoko Konno, Vidal Seegobin, Tsuyoshi Takagi, Engin Volkan, and Jeanine Yutani.

Lastly, we want to acknowledge the love and support of our families. They are the ones to whom we are most indebted.

Mireya Solís, Washington, DC
Barbara Stallings, Providence, RI
Saori N. Katada, Los Angeles, CA

Abbreviations and Acronyms

ABAC	APEC Business Advisory Council
AD	Antidumping
ADA	Antidumping Agreement
AEC	ASEAN Economic Community
AFAS	ASEAN Framework Agreement on Services
AFTA	ASEAN Free Trade Area
AIA	ASEAN Investment Area
ALADI	Latin American Association for Integration (Spanish acronym)
ALBA	Bolivarian Alternative for the Americas (Spanish acronym)
APEC	Asia Pacific Economic Cooperation
ARF	ASEAN Regional Forum
ASEAN	Association of Southeast Asian Nations
ASEAN+3,	ASEAN+China, Japan, and South Korea
ASEAN+6	ASEAN+China, Japan, South Korea, Australia, New Zealand, and India
ASEAN-4	Indonesia, Malaysia, the Philippines, and Thailand
ASEAN-5	Indonesia, Malaysia, the Philippines, Singapore, and Thailand
ATPA	Andean Trade Preference Act
ATPDEA	Andean Trade Promotion and Drug Eradication Act
BITs	Bilateral investment treaties
CAFTA–DR	Costa Rica, El Salvador, Nicaragua, Honduras, Guatemala, and the Dominican Republic
CBERA	Caribbean Basin Economic Recovery Act
CEPA	Closer Economic Partnership Agreement
CEPEA	Comprehensive Economic Partnership in East Asia
CEPT	Common Effective Preferential Tariff
CGE	Computable general equilibrium
CLMV	Cambodia, Lao People's Democratic Republic, Myanmar, and Vietnam

CRS	Congressional Research Service
CSCE	Commission on Security and Cooperation in Europe
CU	Customs union
CVDs	Countervailing duties
DDA	Doha Development Agenda
DIRECON	General Directorate for International Economic Affairs (Spanish acronym)
DMZ	Demilitarized Zone
EACPF	East Asian Competition Policy Forum
EAEC	East Asia Economic Caucus
EAEG	East Asian Economic Group
EAFTA	East Asia Free Trade Agreement
EAI	Enterprise for ASEAN Initiative
EAS	East Asia Summit
EAVG	East Asia Vision Group
ECAs	Economic Complementation Agreements
ECSC	European Coal and Steel Community
EEZ	Exclusive Economic Zone
EFTA	European Free Trade Association
EPA	Economic Partnership Agreement
EU	European Union
EVSL	Early Voluntary Sectoral Liberalization
FDI	Foreign direct investment
FTA, FTAs	Free trade agreement(s)
FTAA	Free Trade Area of the Americas
FTAAP	Free Trade Area of the Asia-Pacific
GATS	General Agreement on Trade in Services
GATT	General Agreement on Tariffs and Trade
GCC	Gulf Cooperation Council
GDP	Gross domestic product
GTAP	Global Trade Analysis Project
HS	Harmonized System
IAPs	Individual action plans
ICN	International Competition Network

IISS	International Institute for Strategic Studies
ILO	International Labor Organization
IMF	International Monetary Fund
IPR	Intellectual property rights
ISI	Import-substitution Industrialization
JACEP	Japan–ASEAN Comprehensive Economic Partnership
JFTC	Japan's Fair Trade Commission
JSEPA	Japan–Singapore Economic Partnership Agreement
KMT	Kuomintang
KORUS FTA	South Korea–US Free Trade Agreement
LAIA	Latin American Integration Association
M&A	Mergers and acquisitions
MAI	Multilateral Agreement on Investment
Mercosur	Southern Cone Common Market (Spanish acronym)
METI	Ministry of Economy, Trade and Industry
MFN	Most favored nation
MNC	Multinational corporation
MOAF	Ministry of Agriculture and Forestry
MOCIE	Ministry of Commerce, Industry, and Energy
MOFA	Ministry of Foreign Affairs
MOFAT	Ministry of Foreign Affairs and Trade
MOFE	Ministry of Finance and Economy
MUSBC	Mexico–US Business Committee
NAFTA	North American Free Trade Agreement
NATO	North Atlantic Treaty Organization
NEACD	Northeast Asia Cooperation Dialogue
NGO, NGOs	Nongovernmental organization(s)
NIEs	Newly Industrializing Economies
NIEs4	Newly Industrializing Economies of Hong Kong, South Korea, Singapore, and Taiwan
NTBs	Nontariff barriers
NZ	New Zealand
OECD	Organisation for Economic Co-operation and Development

OMT	Office of the Minister for Trade
P-4	Pacific-4 (Chile, Singapore, New Zealand, and Brunei)
PRC	People's Republic of China
ROK	Republic of Korea
ROOs	Rules of origin
RTA, RTAs	Regional trade agreement(s)
S&D	Special and differential treatment
SACU	Southern African Customs Union
SPS	Sanitary and phytosanitary
TAC	Treaty of Amity and Cooperation
TIFA, TIFAs	Trade and Investment Framework Agreement(s)
TPA	Trade Promotion Authority
TRIMs	Trade-related investment measures
TRIPS	Trade-related aspects of intellectual property rights
TRQs	Tariff-rate quotas
USCFTA	US–Canada Free Trade Agreement
USTR	United States Trade Representative
WCO	World Customs Organization
WTO	World Trade Organization
WWII	World War II

Notes on Contributors

Aldo Flores-Quiroga is Clinical Professor at the Claremont Graduate University in California, and Affiliate Professor at the Center for Economic Research and Teaching (Centro de Investigación y Docencia Económica, CIDE) in Mexico City, where he teaches courses on public policy, international political economy, and economic development in Latin America. His research on the political economy of trade and exchange rate policy in Mexico has been published in Spanish and English, and includes "Proteccionismo versus Librecambio" (Fondo de Cultura Económica, 1998).

Saori N. Katada is Associate Professor at the School of International Relations, University of Southern California. She is the author of *Banking on Stability: Japan and the Cross-Pacific Dynamics of International Financial Crisis Management* (University of Michigan Press, 2001), which was awarded the Masayoshi Ohira Memorial Book Award in 2002. She also has two coedited books and numerous articles to her credit. Her current research focuses on the trade, financial, and monetary cooperation in East Asia. She received her PhD in Political Science from University of North Carolina at Chapel Hill.

Min Gyo Koo is Assistant Professor in the department of public administration at Yonsei University, Seoul, Korea. Dr. Koo has published his research in a wide range of journals, and is the coeditor of *Asia's New Institutional Architecture: Evolving Structures for Managing Trade, Financial, and Security Relations* (Springer, 2007). He is currently completing a book manuscript, *Island Disputes and Maritime Regime Building in East Asia* (Springer, forthcoming in summer 2009). He obtained his PhD from UC Berkeley.

Mike M. Mochizuki holds the Japan–US Relations Chair in Memory of Gaston Sigur at the Elliott School of International Affairs in George Washington University. Previously he was a senior fellow at the Brookings Institution, co-director of the Center for Asia-Pacific Policy at RAND and has taught at the University of Southern California and at Yale University. Besides numerous journal articles, his recent books include *Japan in International Politics: The Foreign Policies of an Adaptive State* (2007) and *The Okinawa Question and the U.S.–Japan Alliance* (2005).

Junji Nakagawa is Professor of International Economic Law at the Institute of Social Science, University of Tokyo. He has written and edited more than 20 books and about 100 articles and book chapters in the field of international trade law, international investment law, and international law for economic development including *International Harmonization of Economic Regulation* (Yuhikaku, 2008, in Japanese), *Anti-Dumping Laws and*

Practices of the New Users (Cameron May, 2007), and *Managing Development: Globalization, Economic Restructuring and Social Policy* (Routledge, 2006). He received his PhD in law from the University of Tokyo.

Cintia Quiliconi is a doctoral candidate in Political Science and International Relations at the University of Southern California. She holds a master's degree in Politics from New York University and a master's degree in International Relations from FLACSO-Argentina. She is also associate researcher and professor at FLACSO-Argentina and a member of the Latin American Trade Network. Her latest publications include: "US–Latin American Trade Relations: Path to the Future or Dead-End Street?" in R. Higgott and I. Malbaci (eds) (2008) *Political Consequences of Anti-Americanism.*

Mireya Solís is Associate Professor at the School of International Service of American University. She has authored *Banking on Multinationals: Public Credit and the Export of Japanese Sunset Industries* (Stanford University Press, 2004) and co-edited *Cross-Regional Trade Agreements: Understanding Fragmented Regionalism in East Asia* (Springer, 2008). She is a recipient of the Young Scholar Award from the Association of Japanese Business Studies, and Fulbright and Ford Foundation scholarships. She received her PhD from Harvard University.

Barbara Stallings is William R. Rhodes Research Professor at the Watson Institute for International Studies, Brown University. She is the editor of *Studies in Comparative International Development.* Previously, she was Director of the Economic Development Division of the UN Economic Commission for Latin America and the Caribbean in Santiago, Chile (1993–2002) and Professor of Political Economy at the University of Wisconsin-Madison (1975–1993). Her most recent book is *Finance for Development: Latin America in Comparative Perspective* (Brookings Institution Press, 2006).

Takashi Terada is a Professor of International Relations at Organization for Asian Studies, Waseda University. Previously, he was an assistant professor at the Faculty of Arts and Social Sciences, National University of Singapore. His most recent works include *Asia-Pacific Economic Cooperation: Critical Perspectives on the World Economy* (Routledge, 2007, 5 volumes), coedited with Peter Drysdale. He is the recipient of the 2005 J. G. Crawford Award. He received his PhD from Australian National University.

Shujiro Urata is Professor of Economics at Graduate School Asia-Pacific Studies, Waseda University; Faculty Fellow at the Research Institute of Economy, Trade and Industry; and Research Fellow at the Japanese Centre for Economic Research. He has been affiliated with the Brookings Institution and the World Bank, and has published and edited a number of books and articles on international economic issues. He received his MA and PhD in Economics from Stanford University.

Carol Wise is Associate Professor in the School of International Relations at University of Southern California. She has held the Carleton University Fulbright Chair in North American Studies, the Haynes Foundation Faculty Fellowship, the Earhart Foundation Fellowship, and the Woodrow Wilson Center's Public Policy Scholarship. She has written widely on issues pertaining to Latin American political economy, including four edited collections, and is currently completing a book on the decline of US influence in Latin America and the concomitant rise of China as a major trade and investment partner in the region.

Jian Yang is a Senior Lecturer in International Relations at the University of Auckland. He is the author of *Congress and US China Policy: 1989–1999* (2000). He has also published on international relations in the Asia-Pacific, Chinese politics, environmental politics, and human security. He holds the Auckland Branch chair of the New Zealand Institute of International Affairs; he is also New Zealand National member of Council for Security Cooperation in the Asia-Pacific and an Associate Editor of *The Journal of Human Security*. He received his PhD from the Australian National University.

1
Explaining FTA Proliferation: A Policy Diffusion Framework

Mireya Solís and Saori N. Katada

Introduction

In the past 15 years, the world trading system has experienced a major transformation with the rapid proliferation of free trade agreements (FTAs),[1] whereby members make special exemptions to the "most favored nation" principle of the World Trade Organization (WTO) and exchange preferential market access commitments. The increase in FTAs has indeed been phenomenal: from 80 such agreements reported to the WTO or its predecessor organization between 1948 and 1988, to 402 by July 2008 (see Figure 1.1). This FTA boom is all the more remarkable given the many doubts about the intrinsic value of these agreements: the low volumes of trade and investment covered, the red tape of crisscrossing rules of origin (ROOs), the asymmetrical bargaining dynamics that favor industrialized nations over small developing countries, and, in many cases, the low utilization of trade preferences. How then can we explain the rapid expansion of FTAs when their benefits are so much in doubt?

Other scholars have also found the brisk pace of FTA proliferation puzzling, and have mostly described it as a "rise of regionalism," which may undermine the nondiscrimination principle of the multilateral trading system. We argue in this book, however, that this conventional wisdom yields only a partial understanding of the drivers of FTA proliferation and its most important consequences. We posit that in order to understand the rapid expansion of FTAs, it is essential to factor in how these different sets of preferential trade agreements are *interconnected* (either because they generate externalities on nonmembers or because they disseminate novel policy paradigms). Next, we argue that understanding the causes of the rapid increase of FTAs is essential not only because of its impact on the WTO, but also because of its influence on the nature of regional integration––remarkably enough, a very important topic that has remained under the radar. FTAs can work *for* or *against* the emergence of coherent regional blocs, and we must explore which conditions favor one outcome over the other.

1

In order to analyze FTA proliferation, then, it is essential to explore diffusion dynamics arising from the interconnectedness of preferential trade negotiations, including but going beyond traditional economic considerations. For these purposes, we anchor our analysis of FTA proliferation in diffusion models, which have already demonstrated their usefulness in explaining the spread of economic and political liberalism (Elkins and Simmons, 2005; Simmons et al., 2006). We argue that the waves of bilateral trade agreements in the world economy approximate well the condition of "uncoordinated interdependence," as developed by diffusion theorists. In other words, the policy choices of governments are influenced by the actions of their peers, either because they alter the material payoffs or because they disseminate new information about the impact of these policies (Elkins and Simmons, 2005). In the process of analyzing FTA proliferation, we focus on two of the most powerful diffusion mechanisms, emulation and competition, to explore the extent to which policy paradigms propagated by like-minded elites or competitive goals articulated by business and government officials have contributed to the dissemination of FTAs. Furthermore, we offer a much broader conceptualization of competition than the one articulated by the diffusion literature as we take into account not only economic rivalry, but also competitive pressures arising from security and legal objectives as fueling interest in FTA negotiations.

The extent to which the competitive hypothesis is confirmed over the emulation hypothesis in the country case chapters has significant implications for a bedrock expectation in the FTA literature: that these preferential trade agreements promote regional integration.[2] Instead, if the competitive incentives behind FTA proliferation predominate, these preferential trade agreements may weaken the emergence of coherent trade blocs in several ways: eroding preferences created by earlier FTAs, diluting regional solidarity as individual members of existing trade groups negotiate separate trade deals with larger nations, and encouraging cross-regionalism or the development of competing FTA networks within the same region. An FTA competition that undermines, rather than strengthens, the emergence of a regionally coherent trade area is an intriguing proposition assessed by this book.[3]

In sum, this volume investigates a number of central questions regarding the nature of the international trading system and the future of regional integration: What is driving the worldwide explosion of FTAs? What explains the intense interest of so many states in FTAs despite their ambiguous benefits? Can FTA networks be the foundation for much more ambitious projects of regional integration and collaboration? We examine these important questions through a novel analytical approach that highlights the sources of policy diffusion.

The FTA strategies of important trading nations located on both sides of the Pacific Rim offer an ideal venue to test these arguments. Western Hemisphere countries, such as the United States, Mexico, and Chile, have been at the forefront of the FTA wave as they have negotiated multiple preferential deals at the bilateral and subregional level, while a region-wide FTA has remained elusive. Moreover, these active preferential traders have also signed FTAs with East Asian counterparts, which only recently launched an FTA track in their trade strategies. In fact, as the APEC (Asia Pacific Economic Cooperation) project, which sought to voluntarily liberalize trade among the Pacific Rim member countries, lost steam in the late 1990s, these cross-regional FTAs have acquired a much more central role in structuring trans-Pacific economic relations. The policy shift is especially remarkable for East Asian countries such as Japan, Korea, China, and the Association of Southeast Asian Nations (ASEAN), which are now putting aside their previous reluctance with respect to formal integration, and are rapidly signing FTAs that award preferential market access, impose binding commitments, and embrace some WTO-plus commitments.

To understand these developments, we argue that it is important to assess the extent to which the FTA policies of Pacific Rim countries are influenced by the externalities generated by prior actions of their peers; whether FTA diffusion in both the Western Hemisphere and East Asia approximates better the expectations of ideational emulation or economic competition; and within competitive dynamics, the extent to which governments' FTA policy is affected by the need to respond to multiple competitive pressures (economic, political, or legal).

This framework chapter is organized as follows. First, we review the general literature on FTA negotiation and the more specialized scholarship on the policy shift in favor of preferential trading in the Pacific Rim to highlight the contribution that our focus on the diffusion dynamics of FTA proliferation can make. Second, we offer an empirical overview of the rapid spread of FTAs. Third, we develop a model of FTA diffusion that contemplates two hypotheses— emulation and competition. Fourth, we discuss the implications of endorsing a multidimensional concept of competition that factors in economic, security, and legal pressures as triggers for preferential agreements. The final section summarizes the individual chapters in this volume.

Conventional views on FTA proliferation

Three schools of thought have heavily influenced our understanding of the central driving forces of FTA negotiation: economic interdependence, domestic lobbying and rent seeking, and state autonomy.

Economic interdependence

Neofunctionalism focuses on economic interdependence and argues that trade concentration is the most important spark for regional integration. Governments initially agree to pool sovereignty to manage the technical issues created by expanding economic transactions. But integration quickly acquires a life of its own due to the dynamics of functional spillover, for example, integration in one sector increases pressure to integrate other related industries.

Supranational and subnational actors, therefore, are the main engines of the integration locomotive (Haas, 1964). Mattli (1999) uses neofunctionalist logic to explain the demand side of regional integration: as flows of intra-regional trade and investment increase, private actors will call for the creation of supranational institutions that allow them to reduce the uncertainty and the transaction costs surrounding these cross-border economic transactions, and to reap the benefits of economies of scale.

While neofunctionalism identifies a powerful force for regional integration, it faces serious difficulties in explaining the timing of regional integration initiatives beyond Europe and the more specific choices countries make in selecting their trading partners. Economic interdependence is, in fact, a poor indicator of shifts in favor of regionalism. For example, intra-regional trade has consistently been higher for East Asia than for North America (as of 2003, 54% in East Asia and 46% in North America), and yet the United States, Canada, and Mexico moved much faster to negotiate a regional trade agreement (North American Free Trade Agreement, NAFTA) than the nations of East Asia.[4]

Domestic lobbying and rent-seeking

The role of domestic lobbies in pushing for trade-diverting agreements that yield rents for specific producer groups constitutes another line of analysis. Grossman and Helpman (1995) have led the way in developing formal models to explain when FTAs will be politically viable and the likely characteristics of these preferential trading agreements after clearing the political market. They deem possible the successful negotiation of an FTA only under three scenarios: (1) the benefits from trade creation win the support of consumer groups while import-competing industries fail to coordinate their opposition to the accord, (2) gains to exporters far surpass losses to disadvantaged industries, or (3) liberalization exemptions are carved out to protect sensitive sectors. These authors consider the latter two options far more likely since protection for most sectors is the political recipe to muster domestic support for preferential trade agreements. On the one hand, exporters protected by stiff ROOs and hefty external tariffs will endorse an agreement that guarantees them access to higher-priced regional markets. On the other hand, import-competing industries will not mount an opposition campaign if they are promised sectoral protection. Baldwin's (1997) "domino effect" model describes how the negotiation of trade-diverting agreements triggers a chain reaction of subsequent FTA enlargement, or the negotiation of alternative trade blocs, as disadvantaged non-member producers seek to minimize the trade and investment diversion caused by previous FTAs.

Models of domestic lobbying for (and to counter) trade-diverting FTAs offer a powerful account of the importance of sectoral rent-seeking in the search for preferential market access. The trade-diversion motive can only explain a subset of such FTAs, however, and it is quite clearly irrelevant in other instances. For example, Japan's first ever preferential trade agreement with Singapore (in force since 2002) was not informed by the desire to counter trade diversion since Singapore is already one of the most open economies in the world. More generally, domestic lobby arguments are hard pressed to explain the construction of regional institutions to satisfy proactive state agendas at the political level, such as to ameliorate regional tensions, favor allies, partake in trade and investment rule-making, and fend off against domestic lobby groups through the familiar "tying of hands" in international agreements.

State autonomy

Intergovernmentalism focuses on the autonomous objectives of states in embarking on official trade negotiations. According to this approach, states consent to pool sovereignty via regional integration to achieve joint gains that cannot be realized with purely national measures, or to gain leverage over domestic interest groups (Moravcsik, 1993). Alliance and security concerns are also part of the state calculation in engaging in more intense trade relations (Gowa, 1984). Dominated by the state agenda, regional integration proceeds as a series of "celebrated bargains" between heads of state. Preference convergence between political leaders is therefore an important precondition for regional integration. Power asymmetries are important in that the largest states in the bloc dominate negotiations. Policies adopted represent the lowest common denominator, the minimalist position on integration by one of the largest members. Small states will be persuaded to support the integration package through side payments, whereas recalcitrant larger states will be brought in through the fear of exclusion. Finally, states will grant any loss of discretionary power only after carefully weighing the benefits of integration, and they will consistently adopt safeguards (consensus voting rules for instance) to make sure national interests are not overridden by regional institutions (Moravcsik, 1991).

Critics of intergovernmentalism point out that its narrow depiction of regionalism as a series of discreet summitry events leaves out ongoing processes (market exchange), assumes away problems of implementation of high-level official bargains, and fails to explain the reasons behind the convergence of regional integration preferences among key members (Mattli, 1999: 29). Moreover, states are not interested only in supplying an integrated governance structure to lower risk and transaction costs (although an important goal in its own right). They also aim to achieve other economic and security diplomatic goals. Economic integration negotiations can serve as confidence-building measures to improve relations between potential rivals. States may embark on FTA diplomacy in order to bid for regional leadership through economic cooperative endeavors. Preferential trading blocs can also help states accomplish their foreign policy objectives in other forums, such as pushing for new rules on trade and investment that can later be incorporated at the multilateral level (World Bank, 2000b).

As this brief overview has shown, theories of regional integration have yielded a number of propositions regarding the incentives to negotiate FTAs.

From neofunctionalism, we should expect high levels of economic inter-dependence to energize the private sector to demand a regional economic governance structure that reduces transaction costs. From domestic lobbying models, we should expect industries to lobby for FTAs that offer rents through preferential market access or that aim to dissipate these rents by negotiating countervailing FTAs. And from intergovernmentalism, we should anticipate governments to be firmly in control of the integration agenda and to use these agreements to gain leverage over domestic interest groups.

Within the regionalism literature, we believe that Baldwin's domino effect has addressed the issue of FTA proliferation most effectively by highlighting how trade and investment diversion effects from initial FTAs can generate a chain reaction of subsequent preferential trade agreements. Yet we believe that diffusion models can shed new light on the dissemination of FTAs in at least three important ways. First, we can factor in the interplay of multiple com-petitive objectives in FTA negotiation, which go beyond the defensive economic interests of the domino theory, and include regional leadership contests and dissemination of alternative standards in regional integration. Second, our project posits an alternative hypothesis about FTA proliferation, which focuses on the role of ideas or policy paradigms as countries emulate successful FTA strategies of leading reference nations. In this way, our study entertains an alternative explanation for FTA diffusion with a markedly different expecta-tion about the nature of regional integration. If competition is the dominant force behind diffusion, we expect the recent FTA proliferation to work against the emergence of coherent regional integration projects. But if emulation prevails, we anticipate that bilateral FTAs will be supportive of region-wide inte-gration efforts. And third, this project looks more directly into how domestic policy formulation processes influence the manner in which governments respond to external diffusion pressures.

Current understanding of FTA proliferation in the Pacific Rim

First movers: FTA strategies of Western Hemisphere nations

Latin America's "old regionalism" did not produce substantive integration.[5] The predominant developmental model in the region during the 1960s and 1970s—import substitution industrialization—implied that the goal of creat-ing a preferential regional market would be achieved by maintaining exter-nal protective barriers, restricting foreign direct investment (FDI), allowing extensive national industrial planning, and exempting multiple sectors from liberalization (Devlin and Giordano, 2004). The staunch US support for the multilateral liberal economic system, and its suspicion of "parochial and local regionalism," further limited the chances of far-reaching hemispheric integra-tion (Feinberg, 2002: 127).

In the second half of the 1980s and early 1990s, a window of opportunity opened for the emergence of the "new regionalism" in the Western Hemisphere. The 1989 Canada–US FTA, spurred by Canadian concerns over US protectionism, was the first step (Baldwin, 1997). But it was Mexico's subsequent request in 1990 to negotiate an FTA with the United States (which became the trilateral NAFTA) that marked the turning point in the spread southward of the new type of FTA: a North–South trade agreement that endorses a hard law approach to the preferential liberalization of goods, services, and capital flows. Mexico's initiative reflected a much broader shift among Latin American countries in favor of neoliberal policies that emphasized the promotion of exports and FDI inflows.

The broad desire to create more outward-looking economic integration agreements was noticeable in the 1991 formation of the four-country (Brazil, Argentina, Paraguay, and Uruguay) Mercosur. It endorsed the notion of open regionalism, projected the creation of a customs union with a common external tariff, and attempted intra-regional tariff liberalization and FDI promotion. Moreover, spurred by the desire to replicate Mexico's preferential access to the US market, Chile began to explore NAFTA membership and launched a very active FTA strategy (as Mexico had done) in order to diversify its market access. The most ambitious project for region-wide integration, the Free Trade Area of the Americas (FTAA) launched in the 1994 Miami summit, reflected the desire among Latin American countries to pursue integration with the United States to secure market access and FDI inflows, lock in macroeconomic reforms, and consolidate democratic rule (Feinberg, 2002).

At the turn of the century, however, the prospects for subregional and regional integration began to falter. The 1999 Brazilian devaluation and the 2001 financial turbulence in Argentina triggered bitter competition between Brazil and Argentina, and both reverted to protectionist measures. Mercosur also exhibited other fundamental weaknesses such as lack of institutionalization and meager macroeconomic coordination (Preusse, 2004: 131). The FTAA negotiations did not make the 2005 deadline and are currently in limbo. Oliveira (2007: 125) argues that the fundamental reason for this breakdown in the negotiation process is that Latin American countries are not willing to forego their development status (as Mexico did in NAFTA), and want the concession package to reflect the huge North–South asymmetries in the region.

The 2001 shift in US trade policy in favor of "competitive liberalization"[6] (the negotiation of bilateral FTAs with certain nations in order to stimulate negotiations in other trade fronts) also drastically reduced the incentives for Latin American countries to pursue the FTAA. Instead of perceiving the FTAA as the best way to secure preferential access to the US market, many of them opted for the faster bilateral route (Zabludovsky and Gómez, 2007: 99). With competitive liberalization, FTAs have become a cornerstone of US trade strategy and not a mere *ad hoc* deviation from multilateralism. The active FTA policies of the United States, Mexico, and Chile have generated a veritable boom of preferential trade agreements in the hemisphere and later on with Europe. More recently, these Western Hemisphere countries have set their sights on East Asia, the newest theater for the dramatic proliferation of preferential trade agreements.

The latest bandwagon: East Asia joins the FTA boom

Prior to the 1997 financial crisis, East Asia was commonly praised as a high-performing region, where webs of trade and investment had been established not through formal intergovernmental agreements, but rather through the private sector and, more specifically, through Japanese multinational corporations or by business networks of the overseas Chinese (Hatch and Yamamura, 1996). Even the region's most ambitious project of trade liberalization, APEC, seemed to confirm this regional distaste for formal and preferential integration. APEC promised to deliver trade and investment liberalization by the year 2020 based on voluntarism, nonbinding commitments, and most importantly, non-discrimination (Higgott and Stubbs, 1995).

Since the late 1990s, however, East Asian countries have negotiated multiple FTAs, which award preferential market access, impose binding commitments, and embrace numerous WTO-plus commitments. The key question is why? In search for answers, the growing literature on East Asian regionalism has focused on three main aspects: the triggers for policy change, the drivers of the FTA policy track, and the likely consequences of FTA proliferation for the construction of broader regional institutions and the multilateral trading system. Regarding the origins of regional institution building in East Asia, Pempel (2005: 9–11) argues that the region is ripe for cooperation today due to long-term changes, which include increased economic interdependence in East Asia, China's reintegration into the region, and growing cooperation among countries belonging to ASEAN. Other accounts of FTA proliferation in the region focus on a number of recent external shocks. These shocks raised serious concerns about the performance of international trade institutions, including the WTO, APEC, and the ASEAN Free Trade Area or AFTA (Aggarwal, 2006; Krauss, 2003: 317–18; Dent, 2003) and/or challenged the wisdom of exclusively pursuing *de facto* market integration in a world characterized by growing trade blocs and financial instability (Aggarwal, 2006; Lincoln, 2004).

A heated debate has ensued regarding the essential drivers of East Asia's turn to FTAs. Some analysts emphasize the fact that FTA diplomacy is by no means a repeal of statist policies. Bowles (2002: 259–60), for example, explains Japan's recent economic bilateralism as the use of a new mechanism to achieve goals long sought by a developmental state: promotion of a division of labor in East Asia where Japan plays a key role as supplier of technology and capital, where intra-regional exports provide new stimulus to economic growth, and where Japanese subsidiaries in the region capture a sizable portion of the intra-regional trade. Through a broader examination of bilateral FTAs among Asia-Pacific nations, Aggarwal and Koo (2005) reach the conclusion that interest group politics has not been a very powerful driver of these initiatives, thereby reinforcing the conclusion that the strong state is at the center of these bilateral trade negotiations.

And yet, other scholars have portrayed interest group lobbying and non-state actors as powerful agents influencing the actual content of FTAs. For instance, Katzenstein (2006) argues that the porous region of East Asia is experiencing a process of hybrid regionalism whereby new and mostly non-state actors heavily influence this process. Similarly, Munakata (2006a) concludes that East Asian governments have finally started to engage in FTAs to "catch up with the market." In the specific case of Japan, the industrial sector through its umbrella organization, Keidanren, has been pivotal in launching an FTA track in Japanese trade policy (Solís, 2003; Yoshimatsu, 2005). At the same time, the agricultural lobby has very skillfully defined the upper ceiling for farm liberalization (Mulgan, 2005; Solís and Katada, 2007a). Ravenhill's (2005) analysis of the essential features of Asia-Pacific bilateralism reaches similar conclusions in that these agreements are plagued with sectoral exemptions for sensitive sectors, so much so that they might not be compatible with Article 24 of the WTO, which requires FTAs to cover "substantially all the trade" between the countries under the agreement.

Finally, recent scholarship on East Asian regionalism has explored the impact of bilateral FTAs on broader regional trade initiatives and the multilateral trading system. As Aggarwal (2006: 20) puts it, it is important to analyze whether these FTAs are nested in broader agreements or whether they overlap by endorsing different principles of trade liberalization. Dent (2003) offers an optimistic account of how crisscrossing bilaterals (which he labels "lattice regionalism") will create momentum for broader regional integration because there is convergence on the trade liberalization mode (preferential agreements based on specific reciprocity), and because there is strong pressure to streamline the "noodle bowl." Ravenhill (2005), however, reaches the opposite conclusion in that trade-diverting bilateral agreements have weakened the domestic coalition in favor of liberalization (by creating vested interests that endorse preferential export access and protection of weak sectors), thereby undermining the momentum for multilateral liberalization.

In sum, the existing literature on regional integration in the Western Hemisphere has clarified the importance of the shift toward a more open developmental model in Latin America in explaining the new popularity of FTAs. It has also analyzed the causes and the impact of the emergence of "competitive liberalization" in US trade policy. The recent surge of scholarship on East Asian regionalism has helped clarify the external triggers behind the policy change, the importance of domestic politics in each country's FTA approach, and the ways in which emerging FTAs mesh (or not) with already existing trade governance frameworks. We seek to build upon these insights, but we argue that the scholarship to date has neglected a fundamental aspect of FTA proliferation in the Pacific Rim. That is the interconnection among different sets of FTA negotiations both within regions (Western Hemisphere and East Asia) and across them. In other words, it is important to assess the extent to which the FTA policies of Pacific Rim countries are influenced by the externalities generated by prior actions of their peers; whether FTA diffusion in the region approximates better the expectations of ideational policy diffusion or economic competition; and within competitive dynamics, the extent to which governments' FTA policies are affected by the need to respond to multiple competitive pressures (economic, security, or legal) that may or may not be compatible at different points in time.

The state of play in FTA proliferation

The temporal clustering of FTAs is unmistakable. Figure 1.1 shows the rapid increase in the cumulative number of preferential trade agreements since the early 1990s. It also shows the traditional S-shaped curve found in studies of innovation diffusion in diverse settings (Gray, 1994; Simmons et al., 2006).

A look at the types of countries partaking in the FTA proliferation also generates interesting findings. Up to the late 1980s, the most common type of FTA involved industrialized nations, but since then we find more diversity in the types of partnerships established through FTAs: North–South and South–South trade agreements. For instance, in the 2000s (as of March 2007), out of 113 FTAs notified to the WTO, 50 (44%) were between developed and developing countries, and 34 (30%) were among developing countries (see Figure 1.2).[7] These figures then corroborate a widening acceptance of FTAs in the developing world (of the developing country WTO members, only Mongolia is not part of at least one FTA). There is also growing interest among industrialized nations in negotiating preferential market access with countries at much lower income levels.

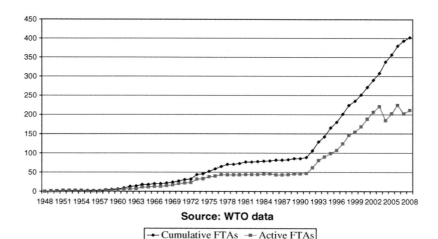

Source: WTO data

— Cumulative FTAs   — Active FTAs

Figure 1.1   FTA diffusion: S-curve

Figure 1.3 shows that throughout the postwar period, and certainly during the latest wave of free trade agreements, the vast majority of the new FTAs were "greenfield" agreements established among new sets of countries, rather than representing expansion of the old ones. In fact, most of the accessions

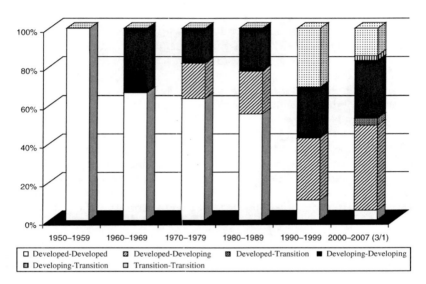

Figure 1.2 FTA partnerships among developed and developing countries

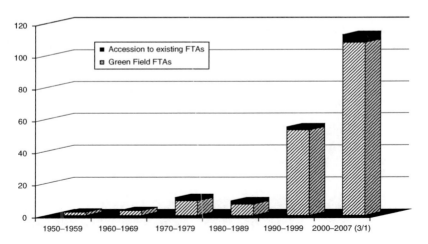

Figure 1.3 FTA diffusion: Enlargement versus proliferation (number of FTAs reported to the GATT/WTO by decade)

involved rounds of enlargement in the European integration process, whereas elsewhere in the world the dominant trend by far was the negotiation of alternative FTAs. Geographically speaking, the majority of the recent FTAs are cross-regional FTAs. In the first half of the 2000s, for example, 58 (51%) out of 113 FTAs were cross-regional (Solís and Katada, 2007a).[8] These two observations do not bode well for the expectation that FTAs will yield region-wide coherent integration blocs, and they again underscore the importance of assessing whether this clustered and fragmented pattern of FTA diffusion results from competitive dynamics to be explored in more detail shortly.

Finally, a striking fact of the recent wave of FTAs is that they only cover a modest volume of trade. As illustrated in tables in the country chapters, only a few FTAs such as NAFTA cover a large proportion of trade for contracting parties. Therefore, standard arguments about the desire to maximize aggregate welfare gains by negotiating with large economic partners as the main motivation for preferential trade agreements cannot account for most FTA agreements in recent years. Instead, we propose to tease out alternative mechanisms to explain FTA proliferation, which include the dissemination of policy paradigms through cross-country policy networks or the multiplier effect of strategic interaction among states and interest groups as they maneuver for competitive advantage.

The analytics of FTA diffusion

Our central objective is to explain the dissemination of FTA policies by using diffusion models. Diffusion occurs when "the prior adoption of a trait or practice in a population alters the probability of adoption for remaining non-adopters" (Strang, 1991: 325). As Garrett et al. (2008: 344) have argued, diffusion models challenge the conventional *modus operandi* in political science of explaining policy outcomes as domestic responses to common external shocks. Instead, the diffusion literature takes "Galton's problem" (the interdependence of government choices)[9] seriously and makes it the central analytical focus (Braun and Gilardi, 2007). Therefore, in developing a diffusion argument to explain FTA proliferation, we posit here that a government's decision to pursue this policy innovation is influenced by the actions of other countries and is not determined purely by domestic factors.

The next analytical task, of course, is to ascertain the ways in which prior actions of governments affect the likelihood that other countries will follow suit with similar policies. The literature recognizes four main mechanisms of diffusion: (1) "competition" as a horizontal economic process whereby countries adopt policies to enhance their attractiveness vis-à-vis competitors, (2) "coercion" as strong countries pressure or manipulate incentives to force weaker countries to adopt a practice, (3) "rational learning" as countries adopt a policy after they assess it objectively and learn that it produces benefits, and (4) "emulation" as countries adopt policies that they deem appropriate, frequently following the lead of strong countries or socio-cultural peers (Simmons et al., 2006; Dobbin et al., 2007).

The diffusion literature has already made significant contributions to our understanding of the cross-border dissemination of economic and political liberalism (Elkins and Simmons, 2005). Nonetheless, this literature is still confronted with the challenge of clearly demarcating among the alternative mechanisms that increase the likelihood of policy convergence. For instance, soft coercion or emulation are hard to distinguish, given that in both cases, powerful countries emerge as the key focal point of policy convergence. Rational learning and competition may also be difficult to separate since countries may pursue policies that have proven successful in order to keep up with competitors. At the same time, epistemic communities are considered important vehicles for the dissemination of policy paradigms both in the rational learning and in the emulation mechanisms.

For these reasons, we propose to conflate these mechanisms into two distinct possibilities: emulation and competition. As Dobbin et al. (2007) argue, emulation offers a constructivist understanding of policy diffusion since it focuses on the role of ideas and the importance of social acceptance of the dissemination process. Policies diffuse not because of an objective examination of their effectiveness, but rather because of the meaning they hold for policy makers and by notions of their appropriateness. Policy paradigms offer cognitive maps that greatly influence policymakers, since they provide "a framework of ideas and standards that specifies not only the goals of policy and the kind of instruments that can be used to attain them, but also the very nature of the problems they are meant to be addressing" (Hall, 1993: 279). Simmons et al. (2006: 801) distinguish three main emulation processes: (1) powerful countries that are used as examples, (2) epistemic communities advocating particular policies, and (3) influence from socio-cultural peer groups. In the first instance, leading countries become the key reference point as policymakers will copy from "the largest, richest, or fastest-growing countries" (Dobbin et al., 2007: 452). In the second case, as professional economists endorse new policy paradigms, they influence the adoption of policies in areas as diverse as privatization strategies in Latin America and Europe (Meseguer, 2004) or European monetary integration (McNamara, 1999). Swank's (2006: 859–60) work on the dissemination of tax reform views emulation along the lines of the third mechanism, in that shared cultures and political histories pave the way for dissemination in a manner he portrays as akin to what the sociologist Castles described in his work about "families of nations."

Furthermore, the role of ideas in promoting regional integration or the spread of FTAs is receiving greater attention. Acharya (2000), for instance, focuses on the importance of regionalist discourses to the process of region building. Oyane (2003: 107–8) describes the recent wave of FTAs in East Asia as one more example of policy bandwagoning. The World Bank (2000b) concurs that policy mimicry seems to be an important factor behind the spread of regionalism. Just as in the past, Keynesianism or trade liberalism became entrenched concepts influencing policy-making, the idea of preferential trade agreements shapes the way policy makers define their interests and plot their foreign economic strategies. Policy networks (composed of epistemic communities in universities and think tanks and/or technocratic bureaucratic elites) become critical channels through which emulation and dissemination of ideas take place. These channels are expected to aid the rapid diffusion of ideas regarding regional preferential trading arrangements among like-minded countries with social, cultural, and historical ties.

The competitive diffusion of policies, by contrast, takes place when a country's actions generate externalities for others, thereby creating an incentive to respond in kind (Braun and Gilardi, 2007). When a competitor adopts a policy, the other country follows suit to remain attractive to foreign capital or to avoid loss of market share. More than national efficiency gains, competition arguments "stress the differential attractiveness of certain policies to investors and buyers in international markets" (Simmons et al., 2006: 792). So, concern with investment diversion encourages developing nations to use bilateral investment treaties (BITs) to generate credible commitments on the fair treatment of foreign capital and outbid other potential hosts (Elkins et al., 2006: 825). Competitive diffusion models share several assumptions: (a) the policy innovation has the potential to influence material outcomes (FDI inflows, market share), (b) these effects can be felt in the short to medium term so it makes sense for elected officials to adopt the new policies and claim credit, (c) countries know which nations they are competing against and how intense the competition is,[10] and (d) competition is a horizontal process amongst one's peers (Simmons et al., 2006: 792–3).

The diffusion literature, therefore, defines competition exclusively as an economic phenomenon that mostly affects countries lacking credibility or capital (mostly developing nations). In our view, however, competition—understood as the quest for relative advantage—is a multidimensional phenomenon comprising economic, political, and legal elements, which affects both large/industrialized nations and small/less advanced countries competing with their peers to secure preferential access abroad for their internationalized business sectors, to gain regional status, or to become more influential in defining the direction of the multilateral trading system. In short, the process involves complex strategic calculations on the part of states as they engage in FTA negotiations. Therefore, there is no guarantee that governments in the region will pursue coherent region-wide FTAs, as each country is influenced by a particular set of competitive pressures.

After clarifying the concepts of emulation and competition, we proceed to flesh out three testable hypotheses:

Non-diffusion hypothesis.   A country's decision to launch an active FTA policy is not affected by the prior decision of other countries to negotiate preferential trade agreements (this is the null hypothesis for a diffusion model: independent decision making). Forerunners of FTA negotiation, therefore, launch the new trade policy track as a response to an external shock and/or a domestic political realignment, but *not* because they are trying to copy or neutralize the FTA policy of other nations.

Emulation hypothesis.   Countries will copy the FTA policies of their socio-cultural peers (identified by "psychological distance": common language, religion, history) or of leading nations, as cross-national policy networks play a pivotal role in the embracing of an FTA track. FTA policies that disseminate through emulation should be "omnidirectional" (that is to say, once preferential trade agreements are deemed an appropriate international trade instrument, governments should be interested in negotiating as many FTAs as possible with little concern about sequencing) and "homogeneous" (FTAs should comprise standard rules that closely mirror those of reference nations).

Competition hypothesis.   Countries will counteract the FTA policies of their competitors (identified by "competitive distance": competition over markets and capital, status/leadership contests, and articulation of alternative models of economic integration). Business and economic bureaucrats concerned with trade and investment diversion and/or politicians and foreign affairs officials focused on the foreign policy implications of FTAs should be the main agents behind the country's trade policy shift. FTA policies that spread through competition should be more "selective" (that is to say, the pattern of counterpart choice, market access commitments, and rule-making in FTAs should reflect the desire to create or restore competitive advantage) and "heterogeneous" (FTAs should comprise a distinct package of trade and investment rules).

These hypotheses, therefore, generate distinct expectations as to how and when countries will be sensitive to the actions of others (either reference nations or competitors); which domestic constituencies will champion the policy shift; and what are the observable implications of either emulation or competition in FTA outcomes. Moreover, these competing hypotheses also hold opposing views on the prospects of regional integration. While emulation should lead to a more coherent regional free trade area, as countries imitate their cultural peers in adopting more homogeneous trade agreements, competition should produce fragmented and inconsistent FTAs within the same region or cross-regional agreements (see Table 1.1).

In order to operationalize these variables, we have constructed aggregate measurements of competitive distance. The intensities with which pairs of countries compete in third markets, which has been arrived at by comparing the similarities in their export profiles (by market of destination), can be seen in Table 1.2. If two countries mostly export to the same markets, they should report higher ratios. It can be seen that there is very intense competition (dark shade) between Japan and China, Mexico and the United States, as well

Table 1.1 FTA diffusion: Emulation versus competition

Diffusion pressures	Domestic policy-making process*	Country FTA outcomes	Regional integration outcomes
Emulation			
Prior actions of socio-cultural peers or leading nations increase information about a policy and pave way for its social acceptance	Policy networks (epistemic communities in universities/think tanks and/or technocratic bureaucratic elites) advocate the FTA policy shift	*Omnidirectional* (negotiate with as many partners as possible with little concern about sequencing) *Homogenous* (negotiate FTAs with standard rules that mirror closely those of reference nations)	Coherent regional integration process as shared views on the merits of FTAs and homogenous agreements pave for the wave for rounds of enlargements
Competition			
Prior actions of competitors that • create trade and investment diversion, and/or • increase the relative influence of rival states, and/or • disseminate alternative models of regional integration	Business groups, economic bureaucrats, politicians, or foreign affairs officials push for FTA policy shift	*Selective* (choice of partners, timing of negotiations, and market access commitments reflect strategic calculus to advance competitive advantage) *Heterogenous* (push for distinct packages of trade and investment rules)	Fragmented regional integration process as competitive dynamics produce preference erosion of earlier FTAs, weaken the solidarity of existing regional subgroups as individual members negotiate separate trade deals, encourage cross-regionalism and/or the development of parallel FTA networks

* The model is agnostic on whether the policy-making process is top-down or bottom-up and expects national variation in decision-making patterns.

Table 1.2 Competitive distance: Similarity in export profiles by market of destination (average 1995–2005)

	China, P.R.	Japan	US	Mexico	Korea	Malaysia	Singapore	Thailand	Indonesia	Philippines	Chile
China, P.R.	1										
Japan	0.996	1									
United States	0.751	0.755	1								
Mexico	0.664	0.667	0.884	1							
Korea	0.314	0.316	0.419	0.473	1						
Malaysia	0.210	0.211	0.279	0.316	0.667	1					
Singapore	0.164	0.165	0.219	0.247	0.523	0.784	1				
Thailand	0.140	0.141	0.187	0.211	0.446	0.670	0.854	1			
Indonesia	0.114	0.115	0.152	0.172	0.363	0.544	0.694	0.812	1		
Philippines	0.091	0.091	0.121	0.137	0.289	0.433	0.552	0.647	0.796	1	
Chile	0.039	0.039	0.051	0.058	0.123	0.185	0.235	0.276	0.339	0.426	1

■ = 0.99–0.80; ▨ = 0.79–0.60; ▨ = 0.59–0.40; □ = 0.39–0.20; □ = 0.19–0.00.

The competitive distance is calculated based on the following method:
1. The export profile of each country is first estimated through a weighted sum of each of its trading partner's export share multiplied by that partner's share of world imports.
2. Next, the export profiles of pairs of countries are compared as a simple ratio. The higher the ratio, the more similar is their distribution of exports by market of destination.

Source: IMF, Direction of Trade Yearbook.

as Thailand with both Singapore and Indonesia. The country that reports the lowest ratios of competition is Chile.

Another way to measure the sensitivity of countries to developments in selected overseas markets is by ascertaining their export concentration. For instance, in Table 1.3, extreme dependence of Mexico on the US market (82% of all its exports) is seen; for all other countries listed in the table, the US is a main outlet for their products. The Japanese market is also important for many of the Northeast and Southeast Asian countries listed in the table. Any decision of these large markets to grant trade preferences to third parties should weigh heavily on these exporters.[11]

Going beyond the insights of these aggregate figures, we opt for process tracing methodology to assess whether a country's FTA policy is influenced by emulative or competitive diffusion forces. This qualitative methodology captures the less easily quantifiable signs of emulation and competition, such as the emergence of policy paradigms, intense industry rivalries that are not captured by aggregate levels of economic exchange, diplomatic contests to enhance regional influence or security, and attempts to disseminate new rules on trade and investment. Our qualitative methodology informs the structure of all country chapters in Parts 2 and 3, as they test the alternative hypotheses outlined above. In so doing, these chapters ask three basic questions: (a) What triggered the policy change (exogenous change and independent response or the actions of socio-cultural peers or competitors)? (b) How were the international pressures for diffusion channeled through the domestic policymaking process (who mobilized in favor of FTAs—policy networks, business lobbies, or politicians—and/or is the decision making process top-down or bottom-up?) (c) To what extent do FTA outcomes (in terms of the timing and selection of countries, market access, and rules commitments) approximate better the expectations of emulation or competition mechanisms?

Competition as a multidimensional concept

Besides fleshing out three alternative hypotheses of FTA proliferation, this study contributes to the diffusion literature by fine-tuning the concept of competition as a multidimensional process comprising economic, security, and legal motivations. In order to understand more fully how FTAs can be used to advance competitive goals along these issue-areas, three thematic chapters explore in depth the different logics of FTA competition. We summarize briefly these logics below, in order to discuss the implications of adopting a more expansive view of the range of competitive pressures and goals at stake in FTA proliferation.

Economic competition

Contrary to the most favored nation principle of the WTO, the essence of FTAs is the exchange of trade and investment preferences that are not made

Table 1.3 Key destination markets of selected exporters

Importer	Exporter										
	China, P.R.	Japan	United States	Mexico	Korea	Malaysia	Singapore	Thailand	Indonesia	Philippines	Chile
United States (17%)	25.88	26.23	—	81.83	19.39	20.43	16.41	20.16	16.06	26.25	17.46
Germany (8%)	4.64	4.62	5.10	0.94	3.27	2.98	3.37	3.13	3.61	4.30	4.15
Japan (5.4%)	12.84	—	8.68	1.29	10.03	10.47	5.55	14.24	23.78	14.54	13.53
France (5.1%)	1.92	1.62	2.98	0.38	1.16	1.23	2.05	1.67	1.43	0.79	3.64
United Kingdom (5%)	2.07	2.98	5.16	0.51	2.44	2.79	4.05	3.14	2.54	3.34	3.03
Italy (3.8%)	1.71	1.07	1.45	0.20	1.31	0.58	0.39	1.22	1.65	0.44	4.22
Canada (3.6%)	2.28	2.17	19.73	5.45	1.89	1.42	0.83	1.56	1.04	1.73	2.44
China, P.R. (3.6%)	—	10.21	3.34	0.59	16.94	6.79	6.61	7.09	6.59	8.27	7.06

Each cell in the column shows that share of an importer in the total exports of an exporter. For example, 25.88 percent of China's exports go to the United States. Importers are sorted by their share of total world imports (percentages in parentheses after the name of the country).

available to third parties. Preferential liberalization, therefore, creates new incentives for private sector lobbies and governments to achieve competitive goals through these agreements. On the economic front, these objectives include improved market access through tariff and investment liberalization, the harmonization of product standards, policy coordination in areas such as competition and antidumping, or the elimination of non-tariff barriers (NTBs). Because these concessions are only extended to FTA parties, they enable member companies to out-compete their rivals through preferential treatment. FTAs also offer a potent form of nontransparent protectionism through ROOs that can be manipulated to disadvantage non-member producers. Excluded parties, therefore, have a strong incentive to negotiate countervailing FTAs to minimize the effects of trade and investment diversion.[12]

These series of moves and countermoves of FTA negotiations create another competitive element that has received less scholarly attention: "concession linkage." With the rapid multiplication of FTAs, preference erosion has become a real problem because the initial advantages secured by members of the first FTA are undermined when similar benefits are extended to other countries through subsequent preferential trade negotiations. Governments have adjusted to this possibility by introducing renegotiation clauses and periodic updating of preferences. FTA concessions are, therefore, not fixed, but can be adjusted over time. Concession linkage also has signaling effects that influence a country's bargaining behavior because tariff concessions in current FTA talks become the minimum baseline for future FTA negotiations. This "shadow of the future" frequently persuades governments to adopt more defensive positions in on-going FTA talks, lest they lose bargaining power in subsequent FTAs.

In sum, FTAs offer interest groups and governments the ability to get ahead in international economic competition in several different ways: preferential trade and investment access, onerous ROOs for non-members, targeting of rents for investors and exporters while maintaining the mantle of protection for uncompetitive sectors, and concession linkage to secure better deals in subsequent trade talks.

In Chapter 2, Shujiro Urata reviews the theories of economic determinants of FTAs and empirical analyses of the welfare impacts of these agreements. He finds that defensive economic motives (the perceived need to counter trade diversion) have largely fueled the FTA wave in East Asia, and that this competition has been most acute between Japan and China.

Political/security competition

FTAs are also pursued to achieve noneconomic foreign policy objectives. Traditionally, this agenda has been discussed in terms of alliance politics. FTAs can affect interstate alignment patterns by establishing closer economic links with security partners, employing them as confidence building measures vis-à-vis rivals, or using them instead to isolate competitors by excluding them from economic cooperation agreements negotiated with other nations.

FTAs can also be used to increase a country's political influence or status. The degree of ambition on this front is heavily influenced by a country's power resources (both hard and soft forms of power).

For major powers, then, it is about emerging as credible regional leaders capable of acting as focal points in the integration process. This process defines the membership of regional blocs, the sequence of the integration movement, and the offering—if necessary—of side payments. Political rivalry among major powers, therefore, can inhibit the emergence of encompassing FTAs. For secondary powers, FTAs are a good instrument to reduce political-security vulnerability and/or to reinforce security ties with patron states. FTAs also offer the opportunity of acquiring greater visibility in the politics of international trade as medium-sized nations establish themselves as trade hubs. Chile, Mexico, South Korea, and ASEAN have emphasized this goal.

In Chapter 3, Mike M. Mochizuki applies the insights of major IR (international relations) traditions (offensive/defensive realism and commercial liberalism) to understand the political-security dimensions of FTA proliferation in the Asia-Pacific. He finds that the large powers (United States, Japan, and China) have not used FTAs among themselves to counter competitive pressures, and have instead signed FTAs with smaller states to hedge against negative security trends. So far, large power competition has prevented the predominance of any hegemonic FTA project.

Legal competition

The difficulty the WTO has experienced in adopting trade rules on "new" issues, such as investment protection, competition policy, and labor or environmental standards, has created an incentive for some countries to compete through their FTAs in the definition and dissemination of new rules in these areas. FTAs offer several advantages in this endeavor. First, it is easier to reconcile the preferences of a small number of partners. Second, it is possible to select "common view" partners with similar policy positions. Third, because many of the recent FTAs pair industrialized with developing nations, the larger party uses its asymmetric market power to gain control over the negotiation agenda (Pekkanen et al., 2007). Developing nations are prepared to make concessions bilaterally (such as the incorporation of the new issues in international trade and investment) that they are unwilling to make multilaterally, lured by the prospect of preferential access to important export markets and the desire to attract inflows of FDI (Ethier, 1998). But there is a strategic calculation as well: holding out on multilateral commitments increases the attractiveness of these developing nations as FTA partners since only through preferential trade negotiations will they endorse some WTO-plus commitments such as investment protection.

The race to push for the adoption of new rules on trade and investment through FTAs is guided by two fundamental objectives. One, which we label standard setting, seeks the dissemination across several FTAs of a new rule or standard that can later be incorporated more widely at the multilateral level (for example, intellectual protection, investment protection, or antidumping disciplines). The second objective is a strategy of lock-in, whereby nations offer alternative models of FTAs that differ in the degree of legalization, escape clauses, and the scope of WTO-plus commitments. For both legal strategies, early-mover advantages are very strong. The first preferential negotiations usually set important precedents so that the first commitments become default approaches guiding subsequent negotiations. Thus, the term "race" quite literally describes FTA proliferation.

In Chapter 4, Junji Nakagawa traces the impact that failure of multilateral rule-making (through a stagnant Doha Round and the collapse of the Multilateral Agreement on Investment) had in persuading East Asian nations to join the global trends of regionalization and legalization. Instead of a blanket acceptance of hard law, however, the FTA strategies of countries in the region have ranged from highly legalistic to modest rule-making. This marked diversity in the legalization approach of Asia Pacific nations represents a fundamental challenge to the coherence of the integration effort.

Implications

The decision to adopt a multidimensional characterization of competition that goes beyond defensive economic interests has important implications for the analysis of FTA proliferation. First, it raises the possibility that the rapid spread of FTAs is due to their "flexibility benefits." In other words, governments approve of the fact that they can pursue multiple goals through FTA diplomacy in ways that may not be possible through other instruments. This is clear particularly in contrast to BITs: through FTAs, policymakers can simultaneously push for trade and investment liberalization, and due to their deeper integration agenda including economic cooperation clauses, they can more effectively boost diplomatic relations with selected countries. Consequently, and more problematic for the analysts, FTAs may frequently be "over-determined" since they may be animated by different competitive pressures. We believe that the task of sorting out the weight of these competitive pressures triggering individual FTAs should begin with a clear demarcation of the competitive goals at stake in each issue area as the thematic chapters in this volume do. Furthermore, there could be a marked contrast among governments regarding the type of competitive pressure that triggers the FTA shift. Finally, the conceptualization of competition as a multidimensional process underscores potential tradeoffs among competitive goals and, in such cases, the need for governments to negotiate among contradictory competitive objectives.

Overview of country chapters

The country chapters in this volume examine how diffusion dynamics have influenced the FTA policies of countries on both sides of the Pacific Rim. Early on, the United States, Chile, and Mexico made FTAs a main pillar of their trade diplomacy. As they were among the first movers in this process, they operated on an autonomous (non-diffusion) basis. Given its weight as the world's largest market, the US policy shift in particular—as crystallized in NAFTA—jolted its trade partners. As discussed by Cintia Quiliconi and Carol Wise in Chapter 5, the competitive liberalization campaign that the United States launched in the 2000s aimed to achieve key competitive goals: the dissemination of new rules on trade and investment that could be adopted later at the multilateral level, which in the Western Hemisphere generated a "coalition of the willing," as only a subset of Latin American nations were willing to endorse the US FTA formula; and preventing China's domination of the regional integration process in East Asia. In Chapter 6, Barbara Stallings analyzes how Chile adopted an autonomous FTA strategy putting it to a distinct political use in the early 1990s: by reintegrating itself into the region after long years of authoritarian rule. Economic competition was also of great importance vis-à-vis emerging Latin American markets: Chile attempted to capture FDI inflows from industrialized nations and to strategically place itself as a bridge between East Asia and South America. In Chapter 7, Aldo Flores-Quiroga discusses the bottom-up pressures from Mexico's business community to negotiate NAFTA in order to secure market access and investment flows. The Mexican government then continued to negotiate multiple FTAs to diversify economic relations, compete for foreign capital, and foster diplomatic relations with Latin American partners.

In East Asia, Singapore played a key role for the region to adopt an FTA strategy. As Takashi Terada discusses in Chapter 8, political and economic uncertainty in the region after the Asian financial crisis, which also stalled the ASEAN integration movement, motivated Singapore to venture into FTA negotiations with advanced countries such as the United States and Japan. Such a move exerted competitive pressures on other large ASEAN countries to follow suit, and ASEAN as a grouping attempted to become an FTA hub. Korea was also influenced by these external challenges, and as Min Gyo Koo discusses in Chapter 9, its more moderate attempts to emulate the FTA policies of other countries soon gave way under the Roh Moo-hyun administration to a proactive FTA strategy of negotiating with the United States and the EU. While the top-down policymaking process allowed the policy shift, the domestic backlash in Korea (and the United States) has so far hindered Korea's attempts to become an FTA hub of the region.

In Chapter 10, Mireya Solís argues that Japan has used FTA policy to offset trade and investment diversion from other FTAs, disseminate its own FTA formula in East Asia, and compete with China in cementing relations with Southeast Asia. But the Japanese government has been confronted with a major dilemma: whether to negotiate a bilateral FTA with China to maximize economic gains or to emphasize political competition and develop rival FTA networks in the region. Finally, in Chapter 11 Jian Yang argues that while China is keen to emphasize the absolute gains from trade liberalization, its selection of FTA partners and the timing of trade negotiations show that competition, both economic and political, is driving the Chinese strategy. Economically, China is using its FTAs to enhance the efficiency and productivity of Chinese enterprises and to disseminate its acceptance as a market economy. Politically, FTAs are an important instrument in China's pursuit of influence and security goals.

Notes

1. These trade agreements represent the exchange of trade/investment preferences to selected members, and PTAs (preferential trade agreements) might be a more accurate acronym. We have decided to use FTA, however, given that it is the more familiar term. We should also note that the WTO uses a different nomenclature, regional trade agreements or RTAs, to refer to the preferential trade agreements of interest to this project: customs unions and FTAs.
2. Indeed, they are typically characterized as the first step in the path towards regional integration, which would later include the creation of a customs union, then a common market, and finally a monetary union (Balassa, 1961).
3. Our thinking on this issue was greatly influenced by the comments of Richard Stubbs and T. J. Pempel at a 2007 ISA (International Studies Association) panel.
4. Figures are from Kawai (2005, 31–2).
5. See Stallings (2009) for a brief history of regional integration endeavors in Latin America. The most notable initiatives were the Central American Common Market (1960) and the Andean Group (1969). Broader, but less effective was the Latin American Free Trade Area (1961, transformed in 1980 into the Latin American Integration Association or ALADI).
6. The competitive liberalization strategy reflected the concern with falling behind in the FTA race given the difficulties in obtaining fast track authority after NAFTA; the desire to obtain market access concessions from countries competing for preferential treatment in the US market; and the attempt to maximize leverage by pursuing concurrent trade negotiations bilaterally, regionally, and multilaterally. See Evenett and Meier (2008).
7. As per the WTO, developed economies include Canada, US, EU, EFTA, Japan, Australia, and New Zealand. Transition economies are the former USSR, Eastern and Central Europe, the Baltic States, and the Balkans.
8. We relied on the World Bank's regional criteria to define which country belongs to which region, thus what constitutes a cross-regional agreement.
9. In statistical analyses, this is usually identified as a problem of spatial dependency or autocorrelation.
10. The intensity of a rivalry is measured by competitive distance among countries: the similarities among a) their export patterns in terms of market destination, b) their product profiles, and c) their educational and infrastructural resources (Elkins et al., 2006).
11. These tables merely provide a baseline, however, since they do not capture rivalry in specific products or the role of MNCs and intra-firm trade, both of which influence trade competition.
12. Manger (2009) explains the proliferation of defensive North–South FTAs by highlighting the role of MNCs seeking preferential investment access in developing countries to reap early-mover advantages and/or to reduce production costs in fragmented production chains.

Part I Thematic Chapters

2
Exclusion Fears and Competitive Regionalism in East Asia

Shujiro Urata

Introduction

In the twenty-first century, East Asia has finally caught up with the frenzy of free trade agreements (FTAs). The rest of the world had begun to actively look at FTAs as a means of promoting trade liberalization since the early 1990s, when multilateral trade negotiations under the General Agreement on Tariffs and Trade (GATT) were making little progress. Interest in FTAs increased even after the establishment of the World Trade Organization (WTO) in 1995—which succeeded the GATT—with a broader coverage and stronger legal foundation, especially after the new multilateral trade negotiations (the Doha Development Agenda, DDA) entered into the deadlock. Indeed, the cumulative number of FTAs reported to the GATT/WTO since 1949 increased from 86 in 1990 to 165 in 1995, to 251 in 2000, and further to 404 as of August 10, 2008.[1]

In East Asia, the ASEAN Free Trade Area (AFTA) was enacted in 1993 but this was the only major FTA in the region until the Japan–Singapore FTA was implemented in 2002. Since then, East Asian countries have become very active in establishing FTAs in the twenty-first century. This chapter analyzes the manner in which economic competition factors have spurred FTA proliferation in East Asia, and the economic impact of such agreements. The analysis finds that competition among East Asian countries, especially between China and Japan, for obtaining market access in East Asian countries and for gaining a leadership role in East Asian integration have been crucial factors leading to the proliferation of FTAs. Specifically, East Asian countries hurriedly entered into FTA negotiations with other East Asian countries because of the concern of the negative effects of FTA exclusion. On the other hand, empirical analyses have found that FTAs promoted trade between and among FTA members in many FTAs, while the negative impacts from being excluded from FTAs are rather limited. This contrast suggests that the fears of exclusion as envisaged by policymakers and business people—and not the actual negative effects from alternative trade agreements—are fueling FTA proliferation in the region.

The structure of the chapter is as follows. The second section examines the impacts and determinants of the formation of FTAs mainly from a theoretical aspect. The third section examines empirically the changing patterns of trade and foreign direct investment (FDI) in East Asia by focusing on their intra-regional relationship. This section also summarizes trade liberalization experiences up to the end of 1990s, which contributed to increasing trade and FDI in East Asia. The fourth section examines the developments of FTAs in East Asia, as an FTA became an important trade policy tool for East Asian countries. This section also empirically evaluates the quality and the impacts of FTAs. The final section presents some concluding comments.

Economic analyses of FTAs

Contrary to the most favored nation principle of the WTO, the essence of FTAs is the exchange of trade preferences that are not made available to third parties. Preferential liberalization, therefore, creates new incentives for private sector lobbies and governments to achieve competitive goals through these agreements. These objectives include the desire to gain preferential access to a main market of destination, to counter the trade and discrimination effects from existing FTAs, and to leverage tariff concessions in one FTA negotiation into more substantial gains in subsequent trade talks. These are some of the economic motivations behind the formation of FTAs.

This section reviews the economic literature on FTAs. Specifically, I first review the studies that analyzed the impacts of FTAs with an observation that a government forms an FTA if the perceived net benefit (benefits–costs) of an FTA outweighs the costs. The theories reviewed here are rather basic, but it is important to grasp them well in order to understand actual developments. Then I turn to economic studies, which explicitly analyzed the factors leading to the formation of FTAs. These studies, which explicitly incorporate government behavior, are rather new but have shed light on the factors determining the formation of FTAs.

Economic impacts of FTAs

One can classify the economic impacts of FTAs into two groups: static effects and dynamic effects.[2] Static effects are 'trade creation effects,' 'trade diversion effects,' and 'terms of trade effects,' while the dynamic effects include 'market expansion effects' and 'competition promotion effects.'

'Trade creation effects' result from the elimination of trade barriers among FTA members and, therefore, the new trade created among them, resulting in an improvement in resource allocation. 'Trade diversion effects' address the ways that FTAs replace highly efficient products of nonmember countries by imports from less efficient FTA members. In general, and from the viewpoint of FTA members, 'trade creation effects' have positive impacts while the impacts of 'trade diversion effects' are ambiguous. Despite ambiguity of the impacts of FTAs on FTA members, one can derive several important policy implications from the analysis of trade creation and trade diversion. To reduce the negative impacts caused by trade diversion, tariffs on non-members or most favored nation tariff rates should be low. To maximize the scope for trade creation, a country should form an FTA with a highly productive country. Having pointed out the ambiguity of the impacts of FTAs, it has been proven theoretically that any FTA can be welfare-improving if it is properly formulated.[3]

The above analysis of trade creation and trade diversion effects can be applied to a small country, which does not have any influence on international prices or the terms of trade. As such, the terms of trade effect of FTAs is not considered in the above analysis. For a large country or a large FTA group consisting of FTA member countries, the formation of an FTA enables a large country or a large FTA group to gain as it improves its terms of trade by expanding trade between FTA members at the expense of its trade with nonmembers.

Beyond the economic impacts of FTAs on their members, it is important to recognize that the static impacts of FTAs on non-FTA members are negative. Non-FTA members suffer from welfare loss because trade diversion effects reduce the level of their exports to FTA members, and because the terms of trade effect would reduce nonmembers' welfare when the terms of trade for non-FTA members deteriorate. Indeed, as we will discuss below, the emergence of negative impacts of FTAs for non-FTA members leads to competitive FTAs and the proliferation of FTAs, as non-FTA members try to cope with the negative impacts by creating new FTAs or joining existing FTAs.

As for the dynamic effects of FTAs, both market expansion effects and competition promotion effects contribute to economic growth of FTA members. 'Market expansion effects' involves expanded market size needed to achieve efficient production/distribution and economies of scale. 'Competition promotion effects' result from market integration in ways that would make regionally oligopolistic industries more competitive, thereby achieving higher productivity through the introduction of competitive pressures. For non-FTA members, these effects are likely to have positive impacts as economic growth of FTA members tends to promote the exports of nonmembers to the members.

There are two important issues arising as a result of the proliferation of FTAs that I will discuss before turning to the empirical investigation. One is the 'spaghetti bowl effect' and the other is 'hub-and-spoke' FTA system. The 'spaghetti bowl effect,' coined by Bhagwati (1995), refers to a situation where numerous and crisscrossing FTAs with different rules of origin (ROOs) increases transaction costs and facilitates protectionism, thereby reducing the welfare of both FTA members and nonmembers. ROOs play a key role in determining the impacts of FTAs on foreign trade, since FTAs give preference to the products produced in FTA partner members and the nationality of the products are determined by ROOs. Although the spaghetti bowl effect (in East Asia, some observers call it the 'noodle bowl' effect) attracted a lot of attention of researchers and policy makers, its negative impacts may be exaggerated because the 'spaghetti bowl' effect may not increase trade cost from the pre-FTA level and thus it does affect trade. In other words, trade can increase if preferential treatment is applied under an FTA, while trade remains the same if preferential treatment is not applied because the product in question does not qualify as local product without passing the ROO test.

Thus, the cost of the 'spaghetti bowl effect' due to different ROOs applied in different FTAs could be overstated. It is important, however, to point out that ROOs have become an important tool for protectionists to restrict trade. Under an FTA treaty, products qualified as local products by passing ROO test can be exported to an FTA partner country without facing import tariff. Under such situation, the FTA partner interested in protection adopts very stringent definition of ROOs, in order to restrict imports. Indeed, in many FTAs, countries have established very complicated and restrictive ROOs.

A hub-and-spoke FTA system has emerged in many parts of the world. In East Asia, for example, Singapore has become a hub with many bilateral FTAs involving spoke countries. The Association of Southeast Asian Nations (ASEAN) is likely to become a hub region, when it forms 'bilateral' FTAs with various spoke countries including China, Japan, Korea, and possibly India, Australia, and New Zealand. The benefits to the hub country are likely to be greater than benefits to the spoke countries, because a hub country is able to reduce the negative impacts of trade diversion while spoke countries cannot do so. To understand why, one should keep in mind that unilateral trade liberalization, which is essentially identical to having FTAs with all the countries, does not give rise to the trade diversion effect. For a spoke country, the welfare implications depend on whether the exports of the new spoke are complements or substitutes to those of old members. If they are substitutes, existing spoke countries may be harmed by an erosion of their degree of preference in the hub market. If they are complements, the initial members tend to gain.[4] Therefore, the hub-and-spoke dynamics create incentives for countries to become an FTA hub in order to ensure positive gains.

In addition to its impacts on trade, an FTA also affects other foreign economic activities such as FDI. As the FTA eliminates regional trade barriers and expands market size, FDI is likely to flow into the regional market in the expectation of selling more products. This is FTA's investment creation effect. Investment may also be undertaken in member countries at the expense of investment in nonmember countries because of increased attractiveness of member countries for investment. This is FTA's investment diversion effect. These observations indicate that FTAs would promote economic growth of FTA members by enabling them to attract FDI, which would bring the members various factors needed to achieve economic growth such as funds for fixed investment, technology, and management know-how. The spaghetti bowl effect due mainly to complicated ROO systems would affect investment negatively as these distort investment decisions of firms which face difficulty in meeting ROO requirements.

Determinants of the formation of FTAs

The findings from the studies above on the expected impacts of FTAs highlight the factors determining the formation of these trade agreements. More specifically, an FTA is formed if the government believes the benefits of the FTA exceed its costs. According to the theories/models analyzed above, the benefits of an FTA arise from the trade creation effect, terms of trade effect, market expansion effect or economies of scale effect, and competition promotion effect, while the costs emerge from the trade diversion effect.[5] As discussed, many of those impacts are not determined a priori, but are influenced by FTA partner selection. Thus, it is imperative to examine the characteristics or relationships of potential FTA partners. Although rigorous theoretical investigations are lacking, several conditions for beneficial FTAs have been discussed from the static point of view, which include broad membership, high pre-FTA tariffs among members, low pre-FTA tariffs vis-à-vis third countries, and substantial overlap between FTA partners' production bundles.[6]

In general, however, the trade diversion effect motivates an excluded country to form a new FTA in order to avoid reduced export opportunities as it is discriminated against by FTA members in their markets. Indeed, overcoming the trade diversion effect is a very important factor behind the proliferation of competitive FTAs. The terms of trade effect is another factor leading to the formation of FTAs. Small countries attempt to increase their welfare levels by becoming 'large' as they eliminate cross-border trade barriers through FTA formation.[7] The incentive is that a 'large' country can exploit the benefit in the form of terms of trade improvement.

Very few empirical studies on the formation of FTAs have been conducted. One of them is by Baier and Bergstrand (2004), which examines the economic factors affecting the formation of FTAs for 54 countries. They find that the probability of the formation of an FTA increases when two countries are in close geographical proximity, both relatively large and similar in economic size. They also confirmed that the likelihood of an FTA between a pair of countries is higher if one or some of the following conditions are met: the more remote a pair from the rest of the world, the greater the difference in capital–labor endowment ratios between two countries due to the gains from traditional comparative advantage, and the less the difference in capital–labor endowment ratios of the member countries relative to that of the rest of the world due to less inter-industry trade diversion.[8]

One of the problems of the theories/models discussed in the previous section for the analysis of the determinants of FTA formation is the exclusion of policy variables such as the presence of other FTAs in the discussions.

Accordingly, the analysis neglected the political and strategic interaction of the governments in the formation of FTAs.

In order to deal with the problem, recent models explicitly take into account government behavior. For instance, Grossman and Helpman (1995) assume that governments respond to political pressures from industry-special interests but also pay some attention to the effect on the average voter. Using this framework, they show that the government endorses an FTA in two types of situations. One is when the FTA would generate substantial welfare gains for the average voter, and adversely affected interest groups fail to coordinate their efforts to defeat the FTA. The other is when an FTA would create profits for actual or potential exporters in excess of the losses that would be suffered by import-competing industries, plus the political cost of any welfare loss that might be inflicted on the average voter. They also show that the formation of an FTA is likely when there is a relative balance in the potential trade between the FTA partners. Furthermore, they show that the prospects for an FTA agreement improve, if some industries can be excluded from the agreement.

Indeed, several studies found that many FTAs in East Asia excluded sensitive sectors. Ravenhill's (2005) survey of early FTA initiatives in the Asia-Pacific leads him to conclude that these governments are lured by the goal of achieving 'liberalization without political pain.' Industrialized nations seem increasingly interested in bilateral FTAs with small trade partners because they can offer economic rents to specific producers through preferential treatment; while keeping off-limits the most sensitive sectors (Pekkanen et al., 2007). This combination of targeted rents for exporters and investors with exclusions for import-competing sectors provides a powerful impetus in the FTA race.

Endoh (2005) extends the analysis of Grossman and Helpman by incorporating Cournot-type monopolistic competition and introducing tariff revenue increases as one of the government objectives. In addition, he considers that the quality of the government—defined as the extent of its acceptance of requests from the industry—affects FTA decisions. According to Endoh, an FTA is likely to be formed between two countries under the following conditions: the countries' sizes are large but similar, the countries have high quality governments, and the countries are in geographical proximity to each other. Finally, he demonstrates that the incentive for a country to form an FTA increases with the number of FTAs it has established. The reasoning behind this observation is as follows. A new FTA gives benefits to exporters as they expand their exports in the FTA partner's market, and so exporters desire new FTAs. FTAs incur losses to domestic producers as competition from imports increases. Under the model framework, one can show that the additional cost to domestic producers declines with the number of FTAs weakening the opposition to subsequent FTAs. Combining these two effects, one finds that additional net gain (benefits–costs) for a new FTA increases. This finding may be interpreted as the 'domino effect' discussed by Baldwin (1995). Endoh's empirical analysis of 118 countries for the year 2002 confirmed all the expected relationships discussed above. It is particularly noteworthy that Endoh corroborates that the greater the number of FTAs established by a country in question, the more likely it is for that country to have another FTA.

Having laid out the main theoretical findings on determinants and impacts of FTAs, I turn to the empirical analysis by examining first the situation in East Asia before the FTA wave and the subsequent pattern of FTA proliferation in the region.

East Asia prior to the FTA race

East Asia experienced substantial changes in the patterns of foreign trade and FDI in recent decades.[9] One is increased intra-regionalization in foreign trade. Another is increased share of machinery, especially electronic machinery, in foreign trade and FDI. The third distinguishable pattern is the increased role of multinational corporations (MNCs) in international trade, intensifying the linkage between FDI and foreign trade. These observed patterns appear to reflect the formation of regional production networks by MNCs. These changes in international trade and FDI in East Asia are mainly promoted by trade and FDI liberalization policies pursued by East Asian countries.

Changing patterns of foreign trade and foreign direct investment in East Asia

A rapid increase in intra-regional trade in East Asia is clearly discernable in Table 2.1.[10] Intra-regional trade in East Asia increased 2.19 times in ten years from 1995 to 2005, while world trade expanded only twofold. As a result of rapid expansion in intra-regional trade, the share of East Asia's intra-regional trade in world trade increased from 12.3 percent in 1995 to 13.2 percent in 2005. The magnitude of East Asia's intra-regional trade is significantly larger than North American Free Trade Agreement's (NAFTA) intra-regional trade, but substantially smaller than that of the European Union (EU). In 2005, the shares of intra-regional trade in world trade for the NAFTA and the EU were 7.7 and 25.4 percent, respectively.

During the 1995–2005 period, East Asia's intra-regional trade grew faster than its overall trade, as its exports and imports increased 2.08 and 2.03 times, respectively. As a result of rapid expansion of intra-regional trade in East Asia, the share of East Asia in overall exports and overall imports increased from 47.4 and 54.7 percent in 1995 to 49.9 and 59.1 percent in 2005, respectively. The importance of intra-regional trade for the region's trade in East Asia is greater compared to the NAFTA (55.1 percent for exports and 38.3 percent for imports, both in 2005) but smaller compared to the EU (66.3 percent for exports and 66.1 percent for imports).

Table 2.1   Changing patterns of East Asia's trade from 1995 to 2005

| | | Change from 1995 to 2005 | | Share of world trade | | Share of region/country's total trade | | | |
| | | | | | | Exports | | Imports | |
		Exports	Imports	1995	2005	1995	2005	1995	2005
East Asia	East Asia	2.19	2.19	12.3	13.2	47.4	49.9	54.7	59.1
	China	3.96	3.74	1.8	3.3	7.4	14.1	7.2	13.4
	Japan	1.81	1.49	2.9	2.3	8.5	7.4	16.1	11.9
	NIEs4	1.92	2.14	5.4	5.3	21.8	20.1	22.6	23.9
	ASEAN4	1.78	2.31	2.3	2.2	9.8	8.3	8.7	9.9
	NAFTA	1.78	1.22	5.0	3.8	24.0	20.5	16.8	10.1
	EU25	2.11	1.49	3.5	3.1	14.9	15.1	14.0	10.3
	World	2.08	2.03	24.3	24.4	100.0	100.0	100.0	100.0
China	East Asia	3.74	3.96	1.8	3.3	55.7	40.6	66.8	59.6
	China	—	—	—	—	—	—	—	—
	Japan	2.95	3.65	0.5	0.8	19.1	11.0	15.0	12.4
	NIEs4	3.97	3.72	1.2	2.2	32.9	25.5	48.1	40.3
	ASEAN4	5.72	8.26	0.1	0.4	3.7	4.1	3.8	7.0
	NAFTA	6.82	3.53	0.4	1.1	17.8	23.7	9.6	7.7
	EU25	7.08	3.31	0.4	1.0	13.6	18.9	13.3	9.9
	World	5.12	4.44	2.9	6.8	100.0	100.0	100.0	100.0
Japan	East Asia	1.49	1.81	2.9	2.3	41.7	46.4	37.9	43.4
	China	3.65	2.95	0.5	0.8	5.0	13.4	9.6	18.0
	Japan	—	—	—	—	—	—	—	—
	NIEs4	1.30	1.29	1.6	1.0	24.7	24.0	16.9	13.8
	ASEAN4	1.00	1.61	0.9	0.5	12.1	9.0	11.4	11.6
	NAFTA	1.15	0.88	2.0	1.0	29.7	25.5	24.9	14.0
	EU25	1.22	1.26	1.1	0.7	16.1	14.6	14.6	11.6
	World	1.34	1.58	7.3	5.1	100.0	100.0	100.0	100.0
NIEs4	East Asia	2.14	1.92	5.4	5.3	48.4	57.2	58.0	63.0
	China	3.72	3.97	1.2	2.2	13.1	26.9	9.9	22.2

Group	Region								
	Japan	1.29	1.30	1.6	1.0	9.4	6.6	22.0	16.3
	NIEs4	1.55	1.55	1.6	1.2	14.9	12.7	16.1	14.1
	ASEAN4	1.80	1.86	1.1	1.0	11.1	11.0	10.0	10.5
	NAFTA	1.32	1.13	2.0	1.2	22.2	16.2	16.0	10.3
	EU25	1.73	1.35	1.4	1.1	14.1	13.4	13.1	10.0
	World	1.81	1.77	10.1	8.9	100.0	100.0	100.0	100.0
ASEAN4	East Asia	2.31	1.78	2.3	2.2	51.4	54.7	62.3	69.9
	China	8.26	5.72	0.1	0.4	2.8	10.8	2.7	9.6
	Japan	1.61	1.00	0.9	0.5	17.4	13.0	25.9	16.4
	NIEs4	1.86	1.80	1.1	1.0	25.6	21.9	28.5	32.4
	ASEAN4	3.51	3.51	0.2	0.4	5.6	9.0	5.2	11.5
	NAFTA	1.87	1.16	0.6	0.5	20.8	17.9	12.3	9.0
	EU25	1.82	0.97	0.6	0.4	15.4	12.9	15.7	9.6
	World	2.17	1.59	3.9	3.6	100.0	100.0	100.0	100.0
NAFTA	East Asia	1.22	1.78	5.0	3.8	22.6	16.0	32.5	26.8
	China	3.53	6.82	0.4	1.1	1.7	3.4	2.7	8.6
	Japan	0.88	1.15	2.0	1.0	8.6	4.5	13.5	7.2
	NIEs4	1.13	1.32	2.0	1.2	9.3	6.2	12.2	7.4
	ASEAN4	1.16	1.87	0.6	0.5	3.0	2.0	4.1	3.6
	NAFTA	2.04	2.04	7.8	7.7	46.2	55.1	40.5	38.3
	EU25	1.53	2.32	2.9	2.8	16.5	14.8	16.1	17.3
	World	1.71	2.16	18.0	17.2	100.0	100.0	100.0	100.0
EU25	East Asia	1.49	2.11	3.5	3.1	7.6	6.0	9.8	10.4
	China	3.31	7.08	0.4	1.0	0.9	1.6	1.0	3.6
	Japan	1.26	1.22	1.1	0.7	2.1	1.4	3.5	2.2
	NIEs4	1.35	1.73	1.4	1.1	3.1	2.2	3.7	3.3
	ASEAN4	0.97	1.82	0.6	0.4	1.5	0.8	1.5	1.4
	NAFTA	2.32	1.53	2.9	2.8	7.5	9.1	7.0	5.4
	EU25	1.91	1.91	27.3	25.4	66.1	66.3	68.9	66.1
	World	1.90	1.99	40.5	38.4	100.0	100.0	100.0	100.0

Source: Computed from JETRO's trade matrix.

The changes in intra-regional trade in East Asia from 1995 to 2005 are quite striking, in particular the increased importance of China and the shrinking importance of Japan. The shares of China and Japan in East Asia's exports changed from 7.4 and 8.5 percent in 1995 to 14.1 and 7.4 percent in 2005, respectively, while those for East Asia's imports changed from 7.2 and 13.4 percent to 16.1 and 11.9 percent, respectively. These changes in the positions of China and Japan in East Asia's trade are largely attributed to the differences in economic growth rates of China and Japan.[11]

East Asian countries became more important trading partners for most East Asian countries from 1995 to 2005, as the shares of East Asia in their trade increased. However, it was not the case with China, for which the shares of East Asia in its exports and imports declined. Although the importance of overall East Asia in China's trade has declined, the share of ASEAN in China's trade increased reflecting substantial growth in China–ASEAN trade albeit from a low base. In addition, the importance of the NIEs4 (Hong Kong, South Korea, Singapore, and Taiwan) for China and ASEAN4 (Indonesia, Malaysia, the Philippines, and Thailand) in their trade is crucial. Indeed, the NIEs4 were by far the largest trading partner for China and ASEAN4 in 2005. The importance of the NIEs4 can be partly explained by the roles of Hong Kong and Singapore as *entrepôts*. Intra-ASEAN4 trade has also increased noticeably, as reflected in the increased shares of such trade in the trade of ASEAN4. The AFTA certainly fostered such increase, as trade barriers on intra-ASEAN trade were removed. Finally, though Japan was surpassed by China in terms of the importance as a trading partner for East Asian economies during the 1995–2005 period, for ASEAN4, unlike the case for the NIEs4, Japan still has a larger, though rapidly shrinking, trade share than China.

Another important change took place in the commodity compositions from 1990–94 to 2000–04 (Table 2.2). The changes are especially notable for exports, among which manufactured goods and, in particular, machinery increased remarkably. Among machinery, exports of electronic and electrical machinery grew particularly fast for ASEAN4, NIEs4, and China. Exports of automobiles and auto parts account for much smaller share in the exports for the NIEs4, ASEAN4, and China, compared to electronic and electrical machinery. Among other manufactured exports, textiles and garment either grew relatively slowly or experienced a decline in their share in total exports for East Asian developing economies, although their share is still high for China and the NIEs4.

Turning to the import composition of East Asian countries, one finds relatively small changes when compared to the case for exports. The share of manufactures remained around 70–80 percent throughout the period for East Asian developing countries. Similar to the changes observed for exports, imports of machinery, in particular, electronic and electrical machinery, increased their shares in total imports in many East Asian countries.

Table 2.2 Commodity composition of international trade for East Asian economies with other East Asian economies (percentage share of total)

Exports	East Asia		ASEAN		NIEs		China		Japan		World	
	1990–94	2000–04	1990–94	2000–04	1990–94	2000–04	1990–94	2000–04	1990–94	2000–04	1990–94	2000–04
Agriculture	7.0	4.1	15.7	9.0	4.7	2.3	13.7	5.2	1.1	1.0	12.1	8.8
Mining and fuels	5.4	5.1	16.5	12.6	2.1	3.5	6.4	4.1	1.3	1.7	9.9	11.3
Total manufacture	86.1	88.7	65.2	75.6	92.7	93.2	78.5	90.1	95.8	93.0	74.9	76.9
Chemicals	5.0	6.5	3.8	6.2	5.2	6.8	5.3	4.6	5.6	7.8	9.0	10.4
Leather, rubber, travel goods, footwear	4.0	2.9	2.3	1.7	7.1	3.5	6.9	5.4	1.3	1.2	2.5	2.1
Wood, paper, and furniture	2.3	2.0	4.6	3.3	2.2	1.5	2.0	3.3	0.8	0.6	3.5	3.2
Metal	4.6	4.3	1.7	1.6	5.7	5.1	4.4	5.1	5.5	5.0	5.1	4.6
Machinery	46.6	53.6	37.6	51.0	36.8	52.6	17.4	40.6	71.6	67.1	38.0	41.4
Power generator	1.9	1.7	0.9	0.9	0.9	1.0	0.8	1.1	3.9	3.9	2.5	2.6
Industrial and metal working	6.8	6.3	3.1	3.0	4.7	4.9	2.6	3.8	12.8	12.6	8.3	7.1
Electronic	15.9	19.4	19.5	22.0	14.4	21.6	6.3	22.3	17.7	12.2	7.9	10.2
Electrical	11.1	16.8	11.9	23.2	11.2	18.0	4.0	10.1	12.7	15.2	6.9	9.3
Autos	9.0	7.7	0.9	1.3	3.9	4.9	3.0	2.6	21.8	20.6	9.3	9.5
Other transport	1.8	1.7	1.2	0.6	1.7	2.3	0.6	0.8	2.7	2.5	3.0	2.6
Textiles and garment	12.7	9.1	8.7	5.8	20.6	11.8	29.1	18.3	2.1	1.5	7.1	5.7
Other manufactures	11.0	10.2	6.6	6.0	15.0	11.9	13.4	12.8	9.0	9.8	9.7	9.3
Others	1.5	2.1	2.6	2.8	0.5	1.0	1.4	0.6	1.8	4.3	3.1	3.0
Total	100	100	100	100	100	100	100	100	100	100	100	100

(continued)

Table 2.2 (Continued)

Imports	East Asia		ASEAN		NIEs		China		Japan		World	
	1990–94	2000–04	1990–94	2000–04	1990–94	2000–04	1990–94	2000–04	1990–94	2000–04	1990–94	2000–04
Agriculture	12.9	8.9	8.5	6.9	9.9	6.2	9.3	7.7	23.3	15.6	12.0	9.1
Mining and fuels	15.4	16.8	11.5	13.6	11.5	14.7	7.7	13.7	27.9	25.5	12.2	13.3
Total manufacture	68.8	72.7	76.5	77.5	75.4	77.8	82.3	77.9	45.7	56.7	72.5	74.7
Chemicals	8.8	9.0	8.9	8.6	9.0	8.3	11.7	12.2	7.0	7.3	9.1	10.5
Leather, rubber, travel goods, footwear	2.3	1.9	1.1	1.0	3.6	2.8	1.8	1.2	1.9	2.0	2.4	2.1
Wood, paper, and furniture	2.1	1.7	1.6	1.3	2.2	1.5	2.7	1.5	2.3	2.6	3.4	3.2
Metal	5.3	4.0	6.6	4.6	5.1	4.1	8.6	5.5	2.7	2.1	5.1	4.6
Machinery	34.3	41.8	47.6	52.9	34.4	42.6	42.0	45.0	16.9	27.6	36.0	39.5
Power generator	2.1	1.8	3.3	2.1	1.8	1.6	2.7	2.0	1.0	1.6	2.3	2.5
Industrial and metal working	9.0	6.8	12.1	7.8	8.4	6.4	18.0	10.5	2.9	3.2	7.9	6.7
Electronic	7.5	11.6	10.2	12.3	7.8	13.2	6.6	10.3	4.4	10.1	7.8	9.9
Electrical	9.7	18.1	14.5	25.9	11.4	19.3	5.6	18.6	4.1	8.8	6.8	9.5
Autos	3.7	2.3	4.1	2.9	3.3	1.5	5.7	2.3	3.0	2.9	9.0	9.0
Other transport	2.3	1.2	3.4	1.9	1.8	0.8	3.3	1.5	1.5	1.0	2.2	1.9
Textiles and garment	7.3	5.4	3.7	2.9	10.0	7.0	9.4	4.4	6.6	6.5	6.8	5.5
Other manufactures	8.7	8.9	7.2	6.3	11.0	11.5	6.2	8.0	8.2	8.5	9.7	9.3
Others	2.9	1.6	3.5	2.0	3.2	1.3	0.7	0.7	3.1	2.2	3.3	2.9
Total	100	100	100	100	100	100	100	100	100	100	100	100

Note: NIEs include Hong Kong, South Korea, and Taiwan.
Source: UN, Comtrade.

The increasing share of machinery products, especially electronic and electrical machinery, in both exports and imports for East Asian countries indicates increasing importance of intra-industry trade. Indeed, various studies including Fukao et al. (2003) have found an increasing share of intra-industry trade rather than one-way trade for intra-regional trade dynamics in East Asia. They have also found that a large part of intra-industry trade in East Asia can be characterized as vertical intra-industry trade, under which parts and components with different qualities and characteristics are actively traded.[12]

The importance of parts in intra-East Asian trade was found by a comparison with trade with the US and the EU. Urata (2006) found that East Asia's exports have lower (higher) share of parts (finished products) in its trade with the US and the EU compared with its trade with East Asia. These trade patterns reflect the regional production network, under which parts are traded in East Asia for the assembling of the finished products, which in turn are exported to the US and the EU. Such trade pattern has been described as 'triangular' trade, reflecting that East Asia has become a factory for the world. A closer examination of international trade patterns at disaggregated country levels in East Asia reveals that China has become an increasingly important country for the location of assembling finished products.

FDI inflows to East Asia have increased rapidly since the mid-1980s, and they have exhibited several notable characteristics with implications on trade patterns in East Asia. First, the source of FDI inflows to East Asia extends beyond the region, and unlike the case of international trade, no particular increase in intra-regional orientation was observed (Table 2.3). Out of eight countries, for which data on the sources of FDI inflows are available, only three countries—Indonesia, Thailand, and Korea—saw the increase in the share of East Asia as a source of FDI inflows. Unlike the pattern observed for international trade, where intra-regional trade accounted for approximately 40–60 percent of total trade for all the East Asian economies, dependence on intra-regional FDI varies widely.

Second, somewhat similar to the pattern found for international trade, the machinery sector, especially electrical and electronic sector, received substantial FDI in many East Asian countries (Table 2.4), suggesting close relationship between FDI and international trade.

MNCs, the major suppliers of FDI, have had huge impacts on East Asian economies through various forms including generating production, fixed investment, and employment. Among these activities, their impacts on foreign trade are substantial.[13] For example, the share of MNCs' exports in China's overall exports increased from 29 percent in 1994 to 55 percent in 2003, while the corresponding share for the imports increased from 46 to 56 percent.[14] Although similar information for many other East Asian countries is not available, the contributions of MNCs for many East Asian countries' trade appear substantial, indicating their elevated position in East

Table 2.3   Sources of FDI inflows to East Asian developing economies (%)

	China (actualized)		Indonesia (approved)		Malaysia (approved)		The Philippines (BOP)		Singapore (committed)		Thailand (BOP)		Korea (approved)		Taiwan (approved)	
	1995–99	2000–04	1995–99	2000–04	1995–99	2000–04	1995–99	2000–04	1995–99	2000–04	1995–99	2000–04	1995–99	2000–04	1995–99	2000–04
World	100	100	100	100	100	100	100	100	100	100	100	100	100	100	100	100
East Asia	73.1	61.6	38.3	41.7	45.4	36.4	48.5	37.5	29.0	21.6	52.0	99.1	26.3	26.5	34.8	31.0
Japan	8.3	8.6	14.7	9.7	18.6	11.6	25.4	24.3	29.0	21.6	26.5	42.1	8.8	13.5	17.2	15.2
East Asia (excluding Japan)	64.8	52.9	23.6	32.0	26.8	24.9	23.1	13.3	0.0	0.0	25.5	57.0	17.6	13.0	17.7	15.8
China	0.0	0.0	0.1	10.2	0.7	4.4	2.7	0.0	0.0	0.0	0.0	0.5	0.2	2.9	0.0	0.0
NIEs4	62.9	51.2	17.6	16.6	25.5	19.3	19.2	12.5	0.0	0.0	24.5	53.1	7.3	4.5	14.2	13.3
ASEAN4	1.9	1.6	5.9	5.3	0.6	1.2	1.1	0.8	0.0	0.0	0.9	3.2	10.1	5.5	3.5	2.5
US	8.5	8.8	4.0	1.7	29.7	21.2	20.6	19.1	45.3	42.4	20.4	2.2	31.3	31.5	24.9	16.6
EU	7.7	7.0	24.0	17.0	9.1	30.3	18.7	4.8	23.2	30.8	17.3	−0.2	29.5	21.6	7.5	17.0

Note: The EU includes Italy, UK, the Netherlands, France, and Germany. In the case of Singapore, the EU indicates Europe.
Source: Country data sources.

Table 2.4 Sectoral distribution of FDI inflows (%)

	Malaysia (approved)		Thailand (BOP)		Korea (approved)		Taiwan (approved)	
	1995–99	2000–04	1995–99	2000–04	1995–99	2000–04	1995–99	2000–04
Manufacturing	100	100	100	100	100	100	100	100
Food	2.5	3.5	7.3	7.3	11.9	4.4	3.2	3.4
Textiles	2.6	1.9	4.2	2.6	1.3	0.9	2.8	1.3
Wood	8.2	8.0	a	a	11.3	0.9	0.5	1.6
Metals	8.3	9.6	20.2	13.6	3.6	5.1	12.2	6.9
Chemicals	33.0	17.1	9.3	10.2	18.9	18.5	12.6	10.0
General machinery	2.2	1.7	25.9	32.2	8.7	13.2	3.1	5.3
Electric/electronic machinery	35.4	43.1	26.9	11.9	29.6	35.9	56.9	61.9
Transport machinery	2.9	6.5	b	b	8.8	12.6	5.3	4.0
Others	4.9	8.4	10.9	22.3	5.5	8.4	3.4	5.5
Manufacturing share of total	na	na	39.6	53.5	49.4	36.4	48.6	35.0

Note: For Thailand Wood (a) is included in others and transport machinery (b) is included in general machinery.
Source: Country data sources.

Asia and their well-developed regional and global trading networks. In light of these observations, it is useful to investigate the trading patterns of MNCs in East Asia, in order to deepen our understanding of the changing trade patterns in East Asia. Due to the limited availability of necessary information, I focus the examination on the patterns of trade by Japanese MNCs as an illustration.

An examination of the patterns of trade for the Asian affiliates of Japanese MNCs reveals several interesting patterns. First, Asian affiliates of Japanese MNCs have strong trade orientation, when compared to the affiliates in other parts of the world.[15] In 2004, the share of exports in total sales for the Asian affiliates in the manufacturing sector was 51 percent, significantly higher than 14 percent for the affiliates in North America. Among different sectors, trade orientation is particularly strong for the machinery sectors with the highest orientation registered by the electrical and electronic sector. Transportation machinery exhibits quite a contrasting pattern in that a large share of sales as well as procurement involves transactions in the local market. Low trade orientation found in the transportation machinery stems from several factors. One important reason is import-protection policies applied to the transportation machinery sector, the industry that many countries are eager to develop.

Second, intra-Asia trade dominates trade by Asian affiliates of Japanese MNCs, reflecting strong regional orientation of Japanese MNC strategy, which in turn indicates that Japanese MNCs have contributed to the regionalization of foreign trade in East Asia. Intra-regional orientation is particularly strong for the procurements of the Asian affiliates, as more than 95 percent of their imports come from other Asian countries. Among the Asian countries, Japan is by far the most important trading partner for the Asian affiliates of Japanese MNCs. In this way, the Asian affiliates of Japanese MNCs have engaged in regional production network with China, ASEAN4, and NIEs4, as their shares in Asian affiliates' imports are substantial.

Third, a large portion of trade conducted by Asian affiliates of Japanese firms take the form of intra-firm trade, that is, trade which takes place between MNCs' parent firms in Japan and their affiliates in Asia or between overseas affiliates. For manufacturing, as a whole, in 2001 more than 70 percent of Asian affiliates' exports were destined to their affiliated firms regardless of destinations.[16] Coupled with the observation that a large share of international trade by Japanese MNCs' parent offices is destined to their overseas affiliates, our findings on Japanese MNCs' trade and intra-firm trade in Asia appear to indicate that Japanese MNCs have developed their own production and distribution network in Asia. Furthermore, our findings about a high share of intra-firm trade in Japanese MNCs' trade underscore the closed nature of production and distribution network developed by Japanese MNCs.

In sum, this section has revealed the emergence of regional production network in electronic and electric machinery in East Asia. Such regional production networks have been created mainly by MNCs from Japan, Korea, Taiwan, the US, and the EU, as they break up the production process into various subprocesses and locate each process in a country where the subprocess is conducted most efficiently. This kind of fragmentation strategy has been adopted by MNCs, as they take advantage of substantial diversity in the level of economic development and wages among the East Asian countries.

Changing trade policies in East Asia

The rapid expansion of foreign trade and FDI inflows in East Asia as discussed above can be attributed to many factors such as a buoyant world economy. Nevertheless, one of the most important factors is trade and FDI liberalization pursued by East Asian countries. Liberalization of trade and FDI regimes led to the expansion of exports and inward FDI because it shifted the incentives from import-substituting production to export production, and increased the attractiveness of these countries to foreign MNCs. Foreign trade and FDI policies in East Asia have undergone dramatic changes in the last two decades.[17]

In the 1980s and the 1990s, East Asian countries embarked on unilateral liberalization of trade and FDI policies and deregulation in domestic economic activities as part of more comprehensive structural reform policies. It is true that such policy changes were partly induced by their commitments to the World Bank and the IMF for obtaining economic assistance, but it came largely from the realization on the part of East Asian governments that liberalization and deregulation would promote economic growth.[18]

East Asian countries unilaterally liberalized their import regimes by lowering tariff rates and nontariff barriers from the early 1980s through the early 2000s. As shown in Table 2.5, many East Asian countries reduced their tariff rates from the late 1980s to early 2000s. In spite of substantial reduction in tariff rates, some countries such as Korea and Thailand still maintain relatively high tariff rates. It should be noted that for many countries, the primary sector is relatively more protected than the manufacturing sector.

Those governments also started to liberalize policies toward FDI inflows in the mid-1980s, largely because they realized that FDI inflows would promote economic growth. It is difficult to quantify the restrictiveness of an FDI regime, but it is clear that many East Asian economies have reduced restrictions on market access and rights of establishment by diminishing the number of sectors and industries on the negative list, and have relaxed the limits on foreign equity ownership through expanding most favored nation treatment and national treatment.[19] In addition, a number of economies introduced incentives such as tax breaks to attract FDI.

Table 2.5 Trade liberalization in selected East Asian economies

		Binding coverage	All products		Primary products		Manufactured products		Ad valorem equivalent of nontariff barriers
			Unweighted averages	Import-weighted averages	Unweighted averages	Import-weighted averages	Unweighted averages	Import-weighted averages	
China	1992		40.4	32.1	36.1	14.1	40.6	35.6	
	2004	100.0	9.8	6.0	10.0	5.6	9.7	6.0	1.5
Indonesia	1989		19.2	13.0	18.2	5.9	19.2	15.1	
	2003	96.6	6.4	5.2	8.0	3.1	6.1	5.8	0.5
Japan	1988		4.2	3.6	8.3	4.4	3.5	2.7	
	2004	99.6	2.9	2.4	5.3	3.9	2.4	1.6	1.6
Korea	1988		18.6	14.0	19.3	8.3	18.6	17.0	
	2002	94.4	15.5	9.5	20.9	19.0	7.8	5.0	0.0
Malaysia	1988		14.5	9.7	10.9	4.6	14.9	10.8	
	2003	83.7	7.3	4.2	4.5	2.1	7.8	4.6	1.7
The Philippines	1988		28.3	22.4	29.9	18.5	27.9	23.4	
	2003	66.8	4.5	2.6	5.7	5.0	4.2	2.0	0.4
Singapore	1989		0.4	1.1	0.2	2.5	0.4	0.6	
	2003	69.8	0.0	0.0	0.0	0.0	0.0	0.0	0.5
Thailand	1989		38.5	33.0	30.0	24.3	39.0	35.0	
	2003	75.0	14.0	8.3	16.4	4.4	13.5	9.3	0.3

Source: World Bank, World Development Indicators 2005.

Liberalization of trade and FDI also progressed in regional contexts in the 1990s. Southeast Asian countries launched the AFTA process in 1992 to make ASEAN a competitive region for exports and for attracting FDI. The 1992 agreement provided for the liberalization of tariff and nontariff measures under the Common Effective Preferential Tariffs. The target year for achieving tariff and nontariff liberalization was originally set for 2008, but was later moved forward to 2002. The AFTA has been in effect among the original six ASEAN members—Brussels, Indonesia, Malaysia, Singapore, Thailand, and the Philippines—since January 2002 when the tariff rates were reduced to 0–5 percent, though the exclusion list is long and individual country circumstances vary. Vietnam is to comply with the same tariff standards by 2003, Laos and Myanmar by 2005, and Cambodia by 2007. By 2010, ASEAN is expected to become a complete free trade area, except for Cambodia, Lao People's Democratic Republic, Myanmar and Vietnam (CLMV) which have been given later deadlines. FDI liberalization has been underway after the creation of the ASEAN Investment Area (AIA) in 1998, which provides coordinated investment cooperation and facilitation programs, market access, and national treatment of all industries. But some ASEAN members continue to maintain sizeable sensitive and exclusion lists from FDI liberalization.

The Asia Pacific Economic Cooperation (APEC) forum is another regional framework that has promoted trade and FDI liberalization in East Asia. This trans-regional forum, which was established to promote economic growth in the region, includes not only East Asian economies but also economies in North and South America and Oceania. Following the Bogor declaration in 1994 calling for full liberalization of trade and FDI by 2010 for developed-economy members and by 2020 for developing-economy members, APEC members agreed to prepare and implement individual action plans (IAPs) specifying near- and medium-term liberalization measures. Because voluntarism is the basic principle of APEC in implementing policy measures such as trade and FDI liberalization, peer pressure is to play a crucial role in the implementation of liberalization schemes. All APEC members have made significant progress toward freer trade and FDI regimes. APEC lost its vigor in the late 1990s because it could not help the crisis-affected members. However, APEC regained its attention in 2006, when the United States proposed a Free Trade Area of the Asia Pacific (FTAAP), which is discussed below.

In short, East Asian economies have undertaken trade and FDI liberalization policies, which contributed to the rapid expansion of trade and FDI as well as the formation of regional production networks by MNCs. There still remain, however, various obstacles in foreign trade and FDI. As will be discussed in the next section, one of the factors that have led to the recent surge of FTAs in East Asia is the desire for East Asian countries to overcome high protection barriers to expand business opportunities.

FTA proliferation in East Asia

Rapidly emerging bilateral and regional frameworks in the twenty-first century

East Asia was not active in the formation of RTAs, which include FTA and customs union, until recently. Indeed, AFTA was the only major FTA until Japan and Singapore enacted the Japan–Singapore FTA (formally named a New Age Japan–Singapore Economic Partnership Agreement, JSEPA) in 2002.[20] However, the situation changed dramatically in recent years. Many countries in East Asia began to form FTAs with the countries not only in the region but also outside the region.

Besides AFTA, ASEAN as a group, as well as its members individually, has become active in FTA negotiations with other countries in recent years. One of the FTAs involving ASEAN that has received most attention recently is that with China. ASEAN and China enacted FTA in goods trade in July 2005 and they are currently negotiating an FTA in services trade. ASEAN enacted an FTA with Korea with the exception of Thailand, which did not reach an agreement because of the exclusion of rice, a commodity strong interest for Thailand, from the FTA agenda. ASEAN reached an agreement with Japan and it is currently negotiating FTAs with India, Australia, and New Zealand. Several ASEAN members have become active in establishing bilateral FTAs. Singapore enacted many FTAs with countries such as New Zealand, Japan, Australia, the US, the European Free Trade Association (EFTA), and India, and began negotiations with many countries. Thailand has also become active in establishing FTAs as it has implemented FTA with Australia, New Zealand, and Japan, and is currently negotiating FTAs with several countries. Malaysia enacted an FTA with Japan and it began FTA negotiations with several economies including the US. Both the Philippines and Indonesia signed FTA with Japan separately.

Compared to ASEAN countries in Southeast Asia, the economies of Northeast Asia including China, Japan, Korea, and Taiwan had not been active in FTA negotiation. Recently, however, China, Japan, and Korea have been very proactive in their FTA policies. China implemented FTAs with ASEAN, Hong Kong, Macau, and it is negotiating FTAs with over 20 countries. Japan enacted FTAs with Singapore, Mexico, Malaysia, Chile, and Thailand. It has signed an agreement with Brunei, the Philippines, Indonesia, and ASEAN, and it is currently in negotiations with Australia, India, the Gulf Cooperation Council (GCC), Korea, and others. Korea implemented FTAs with Chile, Singapore, and ASEAN, and has reached an agreement with the US. Korea is actively pursuing FTA policies, as it is currently in FTA negotiations with several countries including the EU, Canada, India, and Mexico.

An idea of an FTA covering East Asian countries has also emerged. At the Leaders' Summit Meeting of ASEAN+3 (China, Japan, and Korea) in 1998, the leaders decided to set up the East Asia Vision Group to study the long-term vision for economic cooperation. The group has presented the leaders with recommendations including the establishment of an East Asian Free Trade Agreement (EAFTA). The Expert Group, which was set up at the recommendation of ASEAN+3 Economic Ministers, presented its recommendations to the Economic Ministers in 2006 to start the process in 2007 toward establishment of an East Asia FTA. The recommendations by the Expert Group, however, were not adopted and the Expert Group was asked to conduct further study.

Japan proposed the Comprehensive Economic Partnership in East Asia (CEPEA), which is an Economic Partnership Agreement including an FTA covering ASEAN+3+3 (India, Australia, and New Zealand). ASEAN+3+3 are also the members of the East Asian Summit. Recognizing the rivalry between Japan and China as will be discussed below, it is very likely that behind the CEPEA idea lies Japan's strategy of taking a leadership role in setting up regional institutions in East Asia, as it was China that had taken an initiative in the EAFTA discussions.

One notable characteristic of FTAs in East Asia is their comprehensiveness on issue coverage. As such, some of the FTAs established in East Asia are termed as Economic Partnership Agreement (for example, Japan–Singapore EPA, JSEPA), or Closer Economic Partnership Arrangement (for example, China–Hong Kong CEPA), and others. These new types of FTAs typically include facilitation of foreign trade, liberalization and facilitation of FDI, and economic and technical cooperation, in addition to trade liberalization, which is included in traditional FTAs. The basic philosophy behind these new types of FTAs is interestingly similar to that of the APEC forum, whose three pillars are (1) liberalization and (2) facilitation of foreign trade and foreign investment, and (3) economic and technical cooperation.

There are various reasons behind the recent surge of FTAs in East Asia. First, the rapid expansion of FTAs in other parts of the world has made East Asian economies realize the importance of establishing FTAs in order to maintain and expand their export opportunities. This market seeking FTAs pursed by East Asian countries is largely of defensive nature. A case in point is Japan's FTA with Mexico. Japanese firms were in disadvantageous position vis-à-vis US and EU firms in the Mexican market because the US and the EU have FTAs, under which their firms have duty-free access to Mexico. Japanese firms put pressure on Japanese government to negotiate an FTA with Mexico to overcome their disadvantage.

Second, countries interested in promoting structural reform to achieve economic growth use FTAs to gain leverage over opponents to liberalization. Third, the Asian financial crisis in 1997–98 prompted East Asian economies to be aware of the need for regional cooperation such as FTAs in order to avoid another crisis.

Finally, rivalry among East Asian economies over market access in potential FTA partners' market, as well as rivalry over gaining a leadership role in the region (as discussed more fully in Chapter 3) has spurred FTA strategies of countries in the region. The rivalry between China and Japan is most notable. Both China and Japan, which are competing to become a 'leader' in the region, are keen on using FTAs to strengthen the relationships with ASEAN, Korea and other countries. Indeed, in November 2002, Japan proposed an economic partnership framework to ASEAN one day after China agreed to start FTA negotiations with ASEAN. It should also be noted that ASEAN, Korea and other countries also consider FTAs as a means to maintain and increase their influence in East Asia.

Empirical analysis of welfare and trade impacts of FTAs

The theoretical models discussed before showed that the economic welfare impacts of FTAs on members are ambiguous, while their impacts on non-members are likely to be negative. Given the indeterminacy of the impacts of FTAs theoretically, it is necessary to examine the impacts empirically. Two types of empirical research have been conducted to examine the impacts of FTAs on members and nonmembers. One is a simulation analysis using computable general equilibrium (CGE) models, and the other is to use econometric methods. Each approach has its strengths and weaknesses.[21]

A CGE model is constructed to mimic the actual working of the economic system by specifying activities of economic agents such as producers, consumers and governments. A typical CGE model covers the world consisting of a large number of countries and a large number of sectors. The most popular CGE model used for FTA analysis is the Global Trade Analysis Project (GTAP) model and the most up-to-date (the year 2001) database used for the GTAP analysis includes 87 countries and 57 sectors. The strength of the CGE model is its theoretical consistency and comprehensive coverage in that it captures all economic impacts through the market mechanism including inter-industry and inter-country impacts of policy changes such as FTAs. At the same time, there are several weaknesses. One is the difficulty in constructing a model that reflects the actual economic system. For example, a typical CGE model assumes perfect competition. Although the perfect competition assumption may not be appropriate in many cases, a lack of knowledge on the type of actual competition forces researchers to make the perfect competition assumption.[22] Another problem is the difficulty in obtaining appropriate data and parameters used for the model. Indeed, the more detailed and realistic the model becomes, the more difficult it is to obtain the appropriate data. The third problem is that the results of CGE model cannot be tested statistically, in order to evaluate the validity of the results.

A large number of simulation exercises have been conducted to investigate the possible impacts of FTAs by using CGE models.[23] Indeed, it has become customary to conduct a CGE model simulation when policy makers formulate FTA policies. The results of CGE studies show two common trends. First, FTA members are shown to gain in terms of economic welfare and gross domestic product (GDP), while non-FTA members generally lose. These findings are consistent with the theoretical predictions. For example, Scollay and Gilbert (2001) obtain the following results from their analysis of an FTA comprised of ASEAN, China, Japan, Korea, Australia, and New Zealand. All the members gain in terms of economic welfare, while non-members such as the US, the EU and Taiwan lose. The world as a whole is shown to gain. Similar patterns of gains and losses are found by Ando and Urata (2007), who examine the static as well as dynamic impacts of FTAs involving East Asian countries using the GTAP model. Their results are reproduced in Table 2.6. Although there are exceptions, they found that the FTA members gain in terms of economic welfare and GDP growth, while non-FTA members lose in both accounts. Specifically, in terms of economic welfare which reflects the level of consumers' satisfaction, Japan is estimated to lose USD$1,569, 776, and 7,625 million dollars, if ASEAN forms an FTA with China, Korea, and China–Korea, respectively, while Japan gains when it forms an FTA with ASEAN. These results from CGE simulations indicate the reasons for competitive FTAs, because a country excluded from an FTA is shown to lose.

Another general trend observed from the results of CGE simulation studies has to do with the number of FTA members or the country coverage. Generally, it is observed that the greater the number of FTA members, the larger the gain from an FTA. This can be seen by comparing the results of FTAs with different country coverage using the same model. Scollay and Gilbert (2001) also find that the welfare gains for the world as well as FTA members tend to increase through wider coverage of countries under liberalization as the coverage of FTAs change from a group consisting of ASEAN, China, Japan, Korea, Australia, and New Zealand to a group of economies belonging to APEC and then to the all the countries in the world. A similar pattern was observed by Ando and Urata (2007) shown in Table 2.6. These observations are consistent with the theoretical analyses in that the scope for trade creation increases and the scope for trade diversion declines with the number of FTA members.

An econometric analysis of the impacts of FTAs typically examines the impacts of FTAs on foreign trade. Specifically, the gravity model, which is constructed on the assumption that the magnitude of bilateral trade depends on the economic size of the two countries and the distance between them, is estimated to examine the trade creation and diversion effects of FTAs. One weakness of the econometric approach in the FTA analysis is its inability to incorporate simultaneous changes in a number of policy variables. For example, econometric analysis finds it difficult to deal with simultaneous removal of tariffs in many sectors from many countries, as they result in a complicated interplay of the effects. Another problem is the difficulty in dealing with a large change such as the removal of tariffs under FTAs, which

Table 2.6   Economic effects of FTAs in East Asia

	FTA partner countries							
	A	A+C	A+J	A+K	A+C+J	A+C+K	A+J+K	A+C+J+K
Static effects only								
Welfare (US $ million)								
China	−241	−211	−731	−524	−623	189	−1,131	800
Japan	−497	−1,569	933	−776	6,555	−2,123	1,783	6,584
Korea	−135	−630	−378	912	−1,761	7,625	640	5,973
ASEAN	2,665	6,646	4,777	2,903	7,355	6,197	5,186	7,107
Change in GDP (%)								
China	0.00	0.02	−0.01	−0.01	0.09	0.01	−0.02	0.13
Japan	0.00	0.00	0.00	0.00	0.01	−0.01	0.00	0.01
Korea	0.00	−0.03	−0.01	−0.02	−0.09	1.12	0.03	1.11
ASEAN	0.07	0.22	0.16	0.10	0.30	0.25	0.22	0.36
Static and dynamic effects								
Welfare (US $ million)								
China	−308	3,575	−872	−690	8,487	5,580	−1,384	11,306
Japan	−265	−1,632	3,038	−516	10,544	−2,208	4,457	11,054
Korea	−184	−1,130	−507	2,514	−3,213	16,046	3,754	14,508
ASEAN	10,603	21,670	20,558	13,033	27,468	22,374	22,779	28,423
Change in GDP (%)								
China	−0.01	0.49	−0.03	−0.04	1.23	0.65	−0.06	1.41
Japan	0.00	−0.02	0.07	0.00	0.18	−0.03	0.10	0.19
Korea	−0.03	−0.21	−0.07	0.55	−0.62	4.15	1.13	4.19
ASEAN	1.93	3.64	3.74	2.44	4.80	3.90	4.17	5.07

Notes: A, C, J, and K indicate ASEAN, China, Japan, and Korea, respectively. The cell with hatching indicates the membership in FTAs.
Source: Ando and Urata (2007).

tends to have substantial impacts not only on trade but also on other economic activities such as production and employment, which in turn would affect trade.

Similar to the case of CGE model studies, a large number of gravity model estimations have been conducted to examine the impacts of FTAs on foreign trade. Many studies found that FTAs promoted intra-FTA trade, indicating the presence of the trade creation effects. For example, Frankel (1997) conducted a gravity model estimation covering 63 countries in the 1965–94 period with a variety of different model specifications. He finds that intra-regional trade in Western Europe, East Asia, APEC, and the Western Hemisphere is significantly higher than the predicted values. A recent study by Baier and Bergstrand (2007) reports very significant trade creation effects as they find that an FTA approximately doubles two members' bilateral trade after 10 years.

Relatively few studies examined the presence or absence of the trade diversion effect. Urata and Okabe (2007) analyze the impacts of selected FTAs on trade by explicitly considering trade between FTA members as well as trade between FTA members and nonmembers. Their results indicate the presence of trade creation effects for most FTAs they study. Specifically, out of 11 FTAs they examine, only three FTAs, ASEAN–China, Singapore–Japan, and Singapore–US, were found to have no significant trade creation effect. As to the trade diversion effect, five out of 11 FTAs were shown to have significant trade diversion effects. These findings indicate that FTAs tend to promote trade between and among FTA members, possibly implying that FTAs are welfare enhancing for FTA members.

Many FTAs are rather new with short history, and thus conducting statistical analysis such as the gravity model estimation faces the problem of insufficient data. Further statistical analysis is warranted and will become feasible with the expansion of the data with the passage of time.

Conclusions

East Asia has seen a rapid proliferation of FTAs since around the turn of the century. For many countries, this is a shift from a single track GATT/WTO-based multilateral trade policy to multiple track trade policy composed of not only a multilateral approach but also bilateral and regional approaches. The analysis in this chapter shows that the new bilateral and regional trade policy was preceded by the intensification of regionalization of economic activities based upon regional production networks and market-driven activities in East Asia. As such, the new trade policy is likely to solidify the on-going regionalization and further promote it.

The economic analysis of FTAs in this chapter identifies several economic reasons leading to the proliferation of FTAs in East Asia. One of the most important factors is a defensive motive on the part of many East Asian governments as they felt disadvantage in foreign markets, where the sharp increase in FTAs led to the discrimination against non-FTA members such as those East Asian countries. To overcome the (perceived or real) negative trade-diversion effects, East Asian countries became active in forming FTAs. This defensive motive has clearly contributed to the formation of many bilateral FTAs in East Asia. In this regard, China and Japan rivalry has contributed to the precipitation of this trend. One important question is whether the pro-liferation of bilateral FTAs would lead to the formation of region-wide FTA. From the view point of economic analysis, the future development depends on the costs and benefits of FTAs to potential FTA members. Such calcula-tion of costs and benefits would be extremely dependent on government policies. In other words, the governments could formulate policies so that FTAs would bring net benefits, leading to the formation of FTAs.

A brief survey of empirical analysis of the impacts of FTAs has shown that many FTAs have contributed to an improvement of economic welfare and economic growth for FTA members, as FTAs promoted intra-FTA trade. In other words, for many FTAs the trade creation effects are detected. Some FTAs are found to produce the trade diversion effects, but in general these seem to be modest. This finding justifies the rationale for many countries to formulate FTAs, which in turn results in FTA proliferation. Due to new and short history of East Asia's FTAs, further investigations and follow up on those FTAs are essential in understanding their determinants and economic impacts.

Notes

1. The figure includes active and inactive FTAs. The figures were taken from the WTO's website on August 27, 2008. http://www.wto.org/english/tratop_e/region_e/summary_e.xls
2. The analysis here is intended to give concise explanation of the major points and therefore lacks theoretical rigor. For a detailed analysis of the economic impacts of RTAs, that is customs unions and FTAs, see, for example, Baldwin and Venables (1995).
3. More accurately, this point is proven for the case of customs union (CU), where the members share common external tariff while they remove tariffs on intra-CU trade. This is known as the 'Mead-Ohyama-Kemp-Wan theorem.' See, Baldwin and Venables (1995) and Bhagwati et al. (1998).
4. Baldwin and Venables (1995).
5. Milner (1997) argues that the scale effect is important for the firms.
6. Winters (1991).
7. See, for example, Riezman (1985) and Kennan and Riezman (1990) for the analy-sis of the terms of trade effect.
8. 'Trade diversion' will be discussed in the next section.
9. East Asia, in this paper, is defined as consisting of the following ten countries and economies: China, Japan, NIEs4 (South Korea, Taiwan, Hong Kong, and Singapore), and ASEAN4 (Indonesia, Malaysia, the Philippines, and Thailand).

10. Many studies have identified the rapid expansion of intra-regional trade in East Asia. See, for example, Ng and Yeats (2003), and Urata (2001, 2005a).
11. The average annual GDP growth rates of China and Japan for the 1995–2005 period are 9.1 and 1.2 per cent, respectively. (Computed from the data obtained from the World Bank's World Development Indicators 2007, CD-ROM).
12. The other type of intra-industry trade is characterized as horizontal intra-industry trade, where products with similar characteristics in quality and price but with different design and other characteristics are traded. Such trade may occur between countries with similar income levels, where consumers have similar taste but also have demand for variety.
13. On the impacts of FDI on trade, see, for example, Urata (2001), Kawai and Urata (1998, 2004), and Urata et al. (2006).
14. China's Statistical Yearbook, various years.
15. See Urata (2006) for more detailed information.
16. In the Ministry of Economy, Trade and Industry (METI) survey, information on intra-firm is collected every three years. The most recent data are available for 2001 in the 34th survey.
17. This section expands Urata (2005a).
18. See, for example, the World Bank (1993) on this point in its assessment of trade policies during the 1980s. The World Bank (2000) notes that the determination to pursue trade liberalization by policy makers in East Asian countries can be confirmed by their unwillingness to retreat into protectionism in response to the crisis.
19. Japan PECC (2002) examined the impediments to FDI in APEC economies, and found that many East Asian economies reduced the number and the level of impediments by liberalizing FDI policies.
20. AFTA was discussed in an earlier section. For discussions on FTAs in East Asia, see for example, Aggarwal and Urata (2006), Urata (2005b), Pangestu and Gooptu (2004), Soesastro (2006), and Sally (2006).
21. On the discussions of these approaches, see, for example, Baldwin and Venables (1995).
22. A few CGE models incorporate imperfect competition, but the models and parameters used in these models suffer from their arbitrariness. For example, the Michigan model developed mainly by Alan Deardorf and Robert Stern incorporates imperfect competition. (Brown et al., 1996).
23. See Ando and Urata (2007) for a survey of the CGE studies on East Asian countries.

3
Political-Security Competition and the FTA Movement: Motivations and Consequences

Mike M. Mochizuki

Incorporating the political-security dimension in an analysis of the prolif-eration of free trade agreements (FTAs) and other preferential trading arrangements in the Asia-Pacific region resonates well with the competition hypothesis tested in this volume. Given that anarchy has been a bedrock assumption in the international security realm, the security studies field has naturally focused on the competitive tendencies in the interstate system. In the debates regarding the means for taming security competition, some posit an unceasing and tragic competition for relative power and a great power quest for hegemony. Others argue that security competition can be tamed through balances of power and mutual reassurance, collective and/or coop-erative security institutions, economic interdependence, or the international spread of democracies.

These divergent theories about anarchy's implications complicate the task of integrating the political-security dimension in an explanation of the FTA movement. Nevertheless it is still possible to pose empirical questions that link the political-security dimension to the FTA movement. To what extent does political-security competition motivate or reinforce a state's FTA policy, in particular, the choice of FTA partners and the timing and/or sequencing of these partnerships? Conversely, to what extent does a state's interest in ameliorating political-security competition drive or constrain FTA policies? Finally, what are the political-security effects of the regional FTA frenzy? Does the proliferation of FTAs in the Asia-Pacific reinforce or even exacer-bate the competitive tendencies in the political-security realm? Or, is the net effect one of taming competition and even promoting cooperation?

The existing literature on the security–economic nexus in general and the linkage between security and FTAs in particular suggests various arguments germane to the above questions (Dent, 2006b: 51–3). Commercial liberalists would argue that FTAs can be an instrument of cooperative diplomacy. Fostering economic integration between states through FTAs can help over-come mutual mistrust and mitigate security competition. The European

Coal and Steel Community (ECSC) forged by France and West Germany is often cited as a prototypical example of how economic integration can promote reconciliation even between so-called "hereditary enemies" (Mattli, 1999). But the ECSC case suggests another logic that is more consistent with political-security competition—namely that FTAs can be one of the economic instruments for bolstering security alliances that are designed to counter potential or actual threats from third parties (Gowa, 1994). Both the cooperative logic of mutual reassurance and the competitive logic of security alliances can unfold bilaterally or multilaterally. In the case of Western Europe, the institutionalization of a multilateral collective defense organization (North Atlantic Treaty Organization, NATO) and the development of an inclusive multilateral cooperative security process (Commission on Security and Cooperation in Europe, CSCE) reinforced the movement towards regional economic integration (the European Community and later the European Union). In East Asia, the US adoption of bilateral alliance arrangements weakened or even impeded the development of regional economic integration processes (Press-Barnathan, 2003).

Another line of argument is that FTAs and other economic integration moves are ways to assert political influence or enhance a state's international status. In the case of great powers, the logic of political-security competition suggests that FTAs might be a factor in hegemonic or leadership competition. As Hirschman's (1980) analysis of the manner in which Nazi Germany used preferential trade links to enhance its relative power in Europe indicates, the existing predominant power might seek to defend its hegemonic status by using preferential trade links to reinvigorate the loyalty and dependence of states already aligned with it, to broaden the network of aligned subordinate states, and to counter hegemonic projects of potential challengers. Conversely, hegemonic challengers might use FTAs to mobilize supportive states and to weaken the influence of the existing hegemon. Even if major powers eschew hegemonic projects, they can still compete for influence to encourage a political-security order that is more favorable to its long-term interests. Of course, such an analysis requires specifying state preferences regarding alternative orders. The pursuit of FTAs for political-security reasons can also exacerbate major power competition and contribute to international instability (Wesley, 2008: 216, 224–5).

For smaller states that have little prospects of becoming great powers, FTAs can serve as tools to reduce their security vulnerabilities or prevent international isolation by deepening economic links with more powerful states. Furthermore, smaller states might form FTAs or pursue other integrationist projects among themselves in order to enhance their collective voice and bargaining power relative to larger states (Grieco, 1996). They can also overcome the disadvantages of smallness by striving to become "trade-hub" nations by serving as the focal point of FTA networks (Ibarra-Yuenz, 2003).

This chapter examines the political-security dimension of the proliferation of FTAs in the Asia-Pacific region in the following manner. First, it provides an overview of the changing regional security environment and identifies the political-security calculations and responses of various key states to establish the strategic context for the FTA movement. It then analyzes the extent to which these political-security calculations have motivated state policies regarding FTAs. Finally, it assesses the implications of the regional FTA movement for competitive and cooperative tendencies in the regional security system.

Evolving security environment in the Asia-Pacific region

Mastanduno (2003) has aptly characterized the Asia-Pacific security order as one of "incomplete hegemony." It is a hegemonic order because the United States maintains a preponderance of both material and nonmaterial power capabilities. US military capabilities remain unrivaled in the region and are forwardly deployed. Despite its historic isolationist tendencies, the United States did not disengage from Asia after the collapse of the Soviet Union. Its extensive bilateral alliance network not only provides military access over long distances, but also augments US capabilities through the defense contributions of allies. America's economic revival after the end of the Cold War and in the face of Japan's economic stagnation reaffirmed US economic and technological primacy. Despite some decline in its international reputation after the Iraq war debacle, most Asia-Pacific states still find the United States attractive as well as its soft and hard powers intact.[1] But the US hegemonic order is incomplete because China's power is rising. Therefore, the cooperative and competitive interactive dynamics between the United States and China is likely to be the key factor in shaping the Asia-Pacific security order. In addition, the strategic calculations and behavior of the other states vis-à-vis both the United States and China will also affect their relative power.

In this era of shifting distribution of power, how then are we to code the strategic responses of states? Concepts for distinguishing state strategies under anarchy include balancing, bandwagoning, appeasement, and buck-passing strategies for dealing with an actual or potential adversary. The problem with this categorization, however, is that it presumes some certainty about which states are adversaries or threats.[2] A state's intentions at a given point in time may not be truly knowable and may depend as much on the perceptions of the other state. Furthermore, a state's intentions can change easily depending on international circumstances, domestic factors, or shifts in relative power resources. For an offensive realist, the changeability of intentions suggests that states ought to identify adversaries by focusing only on capabilities and geographic position. But for a defensive realist, such behavior could lead to worst-case responses and counter-responses that can result in a self-fulfilling prophecy of provoking a potential adversary into becoming an actual threatening adversary. Uncertainty about present and future intentions of potential adversaries may therefore point to mixed strategies that combine elements of different strategies. For example, states can hedge by combining balancing and accommodation (Medeiros, 2005/06; Kang, 2007: 52–4). Accommodation can in turn encompass efforts to engage, integrate, reassure, or even appease potential adversaries.

Whether or not a state has threatening intentions will depend greatly on how a state views the existing international order. According to many power transition theories, if a state is satisfied with the existing order or status quo, that state should not become threatening even as its relative power rises. But if a state is dissatisfied with the existing order and is willing to use force to alter the status quo, then the state is revisionist and is likely to provoke a great power war as the distribution of power shifts (Lemke, 1997). The status quo–revisionist state distinction raises three further issues. The first issue is the specification of what the existing order or status quo is—something that is by no means obvious. The existing order can encompass various factors including the following: (1) the existing power distribution and hierarchy among states, (2) existing territorial boundaries, (3) existing pattern of alliances and alignments, and (4) existing international institutions and their operating rules and norms. Second, there is the issue of what measures a state is willing to use to revise the existing order. The range of possible state action on behalf of a revisionist agenda is quite broad, including the use of force, diplomatic coercion, economic incentives, and persuasion/socialization. Finally, there is the issue of order creation or evolution. In reality (especially in a region as dynamic as the Asia-Pacific), the distinction between status quo and revisionist states is too stark since states in the region are collectively considering the development of new international institutions and processes.

How then are states in the Asia-Pacific region responding to the shifting distribution of power? In addressing this question, we should distinguish between great and secondary powers. Although there is currently no great power in the Asia-Pacific that can militarily challenge the US hegemon, China has the potential of taking on the United States militarily at least in the East Asia region in the future. What about Japan? Although Japan was a great power in the first half of the twentieth century, its pursuit of a tightly constrained defense policy because of antimilitarist norms and its reliance on the United States for security relegates it to the status of a secondary power (Ross, 2006: 357). Nevertheless Japan still has the economic and technological capabilities to become a formidable military power; and if Japan were to pursue a security policy that is independent of the United States, this could alter the regional balance of power. For our discussion here, we will distinguish between the actual and potential great powers on the one hand (the United States, China, and Japan) and secondary states on the other hand (such as South Korea, the Southeast Asian countries, Taiwan, and Australia).

Actual and potential great powers (the US, China, and Japan)

What is striking about these major powers is that all three are pursuing mixed hedging strategies vis-à-vis each other.

Although American policymakers and foreign policy analysts debate whether or not to treat China as a strategic competitor or partner and US policy toward China has fluctuated because of presidential cycles, the center of gravity of America's China policy has been a hedging strategy (Medeiros, 2005/06; Christensen, 2006). On the one hand, the United States has balanced against China by maintaining nuclear, air, and naval military superiority; buttressing its bilateral alliance network (especially with Japan and Australia); expanding military access in the region with bilateral arrangements with countries like Singapore; selling new military systems to Taiwan; and improving relations with India as a potential counterweight to China. On the other hand, the United States has accommodated China by restraining Taiwan from pushing toward formal independence, accepting China into the World Trade Organization (WTO) and other international organizations, cooperating with China to deal with North Korea's nuclear program, supporting China's economic modernization, and engaging China to become a "responsible stakeholder."

China too is pursuing a mixed hedging strategy (Medeiros, 2005/06: 153–9). It is balancing against the United States and the US alliance network by modernizing its military and by preventing the formation of an anti-China coalition in Asia through reassurance and constructive bilateral and multilateral diplomacy. But China is also accommodating the United States. Beijing is willing to join US-supported international regimes, cooperate with Washington to deal with North Korea, and develop a common stance on counterterrorism. Chinese leaders appear willing to accept US predominance for the time being and to use the international stability that American hegemony offers so that China can concentrate on its own economic development. The one issue on which China is willing to confront the United States is any move on Washington's part to support, both diplomatically and militarily, a Taiwanese independence movement. Regarding Japan, China has admonished its neighbor regarding history-related issues, mobilized Asian opposition to Japan becoming a permanent member of the UN Security Council, and criticized moves to strengthen the US–Japan alliance in ways that could be used in a Taiwan scenario. But at the same time, Beijing has been receptive to Tokyo's efforts to prevent a downward spiral in bilateral relations.

Japan is also hedging (Mochizuki, 2007). Tokyo has balanced against China's rise by strengthening its alliance with the United States, by relaxing somewhat its domestic constraints on defense policy, and by furtively discussing Japan's role with the US defense community during a Taiwan crisis. But Japan's balancing against China has been circumscribed (Twomey, 2000). Japan continues to freeze its defense budget and refrains from revising or reinterpreting its constitution so that it can exercise its right of collective self-defense. Japan has accommodated China by assisting China's economic development, welcoming its participation in various global and regional fora, and opposing Taiwan's independence. Since fall 2006, the Japanese government has revitalized its relations with China by avoiding prime minister pilgrimages to the Yasukuni Shrine, by resuming regular high-level exchanges, and by compromising in the Exclusive Economic Zone (EEZ) dispute in the East China Sea. Japan has also engaged in hedging vis-à-vis the United States (Heginbotham and Samuels, 2002). While relying upon its alliance with the United States to hedge against possible military threats, Japan has been developing relations with Asian countries to hedge against economic conflicts with the United States and perhaps even a weakening of the US security commitment to Japan.

How do the three major powers fare in terms of the status quo–revisionist state distinction? While China has become more supportive of existing international institutions and norms and more accepting of US predominance (Johnston, 2004: 77), it exhibits a mild form of revisionism when it promotes regional processes that exclude the United States. Regarding the territorial dispute with Japan, China has so far refrained from threatening military force to seize the Diaoyu/Senkaku islands. China is the most revisionist when it continues to reserve the right to use force against Taiwan, but the actual use of force may depend decisively on whether Taiwan is revising the status quo by moving toward some version of formal independence. Japan appears to be a status quo power unequivocally. It has refrained from considering the use of force to change an unfavorable status quo regarding territorial disputes with both Russia and South Korea. And it supports a continuation of US hegemonic leadership and alliance network in the Asia-Pacific region. Given that the United States is the predominant power in the region, one would expect it to be the most status quo oriented. Washington, however, does display some revisionist tendencies when it considers regime change of rogue states or assertive democratization and human rights policies, but so far in the Asia-Pacific, the US has tempered this tendency especially after its regime change war against Iraq became a quagmire.

Secondary states

There is little evidence that the secondary states in Asia-Pacific are balancing against an ascendant China or the US hegemon. South Korea is accommodating China's rise (Kang, 2007: 55–6, 104–25). Seoul has not exhibited much fear of China's military modernization and has been willing to accept Chinese leadership on many regional issues, especially on how to address the North Korean nuclear issue. South Korea has generally embraced Chinese initiatives for regional institution building. Although South Koreans may disagree about whether to be tougher toward North Korea, even Korean conservatives eschew military balancing against China. This does not mean that

South Korea is bandwagoning with China or balancing against the United States. Even during the Roh Moo-hyun presidency, Seoul cooperated with Washington regarding the US plan to realign military bases on South Korean territory rather than pressing the US to withdraw troops. It also supported the US military operation in the Middle East by deploying a larger defense force than Japan. The election of Lee Myung-bak is likely to lead to a strengthening of relations with the United States as well as a warming of relations with Japan.

The Southeast Asian countries in the Association of Southeast Asian Nations (ASEAN) also show clear signs of accommodating China's rise. The gravitational pull of the Chinese economy as well as the cultural and ethnic linkages have restrained the ASEAN states from directly balancing against China's growing power (Kang, 2007: 126–52). But at the same time, ASEAN is not bandwagoning with China in the security realm. The Southeast Asian countries are engaged in "indirect balancing against potential Chinese (or other aggressive) power by facilitating the continued US security commitment to the region" (Goh, 2007/08: 113–14). Furthermore, ASEAN has been actively promoting multilateral institutions and processes that aim to integrate and socialize China and to moderate great power competition (Acharya and Tan, 2005).

Australia too exhibits a similar mixed strategic response to the changing regional power distribution (Tow, 2005). On the one hand, Australia sees its economic fortunes increasingly tied to China's growth and Canberra has supported regional processes to nurture multilateral cooperation. On the other hand, Australia has revitalized its alliance with the United States after 9/11 and promoted security cooperation with Japan. Canberra has been working with Washington and Tokyo to institutionalize trilateral security cooperation and appears quite favorable to Japan's "normalization" as a security actor (Bisley, 2008). But Australia is concerned about the incipient rivalry between the United States and China, and between Japan and China, and therefore its preference seems to be to encourage what one Australian analyst calls a "Concert of Asia" rather than balancing with the United States and Japan against China (White, 2005). This preference is likely to be stronger with the shift in prime-ministership from John Howard to the Mandarin-speaking Kevin Rudd.

The one state in the region that appears to be balancing against China is Taiwan. To counter Chinese military modernization, Taiwan has been upgrading its own defense capabilities with the help of the United States (Swaine and Kamphausen, 2005). Taipei has also welcomed the recalibration of Japanese defense policy and public attitudes in a direction more favorable to it. Both the governments of Lee Teng-hui and Chen Shui-bian have explored ways to move Taiwan toward independence much to the agitation of China. But even Taiwan has not unequivocally balanced against China. Taipei has been reluctant to commit the budget necessary to purchase some of the advanced weapons systems that the US is willing to sell and Taiwanese business interests have been eager to pursue commercial opportunities in the mainland (Ross, 2006: 383–7). The 2008 election of Kuomintang's Ma Ying-jeou as Taiwan's president suggests in the very least that the Taipei now wishes to ease tensions with Beijing and revive the cross-strait dialogue.

Moderate political-security competition

This brief survey of state political-security strategies confirms competitive dynamics among the three major powers—between China and Japan, and between China and the United States. Therefore, one cannot completely dismiss the pessimistic scenarios of some realists who predict a great power struggle as China grows in power and becomes more of a peer competitor of the US–Japan alliance in the East Asia/West Pacific theater (Mearsheimer, 2006). But for the moment, this major power competition appears moderate with all three states engaged in mixed hedging strategies. None of these major powers are pursuing a stridently revisionist agenda. The Asia-Pacific region has yet to manifest the intense rivalries and conflicts that the more pessimistic analyses predicted soon after the end of the Cold War (Friedberg, 1992/93). We do not see a clear geopolitical divide between the US-led alliance network and a Sino-centric coalition reminiscent of the Cold War.

The secondary states in the regional system are also helping to moderate the competition. Virtually, all these states are pursuing a dualistic strategy of accommodating China's rise and indirect balancing against possible security threats (including from China) by supporting the US alliance network and military deployments. Therefore, while the region as a whole is not engaged in hard balancing against China, it is not bandwagoning with China either—making predictions of a re-emergence of a Chinese-centered hierarchical order premature. Rather, the collective effect of inter-active state strategies points toward working with the political-security umbrella of US incomplete hegemony to accommodate and integrate China's rise so that the competitive tendencies will be tamed and the cooperative dynamics will be facilitated.

Political-security motivations for FTA initiatives

How then have political-security strategies shaped the FTA policies of major powers and secondary states in terms of both the choice of partners and the timing of initiatives?

FTA policies of the major powers

The United States has used FTAs to reward countries that cooperate with its foreign and security policies—as indicated by its FTAs with Israel and Jordan (Schott, 2004a: 369–70). In the Asia-Pacific region and the Western Hemisphere, the key political-security motivation for the Bush administration's support of FTAs was an interest in consolidating a counterterrorism coalition in the wake of the 9/11 attacks (see Chapter 5). After the United States concluded an FTA with Singapore in May 2003, President George W. Bush went to Singapore to sign a strategic partnership framework agreement and talked openly of linking trade to security cooperation (Pang, 2007: 8–9). Bush reinforced this message when he attended the 2005 Asia Pacific Economic Cooperation (APEC) meeting in South Korea by stating that FTAs can promote security collaboration to fight terrorism in Southeast Asia and prevent the proliferation of weapons of mass destruction (Pang, 2007: 21). To help buttress the politically problematic relationship with South Korea and acknowledge Republic of Korea's (ROK) support of the US war on terrorism, the Bush administration worked hard to seal an FTA with Seoul in spring 2007. While strengthening defense cooperation with Australia, the United States also signed an FTA with that country in May 2004. But the Bush administration has shunned New Zealand in its FTA policy, indicating a willingness to punish uncooperative allies.

Competitive political-security calculations vis-à-vis China surfaced after China's FTA initiative with ASEAN (see Chapter 11). Responding to criticisms that the US may be distracted with the war on terrorism while "China was focusing on Southeast Asia like a laser," the Bush administration, in November 2005, issued with seven ASEAN countries a Joint Vision Statement on the ASEAN–US Enhanced Partnership and an agreement to cooperate to conclude a region-wide ASEAN–US trade and investment facilitation agreement (TIFA) (Munakata, 2006b: 124–5). Under the Enterprise for ASEAN Initiative (EAI) framework, the US began to pursue FTA projects with individual ASEAN countries: Malaysia and the Philippines (in late 2002) and Thailand in July 2003 (DeRosa, 2004: 166–7). One US incentive for engaging ASEAN countries individually and collectively has been to help shape ASEAN initiatives for East Asian regionalism so that they do not weaken US influence relative to China. Because of its reluctance to accede to the ASEAN Treaty of Amity and Cooperation, Washington has been hampered in its effort to prevent the emergence of an East Asia summit (EAS) process that excludes the United States and heightens Chinese influence. Therefore, in part to compete with China, the Bush administration has preferred to try to revitalize APEC as the central forum for regional economic integration and float the notion of a Free Trade Area of the Asia-Pacific (FTAAP) (Dent, 2007).

Competitive calculations vis-à-vis China have also motivated Japan's FTA policy (see Chapter 10). Despite the pioneering role of the Japan–Singapore FTA signed in January 2002, Tokyo was jolted by the rapid progress in China–ASEAN discussions. In November 2001, Beijing succeeded in persuading ASEAN to establish an ASEAN–China FTA by 2010. This news energized Japanese trade officials to ask politicians to be more flexible about the liberalization of sensitive sectors lest Japan lag behind in the FTA race, and Prime Minister Koizumi proposed a Japan–ASEAN Comprehensive Economic Partnership (JACEP) during his trip to Southeast Asia in January 2002 (Munakata, 2006b: 118).

Regarding a free trade agreement, however, Japan initially opted to negotiate with ASEAN countries individually rather than with the association as a whole. Some analysts observed that this tact provoked regional distrust or allowed China to take "the regional lead in economic diplomacy" (Kwei, 2006: 133).[3] Nevertheless Tokyo initiated FTA talks with individual ASEAN states in quick succession: with Malaysia in January 2004, with the Philippines and Thailand in February 2004, and with Indonesia in June 2005 (Munakata, 2006b: 120–1).

The Sino-Japanese rivalry has contributed to Japan's ambivalent response to Chinese initiatives for subregional or regional FTAs. When China proposed a feasibility study for a trilateral Northeast Asia FTA (China, Japan, and South Korea) in November 2002, Japan was less than enthusiastic. Such an agreement, if achieved, could provide an economic foundation for trilateral political-security cooperation or at least help to mitigate mistrust among these three Northeast Asian states. It appears, however, that Japanese concerns about the agricultural sector and competition from Chinese state-owned enterprises made Japan reluctant to go beyond think-tank studies of the idea (Munakata, 2006b: 117). Conversely, the political-security disincentives might have been too strong and the political-security incentives too weak to overcome these economic considerations. Rather than negotiate trilaterally, Tokyo has focused on trying to achieve an FTA with South Korea where the strategic payoff for Japan might be greater, namely to prevent a South Korean strategic drift toward China.

In response to a Chinese-backed proposal for an East Asian Summit, Tokyo advocated the inclusion of Australia, New Zealand, and India to dilute China's influence. In 2006, Japan began to shift beyond its bilateral individual-country approach to FTAs by proposing talks for a region-wide East Asia Economic Partnership Agreement (East Asia EPA) commencing in 2008. Similar to its preference regarding EAS membership, Japan called for an East Asia FTA that encompassed Australia, New Zealand, and India as well as the ten ASEAN states and the three Northeast Asian countries of China, Japan, and South Korea (Wijers-Hasegawa, 2006). As part of this strategy to counter China's regional influence, Japan has pushed for an FTA with Australia—despite domestic agricultural opposition—to reinforce the growing security cooperation between Tokyo and Canberra and to balance Australia's growing economic ties with China (Capling, 2008: 33–4).

Finally, political-security competition has also animated China's FTA policies (see Chapter 11). The launching of Japan–Singapore FTA negotiations encouraged China to push for an FTA with ASEAN as a whole. China persuaded the ASEAN states that feared competition from China by offering differential treatment for less developed ASEAN states and an "early harvest" of tariff reduction for agricultural products (Munakata, 2006b: 118–19). Although an urge to "catch-up" with Japan might have been the original impetus for China, some interpreted the move as power play to achieve a leadership position relative to Japan. According to one observer, China may be developing "a useful building block toward ensuring China's leadership role in the region" (Kwei, 2006: 129). But there was a defensive competitive calculation as well. China's FTA initiative toward ASEAN was part of an omnidirectional foreign policy to improve relations with its neighbors and reassure the region about China's peaceful rise and to prevent Southeast Asia from aligning against China (Kwei, 2006: 133; Munakata, 2006: 123). At the same time, China announced in November 2002 its objective to forge an FTA with ASEAN: China and ASEAN issued a joint statement of cooperation on "nontraditional security issues" and the Declaration on the Conduct of Parties in the South China Sea. In October 2003, China then acceded to the 1976 Treaty of Amity and Cooperation (TAC) in Southeast Asia (Gill, 2007: 35–6).

China has also promoted FTAs in Northeast Asia. China's proposal of a feasibility study for a trilateral China–Japan–South Korea FTA did not get much traction, so China shifted gears to seek a bilateral FTA with South Korea (Zhang, 2007: 121). According to some Chinese analysts, the ultimate objective is the creation of an East Asian Free Trade Agreement (EAFTA). To achieve this, Zhang Yunling of the Chinese Academy of Social Sciences has argued for the establishment of three parallel FTAs with each tying one of the Northeast Asian countries to ASEAN: China–ASEAN, Japan–ASEAN, and ROK–ASEAN. Then an EAFTA would be established by unifying "the separated arrangements into an integrated framework." Zhang has also downplayed Sino-Japanese rivalry in this process: "While China would like to see an East Asian FTA in place as early as possible, and is using the China–ASEAN FTA to forge such a grouping, the move is in no way intended to reduce Japanese interests in ASEAN or exclude Japan from East Asia" (Zhang, 2003: 232). But in response to a question about the US role, Zhang reportedly stated that "EAFTA will not invite the US, otherwise it will become like APEC" (Zhang, 2005).

Such statements by Chinese analysts about excluding the United States from the EAFTA have fueled suspicions that Beijing's regional FTA policy might be one element of a long-term agenda to reduce US influence in the region relative to China's. While crediting Malaysia for pushing for an EAS, China has vigorously backed the idea. One of the three conditions articulated by ASEAN for membership in the EAS (signing onto the TAC in Southeast Asia) poses a difficult hurdle for the United States because the TAC might constrain US military options (Gill, 2007: 34–5).

FTA policies of the secondary states

Regarding South Korea, the 1997 regional financial crisis motivated President Kim Dae Jung to improve relations with Japan. In this context, South Korean policy analysts floated an FTA with Japan as a good way to promote more stable and friendly relations between these two countries. Bilateral tensions over historical issues and territorial disputes as well as economic constraints prevented a takeoff in Japan–ROK FTA talks, and South Korea concluded its first bilateral FTA with Chile instead. Nevertheless negotiating an agreement with Chile provided valuable preparation for engaging the larger trade partners, Japan and the United States (Koo, 2006: 145–9). South Korea ended up concluding an FTA with United States in spring 2007 while the talks with Japan stalled in the context of deteriorating bilateral political relations between Seoul and Tokyo. In ROK discussions with the US, buttressing a problematic security relationship served as a strong incentive for the South Korean leadership to make the extra effort not to have the negotiations fail (see Chapter 9). Moreover, the conclusion of the US–Korea FTA gave further impetus to push ahead with the trade talks with Japan and even to argue that an FTA with China was inevitable (President Roh in *Chosun Ilbo*, 23 May 2007). This behavior may reflect a broader geopolitical interest on the part of South Korea to serve as a bridge between China and Japan (Koo, 2006: 149).

In terms of Southeast Asia, the case of Singapore illustrates how a small state's desire to overcome its political-security vulnerability can be a strong motivation for the pursuit of FTAs (see Chapter 8). Singapore harbored a strong sense of vulnerability by being wedged between Malaysia and Indonesia— two large Islamic countries that had at times challenged Singapore's interests. Therefore, the city-state sought to strengthen ties with extra-regional states. Even at the risk of provoking frictions with some ASEAN states, Singapore had a keen interest in using FTAs to anchor the United States and Japan as regional stakeholders (Leifer, 2000: 6). The rise of China also factored into this strategic equation. Singapore signed a strategic partnership agreement with China in 2000 and has signaled its unwillingness to join either the United States or Japan in a strategy to contain China. But at the same time, Singapore has been quite willing to play a hedging game with these three major powers (Pang, 2007: 21–3).

Singapore's move to forge FTAs with multiple extra-regional partners initially provoked intra-ASEAN criticisms that Singapore was undermining ASEAN regional-community building. Rather than blocking such extra-regional initiatives, however, just about all the ASEAN states eventually joined the FTA bandwagon. And Singapore found in Thailand a good partner to trailblaze this movement. As Christopher Dent warns, the "economic Darwinism of competitive bilateral FTAs" has the danger of undermining ASEAN cohesion insofar as Singapore seeks to establish itself as Southeast Asia's "premier entrepot hub economy" (Dent, 2006: 93–6, 104–5). But as long as Singapore, with the help of Thailand, is able to pull the other ASEAN states along, there does not have to be an unraveling of ASEAN. Even as Singapore tries to be ASEAN's hub economy, ASEAN as a whole is striving to be the "hub" for East Asian economic integration and community-building by continuing to promote its own ASEAN Free Trade Area and by collectively engaging non-ASEAN states in FTA negotiations (Ong, 2003: 58). Goh characterizes ASEAN's FTA policy an "omni-enmeshment" strategy to moderate major power competition (Goh, 2007/08: 125, 139–44).

For Australia, the pursuit of FTAs marked a major departure from its commitment to multilateral trade liberalization. This policy shift can be attributed to a realization of neither APEC nor WTO driving liberalization as well as a recognition that FTAs could bring significant economic gains, but important contributory factors are the greater receptivity of Washington to such preferential trade agreements and the possibility that a bilateral US–Australia FTA might put the security alliance with the United States on more solid ground (Bisley, 2004: 251–2). Canberra was also responding to Washington's concerns that Australia might be too accommodative of China's security interests (especially about Taiwan) because of Australia's China economic fever. Therefore, to rebalance its foreign policy between the US alliance and China, the Howard government opted not only to enhance US–Australia–Japan security cooperation, but also to pursue an FTA with Japan as well as with the United States (Capling, 2008: 34–6). But this responsiveness to US pressure did not mean that Canberra was willing to join Washington and Tokyo in a balancing—much less a containment—strategy against China. Prime Minister John Howard noted that "Australia's interests would be best served if the US would allow China a somewhat bigger regional role, in return for China allowing Japan a larger say in regional affairs" (Gill, 2007: 152–3). Similar to ASEAN, Australia has completed or launched FTA negotiations with a variety of partners including China (Ravenhill, 2008: 121–8).

Taiwan's FTA policy is motivated by a strong desire to reduce its vulnerability and political isolation in the context of a rising China and negative trends in the China–Taiwan balance of military and economic power. As Beijing has gradually chipped away at the countries that have diplomatic relations with Taipei, Taiwan has moved vigorously to negotiate FTAs with states with which it still has official relations. Therefore, Taiwan has concluded bilateral FTAs with Panama, Guatemala, and Nicaragua, and a trilateral one with El Salvador and Honduras (Hsueh, 2006). But the big prize would be an FTA with the United States and Japan—both countries that will play an important role in a Taiwan Strait crisis. Although Washington and Tokyo have publicly declared their interest in a peaceful resolution of the Taiwan issue, both capitals have refrained from entering into formal talks about an FTA with Taipei for fear of provoking Beijing. There has been a sharp political divide within Taiwan about how best to deal with China. Although the Democratic Progressive Party (DPP) government under Chen Shui-bian pushed for a more independent Taiwan identity despite strong protests from China and even the United States, the Kuomintang under Ma Ying-jeou has advocated positive dialogue with the mainland. Before being elected Taiwan's president, Ma announced in July 2007 that he would seek some kind of "closer economic partnership" with China similar to the arrangement that exists between China and Hong Kong. As a complement to this new policy, Ma stated that a Kuomintang (KMT) government would also seek FTAs with Hong Kong, Singapore, and South Korea (Ma in *Daily Times*, Pakistan, 3 July 2007).

After assuming office in May 2008, President Ma followed through by commencing FTA negotiations with China (Cha, 2009).

Political-security competition hypothesis: Confirmation and limits

The above survey confirms the hypothesis that political-security competition between the United States and China, and between Japan and China, has been one of the motivators behind the FTA policies of these three major powers. Conversely, the absence of serious discussions of FTAs between China on the one hand and the United States and Japan on the other hand suggest that the incipient political-security rivalry among these three major powers can serve as an inhibitor of FTA policies.

The absence and weakness of other FTA initiatives, however, indicates that there are limits too to the political-security competition hypothesis. First, despite Taipei's keen interest in negotiating FTAs with both the United States and Japan for the strategic purpose of vulnerability reduction, both Washington and Tokyo have been reluctant because of their sensitivities toward Beijing. Second, the United States and Japan have so far not promoted a bilateral FTA with each other. Given the progress in US–Japan defense cooperation since the mid-1990s, one might imagine a US–Japan FTA as a good way to further bolster the alliance as China's power rises. Various US policy analysts have advocated such a bilateral FTA (Fauver and Stewart, 2003: 23–39). For example, the February 2007 sequel to the famous Fall 2000 Armitage–Nye Report on the US–Japan alliance stressed that a bilateral FTA would become "the hub for an emerging network of FTAs in Asia" and yield immense political and strategic benefits by sending a "remarkably powerful signal to the region and world" (Armitage and Nye, 2007: 17–18). But despite such calls, the Bush administration did not embrace this notion as strongly as it did the FTAs with South Korea and Australia. In addition to the domestic political complexity of negotiating a US–Japan FTA, perhaps both Washington and Tokyo did not see a compelling political-security necessity for such an economic agreement given the progress in bilateral security cooperation in recent years and their shared interest in engaging rather than containing China.

The track record of secondary states shows that an interest in reducing political-security vulnerabilities (Singapore) or placating security patrons (South Korea and Australia) can motivate these states to pursue FTAs. What is also noteworthy is that virtually all the secondary states and the ASEAN as a whole are reluctant to use FTAs to reinforce the competitive tendencies among the major powers by aligning with only one major power. In fact, the secondary states are inclined to pursue FTA initiatives with all three major powers as part of their strategic interest in mitigating major power rivalries. Nevertheless, at the same time, ASEAN through its ASEAN+1 agreements has been quite willing to use competition among the larger powers to obtain an economically better FTA deal.[4]

Although this survey of FTA strategies supports the notion that political-security calculations can contribute to the choice and timing of FTA partners, determining the actual power of the political-security variable requires further investigation than is possible in this chapter. For instance, it is not clear if political-security incentives are powerful enough to overcome domestic resistance or divergent economic interests to bring an FTA negotiation to a successful conclusion. The case of the previously unimaginable Australia–Japan FTA negotiations does suggest that political-security motivations might trump formidable domestic political resistance in Japan from the agricultural lobby. But since these talks are still a work in progress, we cannot yet assess the relative power of the strategic variable. One possible hypothesis is that because the competitive strategic dynamics in the Asia-Pacific (especially among the major powers) remains moderate rather than extreme, the power of political-security calculations to trump domestic political and economic impediments to FTAs is likely to be modest. Whether or not the US–ROK FTA wins US Congressional approval will be a good test of this hypothesis.

Conversely, it is worth investigating whether convergent economic and domestic commercial interests are powerful enough to overcome political-security impediments to FTAs. For example, will economic interests between Japan and China or between Japan and South Korea be convergent enough to overcome existing political-security impediments? The recent improvement of Japan–China and Japan–ROK relations suggests that a closer look at the prospects for a Northeast Asia FTA is warranted. When the economic interests are not convergent enough and the political-security impediments are too formidable, FTAs are unlikely to be realized. However, growing economic convergence coupled with a reduction of political-security impediments might present a favorable threshold for an FTA breakthrough.

Regional political-security consequences

How does the varied pattern of intra-regional and extra-regional FTA initiatives matter for political-security relations in East Asia? Is the FTA phenomenon steering the region toward a particular political-security order? Does the FTA movement reinforce or counter regional rivalries?

Competitive tendencies

Insofar as the rise of China is shaping East Asia's strategic landscape, the competitions between China and Japan and between China and the United States will play a defining role in the future regional order. But as noted earlier, the competitive dynamics have been moderate thus far with each of the major powers pursuing hedging strategies and refraining from stridently revisionist agendas. The secondary states have also acted to help moderate this major power competition—or at least to avoid exacerbating this competition.

How then does the FTA movement fit into this evolving strategic dynamic? The three major powers have notably refrained from using FTAs with each other to counter the competitive tendencies between China on the one hand and the United States and Japan on the other hand. Neither a US–China FTA nor a Japan–China FTA has been under serious discussion, much less negotiation. Consideration of a trilateral Northeast Asia FTA composed of China, Japan, and South Korea that could help foster better Sino-Japanese relations has not gotten far as well.

The major powers, however, appear to be using FTAs with third parties to check potential negative strategic trends. To reassure other regional states about China's rise and to prevent the emergence of a broad-based regional coalition to contain China, Beijing has promoted FTAs with ASEAN, South Korea, and Australia and supported an East Asian FTA and an EAS. To try to secure US economic and security presence in East Asia in the face of China's rise, Washington has in turn signed FTAs with Singapore, South Korea, and Australia, launched the EAI for Southeast Asia, and is beginning to refocus on APEC. And to prevent China from gaining a predominant position in East Asia, Tokyo has been negotiating FTAs with individual ASEAN states and ASEAN as a whole, proposing an East Asia EPA that includes Australia, New Zealand, and India, and continuing FTA discussions with South Korea (although progress has been limited).

The competitive interaction of FTA initiatives as mentioned above along with other diplomatic and security maneuvers block for the time being any regional hegemonic projects on the part of any of the three major powers. At the economic level, the United States, Japan, and China may compete for leadership regarding whose model of economic liberalization and integration will become the norm (Dent, 2007: 464–6). But such competition does not directly translate into regional leadership in the political-security realm. Leading or winning the competition regarding regional models of economic liberalization and integration could enhance a state's reputation and influence so that its ideas for a regional security architecture are taken more seriously. But relative military capabilities, alliance arrangements, and a willingness to contribute to collective defense or security will remain critical to regional political-security leadership. Competitive FTA initiatives may also have the effect of *indirectly* mitigating strategic rivalries between China and Japan and between China and the United States. The fact that virtually all the secondary states in the region want to reach out to all three powers indicates that they are reluctant to pick sides in a great power rivalry.

Finally, the restraint that the United States and Japan have exercised in responding to Taiwan's overtures for an FTA show that both Washington and Tokyo are careful not to use FTAs to provoke Beijing about what it considers to be a vital political interest. In other words, even though FTA initiatives may *reinforce* incipient major power rivalries, they have not been used to *exacerbate* such rivalries. As the possible shift in Taiwan's policies suggest,

Taipei could mitigate the problem by pushing for some version of an FTA with Beijing.

Cooperative tendencies

After the end of the Cold War, a number of fledgling multilateral dialogues at both the official and nonofficial levels have emerged to foster security cooperation. They include the ASEAN Regional Forum, the Track-2 Northeast Asia Cooperation Dialogue (NEACD), and the International Institute for Strategic Studies (IISS) Shangri-la Dialogue. Some have even argued that the Six-Party Talks about North Korea's nuclear program provides the basis for establishing a cooperative Northeast Asia security institution. But compared to the resilient US-centered security alliance system in the Asia-Pacific, these multilateral forums are so far primarily talk-shops that are unable to address hard security challenges or even to promote substantial military transparency and mutual reassurance measures. To what extent does the FTA movement aid or hinder the development of regional security cooperation beyond the use of bilateral FTAs to buttress existing alliances?

The FTA bandwagon has been accompanied by increasing voices for regional community-building. Although the creation of a security community for East Asia in the sense that Karl Deutsch originally employed the concept may be illusive in the foreseeable future, optimists believe that regional economic interdependence and integration might eventually provide the material foundations for cooperative security (Wan, 2003: 280–305). To the extent that the FTA movement might promote regional economic integration, the same movement would in turn foster security cooperation. Indeed, the above survey of national cases shows that even with their competitive elements, bilateral FTAs have also been used as tools of cooperative diplomacy and reassurance.

But where the FTA movement becomes most salient for the prospects of regional cooperative security mechanisms are the proposals for various regional FTAs as opposed to bilateral FTAs. A key consideration is the degree of matching between possible security forums on the one hand and possible regional FTAs on the other hand. In the early 1990s, APEC as a region-wide economic forum and the ASEAN Regional Forum (ARF) as a region-wide security dialogue represented a near perfect match on the face of it. Both forums bridged the two sides of the Pacific rather than dividing them. But there was also a difference that prevented them from being mutually reinforcing. Whereas APEC was seen as diluting the role of ASEAN as it tried to bridge trans-Pacific divisions regarding the modality of regional economic liberalization, ARF was firmly anchored around ASEAN norms and concentrated on security issues more relevant to Southeast Asia rather than to Northeast Asia.

As APEC waned in the wake of frictions over the early voluntary sectoral liberalization (EVSL) negotiations and the 1997–98 regional financial crisis, ASEAN reasserted itself in regional economic dialogues through the ASEAN+3 process which excluded the United States. Singapore's FTA trailblazing and the Sino-Japanese competition regarding ASEAN have made ASEAN one of the FTA regional hubs. This is evident in the way both China and Japan are willing to respect ASEAN as a focal point. Both the Chinese concept of an East Asian FTA and the Japanese notion of an East Asian EPA keep the center of gravity around ASEAN. If the East Asian Summit process purports to build upon such a regional FTA project and to have an expansive agenda that includes political and security issues, the absence of the United States becomes problematic. Even if as Japan hopes Australia and India might help to counter China, an EAS without the United States could become the first step in a gradual erosion of US influence. The ball now appears to be in the US court about whether it will make a serious effort to be a part of EAS by signing on to the TAC with some modifications. But the risk of such a move from the perspective of East Asia community-building is that a vigorous US attempt to alter TAC norms (especially regarding non-intervention) with the help of allies like Japan, Singapore, and Australia might be enough to blow apart the fragile EAS community-building project.

There are two alternative paths to regional security cooperation that would give the United States a central role. One is the Northeast Asian path that could build upon the Six-Party Talks and the Track-2 NEACD. The United States could build on its FTA with South Korea to negotiate a "comprehensive economic partnership" with Japan to establish a new gold standard for international economic liberalization. Such an achievement would put the US and its allies in the economic driver seat through FTAs in Northeast Asia. Regional economic liberalization, of course, does not address the critical obstacles to Northeast Asian cooperative security; but if the Six-Party Talks prove successful in putting North Korea on the path of denuclearization, then the time could become ripe for laying the groundwork for a Northeast Asia cooperative security order that is more to America and Japan's liking—one in which China's voice is not predominant and South Korea remains anchored to the US alliance network.

The alternative might be the vision of Pacific community articulated by President Clinton in the context of the first APEC summit back in 1993. But this path would require that the United States, with the help of allies and friends in East Asia, resurrect the goal of a free trade area of the Asia-Pacific and to strengthen APEC as "the pre-eminent regional economic forum" as declared by the United States and Japan in their joint statement on alliance transformation in May 2007 (Joint Statement). Eventually, APEC or a related trans–Asia-Pacific forum could begin to address more forthrightly various security issues. The advantage of this course would be that the United States and its allies would be less constrained by ASEAN norms that have hampered substantive progress in ARF, but this would inevitably take the initiative away from ASEAN and is therefore likely to be resisted. How much other Asian countries would go along with a US-led drive for multilateral security cooperation remains to be seen: if the United States is too overbearing and impatient, the effort could provoke a backlash that could in turn aggravate the competitive tendencies in the region.

Conclusions

This chapter confirms the hypothesis that political-security competition motivated the FTA policies of the major powers in the Asia-Pacific region and affected the sequencing of FTA initiatives. China launched an FTA initiative with ASEAN as a whole to catch up diplomatically with Japan in Southeast Asia, and both the United States and Japan became more energetic about FTAs with individual ASEAN states in response to the Chinese initiative. Although the secondary states in Southeast Asia have been willing to use major power competition to negotiate more advantageous FTAs, they along with South Korea and Australia have avoided exacerbating major power cleavages in their pursuit of FTAs by not siding with one major power to the exclusion of the other major powers. But at the same time, secondary states have embraced FTAs as a means to lessen their political-security vulnerabilities or to bolster their alliances with the predominant power—the United States.

The relative influence of political-security calculations when there are tradeoffs between economic and security interests appears mixed. For example, the conclusion (but not ratification) of the US–ROK FTA agreement and serious negotiations for a Japan–Australia FTA shows that alliance interests might overcome domestic economic resistance to FTAs. But alliance interests have thus far not been strong enough to steer Washington and Tokyo toward a bilateral FTA. Moreover, the major powers have not used FTAs directly as a means to mitigate their competitive tendencies—indicating the limits of commercial liberalism. Sino-Japanese discussions for FTA have not advanced very far, and China and the US are not seriously considering a bilateral FTA. Tokyo and Washington, however, have refrained from provoking Beijing by not responding positively to Taipei's FTA overtures. This restraint, along with the tendency of secondary states to seek FTAs with all of the major powers, has reinforced the moderate nature of regional security competition.

The major powers are competing among themselves regarding their respective visions for regional economic integration. While China has preferred a regional FTA without US participation, Japan has sought to dilute Chinese influence by insisting on the participation of Australia, New Zealand, and India. The United States is concerned that it might be left out of a region-wide FTA grouping and has therefore sought to revive the APEC formula. How this competition plays out and how it affects regional community-building projects remains to be seen. But the bilateral FTA links that the United States has succeeded in forging with a number of individual Asian countries as well as the resilience of the US alliance network in the region suggest that America's "incomplete hegemony" is likely to continue for the time being despite China's ascent.

Notes

1. Whereas the United States has enjoyed unrivaled influence in the Western Hemisphere, the recent emergence of Left-wing governments in Venezuela, Ecuador, and Bolivia has brought increased contestation of US power in the region. My thanks to Mireya Solís for reminding me of this development.
2. An analytical problem occurs if one views threats to be a function of intentions as well as material capabilities and geographic position, not simply the functions of material capabilities and geographic positions. Then, the determination as to which states are threatening and the extent to which they are threatening becomes more uncertain and open to debate.
3. Ministry of Economy, Trade and Industry (METI) official Munakata argues that Japan took this course because its status as a developed country under General Agreement on Tariffs and Trade (GATT) rules about FTAs prevented it from being as flexible as China regarding FTA negotiations with ASEAN.
4. My thanks to Mireya Solís for this important point.

4
Competitive Regionalism through Bilateral and Regional Rule-Making: Standard Setting and Locking-in

Junji Nakagawa

Introduction

The success of the World Trade Organization (WTO) dispute settlement mechanism and the proliferation of investor-state arbitration, together with the regionalization of international trade and investment relations, are the contemporary features of legalization of international economic relations, which draws more and more attention of scholars of international relations and international economic law. An increasing number of free trade agreements (FTAs) and bilateral investment treaties (BITs) are concluded either within regions or cross-regionally.

Earlier, Western Hemisphere countries signed binding preferential trade agreements, and East Asia lagged behind in these trends (both legalization and regionalization) until fairly recently. Many countries in East Asia preferred informal dispute management to adjudication of trade and investment disputes. Also, they preferred multilateral trade liberalization [WTO and APEC (Asia Pacific Economic Cooperation), in particular] to preferential trade arrangement. However, as I discuss below in the first section, they finally made a policy shift toward legalization and regionalization in the early 2000s. Why did East Asian countries join the global trends?

In the second section, I argue that the key to the answer lies in the stalemate of multilateral rule-making, which resulted in standard-setting efforts through bilateral/regional FTAs and BITs in the region. I also highlight the nuance in legalization/regionalization in East Asia among modest, medium, and aggressive legalism in the sense that the latter two approaches prefer mid- to high level legal rule-making in regionalization, while the former prefers more modest rule-making. In the third section, I assert the need to get the modest legalist countries, especially China, involved into more aggressive legalism, so that they may secure a more transparent and predictable business environment.

Finally, I examine the implication of legal competition on the coherence of regional integration in East Asia. My conclusions are that coherent East

Asian and Asia-Pacific regional integration should be sought as an ultimate goal so that all the members of the region, including those exhibiting more modest legalism, should play by the same rules that would enhance robust trade and investment relations within and beyond the region, though, pragmatically, it should be aimed at as a mid-term goal, rather than as a short-term goal to be realized in the near future.

Legalization in international economic relations and the possible use of FTAs for standard setting

Legalization of international economic relations: Why and to what extent?

Legalization of international relations in general, and legalization of international economic relations in particular, is on the rise. By "legalization" we mean obligation, precision, and delegation (Abbott et al., 2001: 17–18). Obligation means that states or other actors are legally bound by a rule or a commitment in the sense that their behavior thereunder is subject to scrutiny under the general rules, procedures, and discourse of international law, and often, domestic law as well. Precision means that rules unambiguously define the conduct they require, authorize, or proscribe. Delegation means that third parties have been granted authority to implement, interpret, and apply the rules; to resolve disputes; and possibly to make further rules.

As Abbott et al. (2001: 21) put it, international trade relations governed by the WTO approach the ideal type of full legalization in the sense that the WTO administers a remarkably detailed set of legally binding international agreements. It also operates a dispute settlement mechanism, including an appellate tribunal with significant authority to interpret and apply those agreements in the course of resolving particular disputes.

The unwillingness of developing countries to sign on to new rules on these issues in the absence of substantial agricultural liberalization in developed nations has in many ways contributed to the current stalemate of the Doha Development Agenda (DDA). In turn, the stagnation of the WTO negotiation process has created a strong incentive for nations to resort to regional and bilateral trade negotiations as an "insurance mechanism"(Mansfield and Reinhardt, 2003). This hedging strategy not only revolves around keeping the momentum for more tariff liberalization, but also, at a fundamental level, aims at deepening the liberalization process through the inclusion of the new rules on trade and investment.

The United States has been one of the most active practitioners of this "bottom-up" approach to international trade and investment rule-making. An early example of this strategy at work was NAFTA's (North American Free Trade Agreement) incorporation of the cutting-edge issues that would later on be incorporated in the WTO, such as intellectual property protection (trade-related aspects of intellectual property rights or TRIPS agreements) and service liberalization (General Agreement on Trade in Services or GATS). NAFTA went even further with the adoption of a host state-investor dispute arbitration mechanism (Chapter 11) that has not been incorporated at the multilateral level (Hufbauer and Schott, 2005: 210–13), and environmental and labor side agreements (Ibid.: Chapters 2 and 3). More recently, the United States responded to the stagnation of the DDA with a strategy of "competitive liberalization," whereby bilateral trade negotiations with countries that agree to negotiate on the issues of critical US interest receive a greater priority (Feinberg, 2005; Quiliconi and Wise, this volume).

Japan has also realized the benefit of FTA negotiation for international rule-making. Take for instance the argument advanced by the leading business association that "using the network of FTAs to disseminate fairer rules on antidumping out to other countries would help strengthen Japan's position in the next WTO negotiations" (Keidanren, 2000: 6). China is another country dissatisfied with current multilateral rules on antidumping, and has used its cross-regional FTA negotiations to reward nations willing to recognize China as a market economy.[1] In this way, China is strengthening its WTO campaign to scrap the application of the nonmarket economy methodology that facilitates the imposition of ad hoc and allegedly politically motivated antidumping duties on Chinese exports, as discussed by Yang in this volume.

Legalization in East Asia and the Pacific: Shift from low- to higher level

If North America provides an implicit benchmark for high legalization, the Asia-Pacific and East Asian regions offered an important example of low legalization or even an explicit aversion to legalization until recently (Kahler, 2001). Before the end of Cold War, the Asia-Pacific region had produced few formal multilateral institutions. A modest wave of institution building in the 1990s [ASEAN (Association of Southeast Asian nations) and APEC] narrowed the institutional difference with other regions, but the density of institutions spanning the regions remains lower than that in Europe or in the Americas. More importantly, those regional institutions constructed with Asian participation remained highly informal and explicitly rejected legalization in their design. Formal rules and obligations were limited in number; voluntary codes of conduct or general principles have been favored over precisely defined agreements; and disputes have been managed, if not resolved, without delegation to third-party adjudication (Kahler, 2001: 165).

Why legalization was low in Asia? One widely accepted explanation is that ASEAN and APEC are set apart from "Western-style" institutions on the basis of radically different Asian *legal culture and institutions* (Kahler, 2001: 176–7). However, this argument fails for several reasons. Most Asian societies, particularly in Southeast Asia, display legal pluralism rather than monolithic legal cultures and homogenous legal institutions. What appear to be cultural differences may in fact represent strategies pursued by political actors.

The "ASEAN (or Asian) way" of managing disputes or favoring informal institutions may result not only from the construction of social myths about harmony and a national past untouched by Western influence but also from conscious political programs to dampen adversarial conflict internally and internationally (Kahler, 2001: 176–7).

The reluctance to legalization in Asia seems to have expired in the 2000s, however. Asian countries are increasingly resorting to the WTO dispute settlement mechanism, though with country-specific nuances—with Korea being the most aggressive user and Japan being more modest in its use of the WTO dispute settlement mechanism (Nakagawa, 2007). Moreover, East Asian countries are finally joining the regionalization race through FTAs and BITs. Especially active are the ASEAN countries, which agreed in October 2003 to economic integration by 2020.[2] In addition, ASEAN and China signed an agreement in November 2004 to liberalize trade in goods.[3] ASEAN countries signed basic FTA framework agreements with Korea in December 2005[4] and with Japan in April 2008.[5] A similar agreement is being negotiated between ASEAN and India (Trade Policy Bureau, METI, 2006: 458).

Starting with the FTA with Singapore (signed in January 2002),[6] Japan has concluded FTAs with chapters on the promotion and protection of investment with the Philippines (September 2005),[7] Malaysia (December 2005),[8] Thailand (April 2007),[9] Brunei (June 2007),[10] Indonesia (August 2007),[11] and ASEAN (April 2008). It is also negotiating EPAs with India,[12] Vietnam,[13] Korea,[14] and Switzerland.[15] Besides FTAs, Japan has accelerated negotiation of BITs. Before 2000, it had concluded BITs with only two East Asian countries [China (1988)[16] and Hong Kong (1997)[17]]. Since 2000, it has concluded BITs with Korea,[18] Vietnam,[19] and Cambodia.[20] In addition, it is negotiating a trilateral BIT with China and Korea,[21] and a BIT with the Lao People's Democratic Republic.[22]

Japan's emphasis on regional/bilateral trade and investment rule-making can first and foremost be understood within the context of its huge trade and investment interests in East Asia. Its foreign direct investment (FDI) in the region rapidly increased in the 1990s. In 1997, when the Asian financial crisis broke out, Japanese investment peaked at 1.58 trillion yen, comprising over 50 percent of its total FDI.[23] This trend continued after the Asian financial crisis, and Korea and the ASEAN 10 also increased their FDI in the region since the early 2000s. From 2000 to 2005, FDI flow from Japan, Korea, and ASEAN 10 to East Asia increased from $8.77 billion to $23.88 billion, while the world's total FDI flow decreased from $1.34 trillion to $0.93 trillion.[24] Trade relations within the region have also grown rapidly. The ratio of intra-regional trade (export and import combined) in East Asia grew from 35.7 percent in 1980 to 55.8 percent in 2005, nearing that of the 62.1 percent of the EU.[25] The deepening trade relations in the region are reinforced by the increasing intra-regional FDI, in the sense that a substantive amount of FDI aims at trading capital and intermediate goods and final products within the region. For those companies of East Asia investing in the region, protection of investment through clear and transparent rules, and their enforcement through investor-state arbitration, are of critical importance. As these were not provided through multilateral forum, they lobbied their governments to secure them through BITs and FTAs.

On the side of host countries of FDI in East Asia, committing themselves to the promotion and protection of investment was deemed necessary to attract FDI: potential host countries are competing for credible property rights protections that foreign investors require (Elkins et al., 2006: 812). BITs and FTAs with investment chapters are one of the most salient means for showing such credibility, as foreign investors deliberate many factors regarding where to invest and whether to invest.[26] Both pushing and pulling powers thus functioned as catalyst to the proliferation of BITs and FTAs in East Asia.

Why then did East Asian countries join the global race toward regional/ bilateral BITs and FTAs? I argue that the key to the answer lies in the failure of multilateral rule-making.

Legal competition in the Asia-Pacific: Multilateral versus regional/bilateral rule-making

Investment rules

Two failed attempts at multilateral rule-making for the promotion and pro-tection of foreign investment in the late 1990s triggered the regional/bilateral rule-making in East Asia. One was the failure of the Multilateral Agreement on Investment (MAI), sponsored by the Organisation for Economic Co-operation and Development (OECD) in 1998.[27] The other failed attempt was "trade and investment" incorporation into the agenda of the first negotiating round of the WTO at its 1999 Seattle Ministerial Conference.[28]

The failure of the MAI negotiation cemented the impression that those developing countries that joined the negotiation, though they were willing to conclude BITs on an individual basis,[29] were still reluctant to commit themselves to multilateral rules for the promotion and protection of foreign investment. On the other hand, the members of the WTO, at its First Ministerial Conference held in Singapore in December 1996, agreed to establish a working group to examine "the relationship between trade and investment" at the first negotiating round of the WTO.[30] However, the Seattle Ministerial Conference failed to establish the working group, and the Hong Kong Ministerial Conference finally dropped "the relationship between trade and investment" from the agenda of the DDA in December 2005.[31]

These failures forced the developed countries in the Asia-Pacific region and their global firms to shift the forum for investment rule-making from mul-tilateral to regional/bilateral forum. In Japan, Keidanren published a policy statement titled *Challenges for the Upcoming WTO Negotiations and Agenda for Future Japanese Trade Policy* in May 1999.[32] While expressing expectations of the upcoming WTO negotiations, it emphasized the importance of strengthening

Japanese governmental efforts to develop a network of BITs and FTAs with investment chapters because they are "extremely important in terms of the foreign business activities of Japanese companies."[33] In response, the Japanese Ministry of Economy, Trade and Industry (METI), for the first time in its history, officially admitted in its *White Paper on International Trade 2000*[34] that regional integration through BITs and FTAs could have economic value for Japan, and that it should be pursued "as a supplement to the multilateral trading system" (METI, 2000a: 39). In August 2000, METI published a special report titled *The Economic Foundations of Japanese Trade Policy – Promoting a Multi-Layered Trade Policy*.[35] It advanced the policy stance expressed in the *White Paper on International Trade 2000* a step further. While admitting that "Japan continues to promote international rule-making on the multilateral level, with policy based on strengthening the WTO-centered multilateral trading system," it noted that Japan "has also begun to develop bilateral investment liberalization frameworks," and announced that Japan would henceforth promote a "multi-layered trade policy" with efforts to strengthen the multilateral trading system and promote regional cooperation (METI, 2000b: Chapter 2, Section 3).

Since then, the Japanese government repeated this "multi-layered trade policy," whose focus was clearly on investment rule-making at the regional/bilateral level. And, as has been discussed above, Japan accelerated negotiations of BITs and FTAs with investment chapters with countries in East Asia and the Pacific Rim (Mexico) where Japanese companies have large investment interests.

A similar policy shift occurred on the other side of the Pacific. The US government, backed by support from its business lobby, accelerated its negotiations of BITs and FTAs with investment chapters with countries that meet the criteria set by the United States, resulting in nearly 40 BITs and 13 FTAs with investment chapters as of August 2008.[36] Mexico and Chile also came to negotiate many BITs and FTAs with investment chapters with their trade and investment partner countries. It is fair to say that not only East Asia but the whole Pacific Rim came to adopt regional/bilateral rule-making for the promotion and protection of foreign investment in the 2000s, as a result of the failure of rule-making at multilateral levels.

Standard setting: Antidumping and trade facilitation

The rivalry between multilateral and regional/bilateral rule-making raises the possibility that a new rule or standard adopted and disseminated by several FTAs will later on be incorporated more widely at the multilateral level. We label this objective as "standard setting" by regional/bilateral channels. This is particularly prominent in the areas of trade rules currently under negotiation within the framework of the DDA where the allegedly insufficient or inadequate WTO rules need reform. The most salient example is the rules on trade remedies (counter-subsidies, safeguards, and particularly antidumping).

As the most frequent targets of the US and EU foreign antidumping actions, East Asian countries, notably China, Korea, and Japan, have been alleging that the United States and the EU are abusing their antidumping laws in violation of WTO Anti-Dumping Agreement (ADA) for protectionist purposes. Korea and Japan have resorted to the WTO dispute settlement mechanism against these laws and practices (Nakagawa, 2007). Moreover, they, together with Hong Kong, Singapore, Thailand, and Mexico, joined the so-called "friends" of the rules negotiation of the DDA, and have made systematic proposals for the tightening of the ADA discipline in order to prevent the abuse of domestic antidumping laws.[37]

With the stalemate of the DDA, some of these countries began to insert special rules on trade remedies which are more stringent than those of the ADA in their FTAs. For instance, Article 6.2 of the Korea–Singapore FTA,[38] while maintaining the parties' rights and obligations under Article VI of GATT 1994 and the ADA (Article 6.2.1), provides for two special rules to be applied between them which are more stringent than those of the ADA: (1) prohibition of the so-called "zeroing"[39] (see Article 2.4.2 of the ADA) and (2) the lesser duty rule (see Article 9.1, second sentence of the ADA). Also, the Korea–European Free Trade Association (EFTA) FTA,[40] while basically retaining all the rights and obligations under the ADA, adopted the lesser duty rule [Article 2.10.1(b)].[41] In addition, the Korea–EFTA FTA stipulates that the parties "shall endeavor to refrain from initiating anti-dumping procedures against each other" and consult "with the other with a view to finding a mutually acceptable solution," though it does not mandate any specific additional legal requirements [Article 2.10.1(a)]. These rules correspond to the proposals of the "friends" of the rules negotiation of the DDA. Ahn (2007: 218) predicts that such "rule diversification" may constitute important precedents for the ongoing DDA negotiation and the development of the trade remedy system under the WTO.[42]

Another area of "rule diversification" or "standard setting" is trade facilitation. Trade facilitation, sometimes called simplification of customs clearance procedure, is the only survivor of the so-called "Singapore issues" of the DDA (Messerlin and Zarrouk, 2000: 586). By the "July Package," the members of the WTO agreed on 1 August 2004 to commence negotiations on trade facilitation within the framework of the DDA.[43] Annex D of the "July package" set the modalities of negotiation. Under this mandate, members are directed to clarify and improve GATT Article V (Freedom of Transit), Article VIII (Fees and Formalities Connected with Importation and Exportation), and Article X (Publication and Administration of Trade Regulations),[44] and to identify their trade facilitation needs and priorities.[45] Since then, many members of the WTO submitted proposals for the clarification and improvement of GATT articles on trade facilitation,[46] as well as communications on their facilitation needs and priorities.[47]

In parallel with the DDA negotiation on trade facilitation, the East Asian countries have incorporated special rules on trade facilitation in their FTAs.

Even before the start of the WTO, trade facilitation was a priority for rule-making/rule-clarification in the region. APEC took up trade facilitation as one of its "pillars" from its start, and has been conducting a series of research and discussion on it (Ravenhill, 2000). The Bogor Declaration, adopted at the third APEC Leaders' Meeting in November 1994, emphasized the importance of trade facilitation because "trade liberalization efforts alone are insufficient to generate trade expansion."[48] Then, the Manila Action Plan (Part 3: Collective Action) adopted at the fourth APEC Leaders' Meeting in November 1996 listed collective action plans for trade facilitation, including (1) harmonization of tariff nomenclature among APEC members to the six-digit level through the adoption of the WCO (World Customs Organization) Harmonized System (HS); (2) provision of a publicly available information manual on APEC members' Customs laws, regulations, administrative guidelines, procedures, and rulings; and (3) computerization of APEC Customs procedures.[49]

As the APEC process slowed down in the late 1990s,[50] East Asian countries, in particular, Japan, shifted the priority negotiating forum on trade facilitation to FTAs. Japan's first FTA with Singapore shared two chapters on trade facilitation. In Chapter 4 on Customs Procedures, each party shall (a) make use of information and communications technology, (b) simplify its customs procedures, and (c) make its customs procedures conform to relevant international standards (for example, those made under the WCO).[51] In Chapter 5 of the FTA on Paperless Trading, each party recognized that paperless trading[52] will significantly enhance the efficiency of trade through reduction of cost and time, and shall cooperate with a view to realizing and promoting paperless trading between them.[53] Similar provisions were adopted in Japan's FTAs with Malaysia (Chapter 4), the Philippines (Chapter 4), Thailand (Chapter 4), and Indonesia (Chapter 4).

Other FTAs concluded in the region followed suit. For instance, Chapter 5 of the Korea–Singapore FTA, titled "Customs Procedures," provides that the parties shall cooperate on, among others, paperless customs clearance [Article 5.13(b)]. For this purpose, the parties shall (1) simplify and streamline customs procedures through the domestic integration of customs systems with other controlling agencies, with a view to enhancing paperless customs clearance and (2) endeavor to provide an electronic environment that supports business transactions between their respective customs administrations and their trading communities [Article 5,13(b)(i) and (ii)]. Enhancing rules on trade facilitation, in particular, simplification and streamlining of the customs procedure through paperless trading, and cooperation aiming at this goal has thus become priority target of FTA negotiations in the region.

Trade facilitation yields large economic benefits, especially when the level of tariffs is low.[54] As multilateral negotiation on trade facilitation under the DDA has slowed, building-up rules and commitments on enhanced trade facilitation through bilateral/regional channels has become an effective way of improving trade facilitation, as those would lead to "capacity building" and "special and differential treatment (S&D)" for developing countries. Nonetheless, such rules and commitments may have regressive effects on the rule-making on trade facilitation under the DDA (such as simplified customs clearance, harmonization of tariff headings, and so on), and they should do so because regional fragmentation of rules on trade facilitation will generate considerable amount of regulatory cost on both governments and firms ("spaghetti bowl").

In effect, several East Asian countries have made many proposals reflecting their rule-making efforts in the region at the DDA negotiation on trade facilitation. To mention a few: Japan, together with Mongolia and Switzerland, made a proposal on (1) prompt publication of all laws, regulations, judicial decisions, and administrative rulings relating to trade in goods and (2) establishment of enquiry points[55]; Hong Kong, together with Switzerland, made a proposal on the reduction/limitation of formalities and documentation requirements (revision of Article VIII of GATT 1994)[56]; and Korea made a proposal on single window/one-time submission of customs documents (revision of Article VIII of GATT 1994).[57] The other rules covered by the bilateral/regional rule-making on trade facilitation, in particular, those relating to electronic or paperless customs clearance procedure, may be taken up at the DDA trade facilitation negotiation in due course. In this sense, trade facilitation, alongside trade remedies rules, has become another area of standard setting for East Asian countries, which could have regressive effects on the ongoing DDA.

Standard setting through regional/bilateral rule-making: Intellectual property

Finally, I focus on protection of intellectual property rights (IPR) where the fit between multilateral and bilateral/regional rules is of great importance. The TRIPS Agreement greatly enhanced multilateral rule-making on the protection of IPR. However, that was not the end of the story. Some of the recent FTAs by Asia-Pacific countries contain chapters on IPR that provide additional and more stringent protection of IPR, as well as intergovernmental cooperation on the enforcement of those rights.

For instance, Chapter 10 of the Japan–Singapore FTA provides for an enhanced cooperation in the areas of IPR protection through (1) exchanging information and sharing experiences on IPR and on relevant IPR events, activities, and initiatives organized in their respective territories; (2) jointly undertaking training and exchanging of experts in the field of IPR; and (3) disseminating information, sharing experiences, and conducting training on IPR enforcement (Article 96.3). Importantly, it also provides for the facilitation of patenting process whereby Singapore shall, in accordance with its laws and regulations, take appropriate measures to facilitate the patenting process of an application filed in Singapore that corresponds to an application filed in Japan (Article 98.1). Such "TRIPS plus" provisions are also contained in the other FTAs concluded by Japan[58] and Korea.[59]

The US FTAs go a step further. For instance, Chapter 17 of the US–Chile FTA contains detailed rules (32 pages) on IPR protection which secure higher level of protection and enforcement than is provided by the TRIPS Agreement in various types of IPR and their enforcement.[60] Similar provisions are contained in all FTAs concluded by the United States since the launch of the DDA.

As there has been no negotiation conducted within the framework of the DDA for the enhancement/tightening of the TRIPS Agreement,[61] such "TRIPS plus" provisions of the FTAs should not be coined as an example of standard setting through bilateral/regional channels as in the case of trade remedies and trade facilitation. However, this means that such provisions will be the only measures available for the enhancement/tightening of IPR and their enforcement in the Asia-Pacific region at least in the foreseeable future.

Competition among different types of legalism

Modest versus medium and aggressive legalism

Finally, another aspect of legal rivalry in the regionalism in East Asia and Asia-Pacific is the rivalry among the legalistic approach taken by the United States, Singapore, and Korea; the medium legalism taken by Japan; and the modest legalism taken by ASEAN countries (except Singapore) and China.

Most of the intra-Asian FTAs to date, especially those including China, are of relatively low quality in terms of issue coverage while the United States consistently seeks (even if it does not always obtain or even accept itself) "gold standard" FTAs with comprehensive coverage over trade and investment (Bergsten, 2007: 2). Our concern lies in whether there is a discrepancy in the extent of legalization in the region, and the answer seems to be affirmative.

For example, the China–ASEAN FTA hardly contains any legal rules for the promotion and protection of trade and investment in the region, besides the broad commitment for comprehensive economic cooperation (Articles 1 and 2) and liberalization of trade in goods (Article 3), and trade in services (Article 4) and investment (Article 5).[62] The China–Chile FTA[63] contains some legal rules, but the coverage is far more limited than that of the FTAs concluded by the United States, Japan, Singapore, and Korea. For instance, the former contains chapters on rules of origin (Chapters 4 and 5), trade remedies (Chapters 6), sanitary and phytosanitary measures (Chapter 7), and technical barriers to trade (Chapter 8), but does not contain chapters on IPR, competition law and policy, trade facilitation, and investment, all of which are the common features of the FTAs concluded by the United States, Japan, Singapore, and Korea.

In this sense, the FTAs concluded by the United States, Japan, Singapore, and Korea are highly legalized than those concluded by ASEAN countries (except Singapore) and China. Why is it so?

One plausible explanation is that ASEAN countries except Singapore are latecomers in legalized international economic relations and are not ready for such legalization. The so-called "ASEAN way" of informal and gradual liberalization has long been maintained (Kahler, 2001: 167–71). China, which acceded to the WTO only as late as December 2001, is also an exception as it has since been trying hard to comply with its obligations under the WTO Agreement and its accession commitments as has been exemplified by a recent surge of complaints filed against China under the WTO dispute settlement mechanism.[64] It is not yet ready to commit itself to "WTO plus" legalization.

Another explanation is that the United States, Japan, Singapore, and Korea, like Mexico and Chile, have made use of their FTAs for enhancing/tightening legal rules for the promotion and protection of trade and investment. As discussed in the preceding sections, under the current stalemate of the DDA, bilateral/regional rule-making through FTAs and BITs is the only viable means for achieving such goals. These countries around the Pacific Rim are trading countries with huge trade and investment stakes abroad; enhancing/strengthening legal rules for the promotion and protection of trade and investment is the priority goal in their economic diplomacy. Hence, we can safely forecast that it will take some time, maybe several years, before China starts moving toward "WTO plus" legalization at regional/bilateral level.

The situation is different in the case of the ASEAN countries other than Singapore. Individually, these countries have committed themselves to enhancing/tightening legalization. For instance, Thailand and the Philippines signed FTAs with Japan, whereby they committed themselves to many "WTO plus" legal obligations. Thailand is negotiating FTAs with similar "WTO plus" provisions with the United States.[65] Vietnam and Cambodia have concluded BITs with Japan, and the Lao People's Democratic Republic is negotiating a BIT with Japan. As ASEAN-wide regional integration initiatives such as ASEAN+3 (ASEAN plus China, Japan, and South Korea) or ASEAN+6 (ASEAN plus China, Japan, South Korea, Australia, New Zealand, and India) are painstaking and are not plausible at least in the near future, these member countries of the ASEAN have opted themselves to individual commitment for higher legalization with their East Asian trading partners.

Finally, Japan lies between the aggressive legalism taken by the United States, Singapore, and Korea and the modest legalism taken by the ASEAN countries except Singapore and China. As discussed in Section 2, Korea–Singapore FTA contains provisions that stipulate more stringent discipline on antidumping measures, while Japan–Singapore FTA does not. Additionally, the FTAs concluded by Japan generally contain chapters on economic cooperation and trade/investment-related technical assistance without formal legal obligations, and they lack WTO-like formal dispute settlement mechanism, which is in stark contrast to, for instance, the NAFTA with formal dispute settlement mechanism (Chapter 20) and a specific dispute settlement mechanism with respect to antidumping and counter-subsidy measures (Chapter 19). Therefore, in comparison with the United States, Singapore, and Korea, Japan's stance toward legalism is more modest.

US/EU versus Japan: Rivalry in competition law and policy

How about legal rivalry in the Asia-Pacific that goes beyond the region, namely, the rivalry of rules originated in the United States and the EU and those devised by Japan? This competition is taking place in an area beyond the coverage of the current multilateral rule-making, namely, competition law and policy.

Multilateral rule-making on competition law and policy has occasionally been attempted but has never been successful.[66] The most recent attempt was the WTO Singapore Ministerial Declaration, whose paragraph 20 announced the WTO members' agreement to establish a working group to study "the interaction between trade and competition policy." However, together with "the relationship between trade and investment,"[67] this "Singapore issue" was dropped from the agenda of the DDA in December 2005.

While multilateral rule-making attempts repetitively failed ever since the early post-World War II (WWII) period, the United States and the EU remained active in the formation and tightening of their own competition laws and policies, and endeavored towards their global diffusion since the 1990s.

Contemporary competition law has its origins in the US Sherman Anti-Trust Act (1890). After WWII, the United States pressured its European allies such as the United Kingdom and Australia, and the recently defeated Japan and Germany to adopt antitrust laws (Jones, 2006: 25–6). With the intensifying international business transactions, extraterritorial application of US antitrust laws caused international conflicts.[68] In order to prevent such conflicts, the United States has concluded bilateral antitrust cooperation agreements with its major trade/investment partners including West Germany (1976), Australia (1982), Canada (1984, revised in 1995), EC (1991, supplemented in 1998), and Japan (1999), under which US antitrust authorities abstain from applying its antitrust law extraterritorially (the so-called "positive comity") (Pitofsky, 1999: 405–9).

The EU has inserted a clause requiring the enactment of a competition law in line with the EU competition law in its Association Agreements with Central and Eastern European countries, and providing them technical assistance for that purpose, as a precondition on the part of these countries to join the EU (Nakagawa, 2004b: 31).

On the other hand, the United States took the initiative in establishing the International Competition Network (ICN) in 2001 (Nakagawa, 2004b: 36–7). The ICN has established working groups on such key issues of international concern as cartels, mergers and acquisitions (M&A), advocacy, and telecommunications, and has produced recommendations and/or "best practices," though individual competition authorities decide whether and how to implement them, through unilateral, bilateral, or multilateral arrangements, as appropriate.[69] As of January 2008, 103 competition authorities of 92 jurisdictions are members of the ICN,[70] which means most of those jurisdictions which have competition laws are its members. Through this multilateral forum and through chapters on competition law and policy in its bilateral/regional FTAs, the United States has attempted to diffuse its own antitrust law and policy globally as "international best practices."

Japan, while actively participating in these movements (ICN, bilateral antitrust cooperation agreements), has been trying to diffuse its Antimonopoly Act to East Asia. Japan's FTAs with East Asian countries contain chapters on competition law and policy,[71] whereby Japan offers technical assistance and information exchange for the enactment and implementation of competition law and policy according to Japan's Antimonopoly Act.[72] Japan's Fair Trade Commission (JFTC) has been providing technical assistance ("capacity building") to, among others, Korea, Thailand, China, Malaysia, Mongolia, Indonesia, Vietnam, the Philippines, Myanmar, and Laos.[73] It also took the initiative in launching an East Asian Competition Policy Forum (EACPF) website forum which provides a platform for sharing and exchanging information and experiences on competition law and policy in East Asia, in 2003.[74]

These activities have so far achieved results to some extent. In particular, the JFTC provided extensive technical assistance to China in enacting its Anti-Monopoly Law in August 2007,[75] whose basic principles and rules are quite similar to Japan's Antimonopoly Act. Also, Japan's technical assistance to Vietnam has contributed to the enactment of Vietnamese Law on Competition.[76]

There are both similarities and differences among the competition laws and policies of the United States, EU, and Japan. For instance, they all prohibit "abuse of monopolistic status" in private business transactions, but there is no unified practice as to what this means, as was exemplified by the different conclusions drawn by the US, EU, and Japanese competition authorities toward Microsoft. Furthermore, they institute procedures to examine whether an M&A is admissible under their competition laws, but there are no common criteria for the examination of admissibility, as was exemplified by the stark difference of conclusions between EU and US competition authorities on the issue of the admissibility of the M&A between Boeing and McDonnell Douglas.

It matters a lot which competition law and policy will prevail. In comparison, the EU competition authorities have come to adopt more stringent application of its competition law. Many private business practices acquiesced under US and Japanese competition laws were sentenced illegal under the EU competition law, and the EU authorities have imposed a large amount of penalties on them (Wils, 2005).

An increasing number of countries/jurisdictions have come to enact competition laws, and the United States and the EU have been most influential in this process in the sense that the former has achieved a modest success in Latin America, Central and Eastern Europe, and Central Europe, while the latter has successfully diffused its competition law to its new members and former colonies in Africa, Caribbean, and Pacific regions. Japan has, thus far, achieved moderate success in diffusing Japanese Anti-Monopoly Act in East Asia.

Implications of legal competition on regional integration

Legal competition contribute and the coherent regional integration of East Asia

Katzenstein and Shiraishi (2006) argue that porous regional dynamics in East Asia tend to discourage a "national model" to dictate regional integration. Is that the case for EPAs and FTAs in East Asia? The answer seems to be both yes and no.

As discussed above, there has been a discrepancy between high legalization and low legalization in East Asia. Under these conditions, regional/bilateral networks of FTAs and BITs will not form a coherent and integrated set of legal rules for the protection and promotion of trade and investment in the region in the foreseeable future. To the contrary, a worse scenario of the accumulation of scattered and contradictory legal rules in the region with gross country bias (few rules in China and ASEAN except Singapore, and wider and more detailed rules in Japan, Singapore, and Korea and their counterparts) is more plausible.

Policy change of China and ASEAN countries other than Singapore in the direction of higher legalization would bring about a better scenario. Individually, these countries have agreed to higher legalization through FTAs and BITs, and the Japanese government plans to conclude either FTAs or BITs with all the members of ASEAN 10 except Myanmar.[77] Although negotiations will take at least a few years, the day will surely come when almost all the ASEAN countries commit themselves to higher-level legalization on trade and investment.

The recent visit of Chinese President Hu Jintao to Japan (6–11 May 2008) is another positive sign. The Joint Statement of 7 May announced that "(t)he two sides resolved to engage particularly in the following areas of cooperation so that Japan and China, which have a major influence on the world economy, can contribute to the sustainable growth of the world economy:

> To promote mutually beneficial cooperation and expand common benefits in a wide range of fields, including *trade, investment,* information and communication technology, finance, food and product safety, *protection of intellectual property rights, business environment, agriculture,* forestry and fisheries industries, transport and tourism, water, and healthcare.[78] (Italics added by the author)

If both governments think seriously about this commitment, they should resume negotiation of the currently stalled Japan–China–Korea trilateral investment agreement,[79] or even about ASEAN+3 (not to mention ASEAN+6[80]) FTA.[81] This will lead East Asia to a coherent regional integration with highly advanced legalization, already starting to take shape on the other side of the Pacific through the networks of FTAs and BITs among the United States, Mexico, and Chile.

The road ahead is, however, still long. Even now, the unorganized accumulation of FTAs and BITs in East Asia is producing an incoherent network of trade and investment rules ("spaghetti bowl"). In order for a coherent regional integration to come into existence, concerted efforts are needed in coordinating and fine-tuning the existing FTAs and BITs, which will lead to region-wide high level rules and institutions for trade and investment promotion. Such a concerted effort will not start in the near future without agreement between Japan and China as to how and with whom to cooperate (for instance, the conflict between ASEAN+3 or ASEAN+6).[82] A coherent regional integration in East Asia should be aimed at as a mid-term goal.

The formation of coherent regional integration in Asia-Pacific is even less realistic, given the slowdown of the APEC trade/investment liberalization process since the mid-1990s and repeated failures since the 1980s to start bilateral FTA negotiation between Japan and the United States, two major trading powers in the region.

A coherent regional integration as the ultimate goal

Such pessimistic scenarios should not mean that countries of East Asia and Asia-Pacific abandon the hope of coherent regional integration. To the contrary, the necessity of such regional integration is all the more urgent now than a decade ago. Persistent efforts of the countries of these regions to conclude bilateral/regional FTAs and BITs since the mid-1990s have resulted in a rather complicated and occasionally conflicting networks of rules and institutions for the promotion and protection of trade and investment, whose administrative costs may increase to the point where the benefits of trade and investment liberalization may be substantially impaired. Such "spaghetti bowl" effect should be diminished by a concerted effort to fine-tune existing rules and institutions and to create unified rules and institutions, either by revitalizing the APEC process, or by starting the Japan–US FTA negotiation, or by inviting the United States (and Mexico, Chile, and other like-minded countries in the Pacific rim) to the forthcoming "ASEAN+" FTA negotiation.

Such regional initiatives should go hand in hand with multilateral rule-making including the DDA. The interplay between bilateral/regional and multilateral rule-making (standard setting and locking-in) will continue even after the conclusion of the DDA, given the differences of speed, subject matter, and membership among these tracks. As shown by the development of European integration and the NAFTA, regional integration can stimulate multilateral rule-making. The WTO is not a panacea for trade and investment rule-making, but neither is the regional initiative solely a spaghetti bowl maker. The world needs a strong and concerted political determination to take both multilateral and bilateral/regional tracks at the same time, based on the belief that higher legalization will achieve fair and transparent business environment which would be for the good of all the people in the world.

Conclusions

Given the stalemate of the DDA and the manifest failure of the MAI negotiation, the resurrection of multilateral rule-making for the promotion and protection of investment is unlikely. The current trend of regional/bilateral rule-making through FTAs and BITs will continue to prevail at least for a foreseeable future. East Asia and Asia-Pacific are no exceptions.

Legalization through regional/bilateral means has both advantages and disadvantages. It is faster than multilateral rule-making, and one can strategically pick and choose like-minded partners. It can have regressive effects on multilateral rule-making (standard setting), and can have locking-in effects on countries with moderate legalism into higher legalization. On the other hand, it may bring about intricate and contradictory network of rules, which might be practically inapplicable ("spaghetti bowl"). It may also enlarge the discrepancy between modest and aggressive legalism in the region, and may thus have detrimental effect on both multilateral rule-making and coherent regional integration.

To avoid such a disastrous outcome while seeking advantages of regional/bilateral rule-making, a concerted effort is needed of leading countries in the region for coordinating and fine-tuning the existing FTAs and BITs. Both Japan and the United States should cooperate to establish such a mechanism. We need pragmatic and forward-looking leadership in international economic diplomacy in East Asia and Asia-Pacific.

Notes

1. Article 2.2 of the WTO Anti-Dumping Agreement (hereinafter the "ADA") provides that "(w)hen, because of the particular market situation..., such sales do not permit a proper comparison, the margin of dumping shall be determined by comparison with a comparable price of the like product when exported to an appropriate third country." Judging from the special market conditions of China, many countries including USA, EC, and South Africa regard it as "non-market economy" and apply third country export price methodology. This has allegedly contributed to the higher dumping margins against Chinese products. See Brink and Kobayashi (2007: 225–6).
2. See Declaration of ASEAN Concord II (Bali Concord II) done in Bali on 7 October 2003. http://www.aseansec.org/15159.htm.
3. Framework Agreement on Comprehensive Economic Cooperation between the Association of South East Asian Nations and the People's Republic of China; signed 6 October 2003, entered into force 21 December 2004. WTO Doc. WT/COMTD/N/20, WT/COMTS/51.
4. Framework Agreement on Comprehensive Economic Cooperation Among the Governments of the Member Countries of the Association of Southeast Asian Nations and the Republic of Korea; signed 13 December 2005.

5. Agreement on Comprehensive Partnership between Japan and Member States of the Association of Southeast Asian Nations; signed 14 April 2008. http://www.mofa.go.jp/policy/economy/fta/asean/agreement.html.
6. The Japan–Singapore Economic Partnership Agreement; signed 13 January 2002, entered into force 30 November 2002. http://www.mofa.go.jp/region/asia-paci/singapore/jsepa.html. Protocol Amending the Agreement between Japan and the Republic of Singapore for a New-Age Economic Partnership; signed 19 March 2007. http://www.mofa.go.jp/region/asia-paci/singapore/jsepa_a/index.html.
7. Agreement between Japan and the Republic of the Philippines for an Economic Partnership; signed 9 September 2006. http://www.mofa.go.jp/region/asia-paci/philippine/epa0609/index.html.
8. Agreement between the Government of Japan and the Government of Malaysia for an Economic Partnership; signed 13 December 2006, entered into force 13 July 2007. http://www.meti.go.jp/policy/trade_policy/epa/html/malaysia_epa_text_e.htm
9. Agreement between Japan and the Kingdom of Thailand for an Economic Partnership; signed 3 April 2007. http://www.mofa.go.jp/region/asia-paci/thailand/epa0704/index.html.
10. Agreement between Japan and Brunei Darussalam for an Economic Partnership; signed 16 June 2007. http://www.mofa.go.jp/region/asia-paci/brunei/epa0706/index.html.
11. Agreement between Japan and Indonesia for Economic Partnership; signed 20 August 2007. http://www.mofa.go.jp/region/asia-paci/indonesia/epa0708/index.html.
12. Negotiation started in January 2007.
13. Negotiation started in January 2007.
14. Negotiation started in December 2003, but it has stalled, due mainly to the disagreement on the modalities of agricultural trade liberalization, since November 2004.
15. Negotiation started in May 2007.
16. Agreement between Japan and the People's Republic of China for the Promotion and Mutual Protection of Investment; signed 27 August 1988, entered into force 12 May 1989. http://www.meti.go.jp/policy/trade_policy/asia/china/html/investment_treaty.html.
17. Agreement between the Government of Japan and the Government of Hong Kong for the Promotion and Protection of Investment; signed 15 May 1997, entered into force 18 June 1997.
18. Agreement between Japan and the Republic of Korea for the Promotion and Protection of Investment, signed 22 March 2002, entered into force 1 January 2003. http://www.mofa.jp/mofaj/kaidan/s_koi/korea02/toUShikyoutei/gaiyo.html.
19. Agreement between Japan and the Socialist Republic of Vietnam for the Liberalization, Promotion and Protection of Investment; signed 14 November 2003, entered into force 19 December 2004. http://www.mofa.jp/region/asia-paci/Vietnam/agree0311.pdf
20. Agreement between Japan and the Kingdom of Cambodia for the Liberalization, Promotion and Protection of Investment; signed 17 June 2007.
21. Negotiation started in March 2007. See http://www.mofa.jp/mofaj/gaiko/investment/jck.html.
22. Negotiation started in March 2007. See http://www.mofa.jp/mofaj/gaiko/investment/j_laos.html.
23. Trade Policy Bureau, METI, 2006: Chapter 3, Section 2, Figure 3-3-17.
24. METI, 2007: 96, Figure 2-1-9.

25. Ibid., p. 98, Figure 2-1-13. The ratio of intra-regional trade of the NAFTA was 43.0 percent in 2005. Id.
26. Studies assert that the pulling power of BITs and FTAs with investment chapters is limited. Neumayer and Spess (2005); Salacuse and Sullivan (2006).
27. See OECD, Multilateral Agreement on Investment. http://www.oecd.org/document/35/0,2340,en_2649_201185_1894819_1_1_1_1,00.html.
28. See WTO, The Third WTO Ministerial Conference. http://www.wto.org/English/thewto_e/minist_e/min99_e/min99_e.htm.
29. The number of BITs began to increase in the late 1980s and the pace was accelerated in early to mid-1990s. See UNCTAD (2000).
30. WTO, Singapore Ministerial Declaration, 13 December 1996, para.20. http://www.wto.org/english/thewto_e/minist_e/min96_e/wtodec_e.htm.
31. WTO, Hong Kong Ministerial Declaration, 18 December 2005. http://www.wto.org/english/thewto_e/minist_e/min05_e/final_text_e.htm
32. http://www.keidanren.or.jp/english/policy/pol102/index.html.
33. Ibid., Section 3(1). For the role of Keidanren in the policy shift of the Japanese government, see Yoshimatsu (2005) and Nakagawa (2006).
34. Available online at http://www.meti.go.jp/english/report/index.html.
35. Available online at http://hqm-swwwg.meti.go.jp/english/report/data/g00W021e.pdf.
36. See http://www.ustr.gov/Trade_Agreements/Bilateral/Section_Index.html.
37. See, for example, the paper titled *Anti-Dumping: Illustrative Major Issues* submitted to the Negotiating Group on Rules of the DDA on 26 April 2002 (TN/RL/W/6) by Brazil, Chile, Columbia, Costa Rica, Hong Kong, Israel, Japan, Korea, Mexico, Norway, Singapore, Switzerland, Thailand, and Turkey.
38. The Korea–Singapore FTA; signed 4 August 2005, entered into force 2 March 2005. http://www.iesingapore.gov.sg/wps/wcm/connect/resources/file/ebbeeb417fbd629/KSFTA_final_KSFTA.pdf?MOD=AJPERES.
39. "Zeroing" is the methodology of calculating dumping margin by which the investigating authority does not include in the numerator used to calculate weighted average dumping margins any amounts by which average export prices in individual averaging groups exceed the average normal value for such groups. The dumping margin is thus calculated higher than otherwise. See Pandey (2005: 3).
40. Signed 15 December 2005. http://secretariat.efta.int/Web/ExternalRelations/PartnerCountries/Korea.
41. It provides that "the Party taking such a decision, should apply the 'lesser duty' rule, by imposing a duty which is less than the dumping margin where such lesser duty would be adequate to remove the injury to the domestic industry."
42. Also see Kawashima (2006) on the regulation of anti-dumping in regional integration.
43. WTO, decision adopted by the General Council on 1 August 2004, para.1(g).
44. Ibid., Annex D, para.1.
45. Ibid., para.4.
46. For the most recent compilation of such proposals, see WTO, Trade Negotiation Committee, Negotiating Group on Trade Facilitation, WTO Negotiations on Trade Facilitation Compilation of Members' Textual Proposals, TN/TF/W/43/Rev.12, 25 July 2007.
47. For a recent list of such communications, see WTO, Trade Negotiation Committee, Negotiating Group on Trade Facilitation, List of Documents, Note by the Secretariat, Revision. TN/TF/W/106/Rev.3, 20 December 2006, pp. 11–2.

48. APEC Economic Leaders' Declaration of Common Resolve, Bogor, 15 November 1994. http://www.apecsec.org.sg/apec/leaders__declarations/1994.html.
49. APEC, Manila Action Plan for APEC (MAPA 1996) Volume III, A. Overview. http://www.mofa.go.jp/policy/economy/apec/1996/mapa/vol3/vol3over.html
50. This does not mean that the APEC process has stalled since the late 1990s. See, for instance, APEC Economic Leaders' Declaration, Shanghai, 21 October 2001, Appendix 1, Shanghai Accord, II. Clarifying the Roadmap to Bogor, Follow up on the Trade Facilitation Principles. http://www.apec.org/apec/leaders__declarations/2001/appendix_1_-_shanghai.html.
51. Ibid., Article 36.
52. "Paperless trading" was defined as "trading using electronic filing and transfer of trade-related information and electronic versions of documents such as bills of lading, invoices, letters of credit and insurance certificates." Ibid., Article 40.
53. Ibid.
54. Wilson et al. (2003: 18) estimate that 0.55 percent improvement of Port Efficiency indicator, 5.5 percent improvement of Customs Environment indicator, and 3.7 percent improvement of E-business indicator would generate an increase in trade equal to complete elimination of tariffs in the APEC region, whose applied rates in the ad valorem term is 6.5 percent in the region.
55. WTO, Negotiating Group on Trade Facilitation, Communication from Japan, Mongolia, and Switzerland, 7 June 2006. TN/TF/W/114.
56. WTO, Negotiating Group on Trade Facilitation, Communication from Hong Kong, China and Switzerland, 4 July 2006. TN/TF/W/124.
57. WTO, Negotiating Group on Trade Facilitation, Communication from Korea, 21 July 2006. TN/TF/W/138.
58. See, for instance, Chapter 9 of the Japan–Malaysia EPA, Chapter 10 of the Japan–Philippines EPA, Chapter 10 of the Japan–Thailand EPA, and Chapter 9 of the Japan–Indonesia EPA.
59. See, for instance, Chapter 17 of the Korea–Singapore FTA and Chapter 18 of the Korea–US FTA (Free Trade Agreement between the United States of America and the Republic of Korea; signed 30 June 2007). http://www.ustr.gov/Trade_Agreements/Bilateral/Republic_of_Korea_FTA/Final_Text/Section_Index.html.
60. See Chapter 17, Articles 17.1 to 17.12 of the United States–Chile Free Trade Agreement; signed 6 June 2003, entered into force 1 January 2004. http://www.ustr.gov/Trade_Agreements/Bilateral/Chile_FTA/Final_Texts/Section_Index.html.
61. To the contrary, WTO member countries agreed to loosen the obligations of the TRIPS Agreement relating to compulsory licensing for drugs for the sake of developing countries. See Decision of the General Council on the Amendment of the TRIPS Agreement, 6 December 2005. WT/L/641, 8 December 2005.
62. For instance, the Framework Agreement does not contain preferential rules of origin.
63. Free Trade Agreement between the Government of the People's Republic of China and the Government of the Republic of Chile; signed 18 November 2005, entered into force 20 January 2007. WTO Doc. WT/REG230.
64. From 18 March 2004 to August 2008, 13 complaints were filed against China, most of which were targeted against China's failure to comply with its WTO obligations including those under the TRIPS Agreement.
65. See http://www.ustr.gov/Trade_Agreements/Bilateral/Section_Index.html.
66. For earlier attempts at multilateral rule-making on competition law and policy, see Nakagawa (2004a, 2004b).

67. See supra n.32 and the corresponding text.
68. See the epoch-making judgment of the US Federal Circuit Court on the ALCOA case. *US* v. *Aluminium Co. of America (ALCOA)*, 148 F.2d 416 (1945).
69. See ICN, About the ICN. http://www.internationalcompetitionnetwork.org/index.php/en/about-icn
70. ICN Membership contact list (January 2008). http://www.internationalcompetitionnetwork.org/pdf/ICN_Contact_List.pdf.
71. See, for instance, Chapter 12 of the Japan–Singapore EPA.
72. Act on Prohibition of Private Monopolization and Maintenance of Fair Trade (Act No.54 of 14 April 1947).
73. Japan, Fair Trade Commission, Technical Assistance Projects Provided. http://www.jftc.go.jp/eacpf/05/technical-a.pdf.
74. East Asia Competition Policy Forum, Profile. http://www.jftc.go.jp/eacpf/about.html.
75. Adopted 30 August 2007, scheduled to enter into force 1 August 2008. For an explanation in Japanese, see http://www.jftc.go.jp/worldcom/html/country/china2.html.
76. Adopted 9 November 2004, entered into force 1 July 2005. For an explanation in Japanese, see http://www.jftc.go.jp/worldcom/html/country/vietnam.html.
77. METI, Japan's Policy on FTAs/EPAs, March 2005, slide no. 9. (Available from http://www.meti.go.jp/english/policy/index_externaleconomicpolicy.html) Also see METI, The Report of the Joint Study Group on the Possible Trilateral Investment Agreements among China, Japan, and Korea (29 November 2004).
78. Joint Statement between the Government of Japan and the Government of the People's Republic of China on Comprehensive Promotion of a "Mutually Beneficial Relationship Based on Common Strategic Interests." 7 May 2008. http://www.mofa.go.jp/region/asia-paci/china/joint0805.html.
79. See: Ministry of Foreign Affairs (MOFA), On the fourth negotiation of Japan–China–Korea Investment Agreement, held in Tokyo on 12–13 March 2008. http://www.mofa.go.jp/mofaj/gaiko/investment/jck2/04_gh.html.
80. See Kawai and Wignaraja (2007).
81. See: The fifth ASEAN economic ministers and the ministers of People's Republic of China, Japan, and Republic of Korea consultation, 14 September 2002, Bandar Seri Begawan, Brunei Darussalam, Joint Press Statement. (Available from http://www.meti.go.jp/english/policy/index_externaleconomicpolicy.html).
82. See Kawai and Wignaraja (2007).

Part II   The Western Hemisphere

5
The US as a Bilateral Player: The Impetus for Asymmetric Free Trade Agreements

Cintia Quiliconi and Carol Wise

The signing of bilateral free trade agreements with Israel and Canada in the 1980s marked the first time that the Unites States (US) had departed from its longstanding commitment to negotiate trade agreements solely within the multilateral arena. This willingness to negotiate bilaterally was then extended with the completion of the North American Free Trade Agreement (NAFTA) between the US, Canada, and Mexico in 1992, which also signified the first time that the United States had completed a free trade agreement (FTA) that included a developing country. Since the Office of the United States Trade Representative (USTR) announced its strategy of competitive liberalization in 2002 (Zoellick, 2001; 2003), similar bilateral FTAs have been negotiated between the US and other countries at varying levels of development. Ostensibly, these bilateral deals are with can-do countries, those that are ready to move forward with further trade and investment liberalization despite the stalemate that has plagued the multilateral Doha Round negotiations at the World Trade Organization (WTO).

US policymakers have been careful to distinguish competitive liberalization as a strategy that is both parallel and complementary to this larger multilateral liberalization project.[1] As such, it is envisioned that the recent slew of bilateral US FTAs will eventually result in a broader and more vibrant network of globalized trade (Colvin, 2004). In this chapter, we single out an overriding feature of these more recent bilateral FTAs that have been negotiated as part of the US competitive liberalization strategy: all have involved small open economies with relatively high levels of trade dependence on the US market, and where the asymmetries are especially steep (Feinberg, 2003). Given these seemingly low economic stakes, our purpose here is to analyze and shed light on both the political and the economic motivations of US trade policy as it has increasingly embraced these more asymmetric FTAs that fall within the domain of North–South and North–North relations.

In particular, we seek to criticize US motives and expectations around competitive liberalization as this strategy is now playing out in Latin America and Asia. At the very least, in the Latin American context these bilateral FTAs are meant to reinforce the neoliberal policies embraced by much of the region in the 1990s, as a growing contingent of Leftist governments (among others Argentina, Bolivia, Ecuador, and Venezuela) have rejected purist market approaches in the 2000s for their failure to spur higher sustainable growth and income gains. At a minimum, in the Asian setting, US bilateral trade deals have been geared toward more explicitly asserting the US presence in these markets in the face of China's rapidly growing political and economic dominance in this region. Given that the first US Asian FTAs were signed with Australia and Singapore—both of which supported the US invasion of Iraq in 2003—some have suggested that these deals were also meant to reward these signatories for their loyalty to the US at this time.[2]

We formalize our analysis of US motives and expectations vis-à-vis competitive liberalization by relying on the conceptual framework laid out by Solís and Katada at the outset of this volume. Our guiding research question is twofold. First, we explore whether the signing of bilateral agreements by the US with individual countries in Latin America and Asia is based on a follower strategy of emulating the economic path of other leading countries, or whether the US FTA strategy is based on independent decision making and not affected by the prior decisions of other countries to negotiate FTAs. Second, we analyze whether the impetus for bilateral negotiations derives from competitive concerns, and if so, the extent to which these concerns lie in the economic, political, and/or legal realms.

Our subject invokes two main paradoxes. First, common wisdom tells us that small countries would be better off by conducting multilateral negotiations where they can form alliances. Second, while the US competitive liberalization strategy assumes that bilateral negotiations are more or less interchangeable with multilateral ones—in fact, multilateralism is based on the principles of nondiscrimination and most favored nation[3]—while regional and bilateral FTAs imply discrimination against nonmembers and the granting of benefits only to members. In light of these concerns, this chapter explores whether US bilateral accords might actually work to deter developing countries, in particular, from upholding their commitment to the multilateral process at the sacrifice of their own competitive gains.

The first section of the chapter maps those trade negotiations in which the US has been involved since the mid-1980s and analyzes how these bilateral agreements evolved into the competitive liberalization strategy; the second section analyzes the ways in which US domestic politics have shaped the US bilateral FTA strategy; the third section examines these FTAs in light of the three hypotheses posed by Solís and Katada in Chapter 1; the fourth section speculates on how US bilateralism has both affected the prospects for regional integration in the Western Hemisphere and emerged as a main venue for the US to insert itself more prominently into the regional integration process in East Asia. We conclude with a critique of the US bilateral strategy in the 2000s.

From multilateralism to the US bilateral strategy

The first two US FTAs were both labeled as special cases at the time: Israel as an isolated strategic ally with a strong domestic political lobby, and Canada as a bordering state with close ties to the US economy through intra-industry trade and investment (Chan, 2005). With the inclusion of Mexico in the 1992 NAFTA agreement, US trade policy stepped even further outside of its traditional comfort zone by negotiating the country's first FTA with a developing country. However, the finalization of the Uruguay Round in 1994 and the subsequent creation of the WTO suggested that the US was returning to the multilateral fold.

In the aftermath of the US–Canada FTA, a rush of foreign proposals came forth petitioning the USTR for the negotiation of similar bilateral trade agreements, for example, with South Korea, Taiwan, ASEAN, and Australia, although no negotiations were started. In the Latin American region, the advent of NAFTA prompted the presidents of Costa Rica, El Salvador, Guatemala, Honduras, and Nicaragua to notify the Clinton administration in 1992 of their interest in negotiating an agreement of this nature. Given Central America's export similarity with a range of low value-added goods that Mexico ships to the US market, the prospect of heightened trade diversion prompted these countries to act. The Central American countries hoped to achieve market access parity within NAFTA, but the US rejected this proposal and conceded to the granting of preferences only on a discretional basis.

One immediate lesson from the highly contentious NAFTA approval process on Capitol Hill was that the US Congress had little taste, and even a lower political learning curve, for the negotiation of bilateral deals. Mexico's December 1994 financial debacle further soured the prospects of passing bilateral FTAs, even if there was no direct connection between NAFTA and the Mexican meltdown (Pastor, 1998). Rather than continue in a bilateral vein, the USTR emphasized trans-regional and regional options, with the explicit understanding that regional agreements negotiated in tandem with multilateral ones would favor the completion of the latter. In 1994, the US both joined the forum on Asia Pacific Economic Cooperation and launched negotiations with 33 other Western Hemisphere countries to complete a Free Trade Area of the Americas (FTAA) by 2005. It was envisioned that NAFTA would be incorporated into the FTAA, which would embrace WTO-plus rules and norms that surpassed the achievements of the Uruguay Round (1986–1994).

Unfortunately, the ability of the US to negotiate the FTAA was hampered by the systematic veto of the fast-track negotiating legislation by the US Congress throughout the 1990s.[4] In fact, it was not until the passage of the "Bipartisan Trade Promotion Authority (TPA) Act of 2002" under the Bush administration that the USTR was given the green light to seek out trade deals in multiple arenas. In the interim, US trading partners had signed many FTAs, meaning that when the Bush administration finally obtained

TPA in 2002 there was a widespread sense that the United States was trailing behind on this dimension. The USTR confirmed that policy dissemination was at least a partial impetus for the US bilateral strategy when he lamented, "[t]here are over 130 FTAs in the world today and the US is a party to only two of them" (Zoellick, 2001).

With TPA approval in hand, the Office of the USTR thus revived the US bilateral strategy with a vengeance under the strong leadership of USTR Robert Zoellick. A first point of business was the completion of the US–Chile FTA, still pending from Clinton's 1994 invitation. However, the choice of Chile for the first US bilateral FTA in Latin America was more than a matter of taking care of unfinished business. Rather, this decision was also based on Chile's consistently high ranking as the most market-oriented country in the region.[5] More than any of the subsequent US FTAs negotiated in Latin America, the US–Chile FTA enabled the USTR to showcase from the start its goal of achieving WTO-plus results [rules surrounding investment, services, dispute settlement, and intellectual property rights (IPR)] in these bilateral deals.

As seen in Table 5.1, since the completion of the US–Chile FTA in 2004, the US has finalized a plethora of FTAs, the bulk of which represent the competitive liberalization strategy and the steep asymmetries that we referred to earlier. In all, the countries involved in these recent FTAs include Singapore, Australia, CAFTA–DR (Costa Rica, El Salvador, Nicaragua, Honduras, Guatemala and the Dominican Republic), Bahrain, Jordan, Morocco, Oman, and Peru; agreements with Colombia, Panama, and South Korea have now been completed but still await Congressional approval.

The clearest articulation of the competitive liberalization strategy that underpins this subsequent wave of US FTAs was offered by former USTR Zoellick in 2004:

> Competitive liberalization offers countries within regions a step-by-step pathway to greater trade reforms and openness with the United States. Both the President's Enterprise for ASEAN Initiative 12 and his plan to work toward a Middle East Free Trade Area start by helping non-member countries to join the WTO...For those more advanced, we negotiate Trade and Investment Framework Agreements (TIFAs) and Bilateral Investment Treaties. We employ these customized arrangements to resolve trade and investment issues, improve performance in areas such as protecting intellectual property rights and strengthening customs operations... Finally, we may negotiate a wide-ranging, state-of-the-art FTA that will help establish a model for a region and incentives for neighbors.
>
> (GAO, 2004: 58)

To summarize, Schott (2006) defines the current US criteria for selecting bilateral partners: First, is whether a given FTA will meet with broad support

Table 5.1 US agreements, preferential agreements, and trade negotiations (as of March 2009)

Regional, bilateral and multilateral	Negotiations underway or beginning shortly	Negotiations concluded and bills pending ratification	Agreements ratified by both Congresses
Multilateral	WTO (Doha Round)		NAFTA with Canada and Mexico, 1994 Caribbean Basin Trade Partnership Act (2000) Andean Trade Promotion and Drug Eradication Act (ATPDEA, 2002, renewed in 2008)
Western Hemisphere	FTAA (stalemate) Ecuador (suspended)	Colombia (2006) Panama (2006)	Chile (2004) Central America–Dominican Republic (CAFTA–DR)–US (US FTA completed with El Salvador, Guatemala, Honduras, and Nicaragua, 2006) Costa Rica (2009) Peru (2009)
Africa and the Middle East	South African Customs Union United Arab Emirates		Israel (1985) Jordan (2001) Bahrain (2006) Morocco (2006) Oman (2006)
Asia and Oceania	Malaysia Thailand	Republic of Korea (2007)	Australia (2005) Singapore (2004)

Source: Authors' update based on data from the Economic Commission for Latin America and the Caribbean (ECLAC) and the Office of the USTR.

amongst members of Congress and their private sector constituents. Second, is if the agreement promotes US trade and investment interests by improving market access; leveling the playing field for US firms, workers, and farmers; and by forging ties with countries most likely to support US objectives at the WTO. Third, the US considers if the prospective partner is willing to undergo the kinds of regulatory and trade reforms needed to comply with US requirements. Finally, the US analyzes if the FTA promotes its foreign policy interests, which is a concrete manifestation of the carrot-and-stick approach to diplomacy. As we argue in the following section, Congressional consideration of each and every one of these criteria has morphed into a virtual political battlefield since the historic NAFTA debates that exploded in the early 1990s.

Bilateralism as an offshoot of US domestic trade politics, 1991–2008

During the spring of 1991, when the senior Bush administration requested a renewal of the fast-track negotiating authority in order to formally launch the NAFTA negotiations, an unexpectedly heated domestic debated ensued— one that was easily on par with that which surrounded the passage of the highly protectionist Smoot–Hawley Tariff in 1930 (Destler, 2005). A main legacy of this period in the early 1990s was the emergence of a blue–green coalition of grassroots labor and environmental activists that managed to insert non-trade issues onto the US trade policymaking agenda like never before.

This grassroots coalition gathered steam on two fronts (Wise, 1998). First was a realistic reaction to the miserable working conditions and badly pol-luted *maquila* factory sites that lined the US–Mexico border. If NAFTA signi-fied the free flow of goods, services, and capital between all three countries, what was to stop the flow northward of environmental pollution and sub-standard working conditions? Why risk the lowering of labor and environ-mental standards that workers and consumers had fought to achieve since the 1930s? To the chagrin of free trade purists (Bhagwati, 2008), it was this coalition that compelled the senior Bush administration to expend political capital on border cleanup and the enforcement of much higher environ-mental standards. With the election of President Clinton in 1992, this ante was upped to include the formal negotiation of labor and environmental side agreements to accompany NAFTA as a quid pro quo for the blue–green endorsement of the 1993 NAFTA implementing legislation.

The second front was largely symbolic, whereby NAFTA came to embody all that was cumulatively wrong with the US political economy at the outset of the 1990s. What had started out as an issue-oriented blue–green coalition in 1991 blossomed into a full-blown anti-NAFTA movement that included everyone from job-seeking college grads to downsized business executives and laid-off factory workers to teachers' unions, pensioners, and welfare mothers. Regardless of the actual effect that NAFTA would have on any of these constituents, they were united in the perception that they had some-how been excluded from the prosperity that surrounded them in the late twentieth century, and they were understandably angry about it.

NAFTA's self-appointed "losers" have thus kept the opposition to further trade liberalization alive, as witnessed across the board in US public opinion polls for more than a decade and, more recently, in the pandering to these constituents by various candidates in the 2008 US presidential primary debates.[6] But beyond this phenomenon of NAFTA coming to symbolize a general sense of downward mobility and free-floating economic anxiety in the US, it is the tenacity of the blue–green coalition and its effect on Congressional deliberations that perhaps best accounts for the testiness of

US trade policy since the launching of NAFTA. Although this coalition won the battle in securing the attachment of labor and environmental side agreements to NAFTA, the lackluster enforcement of those agreements has further prolonged the trade policy war on the domestic side. Much of the fight has centered on correcting the institutional weaknesses in those earlier agreements, namely the obligation of each country to enforce its own existing national laws but with little regard for strengthening and harmonizing North American labor and environmental standards overall (Hufbauer and Schott, 2005).

The irony here is that the demands of the blue–green coalition have increasingly united Congressional members of all political stripes against FTA expansion, either on the grounds that grassroots lobbying for the incorporation of non-trade issues has gone too far and should be resisted (business-backed Republicans) or in protest that these labor and environmental stipulations need to reach much further (Democrats beholden to labor and environment grassroots supporters). A consensus was finally reached that the legislation and practices of potential FTA partner countries must comply with the obligations set out in Chapter I of the International Labor Organization (ILO) Declaration on the Fundamental Principles and Rights at Work, adopted in 1998. With regard to the environment, new trade partners in Latin America are obliged to sign seven agreements on the environment and to accede to existing multilateral agreements (ECLAC, 2007) in this realm.

In and of themselves, political sensitivities around non-trade issues on Capitol Hill need not necessarily result in a bilateral strategy. However, Destler (2007) emphasizes that the rise of bilateralism must be understood in the context of the heightened polarization of the US Congress on trade policy issues over the past decade. He points to the concomitant decentralization of the Congressional committee system and the ways in which this has weakened committee chairmen and sitting members in their efforts to influence US trade policy. Under the combined influence of this organizational shift related to the Congressional legislative process and the steady pressure from below exerted by the ever-expanding blue–green coalition, earlier Congressional reluctance over bilateral deals has gradually evolved into an acceptance that these are now the deals most likely to make it through all of the tedious hurdles on Capitol Hill.

Of special note here is the seeming disconnect between the obsession with non-trade issues on Capitol Hill and the stealth-like focus of the USTR on achieving GATT/WTO (General Agreement on Tariffs and Trade/World Trade Organization)-plus gains in these agreements. Caught in between is a long list of state entities, led by the Departments of Commerce, State and Treasury, which constitute the so-called interagency process in bringing a trade agreement to fruition (Phillips, 2008: 155). In light of the unwieldy organizational web that has gradually come to govern domestic trade policymaking, the list of small open economies that have completed bilateral FTAs with the US (see Table 5.1) may well represent the "politics of what's possible" at this particular juncture.

Dissecting the diffusion hypotheses

Our analysis thus far points to both internal and external factors in explaining the remarkable US shift from staunchly opposing the FTA option over the post-World War II period to its slow embrace beginning in the 1980s. In terms of the policy dissemination framework, we see the US as the trendsetter in the generation of bilateral FTAs that were negotiated in the 1980s and thus a main independent variable for the diffusion of this specific trade strategy beginning in the 1990s. This is especially so for the Western Hemisphere, where Mexico and Chile have followed the US strategy with the negotiation of dozens of bilateral FTAs in the post-NAFTA era.

Going back to Viner's (1950) classic theory on the proliferation of FTAs, at stake is the prospect of triggering greater trade diversion than creation. Given the increase in bilateral FTAs since the beginning of the 2000s, will the US competitive liberalization strategy promote trade creation and a more general liberalization of the world trade system; or is this prompting a pattern of trade diversion in which the beneficiaries of FTAs will resist further multilateral trade liberalization in order to preserve their margin of preference in the US market? Then again, recent literature on economic growth has declared both questions to be outdated.

Lawrence (1996), Rodrik (2007), and others suggest that the yardstick for successful trade and investment integration should instead measure the competitive gains that FTA signatories achieve as a result of deep liberalization of both traditional (agriculture, textiles) and modern (services, investment) sectors of the economy. The early results on US FTAs with Chile and Singapore conform most closely with this last insight. However, we must also bear in mind that every time the US discriminates in favor of a trading partner, it discriminates against all the other countries that continue to trade on an MFN basis (Cooper, 2005). In some cases, such discrimination can provoke a pernicious pattern of competition among countries to be part of the lucky club of US trade partners, regardless of whether the subsequent agreement fosters the kinds of competitive gains that Lawrence (1996) and Rodrik (2007) highlight.

This is precisely what occurred in 2004 when the US sought to negotiate an FTA with the five members of the Andean Community. Venezuela, which has long eschewed neoliberal reforms in favor of a hodgepodge populism based on high oil prices, withdrew its membership altogether and petitioned for entry into the Southern Cone Common Market (Mercosur). Bolivia and Ecuador, both of which had struggled unsuccessfully to implement market-oriented reforms through the 1990s, could not step up to the plate given the

US emphasis on WTO-plus issues. In both cases, domestic politics literally unraveled under this and other pressures, and both countries have soured against US trade negotiations under the leadership of new Left-wing governments. With the finalization of the US–Peru and US–Colombia FTAs in late 2005 and beginning of 2006, both countries seemed to remain the only members of this bloc to successfully survive the competition. However, the reluctance of US Congress to pass the Colombian FTA left Peru as the only country able to implement a bilateral agreement with the US in the Andean region. Simultaneously, the US bilateral strategy invoked bitter reactions from countries such as Brazil and Argentina, which have no preferential deals with the US and tend to view the US competitive liberalization strategy as a matter of divide and conquer.

Indeed, the timing of the US announcement of its competitive liberalization strategy raises questions about its transitional nature, as this coincided with the granting of WTO membership to almost all developing countries that once were mere bystanders in the multilateral sphere. With developing countries now comprising a majority of the WTO's 153 members, this has created a new dynamic in which each multilateral trade round is taking longer and the chances of reaching an agreement by consensus under the single undertaking principle have become increasingly elusive. When explored from this angle, the US bilateral strategy could just as easily be interpreted as one of circumventing this increasingly complex multilateral terrain.

For some critics, then, the new activism on the part of the US in the bilateral sphere generates fear that competitive liberalization may become a permanent rather than transitional means of coping with this broader sharing of power amongst the WTO membership (Cohn, 2007). This scenario lends credence to Viner's (1950) argument that the further spread of discriminatory trade deals means that trade diversion would most likely trump trade creation. However, others have countered against the idea that bilateralism harms multilateralism or deters trade creation, for example, by highlighting the fact that it was NAFTA's ratification in 1993 that brought the EU back to the negotiating table to finally wrap up the Uruguay Round (Wise, 2007).

To clarify, while former USTR Zoellick coined the present strategy as one of "competitive liberalization," we interpret this as less a matter of the US countering trade competition in third-country markets and more the legal component of the competition variable defined by Solís and Katada. Thus, while the US is inviting these small open economies to jointly embrace deeper integration via the negotiation of a bilateral FTA, it is also engaging in bottom up rule-making by enticing counterpart nations to adopt GATT/WTO-plus commitments for the sake of maintaining/improving access to the US market.

Although the initial driver in the diffusion of bilateral policy approaches in the 1980s, the US strategy itself is motivated by quite different domestic and international concerns at various points over the 1985–2008 time period. Beginning with the US bilateral FTAs negotiated with Israel (1985) and Canada (1988), we see the non-diffusion hypothesis as the more compelling explanation for these two agreements. On the international side, the US faced serious concerns on both the economic and security fronts. In the security arena, the US–Israel FTA enabled the Reagan administration to affirm its support for Israel and the FTA was quickly concluded.

The US–Canada FTA is perhaps best understood from the standpoint of mutual necessity: as strong and longstanding trade and investment partners, the growing uncertainties that roiled global markets in the 1980s prompted both the US and Canada to seek economic comfort in an FTA. The international economic position of the US was threatened by stiff trade competition from Japan and the emergence of mammoth commercial and fiscal deficits. As the US fell back into a net debtor status for the first time in the twentieth century, the mood on Capitol Hill turned decidedly protectionist.

It was Canada, faced with its own economic woes and rising levels of US import protection in the 1980s, which petitioned the USTR to launch negotiations for a bilateral FTA. Canada's move was spurred less by concern over the prospect of facing outside competition in the US market and more by fears of being shut out of the US market altogether. As Table 5.2 shows, Canada's trade and investment ties with the US continue to tower over those of all other partners with which the US has signed a bilateral FTA. Hence, the commitment on both sides to formalize this relationship.

With the launching of the Uruguay Round in 1986, it came as somewhat of a surprise when Mexican President Carlos Salinas de Gortari explicitly requested the negotiation of an additional bilateral FTA with the United States in 1990 (Wise, 1998). It was with considerable difficulty that former President George H. W. Bush obtained the necessary fast-track authority to launch the NAFTA negotiations due to concerns over Mexico's developing country status.

Unexpectedly, the NAFTA agreement moved more quickly than the Uruguay Round. Like Canada, Mexico had acted defensively to secure its own position in the US market, but also as a way of locking in its recently implemented market reform program (Pastor and Wise, 1994). The tradeoff was that both partners agreed to the incorporation of GATT-plus features within NAFTA, such as the rules surrounding investment, services, dispute settlement, and IPR. Therefore, it could be argued that the GATT-plus features of NAFTA triggered a process of both legal and economic competition in the sense that key actors in the Uruguay Round negotiations were now keen to close the deal and achieve similar progress on the GATT-plus rules embodied in NAFTA, and economic competition in that European and Asian (especially Japanese) investors and exporters now faced the prospect of shrinking demand for their goods in the US and Mexican markets.

The legal competition variable prompted a long overdue breakthrough at the multilateral level in the design of rules on the new trade agenda,

Table 5.2 The United States' FTA network (as of March 2009)

Partner*	Status	Trade volume in 2007 (percentage of overall total)≅	FDI volume in 2006 (percentage over total)⊥	Issue scope[A]				Trade capacity building
				Investment	Service	Environment	Labor	
Mexico	In force (1994)	11.15	1.94	Yes	Yes	Yes	Yes	No
Canada	In force (1994)	18.02	8.04	Yes	Yes	Yes	Yes	No
Chile	In force (2004)	0.56	0.58	Yes	Yes	Yes	Yes	No
El Salvador	In force (2006)	0.14	0.03	Yes	Yes	Yes	Yes	Yes
Guatemala	In force (2006)	0.23	N/A	Yes	Yes	Yes	Yes	Yes
Honduras	In force (2006)	0.27	0.02	Yes	Yes	Yes	Yes	Yes
Nicaragua	In force (2006)	0.08	0.01	Yes	Yes	Yes	Yes	Yes
Costa Rica	In force (2009)	0.27	0.12	Yes	Yes	Yes	Yes	Yes
Dominican Republic	In force (2006)	0.33	0.06	Yes	Yes	Yes	Yes	Yes
Peru	In force (2009)	0.30	0.48	Yes	Yes	Yes	Yes	Yes
Australia	In force (2005)	0.89	2.61	Yes	Yes	Yes	Yes	No
Singapore	In force (2004)	1.43	4.41	Yes	Yes	Yes	Yes	No

* The table covers all the agreements in the Asian and Latin American regions that are relevant for this project.

≅ http://tse.export.gov/MapFrameset.aspx?MapPage=NTDMapDisplay.aspx&UniqueURL=pbstck551vkuf2mr2kzw0q55-2008-5-10-17-37-33.

⊥ http://www.bea.gov/international/ii_web/timeseries7-2.cfm. Bureau of Economic Analysis, US Department of Commerce, accessed on 11 May 2008.

A USTR (2003a, 2003b, 2007a and 2007b) and webpage. http://www.ustr.gov/.

including the completion of the Uruguay Round in 1994 and the creation of the WTO in 1995; the economic competition variable simultaneously unleashed a frenzy of new bilateral FTAs, led by countries in the Western Hemisphere. When the US joined this fray in the early 2000s, the GATT/WTO-plus NAFTA template re-emerged as the main reference point for the negotiation of these bilateral FTAs (see Table 5.2).

Table 5.2 summarizes the trade and investment ties that underpin the agreements that the US has signed with Latin American and Asian partners, the bulk of which were launched in the past four years. As can be appreciated from the Table, the NAFTA partners are by far the most important for the United States in terms of trade and FDI volume. Yet Table 5.2 also shows that the trade and FDI flows are not as significant for the US in the other cases. Thus, in the post-NAFTA era, US motives around bilateral trade deals appear to be more political and legal in nature and to be geared toward securing certain services and investment regulations related to specific US economic interests. We would also argue that the US FTAs signed with the Central American and Andean countries represent the US assessment that if the new trade issues cannot be agreed upon any time soon within the multilateral and regional arenas (FTAA), then the US will continue to pursue these issues on a bilateral basis.

The regional implications of US bilateralism in the 2000s

Given the short timeline on the revival of the US bilateral strategy under the banner of "competitive liberalization," the jury is still out when it comes to discerning the impact of this strategy on multilateral negotiations. From interviews that we have conducted, for example, with Costa Rican and Peruvian trade policymakers,[7] these small open economies remain committed to the completion of the Doha Round, although they are clearly not in a position to lead the charge in revitalizing it. Rather, this will be up to the so-called BRIC coalition of developing countries, comprising Brazil, Russia, India, and China, which has thus far been successful in laying developing country demands for market access squarely on the table (Cohn, 2007), but less so in actually wrapping up the Doha agreement such that it includes these concessions.

There remains the question as to whether the US bilateral FTA strategy can create momentum for wider regional trade agreements. With just two US FTAs completed in Asia—US–Singapore (2003) and US–Australia (2004)—this question is premature. Moreover, as we argue below, the US FTA strategy in Asia is geared toward fierce legal and economic competition on the part of the US, as China is moving rapidly with the negotiation of FTAs in these regional markets. In other words, the US is acting defensively in Asia and, if anything, would most likely prefer to slow China's FTA momentum in favor of its stronger compliance with international legal norms under the WTO.[8]

It is within its own sphere, that the US has made claims to the linking of bilateral FTAs with a larger regional strategy. In fact, much of the US trade strategy for Latin America seems predicated on this assumption. Destler (2005) argues, for example, that Venezuela's swapping of membership in the Andean Community for entry into Mercosur in 2006 suggests that the ground for a regional project has been hollowed out. Similarly, two frontline Mexican policymakers who participated in the FTAA negotiations, Jaime Zabludovsky and Sergio Gómez Lora (2007), insist that it was the US patchwork of bilateral deals struck with Latin American countries in the 2000s that ultimately derailed the FTAA negotiations. However, they also note that there were other problems even prior to this, not all of which can be blamed on the US.

As early as 1998, at the Summit of the Americas trade ministerial meeting in San José, Costa Rica, the FTAA countries agreed to a "single undertaking" strategy that proved to be the first fatal blow to the negotiations. This essentially extended a de facto veto to each participant, such that the pace and scope of the FTAA negotiations could basically be set by the slowest moving reformers amongst the group. Additional tensions arose, such as the final standoff in 2003 between the US and Brazil over the timing and extent of concessions to be made between issues on the "old" (market access, agriculture, industrial goods) and "new" (services, investment, IPR) trade agendas. But the final straw, as Zabludovsky and Gómez Lora (2007) see it, was the US rush toward bilateralism in 2002 after securing the TPA, spurred by the USTR's sense of urgency to catch up with the rest of the world.

Other trade policy scholars, such as Tussie and Lengyel (2006) argue that a full understanding of its implications will require a more gradual and long-term study of this phenomenon. Down the road, the increased US reliance on bilateralism may provide the necessary structural foundation for regionalism to eventually flourish. This is based on their notion that bilateralism could gradually evolve into plurilateral regional-level agreements that exhibit new forms of cooperation. This would be most expected where there is a dense and overlapping concentration of bilateral agreements, as is currently happening with those FTAs that the US has thus far completed in Latin America. In fact, during our fieldwork interviews we did indeed detect a low buzz in Washington in favor of weaving together the existing US FTAs in the Western Hemisphere into a regional-12 grouping as the first formal step toward plurilateral cooperation since the collapse of the FTAA.

In the short run, the downside of a regional-12 grouping is that the exclusion of the larger Mercosur countries, and Brazil in particular, would seriously undermine the chance to achieve dynamic hemispheric gains along the NAFTA model. These have included increased scale economies related to greater specialization, improved technological capabilities, and more rapid and efficient deployment of those factors for which Mexico has a comparative advantage (Chase, 2005; Hufbauer and Schott, 2005). However, over the long run there is an upside: by negotiating these asymmetrical FTAs based on the achievement of GATT/WTO-plus commitments, the US could eventually leverage these legal and economic competitive gains to revive hemispheric and/or multilateral talks.

Finally, the full recessionary effects of the 2008 international financial crisis cannot be discounted here, even if the nature of its impact is still ambiguous. As in the 1980s, US trade policy could recoil into protectionist measures and this might prompt the various partners to return to the regional and/or multilateral negotiating tables. Admittedly, an end to the stalemate within both arenas would require a major facelift in terms of US leadership, as well as greater US willingness to concede on market access and other items on the "old" trade agenda that are of key importance to the developing countries. On the Latin American side, despite US success at leveraging WTO-plus concessions, these bilateral FTAs have thus far excluded "the areas of trade remedies and agricultural subsidies, and sensitive sectors and products have routinely been 'carved out.'" (Phillips, 2008: 157). Below we analyze this complicated dynamic whereby US FTAs have heavily emphasized the "new" trade agenda in Latin America and Asia, thus at least implicitly relegating the "old" entrenched issues to the multilateral arena.

Latin America

In examining the US bilateral accords that have been negotiated in Latin America during the post-2002 period, all appear to fit with the scenario suggested by Tussie and Lengyel (2006). The US–Chile FTA was at once a case of unfinished business from the 1990s, the eagerness of the US to reward staunch market reformers, and a reflection of Chile's efforts to promote itself as an investment and services hub in South America.

The only US sector to show interest and pressure for the US–Chile FTA in the 1990s was the services sector. However, as EU business interests began to lobby for the negotiation of an EU–Chile FTA, the interests of US investors in the services sector were quickly rekindled (Manger, 2009). Bilateral negotiations between the US and Chile for a FTA began almost at the same time as those with the EU and Chile, and the US–Chile FTA was finally completed in December 2002. The almost simultaneous finalization of the EU–Chile and the US–Chile FTAs lends support to the competition variable as US investors sought to defend their stake—no matter how small—in the Chilean market.

The remaining US–Latin American FTAs that we discuss here—CAFTA–DR, US–Peru, and US–Colombia—represent a very incremental effort on the part of the US to complete asymmetrical FTAs based on the achievement of GATT/WTO-plus commitments in the form of legal and economic competitive gains that can eventually be leveraged at the regional and/or multilateral level. In all these remaining cases, not only is there little threat to the US toehold in these markets, total US trade and investment ties themselves are rather meager. But the asymmetries are such that all the participating countries are looking to defend levels of market access that had been granted at some earlier point by the US Congress for reasons related more to security than to US foreign economic policy.

Such were the roots of both the 1984 Caribbean Basin Economic Recovery Expansion Act (CBERA) and the subsequent Andean Trade Preference Act (ATPA) bills passed by Congress for the explicit purposes of fighting "Communist" guerrillas in the case of the former and eradicating rampant drug trafficking in the case of the latter. Although in the post-Cold War era CBERA was succeeded by the Caribbean Basin Trade Partnership Act of 2000 and ATPA by the Andean Trade Promotion and Drug Eradication Act (ATPDEA) of 2002, the fact is that both the Central American and the Andean countries stand to lose these benefits at any time should the unpredictable winds of the US Congress deem to suspend them at will.

With the collapse of hemispheric and multilateral negotiations, CAFTA–DR quickly became a test case for the US competitive liberalization strategy. A main legacy of the 1984 CBERA was that apparel had "become the dominant export good for all countries except Costa Rica. The United States encouraged this type of trade when it included the Central American countries as beneficiaries under the Caribbean Basin Economic Recovery Expansion Act" (Hornbeck, 2003: 14). The content of the agreement thus focused on investment and market access in textiles and garments rather than trade in a range of goods. Given the fierce levels of import competition that the US apparel industry has faced since China's 2001 entry into the WTO, coupled with the phasing out of the GATT's Multi-fiber Agreement in 2005, those in support of CAFTA–DR were hard-pressed to convince a majority of legislators on Capitol Hill that CAFTA–DR would, in fact, benefit US textile and garment producers.

First, the pro-CAFTA–DR coalition emphasized the potential for the agreement to fortify cross-border production networks between the US and Central American apparel industries, such that greater market access would enable both groups of producers to strengthen ties and link efforts to combat the steady flow of Chinese apparel exports in their markets (House Ways and Means Committee, 2003: 33). Second, the agreement's supporters presented it as an opportune way for US companies to equalize not just their trade preferences, but also rules around investment, services, and IPR. Finally, although the incorporation of labor standards and rules around environmental protection into the US–Chile FTA rendered this a *fait accompli* for CAFTA–DR, lobbyists readily "conceded" on these points while courting the opposition.

The economic stakes for the US might have been small, but CAFTA's political symbolism loomed large given that this would be the first trade agreement to be rejected by the US Congress in more than four decades (Vieth, 2005). The drama that ensued on Capitol Hill regarding the passage of CAFTA–DR (217 to 215 in the Democratically controlled House of Representatives and 54 to 45 in the Senate) confirmed that regardless of the asymmetries involved, henceforth the negotiation of bilateral FTAs with developing countries would be anything but easy. In hindsight, the impetus for the CAFTA–DR FTA was the further diffusion of the competitive liberalization strategy on the part of the US, including the quest to achieve legal and economic competitive goals no matter how small the actors or the inroads actually made.

The lead-up to the US–Peru FTA was similar to that of CAFTA–DR, as were the competition variables that induced both Peru and the US to negotiate. For reasons discussed above, Peru emerged as the most viable candidate for negotiating a bilateral FTA within the context of the US competition liberalization strategy. As seen in Table 5.2, the flow of US FDI to Peru is small, but still nearly double the percent represented by US–Peru trade. On the trade side, 98 percent of US imports from Peru entered duty-free (under MFN tariff rates, various preference programs, including the ATPDEA, and the General System of Preferences) prior to the 2007 Congressional approval of the US–Peru FTA, suggesting that Peru is yet another minor venue for US promotion of WTO-plus rules around investment, services, and IPR, but a venue nevertheless. As with the US–Chile and CAFTA–DR agreements, Peruvian policymakers conceded to US demands for the harmonization of regulatory norms and to broad commercial policy reforms that complied with US standards, and this obviously included the adoption of the same labor and environmental stipulations that were embodied in these other FTAs.

As for the pending US FTAs with Colombia, Panama, and South Korea, a main trade policy priority for the Bush administration was to secure Congressional ratification of the US–Colombia FTA. Although the US–Colombia trade and investment links are no more compelling than those of the US with Chile, CAFTA–DR, or Peru, this agreement continued to face significant opposition from the Democratic Congressional majority based on projected US job losses and human and labor rights infractions in Colombia and was not passed under Bush administration.

Yet despite the willingness of the Colombian negotiators to raise standards across the board, not to mention the billions of dollars in US military and economic aid dispersed to the Colombian government since the late 1990s under the banner of "Plan Colombia," the powers that be on Capitol Hill have been unable or unwilling to embrace the US–Colombia FTA as a logical extension of ongoing US foreign policy toward this drug- and guerrilla-plagued country—a foreign policy approach that has held true for Democratic and Republican administrations alike for at least a decade.

The recent Democratic Party presidential debates have further clouded the prospects for passage, as the candidates called repeatedly for "fixes" to the existing US FTAs before adopting new ones. Yet they have not announced any details on what actually needs to be done (Markheim, 2008). As the bill for the US–Colombia FTA now wends its way through Congress, there is some bipartisan recognition that rejection of the bill would constitute a major foreign policy blunder from the standpoint of US–Colombian relations and, in turn, US security concerns but in the middle of the financial crisis the FTA has vanished as a policy priority for the new Obama administration.

Asia

The agreements between US–Singapore and US–Australia were signed in May 2003 and May 2004, respectively. Again, while some have interpreted these two FTAs as the US reward for the support of both countries with regard to the Iraq invasion, both solidly represent a competitive strategy on the part of the US, one that is driven by the quest to secure more liberal rules on a number of issues that define the new trade agenda, and the US effort to expand market share in countries that are negotiating similar market access arrangements with China. For example, China negotiated a framework agreement with Australia in 2003 and the two countries are currently negotiating an FTA. Additionally, the ASEAN bloc includes Singapore as a member and has negotiated an FTA with China. In contrast with the very small gains attached to the negotiation of bilateral US FTAs in the Western Hemisphere, these two Asian agreements are both materially and symbolically crucial to US efforts to compete with China on its own regional turf. Ironically, although the stakes for the US were far larger with regard to securing these two Asian FTAs, they raised few political hackles on Capitol Hill. This is so for at least two reasons.

First, the US foray into negotiating these Asian FTAs is underpinned by considerably stronger flows of US FDI. As seen in Table 5.2, Singapore's share of US FDI ranks second only to Canada's while Australia ranks third on this indicator among the countries covered in this chapter. Second, the baseline for both countries at the outset of the negotiations was that of economic openness and market orientation. The asymmetries between the US and each of these FTA partners are obviously there, but the pre-existing bias toward competitive liberalization on both sides of the negotiating table rendered these deals easier to reach, and certainly more obtainable that US FTAs with Japan or South Korea.

In the case of Singapore, Dent (2003) argues that many key factors, including the absence of sensitive issues or a large agricultural sector, also allowed for a smooth set of negotiations with the US. For both sides, the services sector topped the agenda and the final agreement basically reflected a trade relationship between two high-technology partners. For the USTR (2002), the highlights of the US–Singapore FTA are new services and investment opportunities for US banks, expanded market access for US insurance companies, a more open and competitive telecommunications market, and the streamlining of customs procedures. From Singapore's standpoint, although the FTA may have been a reaction to the US competitive liberalization strategy, the sophisticated content of the agreement confirms that policymakers there were seeking to set a new pace for WTO-plus achievements rather than emulating the numerous but less penetrating FTAs that have emerged worldwide since the 1990s.

On the US–Australia FTA, the main interests of the US focused on trade-related investment measures rather than services. From the start, the sectors covered in this bilateral relationship were more complicated, as the US–Australia trade relationship is based mainly on a pattern of comparative advantage that mirrors the China–Chile FTA. Like China, the US exports higher value-added manufactured goods to Australia (aircraft and parts, road vehicles, and specialized machinery); like Chile, Australia mostly exports primary goods (meat, beverages, and dairy products) to the US market.

For Australia, the main irritants included US restrictions on beef and dairy imports; for the US, the strains centered on Australia's local content requirements in television programming, sanitary and phytosanitary (SPS) measures, state-sanctioned monopolies in exports of wheat and other grains, and its screening of foreign investments. On some talking points, such as US restrictions on beef and dairy imports from Australia and on Australia's investment screening, the two sides agreed to loosen existing restrictions. On others, such as Australia's SPS measures and state-sanctioned monopolies, they agreed to establish mechanisms for further discussion. However, no agreement was reached in the most contentious areas, such as US import controls on sugar.

Stoler (2004) argues that the US sought an FTA with Australia to increase US FDI in Australia, to encourage the greater integration of business practices in the two markets, to foster competitive liberalization through its demonstration effects in the WTO and other trade fora, and to further solidify an already strong relationship between the two countries. Apart from the competitive impetus engendered by China's negotiation of an FTA with Australia, the US–Australia FTA was politically motivated to the extent that it enabled the US government to showcase its strong bilateral alliance with a main actor in Pacific Asia, a country that is key to the promotion of stability and prosperity in this region. For Australia's part, the conclusion of the US–Singapore FTA a year earlier surely prompted a competitive reaction, an opportunity for Australia to fast-track its goals of achieving greater access to the US market after the long hiatus on US trade negotiations over the preceding decade.

Conclusions

Critique of the US bilateral strategy in the 2000s

In this chapter, we have argued that the US has clearly been a driver in the diffusion of bilateral policy approaches, even if the US strategy itself is motivated by quite different international and domestic variables at shifting points over the 1984–2008 time period. The impetus for US bilateral FTAs signed between 1984 and 1992 (Israel, Canada, and NAFTA) conformed most closely with the non-diffusion hypothesis, which means that the decision to pursue these agreements was not shaped by the prior actions of other countries. Rather, the US–Israel FTA emerged as an expeditious method for the US to promote its political and security goals in the Middle East. In the cases of the US–Canada FTA and NAFTA, Canada and Mexico were the initiators, respectively, as each struggled economically and fought to preserve market access in the face of rising US protectionism and global financial instability. A defining feature of this period is that the US resort to bilateral approaches was convincingly articulated as a parallel strategy, one meant to complement the US commitment to completing ongoing multilateral trade negotiations at the Uruguay Round.

Ironically, although the Clinton administration achieved this multilateral goal in 1994, contentious domestic politics and a hostile Congress worked to deter the completion of further US trade agreements until the signing of the US–Singapore FTA in 2003. In the interim, more than 230 FTAs were negotiated worldwide, many of them involving some combination of developed and developing country membership. Although the US Congress basically benched the US executive for a full decade on the trade policy front, the initial US move to include Mexico in the NAFTA negotiations was the trigger for the wave of asymmetric FTAs that quickly followed. In this respect, the US was the diffuser of the bilateral FTA strategy and those countries that followed in its footsteps adopted this policy as a way of similarly locking in access to key export markets.

With the passage of the Trade Promotion Authority legislation in 2002, the Office of the USTR launched its strategy of competitive liberalization; the USTR has subsequently finalized more than a dozen FTAs, all of which cover market access, investment, services, labor, and the environment. Despite the lapse in negotiating bilateral FTAs in the 1990s, we would argue that the US competitive liberalization strategy still fits the policy diffusion mold in that the US FTA template continues to push harder than most to achieve WTO-plus outcomes.

The motives of US FTA partners in the 2000s closely mirrored the legal and economic competitive concerns of the US, with the added worry of retaining market share in key US sectors. With the exception of the US FTAs negotiated with Singapore, Australia, and Chile, the US competitive strategy has been geared toward liberalizing jointly to achieve higher levels of efficiency and productivity, and less on the encroachment by third parties into a given US export market. In all the Latin American cases, the US is clearly offering up the bilateral FTA option as an incentive for countries to maintain their commitment to market-based economic policies. The one theme that unites these asymmetrical FTAs across North and South is the US goal of achieving WTO-plus commitments that can eventually be leveraged to revive hemispheric talks in the case of the Latin American FTAs, and multilateral talks overall. In the Asian cases, the more developed status of these countries rendered WTO-plus outcomes a *fait accompli*; thus, US motivations are defensive and centered on preserving a toehold in these markets to counter the rapidly expanding Chinese presence.

Our review of the accompanying debates over the longer-run implications of the US competitive liberalization strategy did, however, raise questions about this rosy scenario of trade creation and increasing global prosperity. On this count, we made three cautionary points. First, we clarified the differences between bilateral, regional, and multilateral liberalization, and highlighted the ways in which bilateralism is most biased toward discrimination and trade diversion. Second, we noted the tendency thus far for the US to negotiate bilateral FTAs with very small players in the world economy. In light of the steep asymmetries involved, especially within the Western Hemisphere, it is no wonder that US negotiators have succeeded in winning legal and regulatory concessions involving the implementation of the new trade agenda within these small open economies. Finally, in the process of pursuing its goals of legal and economic competitiveness with these FTAs, the US competitive liberalization strategy does run the risk of becoming an end in itself, rather than a complementary and transitional means for obtaining plurilateral agreements.

The good news is that US policymakers operating out of the USTR in the executive branch of government are now seeking FTAs with bigger players that matter, both in terms of future economic and political gains and for the impact that these larger agreements may have in revitalizing multilateral talks. The bad news, as the Colombia, Panama, and Korea FTAs remain stalled in the legislative queue, is that the US Congress appears oblivious to the stakes at hand. Even more unsettling is the prospect of another US trade policy blackout akin to that of the 1994–2002 period, as indicated by the tone of the Democratic Party majority that now controls the crucial committees for passing these FTAs.

Notes

1. This statement is based on the authors' interview with John Andersen, Senior Director for Western Hemisphere Affairs, International Trade Administration, US Department of Commerce, Washington DC, September 12, 2008; and on confidential interviews conducted at the Office of the US Trade Representative between May and September 2008.
2. Comments made by Edward Lincoln on the panel "Competitive Regionalism," American Political Science Association Meetings, August 28, Boston, MA.
3. A main pillar of the original GATT, the most favored nation norm obligates all GATT/WTO members to apply the same tariffs and rules to all other GATT signatories.
4. Formerly known as the "Fast-track" legislation, Trade Promotion Authority is granted to the executive by the Congress. Once a trade agreement is negotiated

with a foreign partner, the executive sends it to Congress for an "up or down" vote, that is, legislators are not given the opportunity to further amend or modify the bill.

5. The most widely subscribed index for measuring market reforms is the World Bank's *Doing Business* database. See www.doingbusiness.org.

6. See http://www.realclearpolitics.com/articles/2008/06/oooh_the_new_politics. html.

7. Authors' interviews with Eduardo Ferreyros, Vice-Minister of Foreign Trade, Ministry of Foreign Trade and Tourism, 2 September 2008, Lima, Peru; and Doris Osterlof, former Vice-Minister of Trade, San Jose, Costa Rica, 22 September 2008.

8. Authors' confidential interviews conducted with top policy officials at the Office of the USTR, May–September 2008.

6
Chile: A Pioneer in Trade Policy

Barbara Stallings

Introduction

Chile has followed one of the most aggressive trade policies in the world over the last three decades.[1] It has engaged in unilateral trade liberalization, supported and participated in multilateralism, and pioneered in the negotiation of bilateral and plurilateral free trade agreements (FTAs).[2] Its FTA partners have included its neighbors in Latin America, but also the United States, Europe, and Asia. No partner seems too big or too powerful for the Chilean trade juggernaut, and few seem too small or too weak. As two trade experts said recently, "[w]hen it comes to trade and integration policies, Chile seems to be approaching 'the end of the story.' The pioneer of trade liberalization in Latin America and the Caribbean has probably gone far beyond any other developing country.... The journey to free trade ... was not without setbacks, but Chile's trade policies these days are as close to textbook recommendations as they can get" (Mesquita Moreira and Blyde, 2006: 3).

As in the analyses of other countries in the book, three questions will be addressed in this chapter. First, what triggered the FTA process? Second, who were the main actors, and what were the characteristics of the decision-making process? Third, what were the outcomes? The chapter is organized around these questions. The first section looks at the history of Chilean trade policy from the early 1970s to see how and why the FTA process emerged. The second section addresses the three hypotheses presented in the introductory chapter as possible explanations of the FTA process. Was the process primarily an independent one, or did it respond to the actions of other countries through either emulation or competition? The third section explores the outcomes of the FTA process for Chile itself and for regional integration in Latin America. The fourth section concludes.

The argument about the Chilean experience with preferential trade agreements is as follows. Different motives account for joining with different partners, but in all cases the government was the lead actor. During the military regime from 1973 to 1989, Chile undertook a tremendous amount of trade liberalization on a unilateral basis and, by the late 1980s, had the strongest economic performance record in Latin America. With the resumption of democracy in 1990, the government looked for ways to reintegrate the country with its neighbors and began to sign bilateral and plurilateral agreements. These were not particularly important in economic terms in the short run, but they did have some interesting potential for Chile's long-term development strategy. The agreements with the United States and Europe had defensive economic aims in the sense of locking in major markets to avoid future trade diversion. The Asian agreements were aggressive steps to try to get ahead of potential rivals. In all the non-Latin American partnerships, the desire to attract foreign investment has been at least as important as the interest in trade. Chile aims to be a hub for foreign investment in South America, but mainly to obtain the economic benefits. It is an eminently pragmatic country.

A brief history of Chilean trade policy and the role of FTAs

The history of Chilean trade policy can be divided into three phases. The first represents the phase of unilateral opening (1973–89). The second is the phase of preferential trade agreements with Latin American neighbors (the 1990s). The third is the phase of preferential agreements with non-Latin American countries (the 2000s). This schematic is an oversimplification since additional unilateral liberalization also occurred after 1990, but the main emphasis changed toward negotiated opening. In addition, it should be noted that the dates reflect when the agreements went into effect. Negotiations for the some of the non-Latin American FTAs began much earlier, while some are ongoing with Latin America as well as Asia.

Phase 1

At the time of the military coup against President Salvador Allende in September 1973, Chile had a typical Latin American closed economy where the state played a major role. Indeed, it was an extreme example after the three years in which Allende's Popular Unity coalition tried to move toward socialism. In the trade sphere, average tariffs were around 100 percent and sometimes exceeded 200 percent. They were reinforced by other policies, such as quantitative restrictions, multiple exchange rates, and capital controls. Exports relied heavily on copper, and trade represented less than 30 percent of GDP.

Liberalizing trade, then, was one of the main reforms of the military government, and it was done in a very dramatic way. Quantitative restrictions were quickly eliminated, and the government announced a reduction of tariffs to a maximum of 60 percent for 1977. Two years later, a ten percent uniform rate had been established. While exchange rate policy was supposed to compensate for the rapidly falling tariffs, a real appreciation set in after an initial devaluation. In 1979, the rate was pegged against the dollar. Not surprisingly, the trade deficit burgeoned.

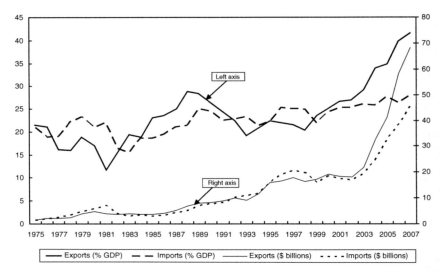

Figure 6.1 Chilean exports and imports: 1975–2007

The trade deficit, together with financial imbalances and international shocks, led to a serious balance-of-payments crisis in the early 1980s. In addition to devaluing the currency, the flat tariff rate was briefly raised to 35 percent with even higher rates for a few individual products. Unlike some of its neighbors, however, the Chilean military survived the crisis; a more prag-matic economic team was installed, and tariffs were again lowered to reach a uniform 15 percent rate by 1988. The impact of these various changes on exports was predictable. After an initial surge, they fell to reach a trough in 1981, but then expanded by almost 20 percentage points of GDP between 1981 and the later part of the decade (see Figure 6.1).

Phase 2

A democratic government returned to Chile in 1990. To the surprise of many, the basic elements of the earlier reforms, including trade liberaliza-tion, were maintained and even deepened. Thus, in 1991 tariffs were reduced across the board from 15 to 11 percent, and in 1998 the congress approved a further five-point reduction over a five-year period. At the same time, important adjustments were made both to domestic and international policies. One of the most controversial changes was the decision to initiate negotiations for a set of preferential trade agreements.

This change came about for several reasons as the new government looked at the world in 1990. First, it was becoming clear that international trade was going to be a key driver of economic growth. Second, at the same time, the multilateral trade negotiations of the Uruguay Round were not going very well. Third, partly as a consequence, both the United States and Europe were looking toward bilateral or plurilateral agreements to improve their trade access. In the light of this scenario, the question for the Chilean government was how to strengthen the export model developed in previous years. Little disagreement existed in light of a national consensus that Chile had done well as a trader and had to continue down that path. There was general agreement too that the country had to deepen its export strategy by expanding the quantity of its sales abroad, raising the quality of the exports in terms of value added, and linking exports more closely to GDP growth (Butelmann and Meller, 1992; Sáez et al., 1995).

The Alywin administration (1990–94) argued that unilateral liberalization and preferential trade agreements are complements, not substitutes. Two main economic roles would be fulfilled by FTAs. First, they would bring about some amount of opening-up on the part of trade partners. By definition, unilateral liberalization affects only the policies of the country itself, and while it may make exports more competitive, it does not open markets. Second, they would lower transaction costs by establishing rules to increase stability, promote transparency, and ensure fulfillment of commitments. In principle, multilateral agreements would serve these functions better, but the time taken by such negotiations and the compromises required led many countries to seek alternatives. In addition to these economic motives, political aims were at least as important. They included the reintegration of Chile into the regional and international system, and recognition of Chile as an important player and a new democracy (Sáez and Valdés, 1999).

Mainstream economists and the right-wing political opposition in Chile opposed the new policy initiative, seeing bilateralism as second best to unilateral liberalization. They pointed out that the effect of signing a number of bilateral agreements would be to replace the uniform tariff with a range of differentiated rates, which would decrease efficiency and lead to increased demands for protection. They were also concerned that bilateral agreements would reduce the likelihood of multilateral liberalization through the GATT/WTO (General Agreement on Tariffs and Trade/World Trade Organization). This opposition was overcome, in part, by continuing the unilateral tariff reduction at the same time that FTAs were being negotiated (Porras, 2003).

Given the decision to expand Chile's trade policy instruments to include preferential agreements, the question was with whom to negotiate. Chile had no single dominant trading partner. Its trade was roughly divided among North America, Europe, Asia, and Latin America, so it needed to open markets across the board. The issue was where to start. The list of Chilean trade agreements through 2007 and some characteristics of each can be found in Table 6.1. The first partners were in Latin America although disagreement existed within the government on whether Latin America should have been at the head of the queue. Nonetheless, agreements were

Table 6.1 Chile's FTA network (as of March 2009)

Partner	Status	Volume		Issue scope				
		Trade[¶]	FDI[‖]	Investment	Service	Environment	Labor	Economic cooperation
Mexico	In force (1992/1999)*	1.3/4.0	0.2/0.3	No/Yes	No/Yes	No/No	No/No	Yes/No
Bolivia[§]	In force (1993)	0.9	0.0	No	No	No	No	Yes
Venezuela[§]	In force (1993)	1.1	0.1	No	No	No	No	Yes
Colombia[§]	In force (1994)*	1.0	0.1	No	No	No	No	No
Ecuador[§]	In force (1994)	1.2	0.0	No	No	No	No	Yes
Mercosur[†§]	In force (1996)	13.9	2.7	No	No	No	No	Yes
Canada	In force (1997)	1.6	18.4	Yes	Yes	Yes[††]	Yes[††]	No
Peru	In force (1998/2009)*	1.6/2.5	0.1/0.04	No/Yes	No/Yes	No/No	No/No	Yes/No
Costa Rica	In force (2002)	0.2	0.0	Yes	Yes	No	No	No
El Salvador	In force (2002)	0.1	0.0	Yes	Yes	No	No	No
European Union	In force (2003)	20.2	38.8	Yes	Yes	No	No	Yes
EFTA	In force (2004)	0.6	2.7	No	Yes	No	No	No
United States	In force (2004)	13.0	26.5	Yes	Yes	Yes	Yes	No
Korea	In force (2004)	4.4	0.1	Yes	Yes	No	No	No
Pacific-4[‡]	In force (2006)	0.2	0.1	No**	Yes	Yes[††]	Yes[††]	Yes
China	In force (2006)	9.3	0.1	No**	No**	No	No	Yes
Japan	In force (2007)	7.7	2.9	Yes	Yes	No	No	No
India	In force (2007)	1.8	0.0	No	No	No	No	No

* Upgraded from ECA to FTA; in force for Mexico and Peru; signed but not ratified for Colombia.

[†] Argentina, Brazil, Paraguay, Uruguay.

[‡] Brunei, Chile, New Zealand, Singapore; formal name is Trans-Pacific Strategic Economic Partnership (SEP).

[§] Not notified to WTO because signed under authority of the LAIA agreement, which was notified to GATT in 1982.

[¶] Chilean exports plus imports with respective partners as share of total Chilean trade for year agreement entered into force; data for Japan, India, and Peru are for 2006.

[‖] Cumulative FDI from 1974 through year agreement entered into force.

** Follow-up negotiations underway.

[††] Side agreements.

Sources: IMF, Direction of Trade Statistics Yearbook (for trade); Chilean Directorate of International Economic Affairs website (for text of trade agreements that provide data on year and scope).

signed with ten Latin American countries between 1991 and 1998: Mexico in 1991; Bolivia, Colombia, and Venezuela in 1993; Ecuador in 1994; the four countries of Mercosur (Argentina, Brazil, Paraguay, and Uruguay) in 1996; and Peru in 1998. These agreements were the so-called Economic Complementation Agreements (ECAs), which were negotiated within the framework of the Latin American Integration Association (LAIA).

The LAIA framework is very flexible,[3] but the agreements tend to be narrow (focused mainly on trade in goods) and lacking in rigor (obligations are not defined in a precise way). The ECAs contrasted with the so-called FTA model that came into being with the North American Free Trade Agreement (NAFTA). The latter is both broader and more specific. Rules for trade in goods have few exceptions and are much more demanding, especially with respect to rules of origin (ROOs). They also include many other issues, such as services, investment, and dispute settlement mechanisms.[4] The Chile–Mexico ECA was upgraded to an FTA in 1998, as was the Chile–Peru agreement in 2009, and the Colombia accord is in the process of upgrading. In this sense, Chile played a role in exporting a new FTA model.

While the spotlight was on negotiating agreements with Latin America, under the surface another set of relationships was being developed simultaneously. In 1991, Chile was the first Latin American country to respond positively to President Bush's Enterprise for the Americas Initiative (Rosales, 2003). Discussions began for an FTA with the United States under President Clinton, but were held up by the NAFTA controversy and the elimination of "fast track" authority. In the meantime, an important intermediate step was taken through an FTA between Chile and Canada that was signed in 1996. It established many of the parameters for the later FTA with the United States, especially with respect to services and investment. Environmental and labor accords were incorporated as side agreements, as had been done with NAFTA.[5]

Phase 3

In the current decade, Chile took a major step forward and began to sign agreements with its largest trading partners. The initial ones were with the traditional partners—Europe and the United States—followed by agreements with Asian countries that had become important export markets. In general, the agreements were broad ones that fit into the category of the new FTA-type trade model, but Chilean officials indicated that they were willing to accept less comprehensive agreements—especially in Asia—if that was all they could get. This was another example of Chile's pragmatism.

The first of the new agreements to be ratified was an Economic Association Agreement with the European Union. It included goods, services, and government procurement as well as liberalization of investment and capital flows, the protection of intellectual property rights, and a binding dispute settlement mechanism. Indeed, the EU called it "the most innovative and ambitious results ever negotiated by the EU" with respect to trade.[6] In addition, it covered many other issues including political dialogue as well as cooperation on industry, science and technology, culture and education, migration, drugs, and so on.

The long-awaited treaty with the United States was not signed until June 2003, nearly 12 years after the idea was first mooted. It built on the Canada–Chile and NAFTA treaties, but added new dimensions. It covered seven general areas: market access, trade remedies, customs rules and standards, services, investment, labor, and the environment. The most controversial issue was the inclusion of labor and environmental provisions within the treaty itself. Chile had hoped to have them incorporated as parallel agreements, but the political reality in the United States made this impossible. Also controversial were Chile's capital controls, designed to avoid short-term speculative flows. Eventually, a compromise was reached that allowed both sides to save face (Hornbeck, 2003; Rosales, 2003).

In the Asian region, Chile has signed agreements with seven countries (Korea, Singapore, New Zealand, Brunei, China, India, and Japan). Four others are under active negotiation (Australia, Malaysia, Thailand, and Turkey) and several more are under discussion. With the exception of the China and India treaties, all are broad, detailed agreements of the FTA type.

The first Asia–Latin America FTA was signed between Chile and Korea in February 2003. The terms with respect to goods were broad; investment and services were also included although with exceptions (Park and Koo, 2007). The next Asian accord was signed in mid-2005 by the so-called Pacific-4 (P-4) group, which was constituted by four small economies: Chile, Singapore, New Zealand, and Brunei. Not surprisingly, this was one of Chile's most complete agreements since both Singapore and New Zealand have very open economies. The coverage was broad, and specific reference was made to the agreement as a model for free trade in the Asian region (Stoler, 2006). It also has an accession clause so that others can join.

The agreements with China (2005) and especially India (2006) were less inclusive. Both were limited to goods, although the China treaty anticipated future negotiations on services and investment; a technical agreement has already been reached. The China agreement provided immediate duty-free entry for the vast majority of Chile's exports. A dispute mechanism was included together with intellectual property and various social topics. The India agreement was much more limited, involving reduction in average tariffs of between 10 and 50 percent on a list of products (Rosales and Kuwayama, 2007). The latest Asian agreement was concluded with Japan, Chile's earliest trade and investment partner across the Pacific. While the agreement was broad, including services, public purchasing, and phytosanitary measures, the trade access measures had many exceptions, especially with respect to agriculture.

Explanations for Chilean FTAs

This book aims to test three hypotheses that might explain a country's FTA strategy: independent decision-making; emulation of leading countries; or competition of economic, political, and/or legal types. The argument here is that Chile does not fit neatly into any of the three. Perhaps not surprisingly, since the country has been signing FTAs for nearly two decades, shifts in motivation have occurred over time and among partners, and the agreements have been motivated by aspects of all three hypotheses.

Insofar as competition is important, we need to answer two main questions: competition with whom and with respect to what? Three competitors, or groups of competitors, might be relevant for Chile. First is a single country, Mexico, which is also Chile's most important ally in the region. Among Latin American countries, only Mexico can match Chile's performance record. Chile has frequently followed Mexico's lead, for example, in the agreements with the United States, Europe, and Japan. Of course, Mexico has a great advantage with its geographical location on the US border, and many partners are interested in agreements with Mexico to gain entrée to the United States. Nevertheless Chile has kept up and, especially in Asia, surpassed its northern friend and rival.

A second set of competitors comprises other South American countries. Brazil is one of those world's giants, which are of interest to all economic players. It also leads an integration group, Mercosur, which includes nearly 300 million consumers (compared to Chile's population of 16 million). But Brazil, another close Chilean ally, has an economy that is basically complementary to that of Chile. The same is not true for Argentina, which is also a Mercosur member. Argentina competes with Chile in many important products—and has not always been a friend. Finally, other emerging market countries, especially those in Asia, are potential competitors in the Asian region itself.

In economic terms, competition is focused on trade and investment. An important share of Chile's exports, the 40-odd percent that consists of copper, does not face a competitive threat, since Chile is the world's largest and most efficient producer. More important is competition over markets for agricultural and agro-industrial products together with services at the present and high-technology industrial products for the future. Competition over foreign direct investment (FDI) is perhaps of greater interest to Chile than competition over export markets. Chile wants FDI in its industrial sector both for the resulting access to technology and the access to markets.

In addition to economic competition, and closely related to it, is a political-economic goal. Chile is interested in positioning itself as the hub for South America's relationships with as much of the rest of the world as possible.[7] This goal holds for trade, investment, and physical infrastructure. The agreements with Latin American neighbors, especially Mercosur, are crucial prerequisites for this plan. What Chile has to offer international partners are its political and economic stability, its good policies, its openness, and its trade links with the rest of the region. This approach is similar to what Mexico is trying to do in the northern part of the hemisphere.

The FTA process has mirrored Chile's strong presidential system. All FTA initiatives have come from the executive branch. Congress has to approve trade agreements unless—as was the case of the early FTAs with Latin American countries—they derive legal authority from existing treaties. Congressional power is limited, however, since treaties can only be voted up or down. Since the mid-1990s, the main center of activity in the trade realm has been the General Directorate for International Economic Affairs (DIRECON, by its Spanish acronym). DIRECON is a highly professionalized office within the foreign ministry, which coordinates closely with the finance ministry and other relevant parts of the executive branch to provide policy advice to the president; it also carries out negotiations.

Relations between the trade apparatus and the business sector are multi-faceted. A private-sector consultation committee is the formal venue for exchange of information and opinion. More important are informal links, especially between DIRECON and the main business associations. The latter have acquired substantial skills in the technical aspects of trade negotiations and are considered as partners by DIRECON. An institution known as the "room next door" was instituted for recent negotiations, meaning that business representatives accompany the negotiators to be kept informed and discuss technical matters. Labor and civil society incorporation has been far less extensive. Overall, a clear pattern has characterized Chilean trade policy—the executive branch takes the initiative and sets the main policies; and the business sector gets involved over details that involve particular sectors and may lobby for small adjustments that will help their members.

The Chilean business sector itself, like most other countries studied in this book, is divided between the industrial and financial sectors, and agriculture. The latter is divided within itself into a very productive export agricultural sector and a more traditional one that mainly produces for the domestic market. As will be seen, it is the latter that has sought protection with respect to many FTAs. In addition, smaller industrial firms have also been threatened by competition, especially in Asian countries.[8]

Latin American FTAs

In 1990, with the return of a democratic government and the decision to expand trade policy to include bilateral and plurilateral agreements, two different sets of partners and approaches were proposed by different ministries. The foreign ministry wanted to use FTAs as an instrument for reintegrating Chile into the Latin American region after 17 years of near-isolation under the military regime. Many foreign ministry officials regarded Latin American regional integration as part of a political project, such as that in

Europe; it would also provide the structure for joint negotiations with the industrial countries and thus greater leverage. This model represented an independent top-down strategy initiated by government officials, whose economic advantages were still far in the future. Chile's main economic links at the time were with the industrial countries. In 1990, approximately 65 percent of Chilean exports were sold to the United States, the European Union, and Japan (calculated from IMF, 1991). Moreover, the vast majority of its foreign capital came from those same countries. Of FDI stock, 53 percent was from the United States and Canada, 27 percent from Europe, and 3 percent from Japan (calculated from Chilean Foreign Investment Committee website). Latin America, by contrast, represented only 13 percent of export sales and 2 percent of capital stock.

In light of this economic structure, the finance ministry advocated negotiation with the United States as the top priority. Specifically, Chile hoped to become the fourth member of NAFTA, which would solidify its reputation as being on the leading edge among developing nations and would also recognize its renewed democracy. Technical studies were begun to pave the way for a negotiation process, and Chile was invited to join NAFTA at the hemispheric summit in Miami in 1994. The majority of the business sector preferred this strategy, seeing it as opening many more opportunities than an approach focused on neighbors considered to be of dubious reliability. The process was cut short, however, by political problems that the Clinton administration encountered in getting the three-member NAFTA agreement approved. External circumstances thus determined that Chile's first decade of FTAs would follow the foreign ministry model.[9]

The first agreement was with Mexico, which had almost no economic links with Chile (0.9 percent of exports and 0.2 percent of investment stock). Mexico was, however, an attractive partner for several reasons. It was a like-minded country in the sense that it was the only other Latin American nation that was not a member of a subregional group. Together with Chile, it was the country that had made the most progress in market-based economic reforms. Moreover, Mexico was negotiating a trade agreement with the United States, and a deal with Mexico could improve Chile's own chances.[10] While the Chilean business sector expressed doubts about the benefits of the proposed agreement, the will of the two presidents prevailed. An Economic Complementation Agreement between the two countries was signed in September 1991 and took effect in January 1992; it was upgraded to an FTA in 1998 (Porras, 2003).

The countries that Chile approached next were its former partners in the Andean Community: Bolivia, Venezuela, Colombia, and Ecuador. These countries were small in economic terms, together accounting for only three percent of Chilean exports. Nor was there much likelihood of their becoming major partners in the foreseeable future. Nonetheless, agreements with them would indicate that Chile wanted to return to the neighborhood after its absence during the military government, which included its exit from the Andean integration group because of the latter's protectionist policies. Perhaps most importantly for the foreign ministry, agreements would help to resolve old political disputes and resentments. As in the case of Mexico, the business community was not enthusiastic about the Andean agreements, arguing that they did not bring much economic benefit, but the government prevailed. ECAs with these four countries were signed in 1993 and 1994; a few years later, Chile signed an agreement with Peru, the other Andean Community member and Chile's largest trade partner in the group (Porras, 2003).

It was not until the middle of the decade that Chile became associated with its largest and most powerful neighbors—Argentina and Brazil—along with their smaller partners in the Southern Common Market (Mercosur). Together, in 1996, the Mercosur countries accounted for 11 percent of Chile's exports and provided about three percent of its investment. From the Chilean government's perspective, Mercosur was complicated for several reasons in comparison to the Andean Community. First, from an economic viewpoint, Mercosur had a high common external tariff and differentiated internal tariffs by products. Embracing these policies would go against Chile's lower, flat rate. Second, in political terms, Mercosur's posture was that all negotiations with other countries or groups would be done by the group as a whole; Chile wanted to maintain its independent negotiating power. Third, unlike other integration groups in Latin America, Mercosur's goal was to work toward a political community, which would move well beyond trade and investment issues. Thus, when first approached to become part of the group at its founding in 1991, Chile declined. In 1996, however, it agreed to become an associate member.

The internal dynamic in Chile leading up to the association agreement was different than what occurred with the other agreements that Chile signed before (and afterwards) since civil society groups played an active role. Indeed, the Mercosur agreement was the most controversial that Chile has ever signed. Government arguments in favor of accession mainly stressed economic reasons for the deal, both proactive (prospects for trade and investment in a large market) and defensive (Mercosur's threat to end existing preferences that were significant for Chile). These views were shared by the industrial sector, which saw Argentina and Brazil as important markets. Moreover, these two countries were the recipients of a large part of the new Chilean investments abroad. The traditional agriculturalists, however, felt extremely threatened since the Mercosur countries were among the world's most efficient producers of wheat, sugar, and vegetable oils, which were also their main products. The agricultural producers and their association, the National Agricultural Association (SNA, by its Spanish acronym), joined forces with politicians representing their districts and threatened to defeat the government's proposal. The agreement was approved only when the government promised payments to the affected groups, amounting to three percent of the 1999 budget (Stefoni and Fuentes, 1998; Aninat et al., 2004).[11]

In summary, Chile's early trade agreements were with its regional neighbors. The explanations were mainly political: a way of reintegrating with the region and helping to damp down old quarrels. Nonetheless, even if the dominant explanation for these early agreements was political, several economic factors should also be highlighted. First, Chile, like other Latin American countries, exports higher value-added goods to the region than to the industrial countries. Thus, the reduction of protection in Latin American markets opened the way for these exports, which could later be sold elsewhere. Second, Chile has engaged in significant outward investment, and almost all of it has been within Latin America. While the ECA arrangements did not deal with investment, in some cases they paved the way for broader, modified agreements. Finally, Chile aims to become an investment hub, especially for FDI from Asia, and regional agreements are crucial in this regard, especially the one with Mercosur as Latin America's biggest market.

US and European FTAs

Chile's early trade agreements with its Latin American neighbors were independent decisions mainly designed to boost foreign policy goals, but the next group of agreements centered on competition dynamics. These agreements returned to the path that the finance ministry had wanted to follow earlier in negotiating with Chile's main economic partners. The United States and Western Europe were also political and ideological partners that Chile admired and wanted to emulate. They were the world's leading democracies and the most developed economies. Being associated with them in trade agreements would enhance Chile's reputation in ways that went beyond purely economic gains (interviews with former Chilean government officials).

Chile's trade goals in the agreements with the US and the EU were mainly defensive—to safeguard access to its largest markets and to prevent others getting better access through later preferential arrangements. With respect to the United States, Mexico was of concern to Chile, especially in terms of industrial goods that Chile hoped to emphasize in the future. Chile's natural resource exports already entered the United States with very low tariffs, but tariff escalation for goods with higher value added made it difficult to compete in the industrial sector. Mexico had already become a member of NAFTA, which guaranteed its access to US markets, and it was possible that its smaller neighbors would also sign agreements with the United States (as they did in 2004). In case of the EU, the main concern was with respect to the former Soviet bloc countries, many of which were candidates for EU membership. Chile hoped to expand its traditional political links with Europe into a stronger economic partnership.

Chile's investment goals were more proactive than its trade aims. It wanted to attract FDI from the United States and Europe to upgrade its exports, and it also wanted to become the investment hub for South America by promoting itself as the most reliable partner in the region. Through the combination, the government hoped that it could recover and maintain the high growth rate it had enjoyed from the late 1980s. Indeed, from 1985 to 1997, Chile had had a nearly-Asian rate of growth (an annual average of 7.4 percent), but growth fell off at the end of the 1990s due to spillover effects from the Asian financial crisis. Recovery of that growth rate was important for social and political as well as economic reasons.

Both the US and European agreements had long gestations. As already noted, a US agreement was on the agenda from 1990. The European agreement dated from that same period through the signing in 1990 of a framework agreement. While this framework agreement involved many social and political topics, its trade relevance was limited. Moreover, Chilean business opinions about the EU were initially negative, especially from traditional agriculture. Industrialists were not interested since almost no industrial exports were sold in Europe. Over time, however, the latter opinion began to change, especially as the possibility of a deal with the United States seemed more distant. When Europe itself became more interested in Latin America at the end of the decade, Chile stood out as a likely partner. With the executive branch pushing hard, little opposition was found in Chile, except from the wine and fishing sectors where the Europeans made stringent demands. A compromise was reached over the former, and the latter was unable to garner support for its complaint, so that an agreement was signed in the May of 2002 (Porras, 2003).

Perhaps stimulated by closer relations between Chile and the EU, the outgoing Clinton administration suddenly invited Chile to begin negotiations for a bilateral trade agreement in January 2001. Once underway, the process was relatively straightforward since it closely followed the format and content of the Chile–Canada and (updated) Chile–Mexico agreements as well as that of NAFTA itself. The main sticking point was the labor and environmental accords, which had to be incorporated into the agreement itself given the political climate in the United States. This prospect aroused a good deal of opposition in Chile, but was eventually seen as a small price to pay. In addition, the traditional opposition from the agricultural sector was muted since the SNA had been taken over by the large farming interests that would stand to benefit enormously from a US agreement. It was signed in June 2003 and went into effect from January 2004 (Rosales, 2003).

Asian FTAs

The region where Chile displayed an aggressive, rather than defensive, competitive spirit was in Asia. The Asia strategy dated back more than two decades. The earliest steps involved Chilean attempts to break into the Japanese market, the most important in the region at that time. In the 1980s, Chile devoted enormous efforts to sell its fruit, other agricultural products, and wine in Japan. With the help of the Japanese trading companies, this was eventually accomplished. The Japanese admired the persistence shown and became good customers. In some years in the 1990s, Japan surpassed the United States as the top destination of Chilean exports, and it began to invest in Chile in modest amounts (Saavedra-Rivano, 1993).

Using Japan as a base, and developing serious diplomatic capacity in Asian affairs, Chile expanded its contacts into many Asian countries through its embassies and its export promotion office, Pro-Chile. Pro-Chile's job was to help potential exporters, especially smaller firms, to move into Asia (and other regions). As an indicator of its Asian vocation, in 1994 Chile became the second Latin American country to become a member of APEC, following the accession of Mexico the previous year.[12] The Chilean government also continued to hone the skills of its negotiators. Indeed, it is said that Korea decided to negotiate Asia's first cross-regional FTA in order to learn the art of negotiation from the Chileans (Koo, 2006).

Korea was Chile's first Asian FTA partner. Both sides were enthusiastic because it appeared that their economies were complementary, and each was eager to gain a foothold in the other's region. In this case, unlike most others in which Chile was involved, the agricultural sector (fruit producers, in particular) was enthusiastic while industrialists, especially in the household appliances sector, were leery. On the Korean side, the pattern was the opposite: farmers felt threatened while industrialists were eager for an agreement since they were being displaced in the Chilean market by US producers. The compromise was that apples and pears were excluded on Korea's side in return for protection for Chilean refrigerators and washing machines. In addition, to get the agreement ratified in Korea, the government promised up to $80 billion in compensation if Korean agriculture was damaged (Park and Koo, 2007).

Other Asian agreements followed quickly. The next was with three smaller economies (Singapore, New Zealand, and Brunei). Originally mooted as an agreement between Chile and New Zealand during the late 1990s, objections by the agricultural sector kept Chile on the sidelines as Singapore and New Zealand signed an FTA in 2000. Two years later, negotiations began among the three, stimulated in part by the close political ties between Chile's president and New Zealand's prime minister. Nonetheless, Chilean agriculture again stalled the process until the agreement was rewritten as a "Strategic Economic Partnership," which would form an alliance among these small countries to share technology and carry out joint ventures vis-à-vis third countries.[13] A very comprehensive agreement, one of its characteristics was openness for others to adhere. Brunei did so in the closing days of the negotiations; in 2008, the United States announced that it would also begin negotiations to join.

Moving from three small partners, Chile next turned to negotiate an agreement with China. China had become one of Chile's top five export markets by 2000, and its share continued to rise. Thus, a particular concern was to establish a strong legal framework for the relationship given concerns about the rule of law in China. Even more than other FTAs, this one had to overcome cultural stumbling blocks (interview with former Chilean negotiator).[14] Some political objections remained on the Chilean side, which were reminiscent of the Korean negotiations. The industrial sector was worried about competition, and a number of China's industrial exports were placed on the ten-year liberalization schedule. Likewise, some of the most interesting export products for Chile (fruits and fish) were put on China's ten-year list. Services and investment were not included, but separate negotiations were foreseen.

While the P-4 agreement was very comprehensive and the China agreement was promising (Stoler, 2006), the Japanese agreement was more partial in the merchandise area. Chile wanted an FTA with Japan since that country remained one of its main trade partners and the most prestigious economy in Asia. According to Chilean officials, Japan was less interested, in part because of its difficult negotiations with Mexico. It was only when Prime Minister Koizumi visited Chile in 2004 that movement occurred, as a joint study group was announced. Also, the fact that Chile had signed FTAs with Korea and China attracted the attention of Japanese businesses, which urged their government to act (interviews with current and former Chilean government officials). The agreement that was signed was more favorable for Japan than for Chile in the trade area. Nonetheless, little or no opposition emerged in Chile.

The agreement with India was of much less immediate import, since it was of the older type where a positive list lowered tariffs on some of each country's merchandise exports. There is a possibility, however, that it will eventually be upgraded to a more comprehensive FTA if economic relations continue to expand. In the meantime, negotiations are underway with Australia, Malaysia, Thailand, and Turkey, and others are under discussion.

This record greatly increased Chile's international prestige, particularly in Asia. While it helped to open markets, the goal was larger and more strategic. Chile's Foreign Minister, when signing the Japan agreement, made this clear: "We began explorations in Asia some years ago. We dared to enter an extraordinarily large, diversified market, and with the implementation of the free trade agreement today—added to the accords that Chile already has with the People's Republic of China, South Korea, India and the countries of the P-4, as well as the network of treaties with other South American countries—Chile is becoming a platform for connection in the Pacific Rim" (Fischer, 2007).

Impact of Chilean FTAs

Table 6.2 shows the cumulative tariff impact of the various preferential agreements that Chile signed in the decade and a half between 1992 and 2007. With the Japanese agreement in 2007, 87 percent of Chile's trade is eligible for preferential treatment.[15] The effective tariff—the amount actually paid by preferential partners, weighted by the size of their markets—is calculated to have fallen from 10.5 percent in 1992/93 to 0.8 percent in 2007. For countries that do not have an agreement with Chile, the rate is six percent.

Chile has signed a large number of trade agreements, but the question is whether they will translate into economic advantage, as hoped by the government.[16] DIRECON produces annual reports on the trade and investment impact of Chile's FTAs. Trade has clearly increased, as shown in Figure 6.1, but it is hard to determine what share of the increase is due to trade agreements as opposed to other factors such as price rises. Going beyond the value of exports, then, DIRECON and Pro-Chile also report data on the number of firms exporting, products sold, and countries that import Chilean goods. Overall, in the period between 1990 and 2007, the number of exporting firms rose from 4,100 to 7,915; the number of products exported from 2,300 to 5,258; and the number of markets from 122 to 189

Table 6.2 Impact of Chile's bilateral and plurilateral trade agreements, 1992–2007

Year	Partner(s)	Percentage of imports liberalized	Effective tariff
1992	Mexico Venezuela Bolivia Colombia	4.2	10.5
1995	Ecuador	7.7	9.9
1996	Mercosur	23.2	8.8
1997	Canada	26.0	8.6
1998	Peru	26.2	8.6
2002	Costa Rica El Salvador	37.3	4.7
2003	EU	56.2	2.9
2004	United States Korea EFTA	76.4	2.1
2006	P-4 China India	84.2	1.0
2007	Japan	87.2	0.8

Source: Schuschny et al. (2007: 10).

(unpublished data provided by Pro-Chile).[17] FTA partners where particularly large increases have taken place include China, Korea, and Mexico (Pro-Chile website).

In terms of Chile's other goal—to increase inward investment flows— government data show no real progress, especially with respect to the Asian region. Japan has the largest investment stock ($1.8 billion), but this amounts to less than three percent of the total, and Japanese investment flows have fallen substantially since around 2000. Investments by other potential Asian partners include China (investment stock of $84 million) and Korea ($40 million). Thus, Chile's main investors continue to be the United States and the European economies (Chilean Foreign Investment Committee website).

In broader terms, a number of studies have been carried out with respect to the welfare gains resulting from the trade accords. Studies exist for the US, the EU, and the Asian agreements. Most of these studies have employed CGE models. In general, they have found modest gains for Chile with the largest gains involving the largest markets. Also, the more extensive the liberalization and the fewer the exclusions, the greater are the gains.[18]

Another type of outcome involves the impact of the FTAs on regional integration. As is pointed out in the introductory chapter of the book, competitive FTAs can undermine regional integration, despite the fact that regional integration has long been an aim in Latin America. To what extent has this occurred? Chilean officials have been and remain concerned about "spaghetti (noodle) bowl" problems, and they have tried to structure their agreements in similar ways to make them compatible. This aim was undermined among Latin American partners, however, by the political goals that were pursued. In addition, the fact that some Latin American agreements are ECAs while others are FTAs exacerbates the problem, although many of the ECAs are being upgraded. At the same time, Chile's agreements with countries in Europe and Asia could be seen—and are seen, especially by Mercosur—as undermining regional integration in Latin America itself.

From the Chilean viewpoint, the Free Trade Area of the Americas was designed to deal with these problems by imposing the same terms on all member countries. The FTAA was initially proposed by President George H. W. Bush as the Enterprise for the Americas Initiative in the late 1980s and reintroduced by President Bill Clinton at the Miami Summit in 1994. The idea was to form a single free trade area to cover the entire hemisphere. Working groups were set up, and significant progress was made. Indeed, one of the arguments heard for the increasing interest in FTAs in Asia was competition from the FTAA.[19]

Political competition between the two largest countries in the hemisphere—the United States and Brazil—began to derail the project in the early 2000s. More recently, the election of a number of governments openly opposed to the FTAA seems to have ended it, at least for the foreseeable future, as two rival blocs have emerged. Venezuela and several of its allies (Bolivia, Cuba, Ecuador, Honduras, and Nicaragua) have formed the Bolivarian Alternative for the Americas (ALBA, by its Spanish acronym). Trade liberalization is not a goal; rather the stated aim is to increase equity and social welfare. Simultaneously, another group—the so-called Arc of the Pacific—brings together many of the countries that wanted to participate in the FTAA. Members are Chile, Colombia, Costa Rica, Ecuador, El Salvador, Guatemala, Honduras, Mexico, Nicaragua, Panama, and Peru. The Mercosur countries are not associated with either group, and some overlap among Central American countries makes it hard to interpret the nature of the developing trends. This combination of competing plurilateral groups, together with a set of bilateral agreements with differing terms, leaves regional integration in a state of uncertainty. Without an FTAA to bring them together, the outlook for a robust integration in Latin America seems more distant than ever.

Conclusions

As this chapter has amply demonstrated, Chile has conducted a very active trade policy over the past 35 years. Initially this policy was based exclusively on unilateral and multilateral mechanisms. In the 1990s, however, the Chilean government began one of the world's most intensive processes of negotiating preferential agreements—although it also continued to lower tariff rates on a unilateral basis and to participate in multilateral negotiations. The years since 1990, in turn, can be divided into two subperiods. During the first, Chile concentrated on negotiations with its Latin American neighbors, mostly for political reasons. During the second, Chile turned to negotiate with its largest markets: the United States, Europe, and Asia. In these latter cases, the motives have been mainly economic. Currently, preferential agreements cover 87 percent of Chilean trade. Trade has increased substantially—in part due to the FTAs—but many of the expected benefits have yet to emerge.

What can be said about the three hypotheses outlined in the introductory chapter—independent decision-making, emulation, or competition—for explaining Chile's preferential trade agreements? All three have been in play at different points in Chile's FTA history. The early ECAs in Latin America were examples of independent, state-led action geared mainly to achieve foreign policy goals. Insofar as economic aims were also involved in these agreements, they were elements of a future international strategy, not competition with anything that had already been done in the region. The agreements with the larger economies, by contrast, were motivated by competition, both to lock in access to export markets in light of present and possible future competitors, but especially for FDI that could support Chile's investment strategy. At the same time, it is possible to argue that some elements of an emulation process were involved in the negotiations with the United States and Europe. As bulwarks of democracy as well as economic success, these countries were the ones with which Chile wanted to be associated.

Three types of competition—economic, political, and legal—were outlined earlier. As a small economy, Chile has mainly been concerned with economic competition, but economic competition itself has various components. Competition over markets has received most of the attention in the literature, but this has been less important for Chile because of an export portfolio heavy in natural resources, where the country is a world leader. Thus, the main trade focus has been forward looking toward guaranteeing market access for services and high-technology industrial goods that Chile plans to emphasize on in the future. As part of this future strategy, Chile is in competition for FDI with countries in Latin America as well as other developing regions. Political and legal competition has been tied to economics. Chile would like to play a leadership role as a bridge between Asia and Latin America. It has also been interested, at least to some extent, in promoting a broad type of FTA model that plays to its strengths in investment, services, and limited exceptions in merchandise trade.

The process of initiating, negotiating, and implementing FTAs in Chile has involved a top-down model with leadership clearly in government hands. Leading actors have been clusters of skilled professionals in the foreign and finance ministries. According to interviews with a former president, the president's main roles have been at the initiation stage and bringing negotiations to a successful close, often through personal communications with leaders of partner countries. Despite some internal divisions, the business community has been an ally since Chilean society generally agrees that the country must continue and expand its export vocation. Moreover, Chilean business is less vulnerable to competition than its counterparts in most countries because early liberalization made firms relatively cost efficient, so FTAs are more often seen as opportunities than threats. The business associations have provided important technical assistance and smoothed differences among their constituents, sometimes by obtaining modest concessions for sectors with particular problems—usually traditional agriculture or small industrial firms. Only in the Mercosur negotiations did business take an active political role since it saw its near neighbors as more relevant than rivals further away. This worked in both directions—the agricultural sector was strongly opposed, while the industrialists were active proponents.

A final question is what other countries, including those from Asia, can learn from the Chilean experience with trade policy in general and preferential agreements in particular. Five lessons suggest themselves.

First, small countries can be very proactive. Perhaps it should be said that they have to be. Much of the literature on small European economies suggests as much. In this sense, Chile bears some resemblance to Singapore in the Asian context.

Second, Chile's experience shows that initial conditions are crucial. The fact that Chile began to negotiate FTAs with a flat tariff rate of 15 percent made an enormous difference in what it sought and was willing to accept. During the previous decade and a half of unilateral liberalization, the costs of resource reallocation had already been paid, and a relatively efficient, export-oriented production sector had resulted. The aim after 1990 was to reap the rewards of prior sacrifices.

Third, preferential agreements should be seen as complements to, not substitutes for, unilateral and multilateral policies. All have something to offer in terms of a country's position in the international system. Preferential agreements are often said to be second best, but they should not be eschewed for this reason. Of course, care must be taken in the way such agreements are negotiated to avoid the "spaghetti bowl" or "noodle bowl" effects; Chile could do better on this count.

Fourth, a successful preferential initiative requires strong institutional support. Expertise about potential partners is very important, and foreign ministries have to modernize themselves on this dimension and with respect to economics in general. Negotiators need to be well trained, and other government agents (such as export promotion agencies) also need to play a part.

Fifth, it is crucial to recognize that trade is not an isolated part of the economy. Chile has done an excellent job in managing its macroeconomic balances, including a number of financial and fiscal innovations. It has done less well with respect to microeconomics. While its large firms are extremely efficient, many smaller firms are still not well positioned for international competition. The government is aware of these problems, but it needs to put more effort into remedying them if Chile is to realize the full potential of its international trade accomplishments.

Notes

1. I would like to thank the following colleagues for helpful discussions about Chilean trade policy: Hugo Baierlein, Alicia Frohmann, Alejandro Jara, Mikio Kuwayama, Ricardo Lagos Escobar, Mario Matus, René Muga, Osvaldo Rosales, Neantro Saavedra, Sebastian Sáez, Verónica Silva, and Manfred Wilhelmy. Of course they are not responsible for the interpretations made in the chapter.
2. Chilean practice is to reserve the term "FTA" for a subset of preferential agreements, which have minimal exceptions for trade in goods and include services, investment, dispute settlement mechanisms, and so on. To be consistent with the terminology in other chapters, however, we refer to all trade agreements as FTAs.
3. One reason for the flexibility was that the Congress did not have to approve agreements signed under the LAIA umbrella. Nonetheless, the executive branch agreed to take the Mercosur agreement to Congress because of its controversial nature.
4. See discussion of the two models in Sáez (2005a). Stoler (2006) discusses some of the same issues with respect to "high quality" agreements in Asia, which include

WTO consistency (substantially all trade barriers removed within reasonable period as well as comprehensiveness). Other criteria deal with WTO-plus commitments: transparency, trade facilitation, simplified ROOs, cooperation, sustainable development, and accession by third parties.

5. Chilean negotiators indicate that Canada was important in a more general way. As one said: "They were our professors and taught us what sophisticated trade agreements were all about."

6. EU website: http://ec.europa.eu/trade/issues/bilateral/countries/chile/index_en.htm.

7. Interviews with several experts on Chile's international economic policy suggest questions about whether this goal is feasible, but is reiterated with great frequency by government and private sector officials.

8. For discussion of the policy-making process, including relationships with the private sector, see Silva (2001, 2004), Porras (2003), Aninat et al. (2004), Aninat and Botto (2005), Frohmann (2005), Sáez (2005b), and Bull (2008). I have also interviewed a number of current and former policymakers about these issues.

9. For an illustration of the nature of this debate, see Foxley et al. (1993).

10. Flores-Quiroga, in the Mexico chapter, refers to Chile as Mexico's "ideal first partner" in Latin America.

11. The amount was $500 million. While this seems like a large amount, it pales before the Korean government's offer to pay its farmers $80 billion over 10 years as compensation for the Chile–Korea agreement, as discussed by Koo in this volume.

12. Chile had joined other Asia-Pacific organizations earlier, including the Pacific Basin Economic Council (PBEC) and the Pacific Economic Cooperation Council (PECC). Chilean negotiators note the importance of APEC, in particular, as a venue for meeting Asian leaders and burnishing Chile's image in Asia. See also Faust (2004) and Wilhelmy (2005).

13. While technological exchange is included in a chapter of the agreement, the idea of an alliance may have been put forth as a way of obtaining support for ratification in Chile (see DIRECON, 2006; interview with former Chilean government official).

14. For example, China initially opposed a dispute resolution clause, saying that countries that are friends do not need dispute resolution mechanisms.

15. How much of this potential trade is actually carried out through FTA mechanisms is unclear. Lack of information, along with difficulties in meeting ROOs requirements, limit the use of preferential trade possibilities. For a general discussion of this issue, see World Bank (2005: 40–2).

16. This has long been a problem with Latin America's top-down integration process. Governments have been signing agreements for decades, but the private sector has not followed through (see Stallings, 2009). Recently in Chile, a variety of bilateral and regional trips and events have been organized to try to get the private sector engaged in exporting, to introduce potential buyers to Chile, and to pursue the investment that is such an important part of Chile's strategy.

17. Interpreting the data on products is complicated by a change in definition in 2002.

18. See Cabezas (2003) on the US agreement, Nowak-Lehmann et al. (2005) on the EU agreement, and Schuschny et al. (2007) on the Asian agreements. Other evaluations include Harrison et al. (1997, 2003).

19. For analyses of the FTAA, see Schott (2001); Estevadeordal et al. (2004).

7
Competitive Regionalism and Mexico's FTA Strategy

Aldo Flores-Quiroga

Introduction

There are two distinct phases to Mexico's modern trade strategy, each representing a different approach to multilateral and bilateral trade negotiations. The first phase (1970–1985) is characterized by two failed attempts at opening the trade regime unilaterally, including an unsuccessful effort to join the General Agreement on Tariffs and Trade (GATT) at the end of the Tokyo Round in 1979 due to domestic political pressures. The country's economic strategy then was inward oriented, and regionalism was not high in the priorities of Mexican policymakers.

The second phase (1986 to the present) combines unilateral trade liberalization, accession to the GATT, and the signing of 12 free trade agreements (FTAs) with countries in the Western Hemisphere, Europe, the Middle East, and Asia. Mexico also formally entered the APEC and the Organisation for Economic Co-operation and Development (OECD) as a full member in 1994. This is when competitive regionalism became a central component of Mexico's new outward-oriented strategy.

The collapse of the strategy of industrialization through import-substitution (ISI) in 1982 is often cited as the cause of this transition,[1] but a broader trend of Mexico's increasing economic relations with the world has also been important. This trend began in the early 1970s when trade represented about 20 percent of Mexican GDP, and consolidated by the late 1990s, as this proportion reached close to 55 percent.

Throughout this period, Mexico signed a large number of economic agreements, ranging from bilateral investment protection, double taxation, financial and customs cooperation and promotion, and limited preferential trade concessions, to full-fledged free trade, with geographically disperse partners.

The existence of a causal relationship between a greater level of international economic intercourse and the formalization of international economic exchanges through legal documents is subject to debate, but there is little doubt that Mexico's adoption of regionalism is a part, if not the expression, of this internationalization trend. A greater demand for policy coordination and collaboration with the country's main trade and investment partners, most notably the United States, followed greater trade and investment flows, a demand which expanded the scope of the agreements, until limited engagement gave way to greater liberalization commitments under the terms of an FTA.

From this broad review, one might rightly conclude that functionalism (the perspective that increasing economic interdependence among countries drives them to pursue integration through formal agreements, which then lead to the adoption of supranational forms of governance) explains much of Mexican international economic policy choices. The story behind Mexico's choice of FTA partners, however, does not correlate *perfectly* with the intensity of economic exchange hinting at the importance of noneconomic factors.

In this chapter, I argue that purely functional explanations are insufficient to understand Mexico's FTA strategy. The Mexican government's decisions were also motivated by a drive to emulate and compete with countries in North America and Europe that were implementing successful integration policies, and countries in Asia that achieved high economic growth rates through export promotion. Moreover, the competitive concerns of outward-oriented producers, in light of integration initiatives north of the Mexican border, triggered their intense lobbying which, despite the challenge from import-competing industries, ultimately influenced policy shifts in the direction of free trade.

Once free trade with the United States took precedence in the Mexican policy agenda, it rapidly transformed into a full-fledged trade liberalization program supported by the signing of FTAs in Latin America, Europe, the Middle East, and Asia. By the mid-1990s, the Mexican government's FTA approach went beyond regional integration: it sought to secure a new policy regime, competitive and credible enough to attract investments from all corners of the world, and to establish alliances with key economic and political partners outside North America.

To account for the country's sequential choice of trade partners, and for its eventual success in reaching FTAs with them, one has to pay attention to Mexico's international economic, political, and legal environment, with an eye to the challenges that have guided its foreign policy toward its neighbors. It is also important to observe domestic developments, since Mexico adopted a competitive FTA strategy to advance its own domestic reform agenda, not exclusively to accomplish foreign policy objectives.

Overview of Mexico's trade negotiations, 1970–2005

Table 7.1 presents Mexico's 12 FTAs to date in chronological order, together with their shares of trade and FDI, covering a total of 43 countries.

Table 7.1 refers to the year of signing, not the negotiation starting date. It does not include negotiations under way (Peru and South Korea) at the time of writing (November 2008), or suspended negotiations (Ecuador or Panama),

Table 7.1 Mexico's FTA network (as of October 2008)

Partner	Status	Volume		Issue scope				
		Trade (percentage of total trade in 1990)‖	FDI (percentage of total FDI, cumulative 1994–2003)°	Investment	Service	Environment	Labor	Economic cooperation
NAFTA*	In force (1994)	69	68	Yes	Yes	Yes	Yes	No
G-3†	In force (1995)	<1	<1	Yes	Yes	No	No	No
Bolivia‡	In force (1995)	<1	<1	Yes	Yes	No	No	No
Costa Rica	In force (1995)	<1	<1	Yes	Yes	No	No	No
Uruguay§	In force (1998)	<1	<1	Yes	Yes	No	No	No
Nicaragua	In force (1998)	<1	<1	Yes	Yes	No	No	No
Chile	In force (1992/1999)	<1	<1	Yes	Yes	No	No	Yes
EU	In force (2000)	15	22	Yes	Yes	No	No	No
Israel	In force (2000)	<1	<1	Yes	Yes	No	No	No
EFTA¶	In force (2000)	<2	<2	Yes	Yes	No	No	No
Guatemala	In force (2001)	<1	<1	Yes	Yes	No	No	No
Honduras	In force (2001)	<1	<1	Yes	Yes	No	No	No
El Salvador	In force (2001)	<1	<1	Yes	Yes	No	No	No
EU (15 + 12)	In force (2004)	15.2	23	Yes	Yes	No	No	Yes
Japan	In force (2005)	5.12	2.7	Yes	Yes	No	No	Yes

* The United States and Canada.

† The *Tratado de Libre Comercio del Grupo de los Tres* (G-3) between Mexico, Colombia, and Venezuela is registered with the Latin American Association for Integration (*Asociación Latinoamericana de Integración*, or ALADI) as Economic Complementation Agreement No. 33. *Source*: http://www.aladi.org/.

‡ ALADI Economic Complementation Agreement No. 31. *Source*: http://www.aladi.org/.

§ ALADI Economic Complementation Agreement No. 60. *Source*: http://www.aladi.org/.

¶ Norway, Iceland, Switzerland, Lichtenstein.

‖ Trade figures refer to 1990 because that is when Mexico launched its FTA strategy. Between then and 2003, the participation of the US in Mexican total trade reached close to 75 percent, after reaching a peak of 81 percent in 2000. The European Union's share declined to around nine percent, with most of the resulting gains going to Asian countries, which increased their combined share from less than five percent to ten percent. China represents the largest proportion of this increase.

° Since the North American Free Trade Agreement (NAFTA) was signed, total FDI inflows to Mexico increased fourfold, from an average of US$3 billion to more than US$12 billion.

Source: Constructed with data from the Mexican Ministry of the Economy and the National Institute of Statistics and Geography.

for reasons explained below. It excludes potential negotiations, for which prospective discussions have started but have not materialized in negotiations (e.g. New Zealand or Australia). If the onset of negotiations were the preferred criterion for constructing the table, the first agreement in the list would have been NAFTA, which launched Mexico's FTA strategy.

The second column reveals that, between 1992 and 1999, Mexico signed FTAs only with countries in the Western Hemisphere: with the United States and Canada to the north, and with a number of Latin American countries to the south. The latter include three from the Andean Pact (Venezuela, Colombia, and Bolivia, but not Ecuador or Peru), Chile, two in Central America (Costa Rica and Nicaragua), and one member of Mercosur (Uruguay). No Caribbean country has signed an FTA with Mexico, nor has any other country from the Southern Cone.

The absence of an FTA with the remaining countries of Latin America does not imply lack of interest, however. By the close of the 1990s, Mexico had signed FTAs with all its neighbors, except for Cuba and other countries in the Caribbean with which it traded little and shared maritime borders. As with the successful FTAs, all negotiations occurred under the framework of the ALADI, a region-wide agreement that allows for the signing of FTAs without the need for a ratification procedure in national parliaments.[2] Negotiations with the countries of the Northern Triangle of Central America were underway and eventually concluded in 2001. For practical purposes, they can be included in the block of Latin American countries that signed FTAs with Mexico. Negotiations with Panama, Ecuador, and Peru started in tandem with the others, but were stalled or suspended by 1998. Panama was conditioning the negotiation of an FTA to its exclusion from the Mexican government's list of tax havens,[3] while Ecuador and Peru experienced economic and political meltdown that forced them to suspend trade negotiations, if not to completely rethink their economic strategy. Negotiations with the other countries of Mercosur, though contemplated, have not moved beyond an agreement on the automobile industry, in good measure because of contrasting visions on the trade rules that must predominate—those of NAFTA or those of Mercosur.

The year 2000 inaugurated the era of Mexico's cross-regional agreements with the signing of the FTAs with the European Union (EU15, expanded to EU27 by 2007) and Israel, followed by the agreement in 2001 with European Free-Trade Area (Norway, Switzerland, Lichtenstein, Iceland). By 2005, Asia entered Mexico's portfolio of FTAs through the completion of negotiations with Japan. But Japan was not the first Asian country to consider negotiating an FTA with Mexico; Singapore took the leading role. The Mexican private sector opposition to a parallel negotiation with the European Union and Singapore stopped this negotiation. Today Singapore is not negotiating an FTA with Mexico, as Mexico's attention shifted to South Korea, partly because the latter is an important source of direct investments in the manufacturing sector, whose companies generate export revenues for Mexico much in the same way as Japanese firms do, and because it deployed an active strategy to obtain from Mexico the same benefits it was giving to Japan—namely, NAFTA parity.

Table 7.1 shows that the relative share of a country in Mexico's total trade, or as a source of FDI, does not explain at the outset the chronological order in which agreements were signed. As the third and fourth column reveal, the EU and Japan were Mexico's second and third largest trade and investment partners, respectively, in the 1990s, but they reached an FTA with Mexico after Chile, Colombia, Venezuela, Uruguay, Costa Rica, and Nicaragua—countries representing less than one percent of the same shares. However, in 1990 Latin America as a whole represented a larger share of Mexico's total foreign trade than Japan. One can argue that this would displace Japan to the third place as Mexico's trading partner, and help account for the signing of FTAs with Latin America before Japan.

Understanding Mexico's FTA strategy

The following list of objectives frequently associated with Mexico's FTA strategy is useful in assessing the three hypotheses laid out in Chapter 1[4]:

- Securing stable access to the country's main export markets.
- Reducing trade diversion caused by other countries' FTAs.
- Mitigating investment diversion effects of other FTAs.
- Increasing access to low-cost inputs to improve competitiveness.
- Diversifying export markets.
- Promoting coalitions of like-minded countries in multilateral trade talks.
- Promoting sub-regional political alliances.
- Increasing the cost of trade-reform reversals—increasing the credibility of trade liberalization.
- Establishing a credible legal regime for investors.
- Reducing inflationary pressures.
- Loosening the grip of dominant local economic and political groups.

For the nondiffusion hypothesis to hold, Mexico's FTA strategy would have to be immune to trade and investment diversion pressures, and decoupled from its multilateral trade diplomacy and regional foreign policy objectives. But, as discussed below, considerable evidence on the timing of decisions, together with numerous remarks and testimonies from government officials and business leaders, supports the view that NAFTA was proposed in reaction to international developments, especially the nascent wave of regionalism in Europe and North America (Flores-Quiroga, 1998). Mexican authorities negotiated succeeding FTAs based on international strategic calculations such as avoiding extreme export concentration on just one market, consolidating competitiveness gains derived from access to low-cost inputs, and even promoting regional development. Domestic factors, while indispensable to explain Mexico's adoption of free trade, cannot *on their own* account for the decision to pursue FTAs. They must be complemented by and linked to international factors.

We are thus left with the emulation and competition hypotheses. Which one is more plausible? The answer is necessarily ambiguous, as the list above already suggests some overlap between the objectives. In choosing trade liberalization through negotiated and reciprocal trade barrier reductions, Mexican economic authorities were responding to international developments *emulating* what at the time seemed to be the new trend in trade policy. But consolidating a credible legal regime was also crucial to Mexican policymakers as they *competed* for foreign capital. Moreover, a key objective was to counteract the potential trade diversion from other FTAs, and to alleviate extreme export concentration through market diversification. Finally, international political considerations were also significant as Mexico used FTAs to increase its leverage in the multilateral trading system and to accomplish foreign policy goals in Latin America. The rest of this chapter explains how these various factors shaped the Mexican government's choices.

Mexico's competitive regional strategy begins

The Mexican government's decision to propose the negotiation of an FTA with the United States—its first venture of this kind—was triggered by a shift in the international strategic environment which, combined with the transformation of Mexican trade policy and politics throughout the 1980s, increased the opportunity cost of not joining regional trade areas.

The two most relevant international events came in 1989: the launch of the US–Canada FTA (USCFTA) and the fall of the Berlin Wall.[5] The first mobilized the members of the country's pro-export lobby in favor of an FTA with the United States. The second added weight to their arguments against import-competing producers, tipping the government's hand toward a proposal for a US–Mexico FTA.

Shortly after the USCFTA entered into force in January 1989, Mexico's outward-oriented entrepreneurs and their US partners expressed their concerns regarding trade and investment diversion away from Mexico. The head of the international arm of Mexico's peak business association, the Foreign Affairs Business Council, conveyed this message to the Mexican president at their annual meeting, with the joint recommendation to negotiate a similar FTA with the United States and softening the laws on foreign investment.[6] He echoed a recommendation that the Mexico–US Business Committee (MUSBC), a prominent bi-national group of businesspersons and academicians, had been advocating for at least two years during the USCFTA negotiations. The group's argument is worth quoting, for it summarizes the position of Mexico's pro-export "lobby"—a loose amalgam of the country's wealthiest businessmen, multinational corporations, and associations representing companies specialized in international trade (but not import-competing producers):

> Confidence attracts capital. Investor confidence is based on dependable, satisfactory expectations about the business environment. In Mexico, legal uncertainty reduces the level of confidence and inhibits long-term investment. The frequent amending of Mexican laws and regulations affecting trade and investment causes a serious lack of confidence among private investors. In Mexico, the legal order and the institutions that support it should be strengthened and given permanence and stability. *Of paramount importance are 1) narrowing the discretionary authority of the government as it pertains to private investment, commerce, and the operations of productive enterprise, and 2) increasing the rights conferred by law on investors.* The objective for the Mexican economy should be to reduce the scope of regulation of the private economy....The government's wide discretionary powers hamper sound economic management in Mexico. *The private economy will feel at risk until it is manifest that there is a long-term commitment to free major parts of the economy from government administration and detailed regulation...*
>
> ... *Adherence by Mexico and the Unites States to the principles of free trade will contribute to create the indispensable trust for long-term private direct investment* in modern factories... [the MUSBC recommends] a careful study of the trade agreement between the United States and Canada since it will, together with *a bilateral agreement between Mexico and the United States,* constitute the basis for increasing the volume of trade and investment between Canada, the United States, and Mexico. *This future trilateral relationship will strengthen North America's competitiveness in an era of global markets.*[7]

By March and June 1989, the MUSBC also proposed specific options for liberalizing US–Mexico trade and investment, contemplating both limited and wide-ranging trade and investment agreements.[8] The link made by the MUSBC between an FTA and a credible investment regime to secure "the principles of free trade will contribute to create the indispensable trust for long-term private direct investment" derived from recent Mexican experience. Economic restructuring attempts in the 1970s and 1980s had proven Mexican institutions incapable of sustaining a trade barrier lowering. As soon as the country's current account deteriorated, even if the proximate cause was an overvalued exchange rate caused by a burgeoning fiscal deficit, the Mexican authorities reversed course and increased tariffs. When fiscal deficits reached crisis proportions, the government was quick to expropriate wealth from private investors, as evidenced by the nationalization of the banking industry in 1982 and its unwillingness to convert dollar-denominated deposits at market rates. An FTA, from the perspective of this free-trade lobby, would help to avoid this conundrum by anchoring domestic policy through an international contract, which could only be reneged at a very high cost.[9] Such an agreement would reduce policy volatility and attract long-term investments.

But the Mexican president at the time, Carlos Salinas, was not yet persuaded. As he told the business leaders upon listening to their proposal, Mexico was not going to join any international economic bloc; it would only seek to secure the Mexican good access in foreign markets through limited tariff concessions. Economic stability and a similar level of development with a target partner, from his perspective, were pre-conditions for even contemplating the negotiation of an FTA.[10]

Salinas also preferred not to enter into a controversial free-trade arrangement with the country's neighbors, or anyone else in 1989, because the most pressing priority for his government was the renegotiation of the terms of its foreign debt payments.[11] To negotiate an FTA while seeking one of the most ambitious debt-restructuring package ever would only complicate matters and create unnecessary issue linkages between both negotiation routes.[12] This much he had in mind when as president-elect in November 1988, he rejected a tentative proposal from George H. W. Bush, then also president-elect, to begin negotiations for a US–Mexico FTA (Salinas de Gortari, 2002).

The Mexican president opted instead for an international economic strategy combining four components: foreign debt renegotiation, attraction of FDI, expansion of preferential trade access to Europe, and management of US–Mexico trade through sectoral agreements. The first two components aimed at improving the country's current account, which was deteriorating fast as an appreciating exchange rate was causing imports to outstrip exports. The third aimed at reducing the strong dependence of Mexican exports on the US market, not only for the sake of trade diversification, but also because US trade protectionism and associated sanctions had been increasing steadily. The fourth sought to continue the policy of facilitating access in the United States for sectors heavily involved in intra-industry trade (automobiles, auto parts), or with strong export potential (steel, chemicals, textiles). Sectoral agreements were the closest policy to bilateral free trade in light of the existing policy regime. The approach to Europe had similar objectives, but it also sought to further political links to counterbalance the strong US influence.

Alas, it was a short-lived approach. Soon after the Berlin Wall fell in November 1989, Salinas realized that Mexico would have an increasingly difficult time attracting investments from Western Europe, now focused on the opportunities offered by Eastern Europe. In one conversation after another, he found little enthusiasm from his European peers to his proposal for a closer trade and investment relationship. His talks with Margaret Thatcher, Helmut Kohl, and Jacques Delors, among others, resulted in the same message: Europe was interested in building its own union; its interest in Mexico as an investment destination would increase only if it were part of a North American trade bloc. Further confirmation of this position came at the 1990 World Energy Forum in Davos, when Salinas noted that it was harder than before to persuade governments and investors of Mexico's attractiveness as an investment destination (Salinas de Gortari, 2002). This led Salinas to decide to move forward with the proposal he had already received from Mexican and US businessmen, European leaders, and the US president to join the North American trade bloc. By jumping on the regional bandwagon, he believed, Mexico would regain lost ground on the international competition for investments. Still at Davos, he instructed his Trade Secretary to express to his US counterpart of Mexico's interest in negotiating an FTA. A few weeks later, key Mexican and US officials were already in secret discussions on how to proceed. When the news broke out, Canada, concerned that it would lose some of its advantages through the USCFTA, requested trilateral negotiations. By the fall of 1990, the three countries were ready to negotiate the creation of the largest free trade area in the world.

Up to this point, Mexico's decision to negotiate an FTA involves competition for FDI as a channel of policy diffusion, with Mexico responding to the integration of the US and Canada, and following the example of Western Europe, by joining the North American regional bloc. It also suggests that there is more at play than top-down decision-making: while the Mexican president decided in the end to propose an FTA (it could not have been otherwise, since legally this decision was his to make), Mexican and American businessmen with access to the halls of power and the media, together with leaders from other countries, took him there.

But the story is even more complex. Salinas was able to respond to the international challenges because during the 1980s four developments inside Mexico had lifted the political and economic constraints against trade liberalization: the arrival in government of technocrats well versed in neoclassical economics, the drive to secure access of Mexican exports in the US market, the unilateral trade liberalization Mexico implemented between 1985 and 1988, and the pressure of the private sector to stabilize trade rules.

Technocrats took charge of economic policymaking soon after the 1982 debt crisis, first as a compact group with President Miguel de la Madrid (1982–88), then as the most prominent Cabinet members with Salinas (1988–94) and Ernesto Zedillo (1994–2000). They replaced the cadre of economic policymakers who in the late 1970s had opposed Mexico's entrance to the GATT and the adoption of export-led strategy.[13] They also included a compact group of market-friendly policy entrepreneurs, with connections to the international financial community, able to push forward a new economic policy framework. They sought to modernize Mexico by emulating the integration experiences of North America and Europe, in particular the positive fate of Spain and Ireland, and the export-oriented success of the Asian Tigers.

Their initial efforts in the 1980s concentrated on eliminating the anti-export bias of Mexican trade policy, while securing better terms of access for the country's exports to the US market. As their power consolidated in the 1990s, their economic program gained roots, and they pushed for a more comprehensive approach: negotiating better terms of access not only with the United States, but also with the rest of the country's main trading partners in Latin America, Europe, and Asia.

The removal of the anti-export bias started in the summer of 1985 with the replacement of import permits with tariffs, and their unilateral reduction over the next three years, with the aim of establishing a "rational" structure of protection—higher tariffs for more elaborate goods. In implementing this program they were careful to obtain the approval of the main business associations.[14] Almost at the same time, they secured the support of the Senate to negotiate Mexico's accession to the GATT, reversing the controversial decision not to join during the oil boom of the 1980s.[15]

Mexico hardly had an alternative but to implement trade liberalization after the debt crisis, as the government could not subsidize export programs in a significant way. Exporters could earn badly needed dollar revenues only if their competitiveness improved through access to low-cost inputs. International financial institutions, such as the IMF and the World Bank, were hinting that a successful renegotiation of Mexico's debt would be conditioned on *credible* trade liberalization.[16]

Moreover, the US government, upon requests from US producers, had begun to impose countervailing duties (CVDs) on imports coming from countries such as Mexico that subsidized their exports.[17] This controversy is particularly relevant for this study, as it forced Mexico to adhere to the GATT, and eventually to the pursuit of FTAs. Mexican producers could have disputed the imposition of CVDs, in principle, by resorting to the "injury test" that allowed exporters to show that they were not engaged in unfair trade, but the US government argued that Mexican exports were not beneficiaries to such a test, because Mexico failed to implement the provisions of the GATT Subsidies Agreement, a prominent outcome of the Tokyo Round.[18]

Mexican exporters hurt by this change in US trade regulations pressured their government to seek some form of agreement to obtain the injury test. It came in the form of a *Memorandum of Understanding between the United States and Mexico Regarding Subsidies and Countervailing Duties* signed in the spring of 1985, in which Mexico explicitly renounced the use of subsidies programs to support exports.[19] Now, the only instruments left to promote exports were the elimination of import permits and the lowering of tariffs (an import tariff is equivalent to an export tax).

Many inside and outside the government realized by then that adhesion to the GATT was all but inevitable: in agreeing to remove export subsidies and unilaterally lowering tariffs, Mexico was already operating under the GATT regime, but without enjoying its benefits in the form of greater access to foreign markets.[20] While the case could be made that unilateral liberalization was welfare-enhancing, it was even better to join the GATT and obtain reciprocal tariff concessions from Mexico's main export partners.

Mexico's search for GATT membership was soon interpreted as a measure to avoid the reversal of trade reforms (Ten Kate, 1992a, 1992b). Unlike previous experiences, no one expected Mexico to ignore its GATT commitments.

By the time Salinas decided to propose the negotiation of a US–Mexico FTA, not only was the world moving in the direction of regional blocs, but Mexican trade policy was recognizably different from that of only a few years earlier. All significant import permits had been phased out. Instead of applying an ad-hoc tariff schedule, tariffs levels were rationalized. The maximum tariff was bound to 50 percent following GATT commitments, but in effect, it declined from 100 to 20 percent. Tariff dispersion decreased notably, with only five tariff levels left. Export subsidies had disappeared. In short, Mexico was a GATT contracting-party, while much of Mexican trade was managed through sectoral agreements with the United States.

These developments transformed Mexico's policy of managed trade in specific sectors into one of freer trade in every sector.[21] Much trade between Mexico and the US had for all practical purposes been liberalized. The only open question was whether two economies with considerable differences in size, diversification, and overall income could integrate successfully. This was new policy territory, for the economic gap between Mexico and the United States was larger than, say, that of Spain and the European Union. But with few available options, President Salinas decided to take the risk of integrating Mexico with the large neighbor in the north through FTAs.

In sum, Mexico's decision to negotiate NAFTA emerged from a governmental response to integration initiatives abroad, driven by the pressure of domestic interests as much as by independent maneuvering by like-minded economic authorities. This response was nonetheless possible only because much work had been done domestically to reform the core of Mexican trade policy and the conduct of trade disputes with the United States.

Choosing additional trade partners

Negotiations for NAFTA, which began in 1990, immediately raised a new concern in Mexican policymaking circles: while the agreement promised to secure access to the country's exports in the US and Canadian markets, it created strong incentives for exporting only to them. Government officials estimated that negotiating FTAs elsewhere would help provide investors with a more geographically neutral export incentive, reduce the vulnerability associated with a high export concentration in just one market, and perhaps integrate productive chains between more countries. Now that free trade was adopted as the new economic paradigm, there was a strong motivation to pursue FTAs with additional countries.

Which countries were ideal partners? From an economic viewpoint, one would expect those with the largest share of bilateral trade and potential investment flows, those whose economic structure allowed for complementarities, and those with a similar level of development. For Mexico in the early

1990s, following the data in Table 7.1, the best candidates were the European Community (not yet a full-fledged union), Japan, and Latin America as a whole. Europe and Japan together represented approximately 20 percent of Mexican trade, while all Latin American countries represented close to five percent.

But the choice was neither clear-cut nor preordained. Even though Western Europe was Mexico's second largest trade and investment partner, its level of development was much higher than that of Mexico, and it was on the other side of the Atlantic. Europe, moreover, was immersed in its own integration dynamic, with an eye on investment opportunities in the recently opened Eastern Bloc. Japan was a reliable and important trade and investment partner as well, but it was far in the Pacific and preferred multilateral to bilateral trade negotiations. For Japan in the early 1990s, an FTA with Mexico was from the outset a non-starter. Brazil, Mexico's main trade partner in Latin America, shared a comparable level of development, but its economic structure did not allow for significant economic complementarities. And it was focused on consolidating Mercosur, where it had a clear leadership. An FTA with Mexico was not even an afterthought.

From a political viewpoint, there were additional dilemmas. Should ideological affinity or regional balancing take precedence over economic interests? If ideology mattered, the best route would be to approach Latin American countries implementing market reforms, or even European countries, whose brand of market capitalism was closer to that of Mexico. If regional balancing was paramount, then it was best to approach Europe as a counterweight to the US, or Latin American countries concerned about the implications of Mercosur and the growing influence of Brazil, for whom Mexico could provide a compensating influence. The former was a form of defensive balancing, the latter offensive.

Security also played a role, making neighboring countries particularly relevant. Assuming FTAs promoted prosperity between their partners, they could serve to reduce migration flows, illegal cross-border activities, and to consolidate economic and political reforms in neighboring countries. This was the logic behind the US government's interest in promoting an FTA with Mexico to start with, and the logic of Mexico in promoting an FTA with Central America.[22]

Competitive pressures, in the legal sense, became important later, to the extent that each additional FTA Mexico signed with a new trade partner in the 1990s locked in essentially the same disciplines regarding tariffs, customs procedures, official norms, standards, trade in services, investment rules, property rights protection, and dispute settlement mechanisms. Mexican FTAs in Latin America followed closely the structure of NAFTA. It was logical to attempt extending them to regional negotiations for an FTAA, or for the Doha Trade Round of the WTO.[23]

Mexico's trade negotiations eventually emerged from the combination of design, itself a result of domestic political arrangements; circumstances; and a degree of path dependence. Not every target country selected according to the aforementioned criteria was ready to begin an FTA negotiation with Mexico, and available resources could only be committed to a limited set of negotiations. International economic competition, domestic policy concerns, and regional balancing became preponderant factors in the early phases of the country's FTA strategy. Once a large share of trade began to take place under the framework of FTAs, international political and legal competition took greater significance.

The Mexican private sector sanctioned all the choices the government made. During the NAFTA negotiations, the government made sure to count with the support of the country's business associations, promoting the creation of a private sector consulting body, which provided assistance and helped keep a cohesive free-trade lobby during the actual negotiation process. Likewise, before the government launched a new trade negotiation, it always sought to obtain this body's compliance so that the policy was seen as consensual rather than an imposition. Compliance was not hard to obtain for most negotiations, since FTAs had become a standard of the new policy regime, except for the cases of FTA proposals with clear competitors, such as Brazil or South Korea. The rest of the FTAs posed relatively minor threats to Mexican businesses. Even then, the volume of trade involved outside Europe and Japan was relatively minor to create major worries among domestic producers. The biggest hurdle—accepting to negotiate with the US—had already been overcome.

Mexico's FTAs after NAFTA

The first partner chosen, and ready, for Mexico's trade diversification strategy was Chile: a small economy with a production structure that complemented Mexico's own (it was more geared toward agriculture than manufacturing), that traded relatively little with Mexico, was run by policymakers with an ideological bent similar to that of their Mexican counterparts, and was less involved in the construction of a South American trade bloc as Brazil or Argentina. Mexico–Chile FTA negotiations took place at basically the same time as the NAFTA negotiations, but were concluded and ratified earlier.

Negotiating with Chile would also help to temper the reaction of other Latin American governments to Mexico's approach to the United States, which from the outset was hardly welcoming. To some in the Southern Cone, Mexico was siding with the United States, breaking the long cultural and political ties with the region as it tried to secure better trade preferences from its neighbor to the north.[24] More seriously, in congruence with article 44 of ALADI, which requires that trade preferences extended to nonmembers should be extended to members as well, Brazil demanded that Mexico automatically grant to the rest of the Latin American region the same trade benefits it gave the United States. Mexico's government was not ready to make such a concession, and even signaled that it would leave ALADI if forced to do so. The tensions eased gradually, but Mexico had to embark on FTA negotiations with the rest of Latin

America to show that it still remained committed politically to the region. This was a significant noneconomic factor influencing the Mexican FTA strategy.

FTA negotiations were faster with those countries where, like Chile, greater potential for economic complementation existed, bilateral trade volumes were small, ideological affinity was more apparent, and domestic political conditions made it easier to reach an agreement, such as Colombia and Venezuela (which together with Mexico constituted the G-3), Bolivia, Costa Rica, and Nicaragua. During the time of the negotiations, these countries had conservative or at least market-friendly governments. Negotiations with the rest of the Latin American countries progressed at a slower pace, or simply stalled, due to factors specific to each. Only Uruguay, sandwiched between the two giants of South America, was interested in diversifying its bets, probably concerned with counterbalancing, by negotiating an FTA with Mexico. In Central America, Guatemala, Honduras, and El Salvador had already begun to negotiate a joint FTA with Mexico, but the process was slow due to their lack of FTA expertise, and due to their concern with implementing the provisions of the peace accords they had recently reached with domestic rebel groups after decades of domestic civil war. Nonetheless, the FTA negotiation was launched in 2001 (Flores-Quiroga, 2001).

By the time negotiations started with the EU and Israel in the mid-1990s, the basic objectives—securing stable access to the country's main export market, anchoring expectations about the course of trade policy, and signaling commitment to market-friendly policies—had for all practical purposes been accomplished mostly through NAFTA. Europe could provide additional investments, export diversification, and hopefully a counterweight to growing US influence.

The approach to Europe involved a more ambitious agenda than that of the preceding FTAs. Europe wanted to include a "democratic clause," a provision that explicitly contemplated the suspension of the agreement should the parties stop being democratic. Since European countries could not all agree to the same type of disciplines for FDI that NAFTA contained, bilateral investment treaties with each relevant EU member had to be negotiated. Mexico and Europe wanted to include official development assistance as part of the framework, a component which was absent from NAFTA, although social cohesion funds had shown to increase the economic growth rate of countries in Europe. The agreement provided for the inclusion of every new member that eventually became a part of the EU, expanding automatically the number of countries with which Mexico would exchange under free trade.

As all of these agreements moved forward, negotiations in Asia, which first focused on Singapore and Japan were encountering difficulties. The governments of Mexico and Singapore began to discuss the possibility of an FTA, only to find that Mexican businessmen would have none of it. They saw Singapore much in the same light as Brazil—a manufacturing powerhouse that would compete with them directly. FTA talks had then to be suspended.

An FTA with Japan was full of ambivalence throughout the 1990s. On the one hand, the Japanese government had not made up its mind about the value of negotiating FTAs, maintaining its preference for multilateral trade negotiations. The Mexican government, on the other hand, felt little urgency to move forward with an agreement. It had NAFTA, a network of FTAs in Latin America, and ongoing negotiations for an FTA with the EU.

There was no urgency until Japanese firms, which exported components to Mexico for the in-bond industry and in turn exported the finished products to the United States, obtained special tariff treatment by the Mexican government—a NAFTA parity of sorts. But as the full provisions of NAFTA were implemented, which in the end were discriminatory to countries without an FTA, the real costs of this ad-hoc accommodation became evident. Japanese firms had to deal with cumbersome administrative procedures and red tape in both Mexico and the United States, which their competitors could avoid. Japanese companies producing in Mexico together with Mexican businessmen associated with them increased pressure to launch a Mexico–Japan FTA that would provide full NAFTA parity.

Private sector pressure, however, was insufficient. It was only when the Japanese government, realizing that multilateral trade talks were going to proceed slowly, opted to negotiate an FTA with Singapore that the door for concluding a negotiation with Mexico finally opened. After a long and tortuous process, the two countries reached an agreement in 2004 (Solís and Katada, 2007b).

By way of summary

Table 7.2 summarizes Mexico's motives behind the selection and timing of FTA partners. It identifies competitive channels of policy diffusion along three dimensions: economic, political, and legal. Economic factors are assumed (and actually observed) to prevail where a large share of Mexican trade is involved at risk of diversion. This puts North America, the EU, Japan, and Latin America as regions at the top of the list, since an FTA with them would cover more than 90 percent of Mexico's total international trade and nearly the total of its FDI.

Political (security) and legal factors are coded where trade covered under the prospective FTA is less than five percent of total trade and FDI (in reality for the remaining countries, it has been less than one percent throughout the period considered). These FTAs involve Central American, Caribbean, and Andean countries for the period 1994–98, where Mexico has strategic interests related to security and regional balancing. As emphasized above, an important reason why Mexico sought an FTA with the Central American countries was to promote economic prosperity in order to reduce incentives for migration or for illicit activities. These agreements also consolidated Mexico's presence in the region.

The legal objectives should be interpreted as potential, in the sense that they can become relevant when multilateral negotiations actually take place.

Table 7.2   Mexico: The drivers of competitive regionalism

Year	Agreement	Competitive channels of policy diffusion		
		Economic	Political	Legal
1986	GATT	X		
1993	APEC	X		
1994	United States and Canada (NAFTA)	X		
1995	Colombia and Venezuela (G-3)		X	
1995	Bolivia		X	
1995	Costa Rica		X	X
1998	Uruguay		X	
1998	Nicaragua		X	X
1999	Chile	X	X	
2000	EU	X	X	
2000	Israel	X		
2000	EFTA	X		
2001	Guatemala, Honduras, El Salvador		X	X
2005	Japan	X		

They apply primarily for Central American countries, which signed FTAs with Mexico and the United States. These FTAs closely resemble NAFTA, which means that all the countries involved already share the same trade and investment rules when they sit at the multilateral negotiating table leading to relatively fewer obstacles if they attempt to form a coalition.

The coding, incidentally, is consistent with current Mexican FTA ventures. Having negotiated with basically all of its most important trade partners, the Mexican government has moved on to negotiate with countries whose participation in Mexican trade has increased significantly in the last few years, most notably South Korea, but not with countries with which it trades little or engages in limited political dialogue, like those in Africa.

In sum, the sequencing of FTA negotiations for Mexico puts economic considerations first, followed by political (security, influence) and legal (potential building of coalitions in multilateral negotiations) factors.

Conclusions

Four conclusions stand out from this review of Mexico's FTA strategy. The first is that this strategy has been undoubtedly driven by factors common to functional explanations, such as the intensity or complexity of economic exchange—as captured by the share of bilateral trade and investment—but competitive dynamics are also at play. Mexican economic authorities proposed to join the North American trade bloc with the explicit purpose of competing for investments, among other reasons. In so doing, they were influenced by the domestic pro-export lobby and by the drive of its technocratic elite to emulate successful economic transformation programs of integrating the domestic with the international market.

Second, despite the relevance of economic factors, they cannot account completely for Mexico's choice of trade partners or the sequence of its FTA negotiations. Regional balancing, political influence, prosperous and stable neighbors, security challenges, and legal relevance also mattered. Equally important, the domestic situation of targeted countries facilitated or delayed the signature of an FTA. These other factors were, however, subsidiary to economic ones: choosing the United States as the first Mexican FTA partner was more due to economic considerations than anything else, as was the choice to negotiate with the EU before, say, the Middle East, with Japan before Malaysia, or with Latin America instead of Africa.

Third, international factors were necessary, but not sufficient, for the development of a competitive FTA strategy. Without Mexico's unilateral trade liberalization and accession to the GATT in the mid-1980s, and without the constant imposition of barriers to trade between Mexico and the United States, which contributed to Mexican trade policy reform, the government would have had a hard time justifying domestically the FTA proposals. These two events contributed to mobilize Mexico's pro-export lobby whose concern with competitiveness provided crucial support for the government's new trade approach.

Fourth, emulation did influence the Mexican government's decisions, but it is difficult to always disentangle its influence from the calculus of economic competition. For instance, emulating international best practices on trade liberalization and investment protection is closely correlated with the desire to become an attractive investment destination and compete for foreign capital. The simultaneity of both influences points to an overdetermined explanation (more than one causal factor working at the same time). Nevertheless the competitive elements were very strong as one can argue that the US–Canada bloc was created as a response to the European bloc, and thus that the Mexican authorities were responding to the competitive strategy of their country's neighbors to the north.

Competition and emulation, regardless of their relative influence, combined to determine Mexico's FTA strategy. Both factors affected private sector lobbying as much as the government's trade initiatives, opening space for a strategic response in the form of liberalization through FTAs.

Notes

1. For accounts of Mexican trade policy during this period see Villarreal (1989), Brailovsky (1989), Blanco Mendoza (1994), and Flores-Quiroga (1998).

2. ALADI was founded in the early 1960s under the name *Asociación Latinoamericana de Libre Comercio* (ALALC, or Latin American Free Trade Association). In the 1970s, the "Libre Comercio," or free-trade part of the name was dropped for the current name ALADI.
3. To prevent money laundering, the Mexican government has classified a number of countries and territories as tax havens. This is due to their relatively low taxation on revenues coming from the financial sector. Companies that declare their residence from one of these places are subject to stricter fiscal monitoring than those from, say, the United Status or Europe.
4. Examples of these perspectives can be found in Pastor and Wise (1994), Heredia (1994) Flores-Quiroga (1998), Thacker (2000), and Fairbrother (2007).
5. The USCFTA was signed in 1988; it started operating on January 1, 1989. The free crossing of Eastern European citizens through the Berlin Wall started on November 9, 1989.
6. Reported in the newspaper *Excelsior* (February 8, 1989). Other businessmen held the same view according to a survey conducted during the first half of 1989: 64 of 100 Mexican manufacturers favored negotiating an FTA with the United States (del Castillo, 1991a).
7. Manuscript published by the MUSBC (1987: 9, 11, 13). Translated from Spanish, my emphasis added. This is an extension of the concepts that other business associations, most notably the influential employers' union, COPARMEX (*Confederación Patronal Mexicana*, or Mexican Employers' Confederation), and the peak business association, CCE (*Consejo Coordinador Empresarial*, or Enterprise (Business) Coordinating Council), which encompasses all other associations, had advanced in previous years.
8. See the policy statements of the MUSBC (1989a; 1989b).
9. To avoid reputation cost by not respecting international commitment, a country would make international agreements the law of the land. This adds another type of cost, for the justification for reneging on an international agreement is that germane constitutional provisions have changed.
10. This was his presidential campaign position in 1988, and he maintained it when he took office (Flores-Quiroga, 1998).
11. The government's debt payments had been suspended in 1982. This episode started the international debt crisis and led to economic restructuring throughout Latin America. See SHCP (1988).
12. This negotiation led to the Brady Plan in late 1989, which accepted two important principles: (1) the totality of the foreign debts of Latin American countries would not be repaid; therefore, they had to be reduced or discounted; and (2) without economic growth the prospects for debt repayment were nil.
13. The Economic Cabinet of the then president José López-Portillo (1976–82) was dominated by economists closer to the tradition of ECLA and Cambridge, institutions which at the time advocated more state involvement in the economy. For an exploration into the determinants of López-Portillo's decision to postpone Mexico's GATT accession see Story (1986) and Flores-Quiroga (1998).
14. Casar (1984, 1989) provides an account of the negotiations between the government and the private sector to launch a structural reform and the agreements they reached in principle. On the structure of Mexican protection at the time, see Ten Kate and De Mateo (1989a, 1989b).
15. Detailed accounts of the process through which it was reached can be found in De la Madrid (1985), SECOFI (1988), and Ten Kate (1992a).

16. Mexico signed with the IMF a Letter of Intent in April 1985 in which it committed to (1) liberalize between 35 and 45 percent of imports before the end of 1985 including reducing tariff levels from 10 to 7 percent and setting most tariffs between 10 and 50 percent; (2) grant automatic import permits of raw materials and machinery parts when the price of domestic substitutes exceed 50 percent; and (3) allow *exporters* to import up to 40 percent of the value of their export revenues without the requirement of any permit, while letting them to import free of duties any good used as input.
17. Weintraub (1990) provides a discussion of this shift in US policy. The US was also objecting to Mexico's industrial promotion programs, especially in the pharmaceutical industry (Flores-Quiroga, 1998).
18. The Subsidies Agreement, already incorporated into US trade legislation, established that direct export subsidies constituted unfair trade, thus liable to face CVDs. An exporter from a country that was a GATT contracting-party could resort to the "injury test" to show that it was not relying on those subsides to gain an unfair competitive advantage, in which case the CVD would be eliminated. But an exporter from a country suspect of using subsidies that was not a GATT contracting-party did not count with that line of defense.
19. The targets included credit, export, energy, and other production subsidies central to the government's industrial promotion policy. Lyman (1989) interprets this episode as an example of a conscious and successful US foreign policy directed at pushing for a transformation in Mexico's trade regime.
20. Testimony by Mexico's Trade Secretary, Héctor Hernández, at the Mexican Senate. De Mateo (1986, 1988) discusses the terms of the debate and the technical issue behind accession to the GATT at that time. See also Bravo Aguilera (1989a).
21. Except petroleum, whose control the Mexican Constitution retains for the State.
22. Most Central American countries had suffered protracted civil wars in the previous decades, whose origin was linked in part to the absence of economic opportunities. Freer trade with Mexico, a much larger market than that provided by any Central American nation to any of its neighbors, had the potential of bringing greater wealth.
23. During the negotiations for an FTAA, the dividing line was essentially determined by the positions of the US and Brazil, which implied a competition between the rules of NAFTA and those of Mercousur. NAFTA-like rules prevailed in Mexico, Central America, the Caribbean, and Chile. Mercosur-like rules prevailed in the rest of South America, except for the Andean countries. See Zabludovsky (2005).
24. For example, see the statement by the President of Argentina, Carlos Menem, when this negotiation was announced.

Part III   East Asia

8
Competitive Regionalism in Southeast Asia and Beyond: Role of Singapore and ASEAN

Takashi Terada

Introduction

When the negotiations for trade liberalization at global and regional levels bogged down, Singapore swiftly engaged in planning for and forging a vast array of free trade agreements (FTAs), culminating in an FTA groundswell in East Asia and beyond. On the role played by Singapore, Prime Minister Lee Hsien Loong, confidently stated that "to say it is because of us may be too strong, but we set an example and we set people thinking. And I think that's also the reason why ASEAN itself is discussing FTAs. There is a demonstration effect" (cited in *The Straits Times*, December 1, 2004). Singapore's interest in signing bilateral FTAs consecutively[1] was partly born out of a fear of its survival as a nation relying heavily on trade for its growth, and also for the reason that FTAs were expected to help Singapore overcome its innate inability to call effectively for diplomatic and economic changes in Southeast Asia to promote trade liberalization in the region and beyond.

There are two aspects of FTA movements in Southeast Asia: (1) bilateral FTAs between ASEAN (Association of Southeast Asian Nations) members and extra-regional countries, and (2) FTAs between ASEAN as a single unit and extra-regional countries. This chapter initially focuses on the first aspect of bilateral FTA diffusion by exploring the impetus behind Singapore's active engagement in FTA negotiations on the basis of examination of three pressures (economic, security, and legal), set out by Solís and Katada, to establish whether Singapore has contributed to the growth of FTAs involving both Southeast Asian and Northeast Asian countries, and if so, how. The chapter also examines the nature of trade policymaking system in Singapore to analyze the alleged little involvement of the business sector in trade policymaking as a common feature in Southeast Asia, demonstrating the predominant role of the state in the FTA-making process. The chapter finally analyses another level of FTA proliferation as ASEAN has served as a hub in the ASEAN+1 FTA networks with five major powers. The origins of this approach can be traced back to China's FTA proposal to ASEAN in 2000 that had resulted from the fear of it being left isolated after the bilateral FTA initiative started by Japan and South Korea in 1998. Given the subsequent reactions of Japan, Korea, and India, China's aggressive diplomacy in Southeast Asia, including the FTA proposal, can be seen as an independent variable against FTA diffusion in this aspect. And, symbolically, the ASEAN+1 FTA movement has been a site for competition where two types of FTAs—China-led traditional FTA with gradual implementation and Japan-led new-age FTA with single undertaking approach—have prevailed, creating further complexities for multinational companies' possible use of the FTAs.

This chapter argues that the impact of bilateral FTAs on Southeast Asia is limited, as only Singapore and Thailand have virtually signed multiple bilateral FTAs. Moreover, the FTAs and ASEAN integration schemes such as AFTA are not well utilized by ASEAN and multinational companies either, representing the perception gap between keener FTA creators in the governments and indifferent users in the business sectors. FTA diffusion certainly occurred in Southeast Asia, but it was Japan-centered as most ASEAN members chose Japan as their first and, in some cases, the only bilateral FTA partner, and thus the concern about trade-diversion effect as a valid explanatory variable is mainly attributed to Japan's larger economic presence as the largest trading partner and investment source to its partner countries. Singapore's efforts to sign an FTA with Japan through diplomatic persuasion and political concession effectively bore fruition and the resultant involvement of Japan into the FTA politics in Southeast Asia is evaluated as an independent variable in the phenomenon of bilateral FTA proliferation in the region.

Singapore's economic, political, and legal impetuses behind the pursuit of FTAs

Singapore has enjoyed the world's highest trade-to-GDP ratio, about 300 percent, a fact that well accounts for its active diplomatic endeavors to facilitate the trade liberalization movements in the GATT/WTO-based multilateral trading system, as well as its efforts at regional levels such as the ASEAN and the Asia Pacific Economic Cooperation (APEC) forums. However, both regional and multilateral negotiations became inert in the late 1990s: the Asian financial crisis in 1997 held up the pace of ASEAN members' liberalization movement and sapped ASEAN's collective strength, while APEC became unwieldy and ill-equipped to handle trade issues effectively, due mainly to the failure of the Early Voluntary Sectoral Liberalization (EVSL) program in 1998. In the multilateral arena, the 1999 Ministerial Meeting in Seattle, during which the increasing influence of developing countries became strong enough to hamper the liberalization movement at the World Trade Organization (WTO), the institution employed a consensus-based decision-making approach among over 150 members.

Under these international and regional trading circumstances, Singapore's interest in bilateral FTAs eventually emerged as a fallback tool, since these

FTAs were supposed to be more effective in promoting trade liberalization. Singapore hoped this trading arrangement could be useful in securing larger markets on a preferential basis, in attracting more FDIs, in strengthening its position as a transportation hub, and in circumventing future protectionism and discrimination movements (Rajan et al., 2001: 10). In fact, in view of the potential cost savings that could be accrued from Singapore's attempt to forge more FTAs, more foreign companies are expected to transfer their production bases to Singapore (*The Straits Times*, March 23, 2003). As Prime Minister Goh (2001) mentioned, in WTO and APEC, even when a consensus is reached, it is done so on the basis of "lowest common denominator," one that holds back more developed economies for the sake of the less developed ones. In some areas where no consensus is reached, a few members would be left out. In comparison, bilateral FTAs would not be prone to these problems as they have only to meet the requirements of the two nations. Singapore's determination in pursuit of bilateral FTAs was epitomized by Goh's statement made at the 2000 APEC Summit in Brunei: "Those who can run faster should run faster. They should not be restrained by those who don't want to run at all" (*Australian Financial Review*, November 16, 2000).

Singapore's choice of Japan and the United States as its second and third FTA partners was attributed to Singapore's expectation to bring more direct economic benefits (see Table 8.1). Japan is the second largest economy in the world, and Japanese companies have an imposing presence in Singapore. Major Japanese manufacturers such as Sony and Panasonic have set up their Southeast Asia operational headquarters in Singapore, forging strong and enduring economic and business networks in Southeast Asia. An FTA with Japan was thus perceived to strengthen these business ties and economic relations through the formalization of *de facto* extensive business, and economic links. For instance, the Japan–Singapore FTA grants Japan-based companies national treatment in Singapore, and allows those companies to freely transfer funds related to investment, in and out of Singapore. Since the 1980s, Japan was consistently among one of Singapore's top three trading partners. In 1999, when the idea of the Japan–Singapore Economic Partnership Agreement (JSEPA) was first considered, Japan was Singapore's third largest trading partner, contributing 12 percent of Singapore's total merchandise trade. On an average, it constituted about 20 percent of Singapore's total imports (MOFA, 2000). On the other hand, through the US–Singapore FTA, Singaporean exporters would be able to save US $110 million per year in duty payments. This would boost Singapore's economic output by at least 0.7 percent a year, while providing Singapore companies access to a wider North American market, thanks to the North American Free Trade Agreement (NAFTA) (*The Straits Times*, August 25, 2002). Therefore, the FTAs with these two economic superpowers were expected to play a catalyst role in increasing Singapore's economic and business presence in the Japanese and US markets, while the trade liberalization momentum at the regional and multilateral levels was almost lost.

Table 8.1 Singapore's FTA network (as of October 2008)

Partner	Status (year)	Trade volume*		FDI volume†		Issue scope‡				
		Export	Import	Inflow	Outflow	Investment	Service	Environment	Labor	Economic cooperation
New Zealand	In force (2001)	0.5	0.2	0.6	NA	Yes	Yes	No	No	No
Japan	In force (2002)	4.8	8.2	1.1	1.0	Yes	Yes	No	No	Yes
Australia	In force (2003)	3.8	1.2	4.6	4.2	Yes	Yes	No	No	Yes
EFTA	In force (2003)	0.3	0.9	NA	NA	Yes	Yes	No	No	No
USA	In force (2004)	9.9	12.3	4.1	3.8	Yes	Yes	Yes	Yes	Yes
Jordan	In force (2005)	NA	NA	NA	NA	Yes	Yes	No	No	No
India	In force (2005)	2.8	2.3	1.4	1.0	No	No	No	No	Yes
Korea	In force (2006)	3.2	4.3	1.5	1.4	No	Yes	Yes	Yes	Yes
Panama	In force (2006)	NA	NA	NA	NA	NA	NA	No	Yes	Yes
Peru	Signed (2008)	NA	NA	NA	NA	NA	NA	NA	NA	NA

* Statistics Singapore, "EXTERNAL TRADE," http://www.singstat.gov.sg/pubn/reference/yos/statsT-trade.pdf. Accessed on October 6, 2008.
† Statistics Singapore, "Total Direct Investment Abroad By Country/Region, 1996–2006." http://www.singstat.gov.sg/stats/themes/economy/biz/investmentabroad.pdf. Accessed on October 6, 2008.
‡ List regarding the issues covered by the specific FTA: (I) Investment, (S) Services, (E) Environment, (L) Labor, and (EC) Economic Cooperation. Asia Regional Integration Center Website. http://www.aric.adb.org/indicator.php. Accessed on November 5, 2008.

Singapore's growing interest in FTAs was spurred not only by trade and investment interest, but also by strategic considerations. Singapore tended to believe that strengthening ties with FTA partners outside the region would secure its presence in Southeast Asia. Leifer (2000: 26) argued that Singapore was born with an innate vulnerability arising from its geopolitical situation: Singapore is "wedged-in" by big Islamic countries like Malaysia and Indonesia. A useful way to counter this vulnerability was by adopting the concept of the balance of power that is "directed to finding and employing ways of compensating for and reshaping to advantage a regional distribution of power," which includes "liberal internationalism in economic policy." For instance, in November 2000, Indonesian President Wahid, unhappy with Singapore's rejection of his proposal to include East Timor and Papua New Guinea in ASEAN, urged Malaysia to form an alliance with Indonesia, with the idea of cutting off Singapore's water supply. This was one of the many unfavorable remarks against Singapore, and allowed Singaporeans to view that their security could easily be jeopardized by their neighboring nations. Antagonism toward Singapore in Malaysia and Indonesia has been a source of primary political fear for Singaporeans. Political unpredictability in both countries has an adversarial effect on Singapore's foreign policy approaches. Therefore, "the multiple involvements of important extra-regional states have been encouraged as a practical way of coping with vulnerability" (Leifer, 2000: 26). Raymond Lim, Minister of State for Trade and Industry and Foreign Affairs, supports this view by stating that "our FTAs allow important nations like Japan and the United States to anchor their presence in the region and ensure that they remain stakeholders here" (*The Straits Times*, March 3, 2003).

Singapore's population is small (just over 4 million), and 99.9 percent of its imports are already tariff-free, thereby implying that there is little incentive for a partner country to eliminate tariffs and grant Singapore preferential market access in return for the same by signing an FTA. Thus, it is no surprise that only six Japanese companies have exported their products to Singapore by utilizing the Japan–Singapore FTA, despite approximately 3000 Japanese companies operating in Singapore (*Nihon Keizai Shimbun*, June 25, 2007). Singapore has thus been forced to convince potential partner countries of the merits of an FTA by incorporating elements that go beyond trade in goods, such as liberalization of services and systems for mutual recognition, and adoption of preferential systems for investments from the partner country. This is a legal impetus behind Singapore's keener interest in FTAs. An important aspect of the appeal of Singapore as Japan's first FTA partner was the fact that it was possible to conclude an economic partnership agreement, a new type of FTA that Japan hoped to promote. Economic partnership agreement (EPA) includes numerous "new age" elements not incorporated in the WTO rules, such as cooperation in the areas of small and medium enterprises, the protection of intellectual property, harmonization of standards in e-commerce transactions, and the facilitation of human movement for business purposes—which are termed "WTO-plus" elements (see Chapter 10 in this volume). Given that both nations enjoyed similar levels of economic development—Japan and Singapore ranked fifth and sixth in terms of GNP per capita in the world in 2000 when the FTA movement commenced—Singapore could be one of the few regional nations which could potentially conclude a "new age" economic partnership agreement with Japan that incorporated areas beyond the elimination of tariffs.

Singapore tended to emphasize the need to constantly stay ahead of neighbors and competitors for its survival in both economic and strategic contexts. Singapore thus tried to act as a trendsetter in FTA diffusion in Southeast Asia by swiftly signing East Asia's first and second bilateral FTAs with New Zealand and Japan, respectively, in 2002. Accordingly, its interest in FTAs mainly emerged as a response to the external shocks such as the stagnation of WTO or the Asian financial crisis, rather than an influence of the proliferation of FTAs in other countries or regions. So the non-diffusion hypothesis of independent decision-making fits the launch of Singapore's FTA policy best.

Yet the "concession-linkage" explanation as part of economic competition hypothesis seems to explain well the FTA diffusion in Southeast Asia when it comes to the revision of the older FTAs, partly by referring to the contents in the newly signed FTAs by other ASEAN members. The Japan–Singapore FTA, signed in 2002 as the first bilateral FTA exclusively by Asian countries, was not a perfect FTA as Japan exempted Singapore's key products such as petrochemicals from the liberalization requirement. Perhaps because Japan had never had an FTA, it was worrisome that its FTA with Singapore might provide other ASEAN members a possible "backdoor" entry to the Japanese petrochemical market; so Japan persuaded Singapore to agree to set up 60 percent of local content threshold, which was stricter than the 40 percent set up in AFTA. Yet Japan later removed tariffs on petrochemicals in an FTA that it signed in 2005 with Malaysia; this motivated Singapore to request Japan for equal treatment, in the follow-up negotiations to review the initial contents of the FTA with Japan five years after the effectuation. Singapore claimed that even if the Japan–Singapore FTA continued to keep tariffs on products, its investors, such as Exxon Mobil, would move their production bases to Malaysia from which they would export their petrochemicals to Japan so that they are able to enjoy nontariff treatment granted under the Japan–Malaysia FTA. Singapore and Japan also agreed to lower the local content requirement from 60 percent to 40 percent, the review that was based on Singapore's concern that higher local content requirement would cause Singapore to lose its attractiveness as an investment destination.[2] Any bilateral FTA signed between Japan and ASEAN members include this review commitment and "concession-linkages" are likely to continue to take place as far as different contents exist among those bilateral FTAs.

Bilateral FTA diffusion in Southeast Asia

The proliferation of bilateral FTAs in Southeast Asia began when Singapore signed the FTA with Japan in 2002, and Singapore hoped, as the then Prime Minister of Singapore Goh Chok Tong expressed, that it would "have a positive demonstration effect on other countries and would hopefully give impetus towards the creation of more FTAs" (*The Straits Times*, October 23, 2000). Singapore's prosperity has been closely associated with the economic growth of Southeast Asia, as well as investment and trade with the major economies outside the region. For instance, when it started pursued FTAs in the late 1990s, Singapore invested most in Southeast Asia among all ASEAN countries and at the same time, absorbed more than half of the total American and Japanese FDIs to Southeast Asia (Rajan et al., 2001: 10). It is thus in Singapore's interest to have an economically stable Southeast Asia; and it especially felt so after the 1997 Asian financial crisis, which seriously hampered ASEAN's economic growth, decreased the liberalization momentum, and collapsed its collective strength and prominence. As discussed earlier, Singapore started its FTA initiatives with a hope that major economies such as Japan and the United States could catalyze wider economic links and cooperation with economies in Southeast Asia, creating greater trade and investment flows for ASEAN members, helping regional economic growth, and creating more employment, given the fact that Japan and the United States were an important source of investment and of technology, and a major export market for the ASEAN economies.

However, when Singapore activated its FTA negotiations in 2000, which included one with Japan and New Zealand, it was viewed as insensitive since other ASEAN economies were struggling to recover from the adverse effect of the financial crisis, and Singapore's image as a self-centered member that cared little about its neighbors strengthened. In fact, Singapore did not consult with ASEAN members about its policy orientation toward bilateral FTAs, and some regional leaders were unhappy. For instance, the Malaysian Prime Minister Mahathir stated that "moves by Singapore to negotiate separate free-trade agreements, were worrisome" (*The Straits Times*, February 27, 2001), while his Trade Minister, Rafidah Aziz noted that Malaysia was "not interested in having bilateral FTAs with anybody" (*The Straits Times*, March 15, 2001).

Yet Thailand soon joined Singapore as the only like-minded country in the region, which began to vigorously pursue FTAs after Thaksin Shinawatra came into power in January 2001. Their shared interest in trade liberalization pushed the bilateral ties between Singapore and Thailand into a "special strategic partnership" (*The Straits Times*, January 19, 2005), founded on their enthusiasm in the pursuit of FTAs. The participation of a major regional economy like Thailand in the FTA movement catalyzed other nations to follow the trend. For instance, Indonesia's "sense of unease...leading to more serious consideration on the need for [it] to do the same" grew when Thailand began to show an interest in negotiating an FTA with Japan (Soesastro, 2004: 4). Their partnership was also instrumental in creating a regional atmosphere that pursued more active engagement in trade and investment liberalization. In September 2003, Thaksin and Goh proposed that the projected date for realization of an ASEAN Economic Community (AEC), which would result in the formation of a single regional market, should be brought forward from 2020. Following this proposal, Goh worked to convince the Philippines, while Thaksin did the same in Vietnam, which resulted in these two countries expressing agreement to the proposal (*Business Times*, October 9, 2003). The group of countries supporting the proposal gradually expanded, resulting ultimately in the earlier formation of a consensus. In this way, Singapore has been able to function as a facilitator not merely with respect to bilateral FTAs, but also with regard to ASEAN regional integration by overcoming its smaller size and limited influence in the region.

Then, Malaysia and Indonesia—believed to be the least enthusiastic nations in the region about bilateral FTAs—developed their interest in FTAs by studying all the pros and cons of the JSEPA, according to Katsuhiko Umehara, then Director of METI (Terada, 2003). A bilateral FTA involves the connotation of creating a partner, whereby either country selects the other country in consideration of economic and political benefits. Japan was already the most important partner for trade and investment as well as the top aid donor for these two countries; these countries recognized that Japan would have a vast market and purchasing power through an FTA, and also recognized the importance of being able to enter tariff-free into the Japanese market, and that within that recognition exists an expectation of bringing in investment and technology transfer from Japan. As a result, Malaysia and Indonesia, as well as Thailand, the Philippines, and Brunei, have signed bilateral FTAs with Japan, a movement that Vietnam subsequently joined. It is also Singapore that set a precedent for Thailand and Malaysia to follow in terms of the choice of FTA partners by signing with other major economies such as the United States and Australia.

One of the most powerful explanations behind the diffusion of bilateral FTAs in Southeast Asia concerns the exclusive nature of FTA whereby the benefits accrued, such as tariff eliminations, come at the expense of the third party countries. The main negative effects of FTAs are considered to be a decrease in nonmembers' exports to members, the deterioration of the terms of trade for nonmembers, and a reduction in members' consumer welfare as the more efficient nonmember producers are displaced by less efficient member producers due to tariff preferences (Viner, 1950; Ethier, 1988; and Chapter 2 in this volume). It is the companies of non-FTA partners that are seen to be greatly disadvantaged in competing with other firms from FTA partners, whose products are able to enjoy tariff-free privileges, leading to the creation of a trade-diversion effect. Therefore, as Solis and Katada argue in Chapter 1, business sectors or interests groups for certain industries in these cases may mobilize to influence trade policy, causing the diffusion of FTAs.

However, it is doubtful that this hypothesis comfortably explains the case of Southeast Asia. First, the business sectors in Singapore, like in many other ASEAN members, do not usually participate in the trade policymaking process, and their voices are not necessarily influential in their governments' pursuit of FTAs. Sally (2004: 27) regards the absence of a systematic incorporation of business inputs as the "Achilles heel" of Singapore's trade policymaking, generating "the passivity of the business sector" in Singapore's FTA movement. This makes it difficult for Singapore to "digest the real business preferences and information," and to enjoy "business feedbacks at home." One of the reasons behind the low business interest in influencing the government's economic policy lies in the fact that the government has excessive economic reach in the market. In Singapore, numerous government-linked companies in which former and current ministers and members of the ruling People's Action Party are involved, enjoy their great market power to the detriment of smaller private companies.

Centralized trade policymaking is, to a differing degree though, a general characteristic across Southeast Asia including Thailand, another key regional FTA player next to Singapore (Sally, 2007: 1602). Although the governments of Indonesia, Malaysia, and the Philippines sporadically consulted with non-governmental sectors including commerce and industry organizations when negotiating their first FTAs with Japan, the influence of those groups in FTA policymaking was limited or unidentified (Azuma, 2007). This stems partly from most ASEAN companies' failure to "see how their businesses benefit from … integration" and, as a result, the ASEAN governments find "no pressure from ASEAN businesses to move faster on regional economic integration," as Severino (2006: 249) comments. These observations support a view that interest group politics is neither necessarily an important factor for the proliferation of FTAs in Southeast Asia, nor directly relevant to FTA diffusion in the region, and that it is the strong state that plays a central role in bilateral trade negotiations (Aggarwal and Koo, 2005).

Another fact that does not help the trade-diversion explanation about FTA diffusion in Southeast Asia is that Singapore and Thailand being virtually the only nations in Southeast Asia which have successfully signed multiple bilateral FTAs, the impacts of their FTAs in trade and investment flows in Southeast Asia are not expected to be so substantial and the actual trade diversion would be limited. In fact, Thailand now abandons FTA-oriented trade policy after the Thaksin government was overthrown by a coup on September 19, 2006, and FTA negotiations with the United States, the most significant FTA for Thailand, have been suspended since then. The smaller element of tariff elimination in JSEPA and other bilateral FTAs of Singapore does not produce such a considerable trade diversion on trading partners. Also, Thailand's bilateral FTAs with Australia, New Zealand, and India, are seen as "trade-light" FTAs, meaning that these FTAs would make little difference to their trade activities due to the low trade volumes; for instance, Australia accounted for 2.3 percent of Thailand's total exports, while Thailand accounted for 1.8 percent of Australia's total exports in 2004 (Sally, 2007: 1609). Thailand's average tariff-cut ratios under the FTAs with Australia and India were merely 0.74 percent for 3,393 items and 6.6 percent for only 64 items in 2005, respectively (*The Nation*, September 9, 2006). Even the Thai-Japan FTA, which is much more significant because of the total trade volume, is seen as "quite weak" mainly because of some exemptions on goods, especially agriculture, and the restrictive ROOs (Sally, 2007: 1611).

The number of Japanese companies, which have used FTAs with some Southeast Asian countries like Malaysia, is also small due to complicated procedures and the expensive cost of certificates of origin required to qualify for duty exemption. This is especially true in the case of automobiles in which the companies need to obtain tens of thousands of certificates for their parts (*Nihon Keizai Shimbun*, June 25, 2007). Average FTA utilization rates by Singaporean companies for its six FTAs (the United States, Australia, Japan, ASEAN, India, and China) are 37 percent in 2006 and 32 percent in 2007, respectively (IE Singapore, 2007). From the standard of European FTAs, utilization rates below 50 percent are seen as "very low" (Baldwin, 2007: 12). In summary, the ASEAN members, except for Singapore, currently do not pursue bilateral FTAs actively; they are yet to be necessarily well utilized and even acknowledged as a useful business facilitator by ASEAN companies, indicating the actual trade diversion is not so substantial.

Conditions and outcomes of bilateral FTA diffusion in Southeast Asia

The composition of FTA diffusion, which includes states' calculation over the choice of their FTA partners, depends on how closely economic and business ties had already been established. States tend to see bilateral FTAs as considerably more effective for strengthening the existing economic relations—through increased trade or investment interaction by facilitating mutual economic benefits and business transactions between two countries—than through a regional and global approach. In this context, Japan's interest in pursuing bilateral FTAs played a key role in the proliferation of this kind of trading arrangement in Southeast Asia given the following conditions which affected FTA diffusion. (1) Japan was the largest trading partner, source of investment and technology, and aid provider to most of the ASEAN members, thereby forging close bilateral economic and business linkages; (2) Japan pursued bilateral FTAs most enthusiastically in Southeast Asia from among all extra-regional countries such as China and Korea; and (3) not all ASEAN members were interested in bilateral FTAs with China and Korea. As a consequence, Japan became the first bilateral FTA partner to most ASEAN members, and the only bilateral FTA partner for Indonesia, the Philippines, Brunei, and Vietnam, despite ASEAN's criticism of Japan's bilateralism.

Japan's considerable economic and business presence in Southeast Asia actually made the trade-diversion effect relevant in the FTA diffusion. The Filipino interest in signing an FTA with Japan originated from a fear of possible trade diversion among its neighbors that "ha[d] started to gain wider access to the Japanese market;" as stated by former Economic Planning Secretary Solita Monsod in one of the Senate hearings on the FTA with Japan: "the presence of these EPAs with [other ASEAN members] and the absence of an EPA with us will inevitably result in at least some amount of trade and investment diversion from us, which we can ill afford" (*Japan Times*, January 22, 2008). Indonesia's interest in an FTA with Japan was also spurred by the concern that Indonesian products would be disadvantaged in Japan, which had already started negotiating bilateral FTAs with other Southeast Asian nations (Sato, 2007).

While Japan was generally seen as a favorite "bilateral FTA partner" by individual Southeast Asian countries, China and Korea were not necessarily considered so; the Philippines, for instance, continued to reject signing the bilateral Early Harvest Program due to a fear of the influx of cheaper agricultural products from China. It was finally signed only through Hu Jintao's historic visit to Manila in April 2005. Vietnam was not happy with a trading deal with China as its official expressed: "Chinese appliances are very popular in Vietnam ... given the oversupply of electrical appliances in China, Chinese manufactures will be able to sell more to Indochina and the rest of ASEAN under the agreement" (*The Straits Times*, May 18, 2002). Thailand is also not expected to sign the Korea–ASEAN FTA while Seoul continues to exclude rice from the tariff-reduction list (*The Nation*, December 10, 2005). Prime Minister Thaksin's offer to exclude rice from a bilateral FTA with Japan illustrates the high priority Thailand attached to securing a trade accord with Japan.

Japan's preference for bilateral rather than regional approaches in its FTA with ASEAN can be evidenced by the fact that the actual negotiation of the Japan–ASEAN FTA was not commenced until April 2005, and lagged much behind China and Korea that have not been interested in concluding a bilateral FTA with any nation in Southeast Asia other than Singapore. In the meantime, there emerged a view in Japan that as AFTA was not a customs union with a common external tariff policy, the ASEAN–Japan FTA might eventually be established through the consolidation of the existing bilateral FTAs between Japan and ASEAN, and that there would be no need of the Japan–ASEAN FTA (JETRO, 2007: 83).

With regards to ASEAN's initial reactions to the ASEAN–Japan FTA, they were concerned that Japan's bilateral FTAs with individual ASEAN members could leave the less developed nations behind as ASEAN members were at different stages of economic development. ASEAN leaders are determined to stay economically united and have expressed suspicions over Japan's intention with some claiming that Japan's FTA policy could cause economic disintegration within ASEAN. Even during the process of drawing up the Joint Declaration in Phnom Penh in 2002, to be signed later by Prime Minister Koizumi and the ASEAN leaders, the ASEAN side was reluctant to accept the initial Japanese draft that stressed bilateral ties. The declaration that was eventually approved by the leaders was rephrased to call for the promotion of FTAs between Japan and ASEAN (*Yomiuri Shimbun*, November 6, 2002). It is another matter that seven ASEAN members have now either signed or are negotiating bilateral FTAs with Japan despite ASEAN's concern about Japan's bilateral FTA approach, which would impact ASEAN solidarity negatively. According to Oike (2007: 15), a Japanese FTA negotiator, this was made possible by the closer bilateral relationships that Japan had already forged with individual ASEAN members over decades through official development assistance (ODA) and investment, unlike any other country; bilateral FTAs were considered by ASEAN members to be a way of securing or increasing economic and technical cooperation from Japan. So those ASEAN members accepted Japan's comprehensive EPA approach—the approach originated in JSEPA which Japan saw an "important intellectual springboard and model for the kind of FTAs and EPAs that Japan should aim for" (Watanabe, 2004)—despite their substantially different economic and industrial structure, compared with Japan.

While Japan's bilateral FTA policy and its closer bilateral economic relations are a major causal factor, Singapore's aggressive pursuit of bilateral FTAs is not so, partly because the trade-diversion effect to be caused by Singapore FTAs would be small and, therefore, would not bother other Southeast Asian economies. Singapore's diplomatic efforts to bring Japan as the region's most significant economic partner to the FTA politics in Southeast Asia is not a direct but a significant factor in the explanation of the FTA diffusion in Southeast Asia. Initially, Singapore's FTA approach toward Japan invited only "negative and, at best, skeptical" (Munakata, 2001: 19) responses, as opposition to changing trade policy direction by forging FTAs still lingered. Singapore's explanations for seeking an FTA during intensive talks in the first half of November 1999 were influential in changing Japan's opposition to an FTA. According to Munakata (2001: 23), a senior MITI official involved in the talks with Singapore, what especially struck the Japanese officials was the demand that Japan should also secure policy options to "complement the WTO." This approach helped Japan conclude that "negative reactions from other countries, if any, would be manageable."

Singapore's tactics in visiting the Ministry of Agriculture, Forestry and Fishery in mid-1999 to convey that Singapore was not interested in agricultural liberalization in Japan was also a significant gesture of Singapore's FTA courtship to Japan. Singapore is not an agriculture-free nation; horticulture is fairly well developed and Singapore is the third largest exporter of cut orchids (after Thailand and Malaysia) in which the main market is Japan. Orchids accounted for around $18 million (60 percent) of the agricultural exports in 2002 (*The Straits Times*, September 20, 2003). The tactics Singapore employed were conducive to create the view in Japan that Singapore was actually one of the few nations that did not cause resistance from the farming sector in Singapore due to the smallest portion of agricultural products in its exports. It is not an exaggeration to say that this persuaded Japan to commence official negotiations with Singapore as its very first FTA partner. As a result, there was only a 14 percent increase in the number of zero-tariff commitments of Japan with regard to agricultural products, and these benefits had already been reached within the WTO framework, meaning that there was no new agricultural product in JSEPA from which Japan agreed to remove tariffs. At that time, there was a belief among Japanese policy intellectuals who supported the promotion of Japan's FTA policy that Japan would not have forged any FTA without successfully concluding negotiations with Singapore.[3] Singapore immensely assisted Japan in successfully launching its bilateral FTA policy, and this move was an initial factor behind the FTA diffusion in Southeast Asia.

ASEAN's efforts toward a unified trading player

Singapore's prosperity has been closely tied to the economic growth of Southeast Asia, as well as to investment and trade with the major economies outside the region. Thus, it is in the interest of Singapore to encourage ASEAN's integration and to link it with larger economies, leading to the eventual establishment of a larger single market in East Asia. Before the 1990s, given that trade structures were competitive, rather than complementary, with similar resource endowments and levels of technological development, which culminated in the production and export of similar primary and labor-intensive products, Southeast Asian countries were not interested in regional integration for two decades after the birth of ASEAN in 1967. ASEAN members shunned the term and concept of "integration" and stuck instead to "cooperation," as seen in official meetings and declarations until the late 1980s. A watershed decision in bringing the concept of regional integration to the agenda was the establishment of AFTA, initiated at the Fourth ASEAN Summit in Singapore in January 1992. AFTA has sought to increase ASEAN's competitive edge as a production base in the world market by eliminating tariff and nontariff barriers within ASEAN and by attracting more FDI to the region.

AFTA is now almost completed with 99.77 percent of the products in the CEPT (Common Effective Preferential Tariff) Inclusion List of ASEAN+6 which has been brought down to the 0–5 percent tariff range.[4] The coverage has expanded and the scope has widened: the AFTA-plus measures include harmonization of standards, reciprocal recognition of tests, and certification of products. The ASEAN Investment Area (AIA) as a framework for promoting inflow of FDI in Southeast Asia was signed in 1998; it binds ASEAN countries to gradually remove investment barriers, liberalize investment rules and policies, grant national treatment, and open industries to ASEAN investors by 2010 and to all investors by 2020.

Despite the progress in implementing AFTA, examples abound of the lack of willingness by member countries toward actual integration: for instance, an exporting country's certificates of origin, which acknowledge that a product is CEPT-certified, are frequently not admitted in the importing country; the necessary documents and formats are sometimes different for each country; and safety standards for electrical appliances are different as well (METI, 2004). Also, there are quite a few commodities that have been put on a Temporary Exclusion List, a General Exception List or a Sensitive List (excluded from any liberalization program perpetually). AFTA has not been utilized either. For instance, only 4.1 percent of Malaysia's exports within AFTA enjoyed the CEPT, while only 11.2 percent of Thailand's imports were under the scheme (JETRO, 2003). Also, the AFTA-plus measures such as AIA, ASEAN Framework Agreement on Services (AFAS), or mutual recognition agreement have not made tangible progress (Sally, 2007: 1601). Consequently, ASEAN leaders' appeals for members' commitment to stronger regional cooperation and for concerted efforts to facilitate regional integration were reduced to clichés. Former ASEAN Secretary-General Rodolfo Severino criticized the organization for having no clear idea about its future direction, saying that ASEAN has been "stuck in framework agreements, work programs and master plans" (*Business Times*, November 5, 2002).

A most fundamental structural problem that has caused the lack of interest in ASEAN's integration schemes is insufficient intraregional links, questioning the viability of AFTA and other economic integration measures within ASEAN. Singapore's Foreign Minister Rajaratnam had already recognized this structural problem in 1973: "economic realities require that regional cooperation must be wedded to external economic participation if ASEAN is to achieve its objectives. It is not intra-regional trade and investment but extra regional trade and investment which will accelerate ASEAN's economic growth" (Severino, 2006: 257). In other words, cooperative schemes that strengthen economic ties with larger extra-regional countries have proved more useful for economic growth. Nearly 80 percent of ASEAN's trade has been with non-ASEAN countries, and the exports of Indonesia and the Philippines to the ASEAN region are less than 10 percent and 6 percent, respectively, while the combined populations of the two nations account for nearly 60 percent of the total population (Pang, 2007: 13–14). Furthermore, 90 percent of FDI has been from non-ASEAN economies, and thus, a high degree of mutual interdependence among regional countries, in terms of trade volumes for instance, is not necessarily a powerful explanatory variable behind the formation of regional integration at least in the case of ASEAN. What has sustained ASEAN's need for the further promotion of integration schemes to attain economic growth is securing external markets and eliciting wider economic cooperation from larger extra-regional states, rather than sharing the benefits to be accrued from intra-regional cooperation. Thus, the fact that Japanese FDIs in China increased in the 1990s, and that this trend became stronger as a result of China's accession to WTO in 2001, was of considerable concern to ASEAN. For instance, Japan's FDI in China during the first half of fiscal 2003 was 35.5 percent on a year-on-year basis, but its FDI in ASEAN fell 14.6 percent during the same period (Kwan, 2004). Perceptibly, it was partly this move that spurred Singapore initially—as Lee Kuan Yew noted—to consider the FTA with Japan as a useful means to counter the economic threat posed by China (*Jiji Press News*, September 5, 2001), and to hope to act as an important catalyst in promoting Japanese investment in Singapore and other areas of the region, blazing the trail for other ASEAN members to attract more Japanese investment through FTA ties. ASEAN, which was concerned that its appeal as an investment destination had already been damaged by the Asian financial crisis, decided to follow Singapore's initial move to push ahead with regional integration in Southeast Asia, while expecting that this would also encourage Japan to negotiate an FTA with ASEAN as a whole, and that such an FTA would stop the trend toward reduced investment by Japan (Lim, 2003: 80).

ASEAN's approach underscores the point that in negotiating FTAs with large countries such as Japan and China, it must improve its international competitiveness by reinforcing the regional integration scheme and becoming an attractive investment destination; this way it would avoid bowing to pressure from these large countries and losing its influence. The fear that ASEAN would be marginalized vis-à-vis larger economies in the regional integration movement was expressed by Prime Minister Goh (2001):

> unless ASEAN, ourselves, get our act together, you may have a very wide income gap between Northeast Asia and Southeast Asia…Then ASEAN will become a marginal group within Asia. That is unstable for Asia. We will therefore in ASEAN try and work to integrate all our economies…Long-term, we will have some kind of East Asian Free Trade Area.

These concerns then urged Goh to propose an AEC plan, which was approved at the ASEAN Summit meeting in Bali, October 2003. This initiative aims to fully deregulate the flow of people, commodities, and currency as well as investment and service markets within the region by 2020 (later it was brought forward to 2015). Furthermore, the countries agreed to create a road map to promote integration in 11 industries, including automobiles and electronics, which make up over half of all trade at the informal Economy Ministers' meeting in April 2004. These proposals intend to change ASEAN's perception as a group of fragmented and relatively small economies unable to enjoy benefits from economies of scale in production despite its integration efforts through the AFTA scheme.

Proliferation of ASEAN+1 FTAs

Ironically, while ASEAN's integration programs such as AFTA got stuck in the mire after the financial crisis, it was China, formerly seen as its ideological threat, which brought in an idea for dealing with ASEAN as a single trading partner and push ASEAN's intraregional cooperation forward. In November 2000, Chinese Prime Minister Zhu Rongji, partly influenced by the earlier move of Japan with Korea and Singapore, surprised ASEAN and East Asia with the proposal of a China–ASEAN FTA, the first trading arrangement in the region to be negotiated with ASEAN as a single entity. China was attaching greater importance to cultivating good regional relations with ASEAN partly to neutralize the containment policy of the Bush administration. China is also said to view ASEAN as an ally in the face of intensifying US pressure over the revaluation of the yuan (*The Straits Times*, October 10, 2003). China's proactive diplomatic approach toward ASEAN is also evident in its 2002 meeting with ASEAN where China agreed to avoid using force to settle any dispute in the South China Sea, a major source of confrontation between China and some member states, such as Malaysia, Vietnam, and the Philippines.

China's immense interest in this FTA also derives from the opportunities that ASEAN's market of 580 million people and its rich natural resources could offer. Moreover, China's basic approach to the region has focused on economic cooperation and mutual gains to dispel the perception of a "China threat." To some extent, it has even become an engine of growth for the region, judging by the trade surpluses most ASEAN countries enjoy vis-à-vis China. Thus, to show its sincerity and goodwill, China offered to unilaterally open its agricultural market to ASEAN's latecomers, five years ahead of the opening of their markets to China. In fact, China's FTA with ASEAN is based on more than just reciprocity since China gives more than it receives, for instance, according most favored nation (MFN) status to Vietnam, Laos, and Cambodia before they even join the WTO (Terada, 2003: 271).

It was the initiative of Japan to negotiate FTAs with Korea and Singapore in 1998–99 that led China to feel isolated in the trade structure in East Asia; as Noboru Hatakeyama (2003) mentioned: "had it not been for the start of JSEPA, there would not have been such strong movements in this area towards FTAs, including those between ASEAN and China." China shortly joined the movement, but not bilaterally: it proposed an FTA with ASEAN in October 2000, on which they officially agreed in November 2001, conducive to the FTA diffusion being extended to Northeast Asia. Japan had not considered the establishment of an FTA with ASEAN as a single economic unit, and the agreement for the establishment of a Japan–ASEAN FTA in 2002 was seen as a response to the China–ASEAN FTA proposal (Terada, 2006a). A Vietnamese official commented that Japan's FTA proposal with ASEAN in January 2002 seemed to be a hastily-put-together affair that was "all show" and had "little substance," and that its main purpose, which was not stated, was to counter the FTA proposal floated by China to ASEAN (*Business World*, February 27, 2002). With the rapid development of China as an economic superpower, its readiness to open its huge market to foreign investors, and its aggressive economic movements into ASEAN, Japan found it necessary to start pursuing an FTA with ASEAN while negotiating bilateral ones with individual members. The FTA approaches of China and Japan toward ASEAN also contributed to South Korea developing an interest in pursuing the same path, as its Trade Minister Hwang Doo-yun expressed in Brunei in September 2002, and led to the final agreement on the establishment of an FTA with ASEAN in 2004. India also proposed an FTA to ASEAN in November 2002, and as in the case of Japan, the initial impetus for its desire to strengthen its economic relations with ASEAN through an FTA was provided by China's FTA proposal. This ASEAN-centered FTA movement has been joined by Australia–New Zealand later, culminating in the formation of five "ASEAN+1" FTAs, perhaps as a basis for the eventual establishment of East Asian integration (see Table 8.2).

One important competitive element in the "ASEAN+1" FTA diffusion is that two different types of FTAs were promoted by Japan and China, and that both were presented to ASEAN, meaning that ASEAN needed to implement two different types of FTA. Japan prefers to use the term EPA to FTA in order to pursue more comprehensive economic arrangements, covering WTO-plus issues including investment rules or mutual recognition standards to facilitate service-related business, in addition to the conventional FTA element of tariff elimination. Japan's FTA model is based on the FTA with Singapore (JETRO, 2007: 52). Meanwhile, the China–ASEAN FTA intends not to remove but to lower tariff rates (less than five percent) on almost all commodities (ASEAN–China Expert Group on Economic Cooperation, 2001), and China and ASEAN, both categorized as developing entities, were entitled to utilize the enabling clause which indicates the exclusion of the Article 24 application. The China–ASEAN FTA was thus allowed to incorporate the Early Harvest Program under which, on October 1, 2003, China started removing all tariffs on 600 agricultural exports of ASEAN such as vegetables, tropical fruits, meat, dairy products, ornamental plants, timber, and palm oil (Wong and Chan, 2003: 511). These concessions on the part of China imply ASEAN's importance in China's foreign policy, as has been discussed earlier; the concessions were instrumental in eliminating ASEAN's concern about China as an FTA partner, thereby creating an impression that Japan was lagging behind China in the FTA competition in East Asia (Terada, 2006a). This impression was strengthened, as Oike (2007: 23), a MOFA negotiator, confessed, since in FTA negotiations with ASEAN, Japan persisted in its comprehensive EPA approach, making demands for WTO-plus elements that caused negotiations to be occasionally bogged down due to the strong resistance on ASEAN's part.

The more competitive element lies in the manner of implementations. Japan's single-undertaking approach, which means that every issue in the agreement is negotiated at the same time, tends to promote trade liberalization more quickly than China's model, which is based on a gradual approach in which trade liberalization on goods is negotiated first, and then followed by the services and investments. Also, Japan's FTAs promise to remove most of the tariffs immediately after the agreements become effective, while China's

Table 8.2 ASEAN's FTA network (as of March 2009)*

Partner	Status	Trade volume[†]		FDI volume		Issue scope				
		Export	Import	Inflow[‡]	Outflow	Investment	Service	Environment	Labor	Economic cooperation
China	Goods (2005) Service (2007)	8.1	10.6	1.8	1.3	Yes	Yes	Yes	No	Yes
Australia/ New Zealand	Signed (2008)	4.2	2.3	NA	NA	Yes	Yes	NA	NA	NA
Japan	In force (2008)	11.2	14.1	20.6	8.3	Yes	Yes	No	No	Yes
India	Negotiation	2.3	1.4	0.8	0.8	Yes	Yes	NA	NA	NA
Korea	In force (2006)	4.4	4.1	2.1	1.7	Yes	Yes	No	No	No

* ASEAN website, "Other Free Trade Area under Consideration." http://www.aseansec.org/13999.htm. Accessed on September 21, 2008.
† ASEAN website, "ASEAN Statistical Yearbook 2006." http://www.aseansec.org/13100.htm.
‡ ASEAN website, "Top ten sources of ASEAN FDIs inflow. Annual: 2004–2005; Cumulative annual: 2001–2005." http://www.aseansec.org/Stat/Table27. pdf. Accessed on September 21, 2008.

approach puts the products into different categories of tariff ratios and removes or reduces those tariffs gradually in accordance with the different categories of products. Thus, the elimination of higher tariffs would take longer in China's FTAs and, importantly, this was modeled after the AFTA approach. This means China's approach was more familiar and comfortable for ASEAN, which made it substantially easy to conclude their mutual FTA negotiations. Japan, as a developed nation, needed to meet the requirements of Article 24 of GATT, which stipulates the mutual abolishment of tariff of 90 percent or more for all trade within ten years, based on the principle of reciprocity, and ASEAN needed to abide by this rule in the FTA negotiations with Japan, unlike the case of the FTA with China, as mentioned above. Now that the FTAs of South Korea and India with ASEAN follow China's model in terms of implementation of liberalization with the product categories and initial liberalisation on goods, Japan's comprehensive and WTO-consistent approach, which the Australia/New Zealand team is following, does not prevail well in Southeast Asia. The result that China wins against Japan in the legal competition in the ASEAN+1 FTA diffusion is mainly attributed to ASEAN that prefers China's model to accommodate the wide gaps prevalent among ASEAN countries in their levels of economic development. The result of competition over the FTA styles, however, may delay the completion of regional trade and investment liberalization in East Asia, which is not helpful in overcoming the "convoy problem," where the least willing member holds back the pace of trade liberalization. In addition, the differences in product coverage and time framework of liberalization between these two types of FTAs in Southeast Asia, together with the bilateral FTA networks that Japan mainly forged, would make it difficult for multinational companies, as potential FTA users, to identify which FTA would be most effective in terms of cost-saving for their business at the bilateral as well as the regional level. Thus, a "spaghetti bowl" effect (Bhagwati, 2008) would be most conspicuously set out in Southeast Asia: a large number of ROOs with specific standards and involving specific procedures would be formulated, and different rules will be applied to a single commodity.

Conclusions

This chapter focused on the role of Singapore to test the validity of the FTA diffusion framework in accounting for the proliferation of bilateral FTAs in Southeast Asia. Singapore's aggressive pursuit of FTA policy partly contributed to the initiation of a "domino effect," with more neighbouring countries extending the circle of FTAs in Southeast Asia and beyond. Yet, as this chapter reveals, most of the ASEAN members chose Japan as their first and only bilateral FTA partner, underscoring Japan's distinctive status as the most significant trading and investment partner as well as aid-giver in Southeast Asia. This "biased" FTA diffusion was mainly attributed to Japan whose initial

FTA strategy, based on those strong economic ties, promoted bilateral rather than ASEAN FTAs, distinguishing its FTA approach from those of China and Korea. Most ASEAN members decided to start FTAs with Japan as a result of the concern about trade diversion to be caused by preexisting FTAs signed by Japan with other regional countries. Accordingly, the FTA diffusion in Southeast Asia was not a result of followers' interest in emulating the FTA model preceded by Singapore or their ambition to compete against it. Singapore's role in this process was to help Japan to start pursuing bilateral FTAs in the region.

Significantly, the bilateral FTA diffusion in Southeast Asia has now extended beyond Southeast Asia. The ASEAN+1 approach was initiated by China's proposal of an FTA with ASEAN in October 2000, following which Japan proposed its own FTA with ASEAN in January 2002. The approach has since been adopted by South Korea, India, and Australia/New Zealand, with the result that today ASEAN functions as a hub for the five ASEAN+1 FTAs. Yet a step toward the commencement for an East Asia FTA negotiation depends on ASEAN's willingness to move beyond this framework. ASEAN as a loose group of relatively small economies inevitably depends on external economies for its growth through FDI and exports, but its institutional significance would be diminished if a larger arrangement such as an East Asian FTA, in which ASEAN could be marginalized, developed rapidly. ASEAN's reluctance to move trade liberalization by itself, or perhaps its inability to take a political initiative toward a wider regional integration as a unified player, can be found in the fact that it has never proposed an FTA to any of those "+1" partners. The lack of willingness and of capability on the part of ASEAN would be a major obstacle to the establishment of region-wide integration in East Asia. Japan and China are fully aware of this sensitivity and of this institutional problem, as seen in their careful support for ASEAN's integration programs (Terada, 2006a: 12). The completion of AEC is thus an initial but pressing step toward the eventual formation of the East Asian FTA.

Notes

1. Singapore has concluded FTAs with New Zealand (2000), Japan (2002), the European Free Trade Association (comprising Switzerland, Iceland, Liechtenstein, and Norway; 2002), Australia (2003), the United States (2003), Jordan (2004), India (2005), South Korea (2005), and Panama (2006). Singapore is presently engaged in FTA negotiations with several countries including Bahrain, Mexico, Canada, Panama, Peru, Sri Lanka, and Ukraine.
2. Personal interview with a senior official from Singapore Foreign Ministry; April 3, 2008, Tokyo.
3. Personal interview with Naoko Munakata, December 15, 2004, Tokyo.
4. Joint Media Statement of the Twentieth Meeting of the ASEAN Free Trade Area Council, Kuala Lumpur, August 21, 2006.

9
South Korea's FTAs: Moving from an Emulative to a Competitive Strategy

Min Gyo Koo

Introduction

East Asian countries' interest in free trade agreements (FTAs) has surged at the turn of the new millennium (Pempel, 2005; Aggarwal and Koo, 2005; Aggarwal and Urata, 2006; Solís and Katada, 2007). In particular, the rise of South Korea's FTA initiative has been remarkable in its speed and scope. Over the past decade, South Korea has successfully concluded FTAs with Chile (2003), Singapore (2004), the European Free Trade Association (2005), the Association of Southeast Asian Nations (2006), and the United States (2007). South Korea has also been negotiating FTAs with Japan, Canada, Mexico, India, the European Union, Australia, and New Zealand. In addition, feasibility studies are under way with China, South Africa, Russia, the Gulf Cooperation Council (GCC), and Mercosur.

The rise of South Korea's FTA initiative marks a significant departure from its traditional focus on global multilateralism. Within South Korea's policy circles, a new consensus has emerged that a preferential approach to trade liberalization is not only complementary to the country's multilateral strategy, but also crucial to its economic survival in a world of competitive export markets. Kim Dae-jung's rise to presidency in 1998 turned the new policy idea into action, as manifested by South Korea's first FTA with Chile in 2003. With the inauguration of President Roh Moo-hyun in 2003, the proactive role of the Office of the Minister for Trade (OMT) further expanded the FTA policy to include both small and large economies ranging from Singapore to the United States.

From an institutional point of view, South Korea's embrace of FTAs has been shaped by a top-down political initiative rather than by a bottom-up demand from various interest groups and the general public. In the immediate aftermath of the Asian financial crisis, South Korea's protectionist veto players such as labor unions and farmers' organizations were temporarily disorganized due to President Kim's neoliberal reform and the International Monetary Fund (IMF) austerity program.[1] Amidst sweeping socioeconomic restructuring, Kim's decision to pursue preferential trade liberalization through FTAs went unchallenged, if not unnoticed, by traditional protectionist interests, as illustrated by the fact that it was not until 2003 that a heated debate started over the ratification of South Korea–Chile FTA (Park and Koo, 2007).

The recent dispute over the South Korea–US FTA (KORUS FTA) indicates that socioeconomic cleavages in South Korea may be much wider and deeper than previously conceived. Most notably, the launch of KORUS FTA negotiations in early 2006 added fuel to anti-American and antiglobalization sentiments by those who had been polarized and marginalized by the globalization of world economy. Some radicals even dubbed the resultant economic liberalization the "second IMF-imposed economic exploitation" at the expense of economically disadvantaged groups and people such as farmers and blue-collar workers.

Shifting interest group demands notwithstanding, South Korea's FTA strategy has evolved primarily through a top-down policy mechanism that can be characterized as "embedded autonomy."[2] Under President Kim, strong executive power and public support for neoliberal restructuring allowed the introduction of new FTA initiative. Under President Roh, the OMT steadily institutionalized the idea and practice of promoting economic reform and strategic partnership through FTAs, while other government agencies provided generous side-payments to those who lost out due to more economic openness.

This chapter investigates the following questions: (1) Have the prior decisions of other countries to negotiate FTAs affected South Korea's decision to pursue FTAs? (2) How has South Korea's FTA policymaking process evolved over the decade in terms of its partner selection, timing, and scope of agreements? (3) To what extent do FTA outcomes conform to the expectations of the emulation and competition hypotheses, as developed by Solís and Katada in Chapter 1?

The main argument of this chapter is that South Korea's embrace of FTAs has evolved from an emulative to a competitive strategy in the post–Asian financial crisis period. Recognizing a dire need to secure export markets through a preferential approach, South Korean leaders have embraced FTAs despite vocal protests from those who would be negatively affected by economic liberalization. The remainder of this chapter is structured as follows. The second section reviews existing explanations that pertain to South Korea's dramatic turn to FTA initiative. The third section shows how and to what extent President Kim's leadership shaped the launch of South Korea's FTA policy, as South Korea was lagging behind its peer countries in East Asia in negotiating FTAs. The fourth section unravels the role played by the presidential leadership and OMT in moving South Korea's FTA initiative from an emulative *but* passive to a competitive *and* proactive strategy. The final section summarizes the main findings and draws policy implications.

South Korea's trade policy and conventional explanations

Since its dramatic economic takeoff in the 1970s, South Korea has benefited from export-oriented industrialization under the auspices of the multilateral trading regime of the GATT/WTO (General Agreement on Tariffs and Trade/World Trade Organization). Since its accession to the GATT in 1967, South Korea's active promotion of the export sector has allowed the once reclusive country in Northeast Asia to aggressively participate in the global market. As a trade-dependent country, South Korea's full support of the world trading system, such as that under the GATT, was not a matter of choice, but of survival. Until recently, together with Japan and China, South Korea remained one of the very few WTO member countries which did not enter into any regional trading agreements as defined under Article 24 of the GATT/WTO (Koo, 2006: 142–3).

However, in the wake of the Asian financial crisis of 1997–98, the illusion of South Korea's unstoppable economic growth was severely shattered.[3] Furthermore, as the 1999 WTO Ministerial Meeting in Seattle failed to launch a new round of trade talks, South Korea came to recognize that the mediocre performance of the WTO and increasing competition in its traditional export markets could hurt export-dependent South Korea. The financial crisis and the debacle in Seattle thus served as a wake-up call to South Korea, making it realize the importance of supplementary mechanisms at the sub-multilateral level to safeguard its economic security (Cheong, 1999; Sohn, 2001).

As shown in Table 9.1, South Korea's FTA track record has been remarkable. Since the signing of the South Korea–Chile FTA in 2003, South Korea has concluded bilateral and minilateral FTAs with Singapore, EFTA, ASEAN, and the United States. These five FTAs together would likely cover about 27 percent of South Korea's total trade, if fully implemented. South Korea has also been negotiating FTAs with Japan, Canada, Mexico, India, EU, Australia, and New Zealand. In addition, a number of feasibility studies are currently under way with China, Russia, South Africa, GCC, and Mercosur. If these prospective FTAs are concluded successfully, they would likely cover up to 67 percent of South Korea's total trade.

Existing literature on South Korea's FTA strategy—and East Asian FTAs more broadly—has largely focused on one of the following questions: (1) What has motivated South Korea's rush toward FTAs, departing from its traditional focus on multilateralism? (2) What are the characteristics of South Korea's FTA strategy in terms of its partner selection, timing, and scope of agreements? (3) How has South Korea's FTA policymaking process evolved within the domestic political dynamics?

As noted by many economists, South Korea has made the policy shift toward FTAs primarily because FTAs are likely to generate substantial economic gains (Cheong, 1999, 2001, 2005; Cheong and Lee, 2000; Schott and Choi, 2001; Sohn, 2001; Sohn and Yoon, 2001; Chung, 2003; SERI, 2003; Nam, 2004).

Table 9.1 South Korea's FTA network (as of October 2008)

Partner	Status	Trade volume* (percentage of 2007 total)		FDI volume† (percentage of 2006 total)		Issue scope				
		Export	Import	Inflow (actually utilized)	Outflow (nonfinancial)	Investment	Service	Environment	Labor	Economic cooperation
Chile	In force (2004)	0.84	1.17	0	0.04	Yes	Yes	Yes	No	No
Singapore	In force (2006)	3.22	1.92	6.21	3.01	Yes	Yes	No	No	Yes
EFTA	In force (2006)	0.30	1.00	2.12	0.06	Yes	Yes	No	No	No
ASEAN	In force (2007)	10.43	9.28	5.68	12.91	No‡	Yes§	No	No	Yes
US	Signed (2007)	12.32	10.43	11.06	16.08	Yes	Yes	Yes	Yes	No
Japan	Negotiation (2003)	7.10	15.76	28.83	1.93	–	–	–	–	–
Canada	Negotiation (2005)	0.94	0.91	0.81	3.90	–	–	–	–	–
Mexico	Negotiation (2006)	2.01	0.28	0	0.56	–	–	–	–	–
India	Negotiation (2006)	1.78	1.30	0	0.92	–	–	–	–	–
EU	Negotiation (2007)	15.07	10.32	26.27	9.07	–	–	–	–	–
Australia	Negotiation (2008)	1.26	3.71	0.14	1.22	–	–	–	–	–
China	Study	22.07	17.66	0.58	30.93	–	–	–	–	–
Russia	Study	2.18	1.96	0	0.97	–	–	–	–	–
Mercosur	Study	1.11	1.01	0	1.11	–	–	–	–	–
South Africa	Study	0.47	0.50	0	0.06	–	–	–	–	–

* The Korean Statistical Information Service (http://www.kosis.kr/).

† OECD.StatExtracts (http://webnet.oecd.org/wbos/index.aspx).

‡ Negotiations for an investment agreement are currently underway as of October 2008.

§ The service agreement was separately signed in November 2007, but is not yet in force as of October 2008.

The so-called gravity model offers a popular economic explanation that links geographic distance and economic size to the choice of FTA partners. In order to reduce the costs related to geographic distance and to maximize the benefits from economic size, the gravity model suggests that neighboring countries form FTAs with each other, thus creating a natural trading bloc (Frankel et al., 1997; Krugman, 1991). From this perspective, the formation of natural trading blocs will improve economic welfare, whereas the formation of unnatural trade blocs between distant and/or small economies will have marginal welfare effects, if any.[4]

Despite its explanatory utility, the gravity model explanation runs into a problem in accounting for South Korea's selection of FTA partners. For instance, the South Korea–Chile FTA is a typical case of an unnatural trading bloc, not only because the Pacific Ocean separates the two countries, but also because Chile's economy is relatively small, and thus the bilateral trade volume between South Korea and Chile will remain insignificant, if not negligible (Koo, 2006: 144). Instead, South Korea would most likely benefit handsomely if it removed existing trade and investment barriers by establishing FTAs with Japan and China (Sohn and Yoon, 2001). Nevertheless South Korea's FTA negotiation with Japan has been stalemated since November 2004, while a prospective FTA with China is still a low priority for South Korea owing to its concern about China's cheap agricultural and industrial products. In sharp contrast, South Korea has been more active in pursuing cross-regional FTAs with distant economies, both small and large (Park and Koo, 2007).

From a noneconomic perspective, the structural changes in the post–Cold War and post–Asian financial crisis period contributed to cognitive changes and the diffusion of new policy ideas (Acharya, 2007; Higgott, 2007; Ye, 2007). More specifically, the proliferation of East Asian FTAs is closely associated with the decline of US economic hegemony in the region. During the Cold War period, trade liberalization was provided for most East Asian countries mainly through the GATT under the auspices of American hegemony. To the extent that the GATT required membership, the provision of trade liberalization was a multilateral club good. But it contained a strong public good characteristic, since East Asian countries were allowed to pay less to get more out of the system. As Higgott (2004: 158) notes, the US certainly saw these institutions as beneficial to its national interest and to its view of world order, but it defined its interests broadly and in a sufficiently inclusive manner that other countries felt able to sign on to a vision that stressed the importance of due process and the rule of law.

Yet in the aftermath of regional financial turmoil, East Asian countries' new appetite for FTAs reflects a convergence of interests in securing bilateral and minilateral club goods. The "trade triangle" that had linked Japanese and overseas Chinese capital, developing East Asian manufacturing capacities, and the US market was in trouble. With traditional mechanisms within the GATT/WTO and America's global economic leadership offering no salient solutions, these countries quickly turned toward FTAs to secure preferential access and create a more diversified export market (Aggarwal and Koo, 2008).

Despite their theoretical and empirical merits, few existing studies have focused on the emulative and competitive aspects of South Korea's policy shift toward FTAs. In an interdependent world, the success of early movers is likely to accelerate the spread of new policy ideas (Baldwin, 1997; Ikenberry, 1990). The rapid diffusion of FTAs in East Asia—particularly the 2001 Japan–Singapore FTA and the 2003 ASEAN–China framework FTA—has affected South Korea's embrace of FTAs in various ways. In a similar vein, the voluntary nature of countries' decision to enter FTAs can be attributed to their fear of exclusion. According to this logic, a country's fear of exclusion from an FTA—especially with a country that has "go-it-alone-power"—motivates the former to voluntarily choose to form an FTA with the latter, even if the former prefers the *status quo* (Gruber, 2000). As will be discussed in further details in the fourth section, the KORUS FTA illustrates that the fear of exclusion in the US market played a significant catalyst role in launching KORUS FTA negotiations.[5] Having these in mind, the following sections unravel South Korea's emulative and competitive motives in the FTA policymaking process.

Emulating peers under Kim

In November 1998, the South Korean government's Inter-Ministerial Trade Policy Coordination Committee formally announced that the country would start an FTA negotiation with Chile, while conducting feasibility studies with other prospective FTA partners such as the United States, Japan, New Zealand, and Thailand. Shortly after the announcement, the Kim government formed a special task force on a South Korea–Chile FTA, which consisted of five working groups, covering market access, trade rules, services, intellectual property, and legal procedures (Chung, 2003: 74; Sohn, 2001: 7).

As many observers have noted, the economic crisis shocked South Korea out of traditional policy patterns and practices. The economic shock temporarily disorganized interest groups that used to veto policy reform, while generating pressure for politicians to change the failed policies (Mo, 1999: 53). Although some farmers' groups and labor unions remained militant, their political influence eroded significantly, as both their absolute and relative shares in the economy continued to decline.[6] In sharp contrast, competitive manufacturing sectors began to show their support for the government's FTA policy.[7]

In the advent of South Korea's near economic collapse, the abundant political capital given to President Kim allowed him to implement sweeping economic reforms, including recapitalizing banks, setting up a public asset-management company to buy up bad loans, overseeing banking reforms, and forcing *chaebol* to purge the debt from their balance sheets by selling entire divisions or going out of business altogether. He also actively promoted several promising industries, such as information technology and biotechnology, through various forms of incentives including grants, bank loans on preferential terms, and the like. Reform efforts thus strengthened the mechanisms for resource allocation through the market mechanism and significantly altered the legal and institutional settings to improve governance (OECD, 2003).

The resultant higher factor mobility generated unintended conditions in favor of trade liberalization through FTAs. The IMF conditionalities and President Kim's corporate restructuring program did create more efficient capital and labor markets, namely more flexible resource allocation based on market signals rather than government directives. Such a development significantly weakened the voice of noncompetitive sectors and factors.[8]

On the one hand, FTAs held strong appeal because it was possible to exclude some politically sensitive sectors from preferential arrangements or to minimize market concessions, thus leaving domestic veto players contained.[9] On the other hand, the Kim government's FTA policy reflected its sense of urgency in the advent of rising competition with its advanced trading partners such as Japan as well as developing ones such as China and ASEAN in the regional and global export market (Bank of Korea, 2001). With the WTO's new trade round stalemated, South Korea desperately needed to expand its trade to new markets by bilateral and minilateral means (Koo, 2006: 148).

Most notably, President Kim was also drawn to bilateral and minilateral FTAs in pursuit of his ambitious initiative to make South Korea a regional transportation hub and international business center.[10] He undertook a dramatic policy shift as part of his ambitious vision and strategic goals for regional cooperation. At the first APT summit meeting in Kuala Lumpur in December 1997, he made public South Korea's aspiration to become a hub country of East Asia by playing a balancer role between regional powers.[11] During the 1999 APT summit, he also proposed the establishment of an expert panel, the EAVG, as the first step to forge a regional cooperation mechanism and to develop APT into a more permanent regional institution.[12]

As long as both China and Japan were eager for regionalism, President Kim could play the role of visionary for an East Asian community by serving as a bridge between the two enduring rivals (Rozman, 2006). Apart from the relatively warm Sino-Japanese relations at the turn of the new millennium, Kim Dae-jung's Sunshine Policy that culminated in the June 2000 inter-Korean summit created a great deal of diplomatic capital for South Korea to actively address the delicate issues of peace and stability in the region.[13]

The adoption of FTAs under Kim's presidency as a new policy tool, and the implementation of sweeping economic reforms, thus supports the emulation hypothesis that countries will copy the FTA policies of their sociocultural peers or of leading nations. To some extent, the embrace of an FTA track under Kim also supports a related hypothesis that FTA policies that disseminate through emulation should be omnidirectional in that the Kim government became interested in negotiating as many FTAs as possible with little concern about sequencing.

To summarize, the economic crisis at the end of the 1990s contributed to the rise of reform-minded Kim Dae-jung and the downfall of many domestic veto holders that had plagued South Korea's economic policy in general and trade policy in particular. These included not only formal institutions such as government bureaucracy and political parties but also societal groups such as labor unions, farmers' associations, and NGOs. Yet it should be noted that the Kim government's FTA policy remained emulative but inherently passive to the extent that it aimed at minimizing potential costs, rather than maximizing benefits, of FTAs.

Competing with peers under Roh

The new policy ideas under Kim greatly inspired his successor, President Roh Moo-hyun. Upon its inauguration in February 2003, the Roh government launched an ambitious initiative aimed at creating a peaceful and prosperous Northeast Asia. He created the Presidential Committee on Northeast Asian Business Hub in order to carry out the initiative including the creation of financial and logistic hubs, and the promotion of cooperation in the areas of business, energy, and transportation. At the same time, President Roh launched the "Northeast Asian Cooperation Initiative for Peace and Prosperity," designed to carry out his long-term vision for creating a new regional order based on mutual trust and cooperation (Presidential Committee on Northeast Asian Cooperation, 2004).

From the outset, however, President Roh's agenda encountered inimical regional geopolitics as a result of the unleashing of the war against terror following the September 11 terrorist attacks in the US. In addition, the simultaneous political leadership changes in the United States, China, Japan, and South Korea put unpredictable pressure on East Asian regionalism.[14] None of the great powers surrounding the Korean Peninsula thus seemed supportive of President Roh's wish, which lacked the same degree of diplomatic and moral attraction as his predecessor Kim had once enjoyed. Each great power kept alive an interest in regionalism, but sought to gain advantage over its rival, thereby leaving very little room for Roh to maneuver (Rozman, 2006).

As noted previously, South Korea's FTA strategy emerged initially as a fraction of President Kim's broader economic and strategic agenda. Under his presidency, the FTA policy was largely designed as an emulative but defensive strategy to cope with the rise of regionalism in other parts of the world. The linkage between FTAs and domestic reforms was not clearly defined or was deliberately minimized. The rather peripheral, if not completely marginal, status of the FTA initiative under Kim was replaced by what amounted to an enthusiastic endorsement of FTAs as instruments of foreign policy. To be sure, the policy shift toward FTAs under Kim did mark a dramatic departure from South Korea's traditional trade policy. Yet it was not until Roh entered office in 2003 that the roadmap for FTAs and detailed action plans for its multi-track FTA strategy were completed. With its ambitious regionalist vision in trouble, the Roh government recognized that bilateral and minilateral FTAs might provide more effective mechanism for realizing its strategic and diplomatic goals (Lee, 2006: 5; MOFAT, 2006).

From an institutional point of view, the empowerment of the OMT demonstrated the renewed enthusiasm and commitment under Roh, as the once beleaguered institution took firm roots within the government with its mission and mandate to initiate and negotiate FTAs.[15] OMT's central position was further highlighted by the appointment of its third Trade Minister, Kim Hyun-chong, in July 2004 (until August 2007) as well as the promotion of its first Trade Minister, Han Duk-soo, to Minister of Finance and Economy (March 2005–July 2006) and later to Prime Minister (April 2007–February 2008).[16]

The KORUS FTA is a good example of South Korea's proactive FTA strategy and the role of the OMT. In February 2006, the Roh government made a surprise move to cut South Korea's annual screen quota in favor of the United States.[17] In addition, it lifted the ban on US beef (the response to an incident of mad cow disease in the United States), proposed modifications to its pharmaceutical pricing system, and revised an automobile remissions regulation to provide a grace period for imported vehicles, thereby paving the way for KORUS FTA negotiations (USTR, 2006: 393–417). After eight formal negotiating rounds since June 2006, the two governments successfully concluded a landmark agreement on April 1, 2007.

By any measure, the negotiation process was not an easy one and the two governments expect an even tougher legislative ratification process ahead. From one perspective, the current debate in South Korea about the KORUS FTA indicates that social cleavages may be much wider and deeper than previously thought. South Korea's protectionist interests, which have slowly been recovering from the upheavals caused by the financial crisis, have now been empowered again by their coalition of convenience with anticapital labor unions and anti-American nongovernmental organizations, whereas pro-liberalization business lobbies are not actively mustering enough political support for the government.[18]

Indeed, South Korea's uncompetitive sectors felt more victimized by KORUS FTA negotiations and, more broadly, by their allegedly neoliberal economic orientation. For those skeptics, therefore, the government's effort to restructure the economy by inviting external pressure—namely FTAs—would only worsen the issue of economic polarization in South Korea, rather than providing an opportunity to upgrade its economy to a more advanced level (Lee, 2006: 6). Some South Korean radicals have dubbed the cross-Pacific deal as "the second IMF-imposed economic exploitation." This indicates that the explicit linkage of FTA policy to neoliberal reforms galvanized the once dormant protectionist veto players.

Amid shifting interest group demands, however, South Korea's FTA strategy maintains its top-down momentum that is centered on presidential leadership and government institutions. Under President Kim, strong executive power and public support for neoliberal restructuring allowed the introduction of new FTA initiative. Under President Roh, the OMT took over the driver's seat from the president who suffered low popularity even among his once-loyal supporters.[19] As a champion of neoliberal economic ideas, the OMT is relatively insulated from the pressure of special interest groups, which in turn prevents this government agency from obtaining sufficient public support for FTAs.[20] Nevertheless the abolition of the Foreign Economic Council under the Presidential Committee for National Economy in early 2006 after its operation as a monitoring body for the previous two years expanded the OMT's institutional authority. In addition, a presidential committee to facilitate a KORUS FTA and to win over its opponents was set up in August 2006 under the leadership of the former OMT minister and the former Minister of Finance and Economy Han Duk-soo, who successfully shielded the OMT from its critics.[21] Above all, President Roh's trust in the OMT and in Trade Minister Kim remained firm and steadfast despite criticism.

Roh's endorsement of the OMT and KORUS FTA negotiations reflected his own sense of urgency. On various occasions, President Roh asserted: "China is surging. Japan is reviving. Trapped between China and Japan, South Korea desperately needs to develop a strategy to cope with current challenges. One of the most effective ways to accomplish this goal is to improve our country's competitive edge against China and Japan in the US market by concluding a KORUS FTA."[22] To be sure, South Korea's falling market share in the United States increased his sense of urgency. For the past two decades, it has fallen from the peak of 4.2 percent in 1989 to 2.5 percent in 2006, while both Chinese and Japanese shares continued to rise (KOTRA, 2007).[23]

For South Korea, the KORUS FTA is the largest FTA ever, as the United States is South Korea's third-largest trading partner. Many studies predict that the KORUS FTA would most likely benefit South Korea's export industries such as automobiles and electronics, albeit at the expense of its less competitive agricultural and service sectors (Schott and Choi, 2001; Sohn, 2001). Undoubtedly, the KORUS FTA has the potential to alter the dynamics of US-South Korean economic relations. In addition, the KORUS FTA has the potential to alter the dynamics of East Asian economic relations. With respect to spillover effects, many in Japan and China have already expressed concern that the US-South Korean accord could put their countries at a competitive disadvantage in the American and South Korean markets. Such recognition might motivate both Tokyo and Beijing to seek FTAs with Seoul and Washington.[24] In spring 2008, both Seoul and Tokyo called for joint efforts to resume the South Korea–Japan FTA negotiations, which have been stalled since November 2004. Meanwhile, private/semiprivate research institutions in Seoul and Beijing began studying the feasibility of a South Korea–China FTA.

In addition to the goal of maximizing the gains from trade and investment, South Korea wanted to hedge against the growing strategic uncertainties in

Table 9.2 Key side-payments under President Roh Moo-hyun

	Target groups	Size of side-payments	In return for
Ratification stage of the Korea–Chile FTA (2004)	Agricultural and fishery industries	Over $80 billion of public and private funds over a ten-year period	partial opening of agricultural and fishery markets
Negotiation stage of the KORUS FTA (2006–07)	Movie industry	$400 million government fund	cutting of annual screen quota in favor of the US
	Agricultural and fishery industries	Cash allowances for seven years	to compensate for up to 85 percent of income losses
		Government subsidies for five years	if they went out of business
	Manufacturing and service industries	Low-interest loans	if they lose more than 25 percent of their sales
		Subsidies of up to 75 percent of their payroll for one year	if they switch into other industries or relocate their employees
		Cash incentives of up to $600 a month to companies	if they hire farmers and fishermen who have been dislocated from their work

Northeast Asia by cementing its security-embedded economic ties with the United States. With the divergence in perspectives on coping with the rise of China, the nuclear adventurism of North Korea, and the general tensions in the alliance, relations between the United States and South Korea have steadily deteriorated in the post–September 11 period. In particular, the US decision to move away from a "tripwire" strategy by shifting troops away from the demilitarized zone (DMZ) to the south of Seoul has raised questions about joint command issues, and the eventual number of troops in South Korea (Aggarwal and Koo, 2007). Under these circumstances, the KORUS FTA may greatly contribute to bolstering diplomatic and security relations between the two traditional allies.[25]

These developments under Roh strongly support the competition hypothesis that countries will counteract the FTA policies of their competitors in terms of market shares and regional leadership, and that business and economic bureaucrats concerned with trade and investment diversion and/or politicians and government officials focused on the foreign policy implications of FTAs should be the main agents behind the country's trade policy shift.

To summarize, in contrast to the emulative *but* reactive approach taken by the Kim government, the multitrack FTA initiative of Roh government has adopted a competitive *and* proactive stance, both domestically and internationally. Most notably, the OMT has institutionalized the idea of pursuing economic reforms and cementing strategic partnerships through FTAs. Its neoliberal leanings notwithstanding, it should be noted that Roh's FTA strategy has in fact built upon South Korea's longstanding embedded liberal tradition. South Korea's developmental state has provided minimum safeguards for uncompetitive sectors and rural areas through multi-layered formal and informal trade barriers, although they were largely exploited in favor of competitive, export-oriented sectors and urban areas.[26] The Roh administration chose to combine generous side-payments with its market opening commitments in order to cushion its citizens from the vagaries of the international economy in return for public support for openness.[27] As summarized in Table 9.2, the success of its proactive negotiations has been achieved by embedded liberalism consisting of generous compensation packages to support those who suffer damages from FTAs.

Conclusions

This chapter has investigated South Korea's dramatic embrace of FTAs in the post–Asian financial crisis period. The motivations of the political leadership as well as the new bureaucratic balance of power have played a significant role in South Korea's rush toward FTAs. Although South Korea's pursuit of FTAs does not necessarily mean that it has completely abandoned the multilateral trading system, the policy departure from multilateralism to a multilayered approach including FTAs is increasingly becoming obvious and significant.

Within South Korea's policy circles, a more favorable view of FTAs as potential building blocks has replaced the traditional view that FTAs are a stumbling block for strengthening global multilateralism. Such a cognitive shift began to take place during the Kim Dae-jung administration and took firm roots under the Roh Moo-hyun administration, particularly the OMT. With a growing confidence in negotiating and implementing FTAs, South Korea's FTA policy has become proactive rather than just being reactive in its goal and partner selection. At the same time, South Korea's FTA strategy has evolved from an emulative to a competitive strategy, thus making the country's FTA track records more interesting in both theoretical and empirical terms.

South Korea's FTA frenzy has been shaped largely by a top-down political momentum rather than a bottom-up societal demand. Most notably, the economic crisis at the end of the 1990s contributed to the rise of reform-minded Kim Dae-jung and the downfall of many domestic veto holders. Such domestic dynamics in turn provided peculiarly favorable ground for sowing the seeds of FTAs as an emulative strategy in the face of burgeoning interest in FTAs in other parts of East Asia. In pursuit of his emulative vision of regional and economic diplomacy, President Kim was drawn to bilateral and minilateral FTAs, which also held political appeal because some sensitive sectors could be excluded from trade liberalization. As a result, South Korea's trade strategy successfully shifted its focus from global multilateralism to regional/cross-regional bilateralism and minilateralism. However, the Kim government's approach was designed to minimize the potential costs of FTAs rather than to maximize the gains from them. It also lacked a clear linkage between FTAs and other reform policies, thus leaving the FTA policy inherently passive without consistent or strategic goals.

To a large extent, President Kim's grand regionalist vision and neoliberal economic reforms inspired his successor, President Roh Moo-hyun. Yet President Roh did not have the luxuries of popular support and diplomatic capacity that President Kim had once enjoyed. More recently, South Korea's protectionist interests seem to have become galvanized and empowered again by their coalition with labor unions and leftist NGOs, whereas pro-liberalization business lobbies have fallen short of providing equivalent political support to the government. Nonetheless, the FTA initiative has become a core element of the Roh government's economic policy reforms. Among others, the enlarged role of the OMT has steadily institutionalized the idea and practice of promoting economic reform and strategic partnership through FTAs.

Indeed, FTAs have been the main agent behind South Korea's trade policy shift since the late 1990s. Its multi-track FTA strategy, which has both emulative and competitive components, has been quite successful in concluding a series of bilateral and minilateral FTAs with countries both within and outside the region. South Korea's success has the potential to greatly alter the dynamics of East Asian FTA frenzy by creating both emulative and competitive spillover effects among its peers. Under the new presidential leadership of Lee Myung-bak, South Korea is likely to continue playing a pivotal role in pursuing FTAs, as the country is close to conclude FTAs with big trading partners such as the EU and India.

However, there is an important caveat to this conclusion. The polarization of South Korean politics in the first half of 2008 over the thorny issue of importing US beef reminds us that FTA policymaking occurs in an environment of multiple, competing international and domestic interests.[28] As elsewhere in the world, FTA games are multilayered in South Korea. As Putnam's two-level-game metaphor indicates, besides making moves on an international game board, policymakers also have to maneuver on a domestic board to obtain support at home for their FTA initiatives. Because moves on one game board affect play on the other, neither level can be ignored. As a result, it is often difficult to know where FTA policy ends and domestic politics begins.

Notes

1. A veto player is a person or group who can effectively block the passage of a piece of legislation. For a more detailed discussion about the effect of veto players on policymaking in general, see Tsebelis (1995) and Cox and McCubbins (2001).

2. Peter Evans originally used the term "embedded autonomy" to demonstrate that successful developmental states in East Asia tend to be immersed in a dense network of ties that bind them to groups or classes that can become allies in the pursuit of societal goals. According to him, embeddedness provides sources of intelligence and channels of implementation, which enhance the competence of the state. In his logic, therefore, the idea of the state as midwife comes to the fore: states foster industry by changing social structures, by assisting in the emergence of new social groups and interests. Evans points out the impressive institutional constructions that went with embedded autonomy in Korea in contrast to the often inconsistent state efforts by Brazil and India to generate local entrepreneurial groups in the 1960s and 1970s (Evans, 1995).

3. Under the IMF-mandated austerity program, the real GDP growth rate plummeted from 5.0 percent in 1997 to −5.8 percent in 1998, while real consumption and investment fell by 8.2 percent and 21.1 percent, respectively, during the same period. After the exchange rate readjustment, South Korea's per capita income fell from $10,037 to $6,823 (Pyo, 1999: 12).

4. For more details about an econometric analysis of the impacts of FTAs, see Chapter 2 of this volume.

5. South Korea decided to start negotiations with the United States despite serious concerns about potentially lopsided negotiations due to the US dominant position in the global economy. Furthermore, South Korea's decision to pursue a KORUS FTA goes beyond the logic of policy diffusion and fear of exclusion. South Korea has not made it a secret that it wishes to use a successful accord with the United States as a diplomatic and economic leverage in regional affairs, particularly in its relations with China and Japan (Aggarwal and Koo, 2006).

6. The share of agriculture, forestry, and fisheries in South Korea's total employment decreased continuously from 17.9 percent in 1990 to 8.1 percent in 2004. The three sectors' share in South Korea's GDP was less than four percent in 2003 (MOFE, 2005).

7. A survey conducted by the Federation of Korean Industries (2001) on member entrepreneurs' attitudes toward FTA showed that 87 percent of the 53 respondents recognized the positive economic effects of FTAs. 94.3 percent of the respondents had concerns about the case where South Korea is left alone while other Asia-Pacific countries are busy negotiating FTA deals with a number of South Korea's trading partners.

8. An OECD survey (2003) notes that flexible factor markets were an important aspect of recovering high growth in South Korea with rapid structural change in the aftermath of the financial crisis. Indeed the financial crisis produced dramatic socioeconomic changes. The South Korean economy experienced huge layoffs as well as wild fluctuations in capital flows until the economy rebounded in 1999. The once-rigid South Korean labor market became more flexible, as indicated by the growing proportion of temporary and daily workers, and the emergence of a dualistic labor market. The proportion of nonregular workers increased from 42.5 percent of total employees in 2000 to 52 percent in 2002.

9. In democracies, domestic politics exert a great influence on the choice of trade forums. For instance, if a government has to appease conflicting interest groups in the domestic political marketplace as economic liberalization proceeds apace, it would most likely prioritize forums that allow it to exert greater control over the pace and scope of liberalization. Using the case of Japan, Pekkanen et al. (2007) aptly demonstrate the importance of the *gains-control tradeoff* in trade forum shopping.

10. Apart from his vision for regional institutions such as the East Asia Vision Group (EAVG) and the ASEAN-plus-three (APT), President Kim announced in his 2002 New Year's message to the nation that his government would shortly launch the Northeast Asian Business Hub State Initiative, while permanently pursuing financial and corporate reforms in a market friendly manner (*Chosun Ilbo*, January 14, 2002).

11. The APT proposal was first discussed in the mid-1990s in preparation of the inaugural ASEAN–Europe Meeting (ASEM). European countries could coordinate their participation relatively easily through the EU, but East Asian counterparts lacked such an institutional arrangement. ASEAN thus asked Japan, South Korea, and China to participate in a preliminary ministerial meeting, which took place in 1995. The ministerial meeting was later supplemented by a summit meeting in Kuala Lumpur on the occasion of the annual ASEAN leaders' meeting in December 1997. After a second leaders' meeting, a year later, the group agreed to make the dialogue an annual affair. Since 1999, the scope of the dialogue has expanded to include separate ministerial meetings under the rubric of APT rather than simply as preparation sessions for the ASEM meeting. For more details, see Stubbs (2002).

12. The EAVG also studied a joint surveillance mechanism for short-term capital movements and an early financial warning system. The group later proposed the establishment of an East Asian Monetary Fund and a regional exchange rate coordination mechanism, with the long-term goal of creating a common currency area. Other recommendations included upgrading the annual APT meetings to an East Asian Summit and establishment of the East Asian Free Trade Area (Moon, 2005).

13. In February 1998, President Kim announced that he would pursue what he called the "Sunshine Policy" with North Korea in hopes of encouraging greater discussion and cooperation with Pyongyang, as inspired by the old Aesop's fable about the sun getting more results than the fierce wind. In December 2000, the Norwegian Nobel Committee, in recognition of his "extraordinary and lifelong works for democracy and human rights in South Korea and East Asia in general, and for peace and reconciliation with North Korea in particular," awarded him the Nobel Peace Prize.

14. The US President George W. Bush and the Japanese Prime Minister Junichiro Koizumi entered office in 2001. Hu Jintao and Roh Moo-hyun were elected presidents of the People's Republic of China and the Republic of Korea, respectively, in 2003. All these leaders were characterized as defiant and dogmatic—rather than pragmatic—in their foreign policy orientation, thus often causing diplomatic spats with one another.

15. As a result of the 1998 government organization reforms that were intended to consolidate institutional support for President Kim's reform agenda, the OMT was formed under the Ministry of Foreign Affairs and Trade (MOFAT) with a mission to comprehensively establish and conduct foreign policies on trade, trade negotiations, and foreign economic affairs. Although its institutional legitimacy was shaky at first, the OMT slowly but steadily set in motion the changes in bureaucratic balance of power, and thus began to play a leadership role in foreign trade affairs (Koo, 2006).

16. For the critics of neoliberal economic policy as well as hardcore Korean nationalists, Trade Minister Kim is a bad choice not only because he advocates neoliberal economic policies, but also because he grew up in the United States and was trained as a US lawyer, which allegedly undermines his nationalist credential.

17. South Korea's screen quota system was designed to stem a flood of Hollywood blockbusters. South Korea cut the quota from the current 146 days or 40 percent

reserved for domestic films to 73 days or 20 percent starting on July 1, 2006 ("Screen Quota Cut Clears Way for Trade Deal with the US," *Chosun Ilbo*, January 26, 2006).

18. In March 2006, for instance, a coalition was formed bringing together some 300 anti-KORUS FTA groups, thus becoming the largest coalition ever on a single policy issue during the Roh administration. Its core membership consisted of farmers and film industry people, who would most likely suffer from a successful KORUS FTA. At the same time, this ad-hoc coalition included a number of anti-American and leftist organizations such as the Korean Federation of Trade Unions, the Korean Teachers and Education Workers Union, and the Korean Federation of University Student Councils. In May 2006, many of these radical groups also organized violent protests against the relocation of the US Forces Headquarters in South Korea from Seoul to Pyongtaek, a small city south of Seoul, leading to charges that the anti-KORUS FTA protests turned into an anti-American movement.

19. The OMT's neoliberal policy orientation has been further highlighted by the appointment of its third trade minister, Kim Hyun-chong, in July 2004 as well as the promotion of its first trade minister Han Duk-soo (1998–2004) to deputy prime minister and minister of finance and economy. The OMT's authority has been expanded as indicated by the abolition of the Foreign Economic Council under the Presidential Committee for National Economy in early 2006 after its operation as a monitoring body for the past two years. In addition, a presidential committee to facilitate a KORUS FTA and to win over its opponents was set up in August 2006 under the leadership of the former OMT minister and the former deputy prime minister Han Duk-soo, who is most likely to shield the OMT from its critics.

20. Of course, this does not mean that the OMT operates in political vacuum. Apart from its critics and public opinion, the OMT closely consults various private business councils as well as the National Economic Advisory Council under the President's Office as well. Yet in contrast to its counterpart ministries in the government such as the Ministry of Finance and Economy (MOFE), the Ministry of Commerce, Industry, and Energy (MOCIE), and the Ministry of Agriculture and Forestry (MOAF), the OMT rarely consults small firms and individual farmers directly, while putting much more emphasis on the feedback from big business and industry associations such as the Federation of Korean Industries, the Korea International Trade Association, and the Korea Federation of Small and Medium Business (Lee, 2006: 7).

21. *Chosun Ilbo*, July 24, 2006.

22. A presidential speech delivered to the Korea Chamber of Commerce and Industry on March 28, 2006. Available from http://news.naver.com/news/read.php?mode=LOD&office_id=023&article_id=0000178504. Accessed on May 3, 2008.

23. In a press conference on August 9, 2006, President Roh reaffirmed his commitment to FTAs and urged his people to embrace the tide of globalization wholeheartedly, instead of trying to dodge what liberals of today's world see as an unstoppable and inevitable phenomenon. In addition, he rejected the flying geese pattern of development based on the Japanese model, and insisted that such economic development strategy had already outlived its utility for South Korea. His assertion, instead, was that South Korea should find its economic future in service industries, departing from its traditional focus on manufacturing (*Yonhap News*, August 9, 2006).

24. "Chinese Premier Hopes for FTA with Korea 'Soon,'" *Chosun Ilbo*, April 6, 2007.

25. Many policy experts in Seoul share this view. For instance, Yoon Young-kwan, who served as the first Minister of Foreign Affairs and Trade of the Roh administration stressed that an FTA with the United States would be a useful means to promote South Korea's role as an economic hub country in East Asia. He argued that a KORUS FTA would be compatible with South Korea's globalization strategy that began in the early 1990s under President Kim Young-sam. For Yoon, it was important for South Korea to improve its competitive edge in high value-added service industries. He also emphasized that cementing economic ties with the United States is strategically important because South Korea's future lies in how to coordinate with Washington to ensure the peaceful resolution of the current North Korean nuclear crisis (A speech delivered to a conference organized by the Association of Junior High and High School Teachers, Jeju Island, July 24, 2006). For the details about the economics–security nexus, see Koo (2008).
26. For more discussions about South Korea's developmental state, see Amsden (1989) and Woo-Cumings (1999).
27. For instance, the ratification of the Korea–Chile FTA in February 2004 was followed by the passage of a special law designed to make up for the potential financial damages to farming and fishing industries due to FTAs. Despite criticism for the government's excessive financial commitment to declining sectors, over $80 billion of public and private funds have been earmarked for farming and fishing rescue programs over a ten-year period (MOFAT, 2004). Other examples include a series of side-payment pledges in the form of government subsidies and grant-in-aid during the KORUS FTA negotiations. In March 2006, the Roh government pledged to provide the Korean movie industry with a government fund amounting to $400 million instead of cutting South Korea's annual screen quota in favor of the US ("Will the Post-Screen Quota Measures Be Effective?," *Chosun Ilbo*, January 27, 2006). The Roh government also committed itself to provide cash allowances for seven years to compensate for up to 85 percent of income losses of farmers and fishermen once the KORUS FTA went into effect. Besides this, Korean farmers and fishermen would receive government subsidies for five years if they went out of business due to the KORUS FTA. Furthermore, to boost investment in agriculture, the Korean government would encourage the creation of private agricultural investment funds, and agriculture-related companies would be allowed to bring in CEOs from outside the industry. The government would also offer low-interest loans to businesses that lose more than 25 percent of their sales due to the KORUS FTA, while they would be eligible for receiving subsidies of up to 75 percent of their payroll for one year if they switch into other industries or relocate their employees. The government would also provide cash incentives of up to $600 a month to companies that hire farmers and fishermen who have been dislocated from their work ("Government to Pay Farmers, Fishermen for FTA Losses," *Chosun Ilbo*, May 18, 2008).
28. In April 2008, the Lee administration decided to resume importing the controversial US beef, which had been banned for fear of mad cow disease. By working so hard on the controversial beef issue, the Lee administration wished to impress both White House and Congress with Seoul's seriousness about removing any obstacles to the ratification of the KORUS FTA on both sides of the Pacific. However, such a wishful thinking backfired as it downplayed public concerns about mad cow disease, both reasonable and unreasonable. As it turned out, the Lee administration remained virtually paralyzed for several months until summer.

10
Japan's Competitive FTA Strategy: Commercial Opportunity versus Political Rivalry

Mireya Solís

Japan's decision to join the FTA (free trade agreement) frenzy is best explained as an instance of policy diffusion whereby the prior actions of other FTA nations created strong pressure for Japan to reverse its half-century of exclusive support for the multilateral system. The literature on policy diffusion has identified two major forces for the spread of economic policies (in this case preferential trade accords): ideational dissemination (emulation) whereby new policy paradigms become predominant, or competition whereby the search for relative advantage induces governments to embrace policies likely to yield economic, political, or rule-making benefits.

In this chapter, I argue that competitive dynamics best explain Japan's FTA policy shift. Japan has used its FTAs to meet three main challenges: (1) to restore or advance the competitive advantage of internationally oriented business sectors in selected overseas markets; (2) to disseminate a distinct Japanese approach to preferential economic integration different both from the American and Chinese FTAs; and (3) to hone its regional leadership credentials vis-à-vis China by reaching out to Southeast Asian nations, and inviting extra-regional partners to integration talks in order to balance China's influence. However, the need to respond to multiple competitive pressures has heavily taxed Japanese FTA policy. The Japanese government has confronted a major dilemma: whether to meet the demands of the business sector to negotiate a bilateral FTA with China that maximizes economic returns, or whether to heed the calls from politicians that see in China an emerging rival and in economic integration an important venue to stake Japan's claim to regional leadership.

Moreover, while the origins of Japan's FTA policy cannot be found in isolated domestic pressures, it is undeniable that national policymaking patterns influence the way Japan articulates its FTA strategy. Japan's fragmented decision-making process, also known as "patterned pluralism,"[1] gives interest groups (e.g., from business and agriculture) influence over the direction of Japanese trade policy. However, two recent developments are likely to influence Japan's ability to meet competitive pressures through FTA policy: the attempts to centralize policymaking in order to decrease the power of the farm subgovernment, and the growing politicization of foreign economic policy with the weakening of the traditional division of economics and politics in relations with China, and the pursuit of security-driven FTAs.

This chapter is organized as follows. The first section highlights the main traits of Japanese FTA policy. The second section analyzes the FTA policy shift in order to assess the competing hypotheses on FTA dissemination: emulation versus competition. The next three sections examine Japanese FTA policy from the vantage points of economic, legal, and security competition. The concluding section discusses the impact of these multiple competitive pressures on Japan's FTA policy.

Overview of Japan's FTA initiatives

Roughly a decade after first entertaining the possibility of negotiating preferential trade accords, Japan has rapidly built an FTA network: as of February 2009, Japan had nine FTAs in effect [Singapore, Mexico, Malaysia, Chile, Thailand, Brunei, Indonesia, the Philippines, and the Association of Southeast Asian Nations (ASEAN)]; had signed preferential trade deals with Vietnam and Switzerland; and was in active negotiations with the Gulf Cooperation Council (GCC) nations, Australia and India (see Table 10.1). This table also shows that bilateral FTAs gained traction first, as Japan lined up trade agreements with individual Southeast Asian nations, and Mexico and Chile, while negotiations with ASEAN as a whole proceeded slowly, and the initiative to launch an Comprehensive Economic Partnership for East Asia or CEPEA (comprising the ASEAN+6 members) has not yet materialized, given the disagreements with China over the core membership of an East Asian trade bloc. On the other hand, the volume of trade and investment flows comprising these bilateral FTAs is rather modest—never exceeding the four percent ceiling (with the exception of the FTA with Korea which is deadlocked), while the ASEAN-wide FTA promises to yield more economic benefits.

Another noteworthy characteristic of the Japanese FTAs is their broad issue coverage. The Japanese government has attempted to include multiple WTO-plus commitments in areas such as intellectual property, government procurement, temporary entry of business people, and customs facilitation. But the trademark issue of Japan's trade agreements is the economic cooperation chapter (covering areas such as science and technology, small enterprises, human resource development, and improvement of the business climate), so much so that the Japanese government has coined a different term to refer to its preferential trade deals: Economic Partnership Agreements. Despite the attempt to negotiate encompassing FTAs, Table 10.1 shows that the implementation of this Japanese formula has not been completely homogeneous. Due to Malaysia's *bumiputra* policy (of giving priority to ethnic

Table 10.1 Japan's FTA network (as of February 2009)

Partner	Status	Trade volume*		FDI volume*	Issue scope				
		Export share	Import share	Outflow share	Investment	Service	Environment	Labor	Economic cooperation
Singapore	In force (2002)	3.60	1.53	1.80	Yes	Yes	No	No	Yes
Mexico	In force (2005)	1.00	0.53	0.70	Yes	Yes	No	No	Yes
Malaysia	In force (2006)	2.60	3.44	0.60	Yes†	Yes	No	No	Yes
Chile	In force (2007)	0.10	0.75	0.10	Yes	Yes	No	No	No
Thailand	In force (2007)	3.10	3.00	2.10	Yes	Yes	No	No	Yes
Philippines	In force (2008)	2.00	1.84	1.10	Yes	Yes	No	No	Yes
Indonesia	In force (2008)	1.50	4.21	1.40	Yes	Yes	No	No	Yes
Brunei	In force (2008)	0.00	0.00	0.00	Yes	Yes	No	No	Yes
ASEAN	In force (2008)	13.30	15.26	14.86	No‡	No	No	No	Yes
Vietnam	Signed (2008)	0.50	0.75	0.20	No	Yes	No	No	Yes
Switzerland	Signed (2009)	0.40	0.99	0.20	Yes	Yes	No	No	No
Korea	Negotiation suspended	6.70	4.92	1.60	–	–	–	–	–
GCC (6)	Negotiation (2006)	0.38	10.63	0.05	–	–	–	–	–
Australia	Negotiation (2007)	2.00	4.09	2.50	–	–	–	–	–
India	Negotiation (2007)	0.50	0.63	0.40	–	–	–	–	–
ASEAN+6	Initiative only (2006)	31.90	42.96	15.98	–	–	–	–	–

* Trade and foreign direct investment (FDI) shares represent averages for the years 1999–2004.

† The Japan–Malaysia FTA does not provide WTO (World Trade Organization)-plus concessions on elimination of performance requirements or on government procurement.

‡ The Japan–ASEAN FTA does not adopt new and binding obligations on investment and services, but calls for a committee to explore these issues one year after enactment.

Sources: Japan Ministry of Foreign Affairs (MOFA) web site; trade data from JETRO (Japan External Trade Organization), 2005; and MOF's trade statistics. (http://www.customs.go.jp/toukei/suii/html/time_e.htm), FDI data from MOF's web site http://www.mof.go.jp/english/elc008.htm.

Malays on government contracts and hiring practices), the trade agreement with Japan does not include WTO-plus provisions on the elimination of performance requirements and excludes government procurement.[2] The FTA with Chile includes provisions on the improvement of the business climate, but does not incorporate a full-fledged chapter on economic cooperation. More importantly, the Japan–ASEAN FTA does not include new and binding obligations on investment and services, but only the vague proviso to establish a committee to explore these issues after the enactment of the agreement.

Finally, a very important trait of Japanese FTAs is the asymmetry in liberalization commitments. Market opening is very high (as evaluated by the percentage of tariff lines to be eliminated or reduced) in industrial goods, but markedly less in agricultural commodities due to longer calendars for liberalization and outright exceptions for agricultural commodities. The percentage of Japanese agricultural tariff lines excluded from liberalization in Japanese FTAs is very elevated: 61 percent with Singapore, 41 percent with Mexico, and 55 percent with Malaysia (Cheong and Cho, 2006).[3]

Summing up, there is no question that FTAs have become a major component of Japanese trade policy with 15 such different negotiations initiated in the last decade. Why then has Japan embraced an FTA strategy? Is the new trade policy a response to isolated domestic pressures (independent decision-making), or on the contrary is it best understood as an instance of policy diffusion (interdependent policymaking)? Are Japan's FTA outcomes (selection of partners, sectoral coverage, and issue scope) better explained by emulation or competition dynamics? The remainder of this chapter explores these issues.

Japan joins the FTA frenzy: Dissemination dynamics

Two main actors (trade bureaucrats housed in the Ministry of International Trade and Industry or MITI [METI since 2001][4] and big business as represented by its peak association Keidanren) pushed for a re-direction of Japanese trade policy to experiment for the first time with preferential trade accords. The actions of these actors were fundamentally oriented by the need to respond to the prior FTAs of other nations deemed to put Japanese companies at a disadvantage in overseas markets. The North American Free Trade Agreement (NAFTA), in particular, sent a powerful message on the negative effects of trade and investment diversion that Japanese firms and the government expected would magnify with the non-stop proliferation of FTAs in the world economy. Competitive pressures, therefore, provided the essential stimulus for FTA diffusion in Japan.

Japanese trade bureaucrats first began discussing the possibility of joining the new wave of FTAs in the summer of 1998 as they were approached by Mexico to explore a bilateral trade deal.[5] The Japanese business community was supportive, and so METI launched a study to assess the merits of embarking on a completely new path for international trade negotiations (Hatakeyama, 2002). METI's internal report noted the importance of developing additional trade policy options—especially in a context of rapidly proliferating FTAs and stagnation in the WTO front—and identified in FTAs as well a good opportunity to pursue domestic structural reform. A main concern for trade officials was that Japan lagged behind, as other countries were developing multi-track trade policies (multilateral, regional, bilateral) to advance their economic interests. Acquiring the same policy tools as their counterparts enjoyed was, consequently, a main motivation to launch an FTA policy.

Although METI's consideration of an FTA track had been triggered by the Mexican overture, the ministry opted for negotiations with Korea first. METI's actions reflected political pragmatism since it considered easier to garner the support of politicians and the public in favor of the new FTA policy if it negotiated first with a neighboring Asian country, and not with a much more distant Latin American nation.[6] Negotiations with Korea bogged down, however, due to concerns about a major expansion in Korea's trade deficit with Japan. In the end, Singapore was selected as Japan's first FTA partner largely due to its offer to exclude agriculture from the talks (Terada, 2006b: 1).

Undeterred by the opposition of the agricultural lobby, Keidanren continued to demand an FTA with Mexico (Keidanren, 1999, 2000; Yoshimatsu, 2005). Japanese firms complained that the absence of a bilateral Japan–Mexico FTA placed them at a disadvantage vis-à-vis their American rivals (and later on European companies as Mexico signed an FTA with Europe in 2000) given the relatively high Mexican tariffs (on average 16 percent) and discretionary changes in Mexico's economic policy that frequently applied *only* to non-FTA firms. But beyond these general concerns, Japanese firms in the automobiles, electronics, and government procurement industries considered NAFTA a serious competitive threat to their operations in North America.

The automobile industry complained that NAFTA's strict rules of origin (ROOs) and the continued imposition by the Mexican government of performance requirements (requiring local production for a limited quota of duty-free vehicle imports) made it difficult to compete with American carmakers with more developed regional production networks and to benefit from the expansion of Mexican auto imports in the late 1990s and early 2000s (Nakahata, 2005). Japanese electronic firms, which had flocked to the Mexican export platform program (*maquiladora*) in the late 1980s to create a major supply base of consumer electronic goods (most notably color TVs) for the US market, were deeply worried by the NAFTA-mandated elimination of duty drawback benefits. And Japanese general trading companies and plant exporters were finally squeezed out of the Mexican government procurement market, when Mexico announced in May 2003 that only FTA firms could tender bids. METI was now ready to push for a more ambitious FTA and widely circulated a report quantifying the economic losses for Japan from NAFTA's trade diversion (in the order of 3.2 billion dollars with 31,824 jobs lost) (Solís and Katada, 2007b: 289).[7]

The successful negotiation of the FTA with Mexico did in many ways open the door for a more active FTA policy since it represented the first occasion in which Japan made WTO-plus concessions in agriculture—with Singapore, Japan merely bound the zero-percent tariffs that were de facto in effect (Lincoln, 2004). This was a major advance considering the strong clout that the agricultural lobby (the iron triangle of agricultural cooperatives, ruling party politicians, and farm bureaucrats) has had over trade policy. The extreme bureaucratic sectionalism and the informal norm of unanimity have given the agricultural lobby veto power over Japan's international negotiations involving agricultural liberalization (Fukui, 1978). In fact, it took an unprecedented top-down intervention by the then Prime Minister Koizumi to break the deadlock over meager agricultural concessions in talks with Mexico. Undoubtedly, some structural changes also facilitated this break-through: such as the contraction of the farming population, intra-agricultural rifts,[8] and changes in the electoral system deemed to weaken the influence of the farm vote (e.g., re-districting to correct rural over-representation, and shift to single member districts to encourage issue-based electoral competition and not pork barrel).

But far from representing the defeat of Japanese agricultural protectionism, FTA policy reflects a political compromise whereby the agricultural lobby does not veto the preferential trade agreements but makes sure that its primordial interests are protected. For instance, in all Japanese FTAs, key primary commodities (rice, sugar, wheat, plywood) are off limits, and even in the case of Mexico, tariff-rate quotas (TRQs) were implemented for the most sensitive products (pork, beef, chicken, oranges, and orange juice) and no preferential tariff for chicken was established by the signing of the agreement, lest Thai trade officials use that preferential tariff in their own FTA negotiations with Japan.[9] The recent launch of FTA talks with Australia could indeed represent a turning point since it is the first time Japan is negotiating with a major supplier of agricultural goods in the Japanese market (representing ten percent of all Japanese agricultural imports). However, the use of "exclusions" and "renegotiations" is likely to continue as Australian trade officials have acknowledged that the sensitivities of Japan's agricultural products ought to be factored in the negotiations (Joint study, 2006: 10).[10]

This analysis of Japan's FTA policy shift underscores the importance of competitive pressures (the perceived need to cope with trade and investment diversion effects from proliferating FTAs), and the central role that internationalized business sectors and trade bureaucrats played in championing the new policy. It also underscores how international diffusion pressures must be directed through domestic policymaking channels, which in the case of Japan, meant the cooptation of the agricultural lobby into the new FTA policy by sheltering the most sensitive commodities from liberalization. Japan's ability to meet international competitive pressures through FTA policy is very much influenced by these domestic political constraints. And these internal political battles are likely to intensify as the degree of ambition in Japanese FTA policy has grown quickly: from the original defensive goals to encompass broader economic, legal, and political objectives.

Japan's FTA policy through the logic of economic competition

From defending to expanding market access abroad

Soon after the initial policy shift, Japanese companies became interested in using FTAs to revamp their production networks in East Asia in order to achieve long-standing goals of integrating and streamlining their regional production networks, and to forestall the advances of rival MNCs in Southeast Asian countries, which in the aftermath of the Asian financial crisis had courted more aggressively FDI and export production to increase foreign exchange earnings (Manger, 2005). FTAs would facilitate local and regional supply of parts (to decrease reliance on expensive imported parts from Japan) and would allow Japanese affiliates in the region to enjoy the benefits of specialization and economies of scale by serving larger regional markets. In this way, FTAs were deemed essential to maintain the competitive presence of Japanese multinationals in the region, especially in countries like Thailand where American firms were awarded national treatment status through the Treaty of Amity and Economic Relations, and where Chinese exporters were to enjoy preferential access through the China–ASEAN FTA (Keidanren, 2003).

Bilateral FTAs with the largest ASEAN nations (Thailand, the Philippines, Malaysia) were important vehicles to achieve both the proactive (rationalization of production networks and development of regional export platforms) and defensive (keep up with the competition from Chinese products and Western multinationals) goals of Japanese companies. Yet in one crucial area the demands of the business community have not been met: negotiating an FTA with China. Given the importance of China as a top destination for Japanese FDI and as an export platform to service regional and global markets, it is not surprising that in every survey of Japanese firms, China is selected as the top priority for FTA talks (JETRO, 2003; Kajita, 2004).

In fact, the Japanese business community has begun to demand preferential trade negotiations with its largest trading partners: China, the United States, and Europe. Korea's FTA negotiations with the latter two industrialized countries caught the attention of the Japanese business community. In particular, given Europe's high external tariffs in products in which Japanese companies face stiff competition from Korean rivals (such as automobiles and electronic appliances), Keidanren expects a major negative effect if Japan does not follow suit with an European FTA (Keidanren, 2007).

Evidently, competition with its two neighbors in Northeast Asia has affected the direction of Japanese FTA policy by increasing the premium of speeding up negotiations with ASEAN, and embarking on FTA talks with the United States and Europe. Reflecting these competitive pressures, METI announced in the spring of 2007 that concrete steps would be taken to launch FTA feasibility studies with these industrialized nations.[11] However, a fierce domestic political battle is to be expected between advocates and detractors of the FTA policy in Japan, given the large adjustment costs likely to ensue from negotiating with these large economies. Once more Japan is confronted with the dilemma of keeping up with international competition via FTAs while dealing with sizable domestic political constraints.

Japan's FTA policy through the logic of legal competition

Japan has abandoned its previous insistence on a consensual approach for regional trade agreements [*a la* the Asia Pacific Economic Cooperation (APEC)] in favor of FTAs with a higher degree of legalization. A major objective for Japan has been to gain leverage in the dissemination of international rules on trade and investment across *all* trade forums. Indeed, a key METI official involved in the 1998 intra-ministry deliberations on FTA policy noted that the countries lagging behind the FTA race were precisely the passive countries in negotiations at Geneva. In his view, FTA policy offered an opportunity to reenergize Japan's trade policy and to adopt a much more proactive position on trade and investment rule-making.[12] In this endeavor, MITI bureaucrats enjoyed full support from large business, as Keidanren from early on pushed for FTAs in order to propagate legal rules facilitating the operation of Japanese businesses overseas (Keidanren, 2000).

Japan's competitive legal strategy through FTAs has aimed to amend WTO provisions deemed harmful to Japanese corporate interests (antidumping), to spread new rules that can later on be incorporated at the WTO level (investment), and to elicit from developing countries, preferential commitments that surpass their WTO obligations in areas such as government procurement or intellectual property protection, and in so doing compete with China for the dissemination of a distinct Japanese FTA model that has a much broader issue scope and a higher degree of legalization.

Regarding the reform of existing WTO rules, the Japanese government and industry have long been dissatisfied with the multilateral antidumping code as they deem that American and European anti-circumvention practices and dumping methodologies result in discriminatory treatment of Japanese companies.[13] Japanese business interests identified in FTAs an opportunity to reform antidumping practices by incorporating in these agreements, clauses on the mutual non-application of antidumping duties, or by adopting new antidumping rules that could later on serve as a yardstick for reform at the WTO level (Keidanren, 2000: 6). And Keidanren monitors closely the treatment of antidumping in other FTAs noting, for instance, that any restrictions Korea is able to elicit in the United States' use of antidumping through KORUS should be incorporated as well in any future Japanese trade agreement with the United States (Keidanren, 2006: 6).

The attempt to use FTAs as standard-setting devices to fill gaps in multilateral regulation has gained traction particularly in the area of investment. Japan, as many other industrialized nations, has been interested in adopting a more ambitious investment code that goes beyond the WTO trade-related investment measures (TRIMs) chapter to encompass national treatment and most favored nation (MFN) status, investor-host state dispute settlement mechanisms, and further elimination of performance requirements (including clauses on mandatory employment of local nationals) (Keidanren, 2006). Initially, Japan had high hopes that such an agreement could be incorporated into the WTO charter as one of the four Singapore issues. But once investment was dropped from the Doha Round due to the opposition of developing countries, FTAs and bilateral investment treaties became the venues to pursue the establishment of international investment rules. Pekkanen (2008) notes a very strong correlation between the model investment chapter in FTAs offered by Keidanren and the actual provisions of Japan's trade agreements with Singapore and Mexico in that they offer nondiscriminatory treatment for multinationals, protection and compensation from regulatory expropriation, eliminate performance requirements, and provide state–state and state–investor dispute settlement mechanisms, among other elements.

Japan is also seeking WTO-plus commitments from its FTA counterparts in government procurement, services, and intellectual property protection. FTA negotiations with countries not partaking in the WTO's plurilateral agreement on government procurement are frequently the only way in which Japanese companies can gain a foothold on these markets and/or be able to offer competitive bids. The Japanese business community has also made national treatment a key priority in its service negotiations in FTAs, and has called for a tightening of enforcement mechanisms against counterfeiting in the intellectual property provisions of FTAs (Keidanren, 2006).

Japan has succeeded in negotiating FTAs with multiple WTO-plus provisions on these areas. However, as noted above, Japan was unable to secure substantial commitments on government procurement, services, and performance requirements in its FTAs with Malaysia and ASEAN. Moreover, it is important to note that Japanese FTAs reflect in fact a mix of legalism and voluntarism, rather than an outright endorsement of pure hard law. Japan has been unwilling to undertake binding and actionable commitments on competition policy, customs procedures, financial services, and economic cooperation. This last chapter in particular contains clauses on human resource development, promotion of small and medium sized enterprises, and improvement of the business climate, which are of interest to Japanese corporations in order to ensure the availability of high-skilled labor and supporting industries, and to gain direct access to host government officials to voice specific grievances hindering the climate of their business operations.[14] But all these cooperation clauses are nonbinding, and there are no direct ties to foreign aid disbursements either. The reason why Japan avoids hard obligations in the economic cooperation chapter is most likely the one-sided nature of these commitments: as the industrialized partner in these FTAs, Japan is expected to make most contributions. The coexistence of legalism and voluntarism in Japanese FTAs, therefore, corroborates Kahler's (2001) depiction of legalization strategies in East Asia as instrumental, in that legalization is a strategy that can be activated or deactivated to suit the competitive interests of corporations and governments.

Japan's legal competitive strategy has yielded an FTA approach different from both the NAFTA model and the Chinese trade agreements. Compared to the United States, Japan has shied away from binding obligations on financial liberalization, has not been interested in incorporating labor and environmental standards, and has emphasized an explicit cooperation/development approach to trade negotiations. On the other hand, Japan's FTAs are more comprehensive in terms of issue scope and legalistic (in terms of defining precise obligations and establishing dispute settlement mechanisms) than Chinese FTAs, which have been characterized as brief, vague, and with an emphasis on conciliation rather than formal dispute settlement (Antkiewicz and Whalley, 2005). In this way, China and Japan are offering different "models" of regional integration and rule-making, and the race is on to see which one disseminates further and fastest. A common perception in Japanese FTA policymaking circles is that China is prepared to negotiate narrower FTAs (affecting mostly tariffs on goods), but that it has skillfully lured East Asia by offering agricultural concessions through the Early Harvest Program. On the other hand, Japan is interested not only in tariff elimination but rule-setting, and the spread of high-quality FTAs is a key priority for government and business.[15] Thus, the dissemination of a distinct Japanese approach to preferential trading is a central concern in Japan's competitive FTA strategy, especially toward China, the other possible focal point for regional integration.

Japan's FTA policy through the logic of political competition

Japan's FTA policy is also influenced by two central concerns of its foreign policy: the maintenance of the US alliance (even as Japan departs from past precedent and now endorses regional integration bodies that do not include the United States), and the need to respond to China's rising stature in the region (which could eclipse Japan in terms of defining the tempo, substance, and membership of the regional integration process).

The slowdown of trans-Pacific cooperation forums [APEC and ARF (ASEAN Regional Forum)] and the proliferation of Asian FTAs do represent a significant challenge for the United States to remain actively engaged in the region, and for the United States and Japan to reiterate the centrality of their bilateral bond. For these reasons, Armitage and Nye's report (2007: 18) singles out the negotiation of a comprehensive bilateral FTA as one of the most effective economic means to strengthen the US–Japan alliance.

On the other hand, Sino-Japanese relations are in a moment of re-definition as both countries are confronted with the new realities of Chinese economic takeoff and military buildup, and rising nationalism in both Japan and China. Wan (2006: 334) notes that Japan and China have moved away from the friendship framework to a situation of limited rivalry in that they both have expanded their political, economic, and military objectives and view each other as an obstacle toward their realization.

Thus, as Japan fleshes out its FTA policy it must aim for a delicate political compromise between shoring up its key security alliance with the United States, displaying a commitment to the construction of Asian regional integration institutions, and striking the right balance between competition and cooperation in its dealings with China. These considerations have influenced Japanese FTA policy in at least three important dimensions: the selection of FTA partners, the competitive courting of Southeast Asian nations, and the attempt to define the contours of an East Asian trade bloc.

Political criteria in FTA partner selection

From the outset, political criteria have influenced the decision to select or bypass certain countries as FTA partners. As mentioned earlier, METI bureaucrats leaned in favor of South Korea as the first FTA counterpart, largely because they deemed this choice an easier political sell among politicians and domestic audiences. In characterizing FTAs as essentially "political coalitions" (Ogita, 2003: 241), METI was hoping to consolidate the new trade policy by pointing to the larger benefits for Japan's regional diplomacy.

The decision in the spring of 2007 to initiate FTA negotiations with Australia after a protracted process of consultations and feasibility studies is also explained along political lines. As Terada (2005: 16) notes, Prime Minister Koizumi decided to launch an official FTA feasibility study in order to reciprocate for the dispatch of Australian soldiers to protect the activities of Japanese Self-Defense Forces in Iraq. The security–economic connection was evident in the joint announcement by both governments to launch FTA talks *and* sign a "Japan–Australia Joint Declaration on Security Cooperation." This is a remarkable initiative for Japan since it had not established a close security partnership in the postwar period with any other country besides the United States. In fact, some agricultural watchers in Japan have decried the security–economic link for sacrificing agriculture for the sake of expanded security ties between Japan, Australia, and the United States (Ono, 2007).

But perhaps the single most important application of political criteria has resulted in the bypassing, so far, of China in the negotiation of a bilateral FTA, despite overwhelming business support for such an initiative. That the central preference of the business community has been ignored is remarkable for a country whose foreign economic policy is usually portrayed as supporting the overseas expansion of Japanese exporters and MNCs (Arase, 1995). The deterioration of bilateral relations with China has clearly limited the ability of Japanese business groups to lobby more actively for this FTA. Indeed, Sino-Japanese frictions increased due to the Japanese Prime Minister Koizumi's visits to the Yasukuni Shrine, territorial disputes over the Senkaku/ Daioyu Islands, and competition over gas deposits in the East China Sea; and they peaked in the spring of 2005 with massive anti-Japanese riots in several Chinese cities. However, broader domestic changes in the formulation of Japan's China policy have also affected the chances of the business community to find a sympathetic ear among Japanese politicians. For instance, Takamine (2002) notes a larger role for Liberal Democratic Party (LDP) politicians more attuned to sagging public opinion of China at the expense of MOFA bureaucrats concerned primarily with stable bilateral relations; and Katada (2007) highlights the important generational change, as many old China hands in the LDP have retired or passed away, and they have been supplanted by younger politicians with more assertive views on China.

Competitive courting of Southeast Asia

Southeast Asia is of great importance to Japan and China to achieve political and diplomatic goals. China is keen to cultivate relations with Southeast Asian countries in order to mitigate containment policies of the United States, discredit the "China Threat" theory, and further isolate Taiwan (Yang, 2003: 315). For these reasons, since 1997 China has been credited with pursuing a "charm strategy" that has included refraining from devaluation during the Asian financial crisis, signing a code of conduct on territorial disputes in the South China Sea in 2002, and signing ASEAN's Treaty of Amity and Cooperation (TAC) a year later (Dreyer, 2006: 545).

Japan has also endeavored to expand its ties to Southeast Asia beyond economic diplomacy in order to mitigate regional distrust toward Japan and to counter China's rising influence. This heightened attention to Southeast Asia is reflected in the Hashimoto doctrine of January 1997, which proposed regular summits with ASEAN leaders to discuss a broad range of issues; or through the New Miyazawa initiative in 1998, which committed 30 billion dollars to six East Asian countries undergoing financial crisis.

FTAs, in particular, afford China and Japan the opportunity to emphasize the joint gains of economic cooperation with ASEAN nations and advance these diplomatic goals (Hoadley and Yang, 2007; Munakata, 2001). The competitive dynamics at work are transparent in the series of moves and countermoves that have characterized Japanese and Chinese FTA policies in the region: the Japan–Singapore FTA increased the interest of the Chinese government on FTAs which resulted in its November 2001 announcement to establish an FTA with ASEAN within ten years, and Japan's swift response in January 2002 with the proposal for a Japan–ASEAN Comprehensive Economic Partnership, and then in 2004 its willingness to sign the TAC as well.

Importantly, there is a widespread perception in the region that Japan lags behind China in its ability to use FTAs to score diplomatic points. This is evident in both the FTA and TAC fronts (Terada, 2006a). For instance, the Japanese government negotiated first bilateral trade agreements with selected Southeast Asian countries, whereas China inked a trade agreement with ASEAN as a whole. According to Munakata (2006b: 121), the Japanese government decided to put on the back burner the ASEAN wide trade agreement due to the stiffer constraints it faced in clearing WTO's Article 24 that requires liberalizing substantially all trade. In contrast, China could negotiate with ASEAN under the more lax enabling clause that applies to FTAs among developing countries.[16] But even after Japan initiated negotiations with ASEAN as a whole in the spring of 2005, disagreements over negotiation modalities, ROOs, and exclusion lists meant that a basic agreement was only reached in August 2007, long after the China–ASEAN FTA had entered into force. Japan also took longer than China to sign the TAC since it worried that it would constrain its ability to promote democracy and human rights in the region and it could have negative implications for its alliance with the United States (Terada, 2006a: 13–14). According to Yeo, it is the "US first, Asia second" mentality which hinders Japan's ability to lead in the path toward East Asian regionalism (Yeo, 2006).

Undoubtedly, one of the most important consequences of the competitive courting of Southeast Asia is the increased leverage of ASEAN nations. Fearing marginalization by negotiating with much larger trade partners, ASEAN countries have deliberately encouraged competition among the larger Northeast Asian nations.[17] This strategy has paid off in that ASEAN's agenda has prevailed in defining the criteria to participate in the latest vehicle to promote regional integration, the East Asia Summit: be a dialogue partner of ASEAN, sign the TAC, and have substantial relations with ASEAN.

Conflicting blueprints for East Asian trade integration

Japan and China have also endorsed different schemes for region-wide integration. In the run-up to the inaugural East Asia Summit (EAS) in December 2005, China insisted that ASEAN+3 should constitute the core group, while Japan proposed the inclusion of Australia, New Zealand, and India. In the end, Japan succeeded in gaining admission for these three countries to the EAS, but the designation of ASEAN+3 as the *main* vehicle for community building (with the EAS playing a supportive role) represented an endorsement of the Chinese view to retain a more narrow East Asian focus in the integration process. Undeterred, Japan announced twin initiatives the following spring: the CEPEA (an ASEAN+6 FTA) and the establishment of an Economic Research Institute for ASEAN and East Asia (to intellectually support ASEAN's secretariat). During the second EAS summit in January 2007, a feasibility study of Japan's CEPEA initiative was launched.

The desire to dilute Chinese influence in the future of East Asian economic integration is a large consideration behind Japan's campaign for an expanded East Asian FTA. First of all, the three additional members are all democracies, and this reinforces Japan's argument that in creating a community, members should share values regarding democracy or human rights protection (Hatakeyama, 2006). In this way, Japan seems to be pointing to the potential weaknesses of China as a regional leader on two central issues: strong rule of law and democratic governance. Second, the inclusion of Australia reflects Japan's desire to upgrade bilateral security relations, consolidate trilateral defense talks including the United States, and counter a rising China (Terada, 2005: 12). Third, the incorporation of India, another large and booming emerging economy, prevents China from becoming the sole spokesperson for developing countries in the EAS.

The race is on, therefore, to see which blueprint for integration (ASEAN+3 or CEPEA) will gain deeper traction.

Conclusions

This chapter has argued that the competitive diffusion mechanism explains best the original policy shift and subsequent evolution of Japanese FTA strategy. Therefore, this concluding section identifies the most important competitive pressures and correlates them to FTA outcomes, discusses how international diffusion pressures are processed through domestic policymaking channels, and addresses the central dilemma for Japanese policymakers as economic and political competition seem to pull FTA policy in different directions.

Competition with whom over what?

In the economic realm, Japanese firms, especially in the automobile and electronics industries, have felt strong competition from their American (and to lesser extent European) rivals both in North American and Southeast Asian markets. As American firms pushed in the NAFTA negotiations for tight ROOs in automobiles and the elimination of duty drawback in the *maquiladora* industry, and as American and European firms benefited from the elimination of performance requirements (such as the Mexican Auto Decree), Japanese firms saw their position in North America deteriorate. A few years later, Japanese companies felt the pinch of competition with American firms closer to home, as some East Asian countries liberalized their investment policies in the aftermath of the Asian financial crisis, and Western multinationals made great inroads (for instance the Big Three

Automakers in Thailand). In order to restore the level playing field, Japanese firms strongly demanded FTAs that awarded similar market access benefits.

The FTA policies of China and Korea have also put strong competitive pressure on Japanese enterprises. The China–ASEAN FTA created concerns of trade diversion in Southeast Asian markets: while Korea's negotiations with the EU could put Japanese auto and electronic firms at a disadvantage since their Korean rivals would enjoy lower tariffs in the European market, and the ratification of KORUS could benefit Korean firms through a looser application of antidumping disciplines.

The competitive nature of the FTA frenzy is also evident in the phenomenon of "concession linkages." Examples of this dynamic abound in Japanese FTAs: the refusal to fix the preferential tariff rate for chicken in the Japan–Mexico FTA until the agreement went into force (due to concern over Japan's negotiation with Thailand); or Japan's intention to upgrade its government procurement commitments with Malaysia if the United States achieves more concessions through its FTA. All these examples point toward one important trend: the resistance to give concessions in one FTA front because of its perceived negative effects on subsequent negotiations. Because through FTAs, governments seek to surpass the concessions already achieved by their rivals; commitments in prior FTAs become *de facto* the negotiation floor in subsequent trade talks, making policymakers more defensive in their earlier agreements as they calculate the impact of "escalating concessions."

In terms of rule-making, the United States and China have been the main targets of competition. Toward the United States, the dissemination of alternative antidumping rules has been an important concern, and the Japanese government has consciously differentiated its brand of FTAs by emphasizing the trade facilitation agenda and economic cooperation clauses. Nowhere is the attempt to propagate a distinct model of economic integration more prominent than in Japan's competition with China to become the focal point of regional integration scheme. Japanese officials have emphasized the higher quality of their FTAs (broader issue scope and binding obligations) as well as Japan's ability as an industrialized counterpart nation to facilitate the development of Southeast Asian countries. Strategic competition with China has also fueled an intense race to cultivate relations with ASEAN, and motivated Japan to invite extra-regional partners (such as Australia, New Zealand, and India) to integration talks in order to balance China's rising influence in ASEAN+3.

Japan's FTA outcomes reflect these multifaceted competitive pressures. Japanese FTAs are *selective* in that the choice of partners, timing of negotiations, and market access commitments reflect the attempt to restore and/or advance various competitive advantages. For instance, the FTA talks with Mexico and Thailand aimed to level the playing field for Japanese companies; the timing of the ASEAN–Japan FTA is explained by the desire to neutralize the political gains China made by initiating talks with ASEAN first; and the ASEAN+6 initiative reflects Japan's strong desire to influence the membership and nature of regional integration in East Asia. Japan's FTA policy is indeed heterogeneous in that Japan is pushing for an FTA approach different both from the NAFTA model and the more informal Chinese FTAs.

However, Japan's FTA formula (meager agricultural concessions and multiple WTO-plus commitments) may be a hard sell in East Asia. Japanese FTA policy is undercut by the Chinese FTA approach which does not comprise binding new rules on trade and investment, and may be more attuned to the traditional "ASEAN way." But the other disadvantage (agricultural protectionism) is self-inflicted, and points to the need to factor in how domestic politics influence a country's response to international FTA diffusion pressures.

International diffusion pressures, domestic policymaking processes

Japan continues to exhibit a fragmented policymaking pattern, whereby strong policy subgovernments and weak bureaucratic coordination give clout to interest groups and generate a cumbersome negotiation strategy as the conflicting interests of internationalized business sectors and protectionist agriculture must be reconciled. These domestic political constraints, therefore, have delayed Japan's FTAs with larger trading partners and/or have generated significant acrimony as smaller FTA counterparts must accept promises of economic assistance instead of market access concessions.

But the domestic politics of Japanese trade policy are in flux with attempts to centralize policymaking and growing divisions among the members of the peak associations for agriculture and business—Nôkyô and Keidanren, respectively (see Solís, forthcoming). One of the most important changes, however, is the growing politicization of trade policy with the more active intervention of politicians attuned to public opinion trends. Consequently, the traditional separation of politics and economics vis-à-vis China has been harder to maintain and the most consistent demand of the Japanese business community, an FTA with China, has gone unheeded. But the Japanese agricultural lobby also suffered a serious blow in the launching of FTA negotiations with Australia, a large exporter of farm products. The agricultural liberalization battle is far from over; however, since the electoral backlash that the ruling party (LDP) suffered in July 2007 has accentuated the domestic political constraints for Japan's trade negotiators.

As the examples above show, the tug of war among contradictory competitive pressures has presented Japanese policymakers with a central dilemma: whether to pursue economic opportunity by signing a bilateral FTA with China (that could become the centerpiece for a more cohesive regional integration project) or to respond to political rivalry by developing a competing and overlapping FTA network. This decision will loom large on the nature of regional integration in East Asia.

Notes

1. Policy in each issue area is decided by stable constellations of interest groups, bureaucracies, and specialized politicians (policy tribes or *zoku giin*). In this distinct type of pluralism, the "government is not weak, but it is *penetrated* by interest groups and political parties" (Muramatsu and Krauss, 1987: 537).
2. Underscoring the interconnectedness of FTA negotiations, Malaysia was concerned that any concession to Japan would become the de facto starting point in subsequent negotiations with the United States and India. For that reason, Japanese officials are waiting to see if the United States pries open Malaysia's government procurement market through its FTA talks, to press for a similar concession during the scheduled five-year renegotiation of the Japan–Malaysia FTA. Interview with METI official, Tokyo, May 2006.
3. Despite these large exclusions, the Japanese government insists on consistency with Article 24 as long as 90 percent of the overall volume of trade is subject to liberalization.
4. For consistency purposes, the remainder of this chapter will use the acronym METI (Ministry of Economy, Trade, and Industry) at all times.
5. Although in the past METI officials had informally discussed the possibility of signing a bilateral trade accord with the United States, no initiative had materialized from those discussions (Munakata, 2006b; Krauss, 2000).
6. Author interview with former senior MITI official, Tokyo, May 2006.
7. Sekizawa (2008) argues instead that business lobbying was very weak, and that the Japan–Mexico FTA was possible through the "politics of public interest." In his view, when mass media reported the GNP and employment losses that Japan would incur if negotiations with Mexico collapsed, public opinion rallied and it was possible to overcome the resistance of agriculture. Sekizawa's observation that Japanese car companies were divided—as firms already producing in Mexico (such as Nissan) were concerned that new arrivals (e.g. Toyota) would enter with more beneficial conditions—is very insightful. However, these divisions do not equal business disinterest. Without an FTA, Japanese car companies with operations in Mexico were constrained by performance requirements that did not apply to their American and European competitors (for instance on the duty-free importation of finished vehicles); electronic firms did not believe Mexico's PROSEC (Programas de Promoción Sectorial) program could compensate for the elimination of *maquiladora* duty drawback since only a few components were offered tariff cuts; and plant exporters were marginalized from the Mexican government procurement market. Moreover, Sekizawa does not explain why in this instance mass media played such a catalytic role. Rather, the widespread circulation of the trade and investment diversion figures reflects the tangible losses that Japanese business expected to incur and the savvy strategy of trade bureaucrats to release such figures to put pressure on the agricultural lobby.
8. For instance, a government strategy has been to foster competitive Japanese agricultural exports in niche markets to weaken the opposition to FTAs. Naoi and Krauss (manuscript) emphasize the importance of these intrasectoral divisions.
9. Interview with officials from Mexico's Secretaría de Economía, Mexico City, May 2005.
10. Labor mobility is another controversial issue in Japan's FTAs with the Philippines and Thailand. The opposition of the Ministry of Labor and the Nurse Association has for instance resulted in strict Japanese certification requirements that will make it unlikely to have a large number of applicants (Pempel and Urata, 2006: 88).

11. Notably absent has been a similar initiative for an FTA with China. In addition to the opposition from agricultural and labor-intensive sectors (textiles), the bilateral FTA with China has been a casualty to political tensions as discussed later.

12. Interview with senior ex-METI official, Tokyo, May 2006.

13. Anti-circumvention refers to the imposition of antidumping duties to goods manufactured by target companies in third countries.

14. The Japanese government has been keen on including the economic cooperation chapter in order to gain the understanding of developing country counterparts regarding modest agricultural liberalization.

15. Interviews with METI, MOFA, and JETRO officials and academics, Tokyo, summer 2005. Obviously, the quality of Japanese FTAs is compromised by the significant agricultural exclusions.

16. Other FTA watchers attribute Japan's decision to pursue the bilaterals first to a bureaucratic split, in that METI preferred the subregional FTA to avoid the deleterious effects of crisscrossing ROOs, but MOFA wanted the bilateral route in order to cement relations with target nations by framing this initiative as a broad diplomatic effort. And according to other FTA experts, since the nature of economic involvement in the region is very different for Japan and China (with substantial Japanese FDI in these countries), it made sense to proceed bilaterally to address more fully the market access concerns of Japanese MNCs in each country. Author interviews with officials from METI, MOFA, JETRO, and Japanese academics, Tokyo, summer 2005.

17. Munakata (2006b: 122) cites Singapore's trade minister George Yeo: "On the question of East Asian FTA, it will be 3+10 rather than 10+3. The economic size of the three is much larger than the ten. ASEAN will be marginalized. Therefore, we prefer 10+1, in a position to deal with Japan, China and ROK separately."

11
China's Competitive FTA Strategy: Realism on a Liberal Slide

Jian Yang[1]

Compared with Europe and North America, East Asia is a latecomer in regional economic cooperation and China is one of the latest in the region. In May 2001, China became a member of the Bangkok Agreement, the first free trade area analogue the country joined. China has moved fast since then. It has (partially) completed free trade agreement (FTA) talks with the ten-member Association of South East Asian Nations (ASEAN), Chile, Pakistan, New Zealand and Singapore, and has signed a Closer Economic Partnership Agreement (CEPA) with Hong Kong and Macau. Beijing is also in FTA talks with Australia, Iceland, Gulf Cooperation Council (GCC), and lately Peru. It has completed or started joint feasibility research for FTAs with a number of countries, including the Southern African Customs Union (SACU), India, Japan, South Korea, and Switzerland (see Table 11.1).

There is no simple explanation for the Chinese interest in FTAs. One may argue that it is a natural development of Chinese trade liberalization. After all, ever since it opened up in 1978, the Chinese economy has become increasingly integrated with the world economy through its ever-increasing trade volume and FDI. China's 15-year pursuit for WTO (World Trade Organization) membership highlights its interest in free trade. Others may point to the fact that Chinese FTA partners are carefully selected and Beijing's interest in free trade can hardly explain the selection process.

This chapter investigates the driving forces of China's FTA offensive. It first investigates China's interest in FTAs, focusing on Beijing's genuine interest in liberal free trade and its realist pursuit for gains. The chapter then examines China's four FTA partners, namely Pakistan, ASEAN, Chile, and New Zealand. The final section of the chapter analyses China's interest in East Asian regionalism represented by an East Asia FTA. The chapter concludes that while China has a strong interest in free trade and Beijing is very much influenced by the FTA strategies of other countries, economic, political, and strategic competition can play a decisive role in China's FTA decisions.

Table 11.1 China's FTA offensive (as of October 2008)

Partner	Status	Trade volume[†] (percentage of 2006 total)		FDI (foreign direct investment) volume[†] (percentage of 2006 total)		Issue scope				
		Export	Import	Inflow (actually utilized)	Outflow (non-financial)	Investment	Service	Environment	Labor	Economic cooperation
Hong Kong	In force (2004)	16.06	1.36	32.11	39.30	Yes	Yes	No	No	Yes
Macao	In force (2004)	0.23	0.03	0.96	0.82	Yes	Yes	No	No	Yes
ASEAN	In force (2005)*	7.36	11.31	5.32	2.82	Negotiation	Yes (2007)	No	No	No
Chile	In force (2006)	0.32	0.72	0.00	0.00	Negotiation	Yes (2008)	No	No	Yes
Pakistan	In force (2007)	0.44	0.13	0.00	0.00	Yes	Negotiation	No	No	No
New Zealand	In force (2008)	0.17	0.17	0.13	0.00	Yes	Yes	Yes	Yes	Yes
Singapore	Signed (2008)	2.39	2.23	3.59	0.75	Yes	Yes	Yes	Yes	Yes
GCC	Negotiation (2005)	1.81	3.11	0.24	0.00	–	–	–	–	–
Australia	Negotiation (2005)	1.41	2.44	0.88	0.50					
Iceland	Negotiation (2007)	0.00	0.00	0.00	0.00	–	–	–	–	–

(continued)

Table 11.1   (Continued)

Partner	Status	Trade volume† (percentage of 2006 total)		FDI (foreign direct investment volume† (percentage of 2006 total)		Issue scope				
		Export	Import	Inflow (actually utilized)	Outflow (non-financial)	Investment	Service	Environment	Labor	Economic cooperation
Peru	Negotiation (2008)	0.00	0.00	0.00	0.00					
SACU	Negotiation announced (2004)	0.61	0.53	0.16	0.23	–	–	–	–	–
India	Study	1.50	1.30	0.00	0.00					
Japan–Korea	Study	14.05	25.95	13.48	0.39					
Japan	Study	9.46	14.62	7.30	0.22					
South Korea	Study	4.59	11.34	6.18	0.16					
Switzerland	Study	0.26	0.54	0.31	0.00					

* Dates of CAFTA agreements coming into force: the framework agreement laying out the CAFTA plan in 2003; Early Harvest Program covering trade in goods in 2005 and trade in services in 2007.

† *Source*: National Bureau of Statistics of China, 2007.

This chapter is largely based on Chinese analysts' publications. It is generally believed that in China "a more pluralistic and competitive policy environment has given analysts at think tanks more influence" (Glaser and Saunders, 2002: 597). Lampton (2001: 8–10) notes that the complexity of foreign policy issues has resulted in the professionalization of China's foreign policymaking, which has given Chinese analysts the opportunity to make significant inputs. To Shambaugh (2002: 581), the published journals of Chinese foreign policy think tanks "provide very important insights into policy debates that are percolating inside bureaucracies, thus offering important 'early warning indicators' of policies to come." Similarly, Tanner (2002: 559) believes that Chinese think tanks are now "some of the most important windows through which foreign analysts can observe China's usually opaque policy-making system."

Domestic politics can play a decisive role in foreign policymaking. China is no exception. However, it has always been a challenge to analyze the influence of domestic politics in Chinese foreign policy. It is particularly difficult to specify the role of public opinion in China which is not a democracy. Nevertheless Lampton (2001: 12) has observed that "some issues and some domestic circumstances allow the [Chinese] leadership less room to operate than others." Although the issue of FTA can have strong domestic implications, it is not a sensitive issue to the Chinese public. The Chinese public is not well informed and therefore can offer little input to China's FTA negotiations. The Chinese business, however, does play a role by participating in the feasibility studies and the subsequent negotiations. However, they are not in a position to publicly air their complaints. It is therefore equally difficult to assess their influence in China's FTA negotiations. For these reasons, this chapter's analysis tracks closely the positions of Chinese analysts as a key indicator of the thinking and rationale behind China's FTA initiatives.

A slide toward liberalism

From the time when China opened up in 1978, Beijing has made a consistent effort to integrate with the international society. One indication is its support for the United Nations and for various international regimes. In the 29 years from 1949, when the People's Republic of China (PRC) was established, to 1977, China was a party to a total of 31 international treaties. In contrast, in the 27 years from 1978 to the end of 2004, China signed 236 international treaties (Rao, 2005: 51).

China's effort to integrate with the international society is a process of learning and accepting liberal norms which are foreign to the Chinese: their world views had been dominated by Marxism–Leninism and a sense of insecurity derived from the "Century of Humiliation" (1840–1945) when China suffered at the hands of foreign invaders. From 1978 onwards China has been exposed to Western liberal norms. The end of the Cold War accelerated China's slide toward liberalism. Medeiros and Fravel (2003: 23) noted in 2003 that "in the last ten years, Chinese foreign policy has become far more nimble and engaging than at any other time in the history of the People's Republic." Evidence of these changes include the expanded number and depth of China's bilateral relationships, new trade and security accords, deepened participation in key multilateral organisations, widening acceptance of many prevailing international rules and institutions, and efforts to help address global security issues.

China's slide toward liberalism is most noticeable in the economic arena, highlighted by its 15-year request (from 1986 to 2001) to join the WTO. And China's trade liberalization has been rewarding. From the time that it started economic reforms in 1978, China has pursued a development strategy of export-led growth. After three decades of economic reforms, the Chinese economy has been transformed from a closed socialist command economy into an open, trade-oriented capitalist economy. From 1978 to 2006, China's trade volume grew more than 85 times: from US$20.6 billion to US$1760.4 billion. China is now one of the countries most dependent on foreign trade.

With China benefiting from free trade, most Chinese economists have been supportive of global trade liberalization, and believe that China should not stop its liberalization process. They often point to the successful examples of free trade and the unsuccessful cases of either protectionism or economic nationalism. One unsuccessful case, in their view, is Latin America. It is noted that during the 1960s and 1970s, under the influence of economic nationalism, many Latin American countries changed their free trade policy and became more protectionist, which resulted in the unsatisfactory economic performance of these countries from the 1980s onwards (Jiang, 2007: 20).

However, China's trade policy experienced some major changes shortly after joining the WTO. While remaining committed to multilateral trade talks, China has become very much involved in FTA negotiations and regional trade frameworks. Chinese analysts argue that FTAs are complementary to multilateral trade agreements or "building blocks" (Bi, 2005: 15). They acknowledge that joining the WTO has accelerated the marketization of the Chinese economy, but that China must further widen and deepen its participation in regional economic integration by means of regional and bilateral trade liberalization agreements.

The stagnation of the WTO talks highlighted the importance of FTAs. "Everyone is talking about FTAs. Everyone is conducting FTA talks. Especially after the Doha negotiations reached a deadlock, the FTA talks concerning China and nations worldwide reached their highest peak," noted a senior researcher at the Institute of Asia-Pacific Studies at the Chinese Academy of Social Sciences ("China–Pakistan FTA to promote bilateral trade," 2006). In Northeast Asia, Chinese observers have noted a trend of moving away from the Asia Pacific Economic Cooperation (APEC) and toward FTAs since the 1997–98 Asian financial crisis (Zhang, Z., 2004: 2; Zheng, 2002: 30–1).

China's interest in FTAs also reflects Beijing's effort to learn the international economic game and to emulate other countries. The Chinese started their economic reforms with little experience and had to, as Deng Xiaoping said famously, "cross the river by feeling the stones." Although Beijing soon accepted the concept of free trade, it still is playing the catch-up game. FTA strategies of the United States and Europe have been particularly influential to China's FTA policy (Zheng, 2003: 5–6; Li and He, 2007: 66–70).

China's shift from WTO to FTA therefore does not necessarily imply a reverse of its slide toward liberalism. However, some major differences do exist between WTO talks and FTA negotiations. In WTO talks, China has not been able to play a dominant role and its goals have been limited mainly to advancing its economic interests. In FTA negotiations, China can be a dominant player and, like other governments, has used FTAs as a vehicle to actively advance a range of national interests: economic, political, strategic, and so on. China's FTA strategy, thus, is also driven by Beijing's often realist calculations centered on strengthening its capabilities in various areas, economic and noneconomic.

China's competitive calculations

To begin with, China's initial interest in FTAs was due to its concerns about being excluded from preferential arrangements. Chinese analysts noted the proliferation of FTAs worldwide. Although the number of FTAs in East Asia remained small, the Asia-Pacific as a whole seemed to be entering into new FTAs faster than many other regions, and with many more to come (Liu, 2005: 6). Even the FTAs among third countries that do not seem related to China could have a strong impact on China. Also, compared with WTO, FTAs cover a broader issue area and are more discriminative against non-partners (Zhang, 2006: 7). The Chinese government was advised to follow the trend and to join the "small group" of FTAs after joining the "big group" of WTO in order to avoid being marginalized (Zhang, F., 2004: 74).

Chinese analysts have listed a number of benefits that FTAs could generate. This includes the effect of economy of scale, improving the structure of the market through an intensified competition, stimulating foreign investment, protecting the continuation of economic reforms through binding agreements, attracting potential investors by signaling the government's trade policy and good relations with FTA partners, creating an insurance mechanism by preventing protectionism, strengthening the bargaining power of FTA partners against a third party, and improving the coordination among different economic sectors by mobilizing FTA supporters. In addition, FTAs would contribute to the settlement of international disputes in security areas (Jiang, 2007: 20–1; Zhang, Z., 2004: 4–6).

These benefits demonstrate the competitive nature of FTA negotiations. The following paragraphs investigate China's competitive FTA strategy by focusing on the economic, political, and legal aspects.

Economic competition

It is generally believed that China's rapid growth of exports is, to a great extent, due to its cheap labor, raw material, and land. China's labor cost in 2003 was just one-fiftieth of that in the United States and Japan. However, China's advantage of cheap labor was offset by its low productivity, which was only 1/25 of that of the United States and 1/26 of that of Japan (Zhang et al., 2003: 122). Meanwhile, the costs of labor, raw material, and land have all been increasing. It is thus imperative for Chinese producers to continue to reduce their costs so that their products stay competitive in the world market. FTAs are most effective in lowering tariffs and thus substantially reducing the costs of both exports and imports. FTAs could also save costs by enhancing the efficiency and productivity of China's somewhat old-fashioned command enterprises, partly due to the effect of scale, and because rationalization and modernization would be stimulated by the new competition.

China also attempts to use FTAs to make good use of ROOs. China's WTO membership is helpful in that China is able to keep abreast of the development of ROOs through its involvement in WTO. However, WTO is not a shield from possible negative impacts of ROOs. China is particularly sensitive to ROOs because a high percentage of its exports are products assembled in China. Although much of the value of the products are generated overseas, they may well be regarded as originated from China and added to China's "trade surplus" which may end up with trade barriers against China (Ma, 2004: 47). FTAs are effective in addressing China's ROOs concerns because China can negotiate ROOs to its benefit. For example, the China–New Zealand FTA includes a 137-page-long annex exclusively on ROOs.

Related to its ROOs concerns are Beijing's efforts to reduce the impact of trade diversion resulting from competing FTAs. The South Korea–US FTA, which was signed on April 2, 2007, alarmed the Chinese to a considerable extent. In addition to the strategic implications of US strategic counterbalance against China, as discussed later, competitive US agricultural products could threaten Chinese agricultural exports to South Korea. With an annual value of about US$3 billion, South Korea is the second biggest market for Chinese agricultural exports after Japan (Song, 2007: 39). On the other hand, American businesses have expressed intention to reduce their imports of textiles and apparel from China, and use South Korea as a replacement ("South Korea: US buyers keen to source more apparel, textiles," 2007).

FTAs will also facilitate Beijing's "go out" (*zou chu qu*) strategy, which pushes its enterprises to go global, by helping Chinese enterprises to access overseas markets. The "go out" strategy itself is due to Chinese realization that to become competitive globally is the only way to survive in today's globalized world. As a member of the WTO, China is obliged to further open up to international trade and investment. This means that domestic enterprises would be subject to competition from foreign firms.

A more immediate effect of FTAs is that they help to address China's concerns about the antidumping (AD) charges against Chinese exporters. Since its accession into the WTO, in late 2001, China has faced an increasing number of AD investigations, to the extent that it appears to be the number one victim of AD investigations.[2] From 1995 to 2006, China faced 536 AD investigations: 2.34 times that of South Korea, which was in the second place with 229 AD investigations. In terms of final AD measures during this period, 375 were directed at China: 2.76 times that of South Korea (136) (World Trade Organization, 2007). One major reason for the large number of AD charges against China has been that many countries do not recognize China as a market economy. All WTO members have 15 years to recognize China's market economy status after it entered into the WTO in 2001. China's FTA efforts could have some immediate impact on reducing the number of AD investigations against it, as a number of the countries, which have launched AD investigations against it, are its FTA partners or FTA negotiation partners, such as Australia, New Zealand, Pakistan, Chile, Indonesia, Malaysia, and the Philippines. China has also completed the China–India FTA feasibility study and is looking into the feasibility of negotiating an FTA with South Korea. Both India and South Korea are active AD players (World Trade Organization, 2007).

Political competition

While economic competition is an apparent factor in China's interest in FTAs, political competition is no less important. In analyzing US FTAs, deLisle (2006) notes that:

> FTAs can serve as an economic instrument in the pursuit of security goals that loom large in US foreign policy.... More crassly instrumentally, they can serve as economic goodies that Washington can dole out to serve political ends of building or reinforcing alliance-like arrangements.

A similar observation can be applied to China. deLisle (2006) actually points out that "compared to the US, the political dimension is even larger for Beijing and the commitment to the relatively radical economic liberalism ideals behind FTAs (or of the broader international trade regime) less established and robust."

Chinese analysts emphasize that China's FTA strategy should help it to "enhance its influence in the international political economy and expand its political and security space" (Zhang, F., 2004: 75). Therefore, China should make FTAs "an important tool for both economic diplomacy and political diplomacy" (Liu, 2005: 10). Thus, Chinese analysts are wary of Japan's effort to negotiate FTAs with China's neighbors. They deem it imperative for

China to "break up the encirclement of Japan's FTA strategy" (Liu, 2005: 10). The reason seems simple: the countries with closer economic relations with Japan will inevitably improve their political relations with Tokyo, which may dilute China's regional leadership potential.

Another political and strategic consideration in China's FTA strategy is Beijing's effort to establish a long-term, reliable supply of overseas resources and energy. According to the Development Research Center of the State Council of China (2005), in the years before 2020, China is expected to experience rapid industrialization and peak demand for its resources. On the other hand, China's per capita possession of resources is far below the world average. For instance, its per capita mineral occupation is about half of that of the world average.

Legal competition

Related to economic and political competition is legal competition. The three can hardly be separated. A Chinese analyst argues that for great powers, to play a leading role in regional economic cooperation is not just for their interests in the region or for internal benefits. More importantly, the great powers are aiming at the external benefits, namely to increase their bargaining chips in multilateral negotiations and, further, to play a leading role in the making of international economic rules (Zhang, Z., 2004: 5). While having benefited from its active participation in global trade and investment, Beijing has long believed that the existing international economic order is a part of the "unfair and irrational" international order. Beijing's view of the "fair and rational" international order is based on its vision for a "harmonious world." Chinese President Hu Jintao elaborated the concept of harmonious world by raising some specific suggestions. Economically, Hu urged the international society to actively push forward the establishment of an open, fair, and indiscriminating multilateral trade mechanism; further improve the international financial system; reinforce global energy dialogue and cooperation; and jointly maintain energy security and the stability of the energy market (Ministry of Foreign Affairs, China, 2005).

China is clearly interested in making changes to the existing international trading system to ensure a "fair and rational" international economic order. Chinese officials have repeatedly pointed out that the WTO decision-making process is dominated by a few states and the views of developing countries are not adequately considered. For instance, as a developing country, China opposes any linkage between trade and labor standards, and the use of environmental standards as a new form of protectionism (Lardy, 2002: 156). One of China's goals in participating in globalization and joining international economic institutions is to shape the rules of the international trading system (Zhang et al., 2004: 12). It is believed that those who set the international rules have vested interests and they have no intention to let China enjoy the benefits automatically (Liu and Gong, 2007: 18). "An unchangeable rule (*tie de faze*) is that those who set rules will benefit from the rules," Chinese analysts emphasize (Han et al., 2005: 7).

However, Beijing is not actively challenging the existing international trading system by propounding a new set of rules on trade and investment. This is partly because China is still learning how to play the international economic game. deLisle (2006) notes that "China has remained largely a 'regime taker'—accepting the existing rules ... and pledging to abide by them." It is unlikely that we see a dramatic change in the near future. While suggesting that China should not accept the unfair requirements forced upon it (Zhang et al., 2003: 221), Chinese analysts have observed that

> China's strategy of actively participating in economic globalization demonstrates that in the process of turning China into a world-class economic power, China accepts the existing international economic order instead of challenging it. Not only does China not challenge this order, it utilizes the order. China will first accept the existing international economic order and then work with other countries, especially the developing countries, to gradually improve it.
>
> (Zhang et al., 2004: 12)

Understanding China's FTA outcomes

Chinese analysts have had a rather thorough discussion about selecting China's FTA partners. They took into consideration economic, political, and strategic factors and believe that Chinese selection of FTA partners should be based on what it can gain in all these areas. "What we can get from the FTA should be the key issue in selecting partners," said a Chinese analyst ("China–Pakistan FTA to promote bilateral trade," 2006). It is generally agreed that priority should be given to China's neighbouring countries, then to the countries that either have an economy complementary to China's and are resource-rich or constitute emerging markets. However, FTA negotiations are two-way communications and China has to be flexible in prioritizing its FTA partners. For instance, in Oceania, Australia is a more ideal FTA partner than New Zealand, as Australia has a bigger market, much more resources, and greater political influence in world politics. In the end, it is New Zealand that has signed an FTA with China.

This section investigates China's FTA partners by October 2008.[3] China's CEPAs with Hong Kong and Macao are different from its FTAs in that both Hong Kong and Macao are its special administrative regions and not sovereign states.

Inside Asia: Pakistan and ASEAN

China's FTA "offensive" is global, with negotiation partners in Latin America, Oceania, South and East Asia, the Middle East, Europe, and Africa.

Chinese analysts term these partners as China's "front posts" (*qianzhan*) in its global FTA strategy. However, as mentioned above, China's neighbouring countries have priority in China's FTA strategy. ASEAN thus became China's first FTA partner and Pakistan was not too far behind.

Pakistan

Pakistan's economic value to China is limited. Its trade with China accounted for just 0.3 percent of China's total trade in 2006. Unlike countries such as Chile, Pakistan can hardly be used as a springboard to other economies. This does not mean Pakistan has no economic potential for China. Chinese investment in Pakistan is believed to increase substantially in the coming years ("Pakistan: China displays growing interest in Pakistan," 2007). Nevertheless Pakistan's value to China is largely political and strategic.

Pakistan has been China's strong ally for decades. It has consistently supported China in the United Nations on issues like China's human rights record and on the issue of Taiwan. It has also played a crucial role in Sino-US rapprochement in the early 1970s. Although China has substantially improved its relations with India, a giant in South Asia who regarded China as a major enemy for most of the years since the 1962 Sino-Indian war, Pakistan's strategic importance to China has by no means declined. After all, Beijing is wary of the US and Japanese attempts to deepen their strategic cooperation with India.

Pakistan's strategic value to China lies not only in its support for China on various political and security issues but also in its vital strategic location. It not only neighbors China, India, and the Arabian Sea, but also is close to the Middle East and Central Asia, two oil-rich regions. The Gwadar Port in Pakistan's Balochistan Province is only 72 kilometers away from Iran, and about 400 kilometers away from the Strait of Hormuz, the only sea passage to the open ocean for large areas of the petroleum-exporting Persian Gulf states. The Chinese hope that they will one day ship Persian Gulf oil from Gwadar overland through Pakistan to China. That will cut transport by 12,000 miles, shaving a month off the journey's time and 25 percent off the fees (Montero, 2007). Perhaps more importantly, it would give China an alternative to the Malacca Strait, an increasingly busy and dangerous strait which is plagued by pirates and vulnerable in times of great power conflicts.

While Sino-Pakistan political and security relations are deep-rooted, their economic relations have been shallow. Chinese analysts conclude that the Sino-Pakistan "all-weather, all dimensional" strategic relationship is seriously unbalanced. It is therefore of strategic importance to strengthen the bilateral economic relationship (Huang et al., 2008: 64–5). In Pakistan, in spite of some economic concerns, the strategic value of an FTA with China is also well recognized. A Pakistani commentary notes:

> Spanning over five and a half decades, the historic bonds between China and Pakistan are the living example of a relationship based

on trust, equity and respect....The FTA is acknowledgement of the realization that to sustain cooperation and...nurture the holistic and strategic relationship, major advances had to be made in the economic fields.

("Pak–China FTA," 2006)

ASEAN

Political competition is also prominent in China's FTA with ASEAN. To be sure, the economic necessities for the China–ASEAN FTA were not difficult to identify. Bilateral trade grew rather rapidly, from US$7 billion in 1990 to US$39.52 billion in 2000. The average growth rate was 18.8 percent. In 2000, the growth rate was as high as 45.3 percent. In 1991, ASEAN's share of China's foreign trade was 5.8 percent. By 2000, it had increased to 8.3 percent and ASEAN had become China's fifth largest trading partner. Meanwhile, the share of China in ASEAN's trade expanded from 2.1 percent in 1994 to 3.9 percent in 2000, making China ASEAN's sixth largest trading partner. In 2002, with China's entry into WTO, China–ASEAN trade increased by 31.6 percent (ASEAN–China Expert Group on Economic Cooperation, 2001: 1). According to the ASEAN–China joint expert group, the China–ASEAN FTA would increase ASEAN's exports to China by US$13 billion or by 48 percent while China's exports to ASEAN would expand by US$10.6 billion or by 55.1 percent. At the same time, ASEAN's GDP would increase by 0.9 percent or by US$5.4 billion while China's GDP would rise by 0.3 percent or by US$2.2 billion in absolute terms (ASEAN–China Expert Group on Economic Cooperation, 2001: 31, 150).

Arguably, both China and ASEAN would benefit from the China–ASEAN FTA in the long term by increasing the economic efficiency and competitiveness of their business sectors, and attract more FDI inflows (Cai, 2003: 401). Some also argued that the pact would, in the longer term, be in China's favor as Chinese manufacturers would break into Southeast Asian export markets, and the Chinese economy would also benefit from a stable supply of commodities and raw materials (Vatikiotis and Hiebert, 2003: 28).

However, the short-term economic impacts of the China–ASEAN FTA on both China and ASEAN were less certain. The impacts could be negative. A key principle for establishing FTAs is the complementarity of the two economies. ASEAN and China were more competitive than supplementary in trade structure. This was reflected in the fact that China and ASEAN were not each other's major export markets. Wong and Chan (2003: 518) note that from 1980 to 2000, the ASEAN-5 (Indonesia, Malaysia, the Philippines, Singapore, and Thailand) received only an average of 6.4 percent of China's total exports while its exports to China constituted only 5.5 percent of China's total imports. From the perspective of ASEAN-5, exports to China in this period accounted for only 2.4 percent of its total exports and its imports from China were just 2.6 percent of its total imports. In terms of investment, the FDI share of the ASEAN-5 in China accounted for only six percent in 2001 (Wong and Chan, 2003: 523). Wong and Chan (2003: 526) hence concluded that "there are more possibilities that China and ASEAN would compete, rather than complement one other."

China's strong interest in the China–ASEAN FTA thus cannot be fully explained by economic interests. More incentives can be found in Chinese political and strategic calculations. Lee Kuan Yew (2007: 25) observed that China's decision-making on the China–ASEAN FTA was "based on strategic considerations that override such competing domestic interests as importers versus exporters and agriculturists versus industrialists." Chinese analysts agree that China's decision was, to a great extent, a politically driven move (Qiu, 2005: 8–13).[4]

First of all, to promote China's peaceful rise is particularly important in East Asia. While China has contributed a great deal to trade within East Asia, its export competition with the newly industrialized economies in the region has increased from 8 percent in 1990 to 20 percent in 2002 (He and Hu, 2006: 5). It is therefore, for reasons of strategic implications, important to coordinate economic interests with the ASEAN states.

Southeast Asia is geopolitically significant to China, not only because much of China's trade and oil from the Middle East passes through the region but also because of conflicting maritime claims. China, as a rising power, has been a strong supporter for multipolarity in world politics and ASEAN is crucial in that respect. Southeast Asia is also important in China's effort to counter a perceived US containment-of-China strategy and to marginalize Taiwan politically.

To cement closer economic relations with ASEAN would increase China's regional influence at the expense of the United States, Japan, and other major economic powers. The FTA deal was just part of Beijing's concerted effort to embrace ASEAN from all directions. In November 2002, when China and ASEAN signed the China–ASEAN FTA, they also signed off on three other agreements, including agreements on cooperation in new areas like drug trafficking, agricultural cooperation, and a landmark declaration on territorial disputes in the South China Sea. It was thus observed that "China moved ahead of rival Japan in setting the stage for economic and political ties with the region" (de Castro, 2002).

Outside Asia: New Zealand and Chile

New Zealand and Chile have some similarities. First, both are relatively small and open economies, reflecting Beijing's attempt to learn about and try FTA negotiations. Second, both economies are more or less complementary to the Chinese economy. Third, the two countries have had a strong political relationship with China. Finally, both have been leading the support for China's economic integration with the world economy.

New Zealand

New Zealand (NZ) from the very beginning was determined to become the first developed country to sign an FTA with China. Australia, China's priority FTA negotiation partner in Oceania, tried to compete with New Zealand. However, due to their differences on market access, especially for agricultural products, no significant progress has been achieved in Sino-Australian negotiations since the eighth round in April 2007 (Department of Foreign Affairs and Trade, Australian Government, 2008). On the other hand, China has been grateful to New Zealand for its consistent support in the past. New Zealand was the first developed country to sign a WTO agreement with China, the first developed country to recognize China as a "market economy," which was a huge boost to China's effort to advance this cause.[5]

There are a number of other factors for New Zealand becoming the first developed country to sign an FTA with China. As mentioned earlier, the New Zealand economy is relatively small, open, and complementary to the Chinese economy, and New Zealand has a good political relationship with China. It was an ideal country for China to learn about and practice FTA negotiations. Commenting on China's FTA negotiations in March 2003, Long Yongtu, who was chief trade negotiator for China's entry into WTO in 2001, said that "China has just entered into the WTO. We are really not familiar with all these very sophisticated negotiations and also our negotiating capacities are not very strong; so we have to focus on a few things rather than try to do many things at the same time" (Lee, 2003).

What is striking in the China–NZ FTA is that it is China's first comprehensive FTA. According to David Walker, New Zealand's Lead Negotiator for the China FTA, this is because the China–NZ FTA is the first FTA China has concluded with an OECD member country. Both sides were conscious of this fact which is why the Chinese Premier Wen Jiabao and the New Zealand Prime Minister Helen Clark agreed in April 2006 that New Zealand and China would aim to conclude an agreement that was "comprehensive and of high quality" in the mutual interest.[6] The comprehensive FTA may also indicate that legalization is not a high priority in Chinese FTA policy. China is therefore willing to accommodate the preferences of its counterparts for more comprehensive and formalistic FTAs, such as that with New Zealand, or narrower and more voluntaristic FTAs like those with ASEAN, Pakistan, and Chile.[7] The intention of China and both ASEAN and Chile was to later negotiate outcomes on services and then on investment. China has successfully concluded talks on services with both ASEAN and Chile (see Table 11.1).

Chile

Similar to New Zealand, Chile is a relatively small trading partner to China and has a few firsts in its relations with China. Chile was the first Latin American country to diplomatically recognize the PRC, the first Latin

American country to recognize its "market economy" status, and the first Latin American country to conclude WTO membership accession negotiations with it.

Compared with New Zealand, Chile is more important to the Chinese economy. What attracts China perhaps as much as trade opportunities is the fact that Chile is a liberal, cosmopolitan state that has already negotiated full or partial FTAs with over 30 partners in four continents, and that it has a special relationship with the United States. Chile, thus, is an FTA "hub" in Latin America. A good example is Chinese exports of toys to Latin America. Latin America was believed to be the most difficult market for Chinese toy exporters. It was the only region where Chinese toy exporters faced dumping charges. After the signing of the China–Chile FTA in 2005, Chinese toy exports to Chile, Mexico, Argentina, and Brazil increased by 50, 33, 23, and 58 percent, respectively. This is despite the fact that the China–Chile FTA did not come into effect until October 1, 2006. The increase was so dramatic that Chinese analysts called for self-regulations to avoid repercussions (Zeng, 2007: 12–13).

Concerns over competition from the proposed Free Trade Area of the Americas (FTAA) contributed to China's eagerness to conclude its FTA negotiations with Chile. China was worried that the proposed FTAA would generate more competition from Latin American economies in the US market. The Chinese still remember the tariff discrimination that their country suffered after North American Free Trade Agreement (NAFTA) came into effect in the 1990s. Before NAFTA, China had the largest share of the US textile products market. During the first three years after NAFTA was signed by the United States, Canada, and Mexico in 1994, Mexico saw its exports of male shirts to the United States soar by 122.9 percent while those of China declined by 38.1 percent. For sportswear exports, Mexico gained 769.3 percent while China lost 33.8 percent ("China, India to advance feasibility research on regional trade arrangement," 2007). By 1998, Mexico had replaced China as the largest exporter of textile products to the United States. It is predicted that the FTAA will have an even stronger impact on China's exports. An FTA with Chile will give China's traders a beachhead from which to expand their economic activities into the Latin America region and make the FTAA work for China rather than against it (Yang, 2004: 48–50). Pablo Cabrera, the Chilean ambassador to China, said that Chile expected to provide Chinese companies with a new entry point to the American market. "South America, even the whole of America, will become a complete free trade area for China," Cabrera claimed (Liu and Jiang, 2005).

An FTA with Chile also serves China's energy and natural resources security interest. While China is the world's largest copper importer with its copper consumption accounting for about 22 percent of the world total in 2004 (Chen, 2005), Chile is the world's largest copper supplier. Chile produced 4.9 million tons of copper in 2003. About 850,000 tons were exported to China (Zhang, J., 2004). Copper accounted for 30 percent of Chilean exports to China in 2005 (Xinhua, 2006).

China's push for an East Asia FTA

China proposed an FTA with Japan and South Korea in the fourth summit the three countries held in November 2002 in Cambodia. China also proposed a study on the feasibility of an East Asian FTA (EAFTA) at the October 2003 Summit in Bali, and reiterated this at the November 2004 Summit in Laos (Chu, 2006: 3). According to Hu Angang, a leading international political economy expert in China, an EAFTA can be a stepping-stone for an Asia FTA and ultimately an Asia-Pacific FTA (FTAAP):

1. China actively participating in the ASEAN FTA,
2. Establishing a China–Japan–South Korea–Hong Kong FTA,
3. Establishing an EAFTA,
4. Incorporating South Asian countries to establish an East Asia–South Asia FTA,
5. Participating in the establishment of an FTAAP (Zhang et al., 2003: 124).

An FTAAP is a long-term vision, which is politically unrealistic in the foreseeable future. Early in 1993, East Asian countries rejected a US-backed proposal of establishing an APEC-based Asia Pacific Economic Community (Wang, 2005: 20). Just over a decade later, in April 2004, the APEC Business Advisory Council (ABAC) proposed the establishment of an FTA of Asia Pacific. The proposal was partly an attempt to reform the APEC approach, which is based on the nonbinding principle represented by "concerted unilateralism" and "open regionalism." Although controversial from the very beginning, the proposal has received more positive responses from APEC members. Chinese President Hu Jintao also voiced China's support for "necessary reforms" of APEC in November 2004. However, Hu emphasized that the reforms should be based on "full consultation" (Cai, 2005: 38).

China so far has not been enthusiastic about the FTAAP. Economically, China would benefit from the FTAAP as both its main trade partners and the major trade barriers it faces are concentrated in the Asia-Pacific region. However, Beijing has been concerned about the FTAAP's political implications, such as its potential impact on politically sensitive sectors. More importantly, Beijing is not comfortable with the proposed change to the APEC approach. It is noted that China sees APEC as "a consultative and consensual decision-making entity" and that China's willingness to cooperate in APEC does not mean that it is prepared to transfer sovereignty and to pursue extensive institutionalization (Sheng, 2007: 68).

A deeper concern for China could be that the proposed FTAAP may well increase US influence in the region at the expense of Chinese influence.

The Chinese concerns are similar to US concerns about East Asian regionalism. In December 1990, Malaysian Prime Minister Dr. Mahathir Mohamad suggested to the visiting Chinese Premier Li Peng that East Asian countries should form an "East Asia Economic Group" (EAEG). The EAEG was later renamed the East Asia Economic Caucus (EAEC) with the proposed membership of ASEAN, China, Japan, and South Korea. The EAEC would enhance economic cooperation in the region and give countries in the region a collective voice in multilateral negotiations, including world trade. The idea of an East Asian grouping without the United States worried Washington. The then US Secretary of State James Baker III warned of the danger of drawing a line down the middle of the Pacific. Years later, in his memoirs, Baker revealed that "in private I did my best to kill it" (Singh, 2006: 14). Chinese analysts believe that Washington remains concerned about East Asian regionalism, particularly if China takes the leadership role (Wu, 2007: 47–52). And as discussed later, US concerns are not without reason.

Like in Japan and South Korea, business groups in China are enthusiastic about the prospects of a trilateral FTA. According to a 2003 survey, some 85 percent of Chinese companies responded favorably when asked about the desirability of such a trade pact, compared with 76 percent in Japan and 71 percent in South Korea (Yonan, 2004). A March 2004 survey revealed that a total of 69.8 percent of Japanese respondents, 64 percent of Chinese respondents, and 75 percent of South Korean respondents said an FTA among the three nations was necessary ("NW: East Asia FRA crucial, execs say," 2004). Studies by the Mitsubishi Research Institute in Japan (Higashi, 2004: 20) and Nankai University in China (Yu, 2006: 20) came to the same conclusion that a China–Japan–South Korea FTA would benefit all three parties although the findings vary to a considerable extent.

There are reasons to believe that Beijing is genuinely interested in a China–Japan–South Korea FTA. The FTA would be an important stepping-stone toward East Asian regionalism. China's interests in East Asian regionalism are multifold, including securing economic security, encouraging independent foreign policy in Southeast Asia, power balancing against other great powers such as the United States, and neutralizing the potential of Japanese regional leadership (Breslin, 2007: 153–6).

In terms of economic security, Beijing has realized that regional cooperation will help China "to head off potential crises" and to "mitigate the need to rely on the US dominated global financial institutions in times of crisis" (Breslin, 2007: 153). After all, Asia is China's most important trading partner. In 2006, China's trade with Asia accounted for 56 percent of China's total trade.

East Asian regionalism will also help to strengthen China's influence in international economic institutions. Despite its rapid economic growth, China finds its influence limited when acting alone. Regionalism will result in common economic interests in the region and hence the possibility of cooperation and coordination in international economic activities.

Finally, economic cooperation will help advance China's interests in other areas, such as cooperation on security, environmental protection, resources, and development.

China's interest in East Asian regionalism is not purely economical. It can be regarded as China's strategic move to take up a leadership role in the region at the expense of the US and Japanese influence. Arguably, Hu Angang's blueprint is based on China being the leader or one of the key leaders. Chinese competition with the United States contributed to the signing of the US–South Korea FTA. Reports by the US Congressional Research Service (CRS) pointed out the necessity of signing an FTA with Korea as soon as possible in a bid to tackle a Korea–China FTA. "Many American observers worry that Chinese influence over South Korean policy is likely to rise in the future, at the expense of the US," Mark E. Manyin, a CRS senior analyst, said in a 2007 report. Citing public opinion polls, Manyin said, "The growing anxiety among some Americans has come after a sharp decline in favorable views of the US among Koreans while more and more Koreans have favorable views of China" (Kim, 2007).

It appears that China's push for an EAFTA has lost much momentum, mainly because neither Japan nor South Korea is particularly enthusiastic about an FTA with China in the near future. What is more, the East Asian Summit, which involves ASEAN, China, Japan, and South Korea plus India, Australia, and New Zealand, has attracted much attention of East Asian states, particularly Japan, as a new form of East Asian regionalism. Nevertheless China remains interested in the proposed EAFTA.[8]

Conclusions

Before November 2000 when Chinese Premier Zhu Rongji surprised the world with a proposal to establish a free trade area with all ten ASEAN economies by 2010, China had been "more of a follower than a leader when it came to be dealing with multilateral economic arrangement" (Cheng, 2006). Since then, China has engaged in an FTA offensive and is an influential driving force of East Asian regionalism. As a trade-oriented economy, China has a strong interest in promoting trade liberalization.

On the other hand, China has used FTAs to enhance its competition capabilities in various areas. Economically, concrete benefits include lowering costs, expanding exportation, diverse markets, and helping address the anti-dumping concerns. More importantly, China's interest in FTA talks should be examined against the background that "the use of FTAs in geopolitical jockeying is reaching new heights in East Asia" (Caryl, 2007). Political and strategic considerations can play a decisive role in China's FTA decisions. It is no coincidence that China began its FTA initiatives in Southeast Asia where China has had historical influence that it aspires to reestablish, particularly in rivalry with Japan and the United States. At the same time, FTAs can also be useful vehicles for China to promote its "peaceful development" vision and the notion that China's development is an opportunity rather than a threat to other countries. China's FTA negotiation partners include some resource-rich countries, such as GCC and Australia. In terms of legal competition, China is still in its learning curve. Beijing is relatively new to the existing international trading system and has been focusing on how to make good use of it instead of challenging it.

The outcomes of China's FTA negotiations so far have highlighted the competition factor in Chinese selection of FTA partners. In Asia, China's FTAs with Pakistan and ASEAN are mainly driven by strategic and political considerations. Outside Asia, New Zealand became the first developed country to conclude FTA negotiations with China largely because as a small, open economy, it was relatively harmless to the Chinese economy. Also, China intended to reward New Zealand for its exemplary role in supporting China's effort to participate in the world economy. Similarly, Chile is a small and open economy with a strong political relationship with China. But more importantly, it can be China's springboard to Latin America. These cases point to China's often realist calculations although its FTA strategy is in line with its slide toward liberalism at a time when multilateral trade negotiations have not been productive. The cases demonstrate that China has been competing for economic, political, and strategic interests.

Whom has China been competing with then? The target countries can be specific, but not always. In the case of Pakistan, China is competing with other great powers for strategic interests and for its energy security. In ASEAN, China was mainly competing with Japan and the United States for future regional leadership role. China was also competing with "China threat theory" supporters in that the China–ASEAN FTA will substantially improve its image by demonstrating its rise as an opportunity. The competition factor can be applied to the New Zealand case in that New Zealand played an important role in the Chinese campaign for the recognition of its market economy status. Chile, on the other hand, is important to China's broadly defined economic competition in that it can be China's springboard to Latin America.

China has been active in promoting a China–Japan–South Korea FTA, which may lead to an EAFTA. China's interest in an EAFTA is multidimensional. Such an FTA would help to enhance China's economic security. More importantly, the FTA would strengthen China's influence in the region at the expense of other great powers, particularly the United States. So far China has made only limited progress in pushing for an EAFTA. However, as a rising power with a special interest in "peaceful development," China is set to continue its effort to increase its influence economically. Regional economic integration, which helps to strengthen China's competitiveness, both economic and noneconomic, will remain to be Beijing's key strategic interest.

Notes

1. Some sections of this chapter are based on Hoadley and Yang 2007.
2. Although China is subject to more AD initiations and measures than any other country, it is not the biggest victim in terms of intensity relative to trade value.
3. China and Singapore signed an FTA (CSFTA) on October 23, 2008. The CSFTA came into force on January 1, 2009.
4. Author's interviews in Beijing and Shanghai in October and November 2005 also confirmed this point.
5. By October 2007, 76 countries had recognized China's market economy status (Bhuyan, 2007).
6. Author's interview with David Walker on August 25, 2008.
7. Author's exchanges with Chinese analysts in Beijing in early August 2008.
8. Author's exchanges with Chinese analysts in Beijing in early August 2008.

12
Conclusion: FTAs in a Competitive World

Barbara Stallings and Saori N. Katada

Introduction

A large and increasing number of free trade agreements (FTAs) has become a defining feature of global trade in the early twenty-first century. Even countries such as those in East Asia, which were reluctant to engage in FTA negotiations a mere ten years ago, are now avid participants. Although the tangible benefits of FTAs are ambiguous,[1] and they may be undermining multilateral trade negotiations under the World Trade Organization (WTO), the FTA frenzy has continued and accelerated. Thus, we began by asking the following questions. What is driving these FTAs? What explains the intense interest of so many countries in FTAs despite their ambiguous benefits?

In order to address these questions, this volume started with the assumption that most FTAs are interconnected. That is, although the dynamics between FTA partners are important, a government's decision to negotiate an FTA with another country also impacts third countries. Those third countries, in turn, may feel pressured to participate in the FTA process not only because of their fundamental interest in liberalizing trade with certain partners, but also because partners (or rivals) already have FTA relationships with other countries. This interdependence of government decisions points to a process of FTA diffusion in the world. Such FTA diffusion, we hypothesized in the framework chapter (Chapter 1), is caused by emulative or competitive mechanisms, among which competitive pressures are dominant. Moreover, we argued that competitive pressures are multifaceted and should be disaggregated into different types of competition ranging from economic to political to legal.

Beyond trying to explain FTA diffusion, we also asked another important question regarding the impact of FTA proliferation on regional integration. If our claim is correct—that competitive motivations are behind the spread of most FTAs—the conclusion is contrary to the oft-heard assumption that FTAs will gradually lead to wider regional integration (Baldwin, 2006). Indeed, it looks increasingly likely that the FTA proliferation will challenge, rather than facilitate, region-wide FTA networks. For example, the Western Hemisphere has recently experienced the failure of a proposed region-wide free trade arrangement (the Free Trade Area of the Americas or FTAA) due in part to the growing number of inter- and intra-regional FTAs. Likewise, in East Asia, the main existing regional arrangement (the ASEAN [Association of Southeast Asian Nations] Free Trade Area or AFTA) has arguably been undermined by bilateral negotiations with nonmember countries.

In this concluding chapter, we discuss the findings from the three thematic chapters and seven country case study chapters. The seven countries for the case studies were selected because they have been among the most active participants in the FTA process, which enables us to examine the motives behind the rush to FTAs. The second section looks at the contextual factors that have confronted all countries and some that have confronted particular groups of countries. These contextual differences help to explain why FTAs emerged first in the Western Hemisphere and only later in East Asia. Third, we ask if diffusion dynamics have, indeed, been the central force behind the FTA proliferation in the Pacific Rim. A follow-up question concerns the difference between our two types of diffusion mechanisms: emulation and competition. Having confirmed that competition has become increasingly central to the FTA process, in the fourth section, we turn to three different types of competition—economic, political, and legal—and ask under what circumstances one is more important than the others. Section five examines the implications of FTA diffusion dynamics on regional integration in East Asia and Latin America and asks whether the FTA process is more likely to fragment or consolidate regional integration. Section six concludes this chapter.

Contextual factors and FTA proliferation in the Pacific Rim

As seen in Figure 1.1 in Chapter 1, the number of FTAs has accelerated dramatically from around 1990. One reason has to do with contextual factors prevalent in the global economy. A common global factor that has made all of these countries turn to bilateral preferential trade agreements is the stagnation or failure of multilateral trade negotiations. In the late 1980s and the early 1990s, the slow progress of the Uruguay Round of the General Agreement on Tariffs and Trade (GATT) provided early incentives for FTAs. In the current decade, the apparent failure of the WTO Doha Development Round drove many more countries toward bilateral trade arrangements. Some countries opted for FTAs to influence the multilateral process, while others acted to insure against the failure and/or to complement the shortcomings of multilateral negotiations (Perroni and Whalley, 2000).

Of course, not all countries decided to engage in FTAs, even though they shared the same global environment. For example, Brazil and several South American countries have preferred to work through a subregional integration scheme (Mercosur) rather than pursue bilateral agreements. In addition to providing policies to strengthen their domestic productive sectors, Mercosur is also seen as a bargaining tool that will increase its members' clout in international and interregional negotiations (Morales, 2006). Likewise, in East Asia, Malaysia was very reluctant to establish FTAs until the mid-2000s (Hoadley, 2007: 320). Not only was the Malaysian leadership concerned that bilateral FTA initiatives would undermine regional cohesion, but also that they could undermine the country's domestic political strategy with respect to ethnic relations and certain sectors of the economy (Ramasamy and Yeung, 2007). In these cases, domestic political and economic priorities proved more important than the push toward FTAs. This outcome was more likely to be the case where a country had a relatively closed economy with a strong state role. Under those circumstances, productivity was often low, leading to fears about competitiveness, and interest groups could mobilize to maintain the status quo.

For those countries that did adopt FTAs, the timing varied across regions in part due to reaction to these global factors as well as due to the impact of regional factors. Thus, the Western Hemisphere began the FTA process almost a decade earlier than East Asia. As usual, the United States took the lead, turning to FTAs as a way to influence the multilateral negotiations. After early experimentation with FTAs in the 1980s with Israel (1985) and Canada (1988), the latter arrangement was expanded in the early 1990s into the North American Free Trade Agreement or NAFTA (1994). In the 2000s, the United States has been using FTAs as part of a trade strategy to make small partner countries engage in "competitive liberalization." That is, in order to have preferential access to the all-important US market, its FTA-negotiating partners must demonstrate their willingness and ability to "qualify" for an agreement by meeting conditions beyond reciprocal liberalization. Those conditions include a number of "behind-the-border" issues such as labor rules and environmental standards, including amendment of the country's laws to comply with the FTA with the United States (see Chapter 5).

By the early 1990s, the two Latin American countries in our sample were beginning to be influenced by the US moves in pursuit of FTAs. What distinguished them from other Latin American countries was their earlier decision to adopt unilateral trade liberalization (under a military government in Chile or IMF/World Bank conditionality as a result of the debt crisis in Mexico), which made them less reliant on protectionist policies. The purpose of the FTAs in the two countries varied across their multiple partners. FTAs with large countries such as the United States and the European Union were driven mostly by economic interests, while those with their Latin American neighbors were negotiated primarily for political and diplomatic reasons. Neither country stopped there, however, but expanded its horizons across the Pacific Ocean to engage in FTAs with East Asia in the 2000s.

East Asian countries were latecomers in the global FTA frenzy. Nevertheless once the initial reluctance to abandon the multilateral-only position was overcome by events of the late 1990s and the early 2000s, Japan, South Korea, Singapore, and China all began to negotiate FTAs with enthusiasm. The most important catalytic event was the Asian financial crisis (1997–98), which led many Asian countries to reform and liberalize their economies (under, or independent of, the IMF). In addition, the rise of China intensified their eagerness to expand market access and/or to attract foreign investment. During the same years, the most prominent regional trade arrangement, the Asia Pacific Economic Cooperation forum or APEC, was undermined by the failure of its Early Voluntary Sector Liberalization (EVSL) negotiation.[2] And as the WTO talks failed in Seattle in 1999, East Asian governments saw an urgent need to establish an alternative trade strategy so as not to be left out of the new preferential trade access.

In Southeast Asia, the financial crisis was also a significant event, which stalled the momentum behind ASEAN integration as foreign investment inflows and intraregional trade slowed. As an avid promoter of regional trade liberalization, ASEAN member Singapore took the lead in negotiating FTAs, particularly with economically advanced countries such as Japan and the United States. South Korea and Japan also embraced FTAs as the foundation of their trade strategies. The newly elected Korean President, Kim Dae-jung (1998–2003), approached Japan in the fall of 1998 to launch a study in preparation for a bilateral FTA. Although this FTA is yet to materialize, both governments have actively launched FTA negotiations with other countries in Asia and beyond. Both governments, however, have had to choose their FTA partners with care due to internal pressures for agricultural protection. Korea became an aggressive FTA promoter and aspiring FTA hub in the region as it signed (but has not ratified) an FTA with the United States in 2007. Japan has thus far avoided engaging in FTAs with large trade partners such as China or the United States, but has expanded its bilateral and regional FTA network into Southeast Asia. Finally, China's FTA enthusiasm began after its accession to the WTO in late 2001. Many FTAs have been concluded and are currently being negotiated by the Chinese authorities. Partners include countries in the region and beyond.

In sum, the country chapters in this volume as well as the thematic chapters underline the importance of contextual factors in explaining the acceleration of FTAs in the past two decades. The paralysis of the multilateral trade negotiations under the GATT, and later under the WTO influenced most of the countries in their adoption of FTAs. Regional factors, such as the Latin American debt crisis of the 1980s and the Asian financial crisis of the 1990s, were also important. Together they help to explain the difference in timing as the Western Hemisphere was the first to engage in FTAs in the 1990s (or even earlier) and the Asian countries only followed in the 2000s.

Diffusion or non-diffusion: The FTA processes at work

In Chapter 1 of the volume, we posed three hypotheses regarding the sources of the FTA proliferation and the reasons for each country's adoption of an FTA strategy (Table 1.1). In the first hypothesis, a country engages in FTAs autonomously without stimulus from other countries' FTAs. Therefore, no diffusion pressures exist (non-diffusion hypothesis). The second and third hypotheses incorporate diffusion dynamics. In the emulation hypothesis, where a country is assumed to have copied others based on their close social and policy connections, it therefore should negotiate similar FTAs with as many partners as possible. The competition hypothesis, by contrast, assumes that a country moves toward FTAs due to competitive pressures in economic (market access, investment promotion, and averting losses), political (diplomatic considerations and political rivalry), and/or legal (standard setting and rule-making) spheres. They then negotiate agreements on a carefully targeted basis with different terms depending on the partner.

What do the country chapters tell us about these hypotheses? They suggest that all three hypotheses were at work in different countries and at different stages of their FTA engagement. What we want to do in this chapter is to uncover some patterns to explain when diffusion was more important than non-diffusion and when different types of diffusion became more important.

Table 12.1 presents our argument on which hypothesis best explains each country's FTA policy adoption at each stage. As discussed previously, the timing of early and later stages of FTA adoption differed between the Western Hemisphere and East Asia. Nevertheless the table makes clear that some countries were "first movers," acting on the basis of autonomous motives that were often political or to position themselves to take advantage of economic gains in the future. They were not reacting to already-existing FTAs. Examples include the United States and Chile. Most of the East Asian countries, by contrast, entered the FTA scene almost a decade later than Latin America and thus had more opportunities and incentives to emulate others in their early stage of FTA engagement. Examples include Korea and China. Mexico and Singapore fall somewhere between the first movers and emulators. Despite being an early mover, Mexico also emulated the US strategy, especially after joining NAFTA in the early 1990s. Singapore, not an early adopter of FTAs according to Latin

Table 12.1 Explanations for FTA diffusion by country and period

	Early stage of FTA adoption		Late stage of FTA adoption	
	Latin America: (before 1990 to late 1990s)	East Asia: (late 1990s to 2002)	Latin America: (late 1990s to the present)	East Asia: (2002 to the present)
Non-diffusion	United States, Chile			
Emulation	Mexico, Chile	South Korea, Singapore		China
Competition			United States, Mexico, Chile	South Korea, China, Japan, Singapore

American standards, became a first mover in East Asia. What is most relevant for our research, however, is the clustering of *all* the countries in the "competition hypothesis" box in the later stage of FTA adoption. Hence, the main point of our argument is that competitive pressures became more important over time for all the countries.

Among the early movers, the United States was the most important. Triggered by its own serious economic and security concerns, according to Quiliconi and Wise in Chapter 5, the Reagan administration negotiated an FTA with Israel to satisfy both international (Middle East security) and domestic (pro-Israel lobby) demands. This was followed by the US FTA with Canada to guarantee preferential economic access in both countries, which were suffering from economic downturns. The US administration incorporated "GATT-plus" features such as rules on investment, services, dispute settlement, and intellectual property rights in its early FTAs. When Mexico approached the United States for an FTA, which expanded the US–Canada treaty to the three-party NAFTA, it added the new trade agendas on labor rules and the environment.

Other first movers in their respective regions included Chile and Singapore. Although geographically distant, Chile and Singapore share common traits in that they are relatively small and vulnerable to the external economic and political environment. They decided to use FTAs to help mitigate these vulnerabilities. Chile actively utilized FTAs not only to expand its market access and investment potential, but also to regain its legitimacy in the Latin American region after a long period of military dictatorship. Singapore, too, sought to strengthen its economic ties and facilitate mutual economic benefits and business transactions and to overcome its security vulnerability through FTAs.

For most countries covered in this study, however, diffusion mechanisms account for a large part of FTA proliferation. Most of our country analyses reached the conclusion that both emulative and competitive dynamics promoted FTAs. In particular, emulative diffusion was found to have influenced the countries' trade strategy in the early stage of FTA adoption, as the idea of FTAs gained ground within the respective countries' policy circles. For example, in Chapter 9, Koo argues that after the Asian financial crisis, the Kim Dae-jung administration in South Korea learned from other countries. In addition to conducting many FTA feasibility studies, it launched an FTA with Chile to learn negotiating techniques that would be useful in later agreements. Although quite late in joining the FTA moves, China also demonstrated a willingness to learn from what others were doing in FTAs, as it realized that the WTO was deadlocked. Even Chile, one of the early FTA adopters, was influenced by the NAFTA negotiations among the United States, Canada, and Mexico. Chile wanted to negotiate an agreement with the United States, but had to wait for almost a decade as the expiration of the fast-track authority stalled the US FTA process. Despite the influence of diffusion pressures, some of these countries were relatively slow in actually engaging in FTAs during the emulative phase. This was particularly the case for many of the East Asian governments, which had yet to establish broad domestic support for a policy shift. The early FTA adopters, Singapore and Chile, managed to shift their trade policies in favor of FTAs relatively quickly, since those countries were already extremely open.

Competitive pressures started to mount at a later stage as FTAs spread throughout both regions, which triggered more aggressive and targeted FTA strategies and negotiations among the countries studied. As discussed in detail in the section below, the competitive pressures came from multiple channels. For example, Japan was pressured to launch FTAs not only to avoid being shut out of certain markets such as that of Mexico, but also to compete with China for regional leadership, once China began to engage in FTAs with ASEAN. The US administrations since the mid-1990s sought to reactivate fast-track authority (now called trade promotion authority), which would make it easier to use FTAs at both regional and bilateral levels. Both Chile and Mexico expanded their FTA networks to guarantee future market access in, and investment from, industrial countries such as the United States, the EU, and Japan. Even Singapore engaged in competition to establish itself as the FTA hub of Asia.

In Chapter 1, we established emulative and competitive forces of diffusion as alternative hypotheses. The analysis of the country chapters, however, demonstrated that these two diffusion dynamics have frequently manifested themselves in sequence—from emulation to competition. For the majority of those countries, where emulative pressures led policymakers to accept the idea of FTAs at an early stage, increasing competitive pressures drove the policy toward significant expansion.

Types of competition: Economic, political, and legal

Following our argument that competitive pressures have become increasingly important, and indeed can currently be considered as the main motive for FTA proliferation, it then becomes important to ask which aspects of competitive pressure have driven which countries to adopt FTAs more actively. In the three thematic chapters of this volume, the authors have identified the important sources of economic, political, and legal competition.

In Chapter 2, Urata explains that there are contrasting economic motivations with respect to FTAs between those that are included and those that are excluded. A country seeks FTAs actively because of positive gains from inclusion that range from trade creation effects to competition promotion effects. Furthermore, there is a significant gain from FTAs if a country becomes a trade hub and/or attracts more FDI. Meanwhile, those that are excluded become concerned about trade-diversion effects and "relative loss" compared with the countries included in FTAs. Urata emphasizes the importance of FTAs for relatively small countries that try to become large as they eliminate cross-border trade barriers through FTAs. For large countries, the impact of FTAs in increasing their size is limited, although they do benefit from improving terms of trade.

In terms of political competition, Mochizuki (Chapter 3) explicitly distinguishes between large countries (the United States, China, and Japan) and smaller ones (South Korea) in terms of the use of FTAs as a foreign policy strategy. Large countries often use FTAs as an integral part of their mixed hedging strategy toward each other, as each applies balancing and accommodating strategies at the same time, and to entice the support of smaller countries. Meanwhile, the smaller countries often rely on FTAs to reduce their perceived security vulnerability.

The stagnation of the multilateral process has intensified legal competition. Nakagawa (Chapter 4) argues that, without an active multilateral forum, the major players in rule and standard-setting in trade and investment turn to bilateral and regional fora to pursue their "bottom-up" rule-making in fields such as antidumping, trade facilitation, and intellectual property rights. FTAs are often used to specify and implement such rules, and the major powers—such as the United States, Japan, and China—are actively engaging in such competition. In addition, there is legal competition on the global scale among the EU, the United States, and Japan in the field of competition law and policy. Smaller countries are restricted to being rule and standard takers, not makers.

The thematic chapters have identified distinctive patterns based on size (economic or power-based) in the way that countries respond to the three competitive pressures. As we review the country chapters, we look for evidence of patterns regarding how large and small countries respond to and prioritize economic and political/legal motives behind engaging in FTAs.

Table 12.2 demonstrates that country size leads to one important pattern as to how the three competitive pressures influence the countries' choice of FTA partners. The country chapters indicate that as the FTA race enters the competitive stage, economic competition becomes the predominant concern for smaller countries with weaker bargaining power such as Chile,

Table 12.2 Types of competition by size of country

	Type of competition	
	Economic competition	**Political and legal competition**
Small countries	◀── Singapore ──▶ ◀── Chile ──▶ ◀── South Korea ──▶ ◀── Mexico ──▶	
Large countries		◀── Japan ──▶ ◀── China ──▶ ◀── United States ──▶

Mexico, South Korea, and Singapore. Those countries have opted to engage in FTAs with countries that have large markets, especially the United States but also the EU and Japan, to secure market access and FDI. In the Western Hemisphere, Mexico became the typical country that, by participating in NAFTA, has enhanced its economic attractiveness. Once Mexico succeeded in capturing preferential access to the US market, other small, export-oriented countries had to follow suit. Chile had already engaged in trade agreements with its neighbors before the mid-1990s, but NAFTA triggered its concern over market access, leading Chile to engage in FTAs with large countries beyond Latin America. Both South Korea and Singapore obviously had the idea of cementing a strategic partnership to overcome their respective security vulnerability when they launched an FTA negotiation, as noted by Mochizuki (Chapter 3), but both countries also have had intense concern for their market access in the United States, as the US government began expanding its bilateral FTA network. All of these small countries are rule takers when it comes to legal competition. Nevertheless the large number of FTAs that each small country negotiates increases its prospects for becoming a regional FTA hub and enhances its prestige and bargaining power over its economic competitors.

For large countries, such as the United States, Japan, or China, the motivation for their aggressive FTA policies includes both economic and noneconomic goals. An example is China's choice of FTA partners based on whether the partner would recognize China as a "market economy." This not only relieves China's economic pressures in avoiding ad hoc antidumping claims against it, but also gives it a legitimate place in the trading world. The United States, too, has been interested in promoting its political and legal agendas, through multiple FTAs with small countries, in addition to economic gains in trade access when it comes to relatively large countries in Asia. Japan provides another case where politics is clearly relevant but market access, particularly being shut out of existing markets for Japanese industries, is also an important concern. At the same time, the Japanese government is preoccupied with the country's uncompetitive domestic sectors, particularly agriculture, so that it cannot engage in FTAs with countries such as the United States or China that threaten those sectors.

Pressures of political and legal competition are particularly central reasons for large states—those with hegemonic ambitions—to engage in FTAs. For the United States, most of its FTAs—from its early accords with Israel, Canada, and Mexico through its later ones with Asian countries—have been driven by security and political aims. The United States has used FTAs to solidify or strengthen its security relations with distant countries such as Singapore and South Korea. At the same time, China's increasingly active pursuit of FTAs both in East Asia and in Latin America has pressured the United States. The dissemination of their own models of economic integration is also important for the large countries. The US government is keen on solidifying the NAFTA model as the standard for FTAs throughout the Western Hemisphere and into other parts of the world. It is also important for the United States to influence standard setting at the multilateral level. For these purposes, the United States uses its market power to entice countries to compete for FTAs with it.

Likewise, the rivalry between Japan and China—as Solís (Chapter 10) and Yang (Chapter 11), respectively, argue—has pushed these two countries into active FTA negotiations within the Asian region, since both want not only to demonstrate their trade leadership but also to establish their own model of FTA standards. China offers a non-legalistic FTA model that features selective liberalization without clauses on issues like environment and labor standards. Japanese FTAs (called Economic Partnership Agreements or EPAs), by contrast, promote WTO-plus provisions including rules on investment and intellectual property, but they also emphasize trade facilitation and economic cooperation.

The multiple FTA motivations for the large countries have implications for the FTA strategies of the smaller ones. The countries with market (and often financial) power are able to use their economic appeal to gain ground in other areas of competition. An FTA proposed by the United States to small countries such as Singapore or Korea is hard to refuse because of the large economic gains (or possible punishments and losses) those countries expect. Japan and China also use their economic power to gain ground in intraregional FTA competition. At the same time, small countries can achieve their economic goals by taking advantage of political or legal competition among the large countries. For example, as discussed by Flores-Quiroga on Mexico (Chapter 7), small countries can gain advantage by supporting larger ones—in this case, the United States in its legal competition to spread the NAFTA standard. ASEAN nations (Chapter 8), too, have capitalized on the China–Japan competition to become the focal point in regional integration schemes such as ASEAN+3 and the East Asia Summit.

Beyond the role of size, important domestic political elements also help define the way in which countries react and respond to competitive pressures. The country chapters suggest three such elements. The first is whether competitive pressures affect a country's FTA policy in a bottom-up or top-down manner. The chapters on Mexico and Japan identify bottom-up pressures in economic competition where their respective business communities, fearing lack of credibility and investment shortage (Mexico) or trade diversion (Japan), pushed their respective governments to engage in FTAs with certain partners.[3] The other chapters identify a top-down channel of FTA decision-making. Both Chile and Korea started out on the FTA route as their leaders accepted the idea in the early stage through autonomous decision or emulation, and later began engaging in FTAs based on economic competition. In addition, for both of them, recognition as a regional trade hub or a legitimate democratic regime has been an important trigger to engage in FTAs with large economies. In short, although the governments of Japan and Mexico responded positively to some bottom-up pressures that ultimately led them to engage in FTAs, the countries with top-down channels had an easier time converting competitive pressures into action.

A second element has to do with the number and power of so-called veto players in a given country (Tsebelis, 1999; MacIntyre, 2001). Because of the anticipated negative impact of trade liberalization, potential losers from a particular FTA object to the negotiation. A typical case is the domestic agri-cultural opposition in Japan, which has constrained the Japanese government's options in terms of its FTA partners and the speed at which the country can pursue FTAs. Many of the small countries—such as Chile, Mexico, or South Korea—that engaged in FTAs in pursuit of economic goals had gone through economic liberalization and reform prior to launching FTA activism. If they had not, the anti-liberalization opposition could have trumped FTA negotiations with large countries. Political regime type also affects the influence of veto players. For example, authoritarian political regimes in China and Singapore enabled those governments to implement top-down FTA decisions without strong opposition. Therefore, those two countries have been able to utilize FTAs in order to respond to economic and political competition.

Finally, domestic political institutions are important in enabling the executive branch to overcome domestic constraints. The United States, for example, where institutional arrangements allow for both top-down and bottom-up proc-esses, depended on the presence of "fast track" or "trade promotion authority" for the executive branch to realize FTAs. In Korea, President Roh empowered Office of the Minister for Trade, whose relative insulation from interest group pressure allowed the Korean government to move quickly with the controver-sial FTAs, especially the one with the United States. Chile has also made institutional innovations to help its FTA strategy. Over a number of years, it set up new offices to deal with trade issues and trained its negotiators so well that other countries sought to negotiate with it in order to learn negotiating techniques.

In summary, analysis of the country chapters enables us to identify impor-tant patterns of diffusion influencing the adoption of FTAs. Once the early stage of FTA adoption was past, all the countries in our study launched mul-tiple FTA negotiations propelled by competitive pressures. Nonetheless, as we unpack the process of competition into economic, political, and legal pres-sures, we find that competition in the economic realm tended to trigger FTA activism among small countries, while political and legal competition has dominated FTA initiatives among large countries. This does not mean that political factors never enter the calculations of small-country governments or that economic gains are not a factor for large countries, but size is a significant factor in determining causal patterns. This size effect was complemented by domestic political factors—bottom-up versus top-down decision-making, the influence of veto players, and the role of institutions—which cut across the size categories to enrich our analysis.

Implications of FTA diffusion on regional integration

The final and very important question of this study concerns the implications of the rapid increase of FTAs that are triggered by competitive pressures on regional integration. Surprisingly, this question is seldom asked. Investigation into the impact of FTAs (and regionalism) on the global and multilateral trading regime has produced a substantial volume of scholarship. Often it has been framed as an argument about "building blocs" versus "stumbling blocs" (Lawrence, 1996). The logic is confusing, however, because many of these studies unconsciously conflate FTAs with regionalism (Mansfield and Milner, 1999). Even more problematic, scholars tend to assume that FTAs, even strictly bilateral ones, are a forward step toward region-wide free trade (Baldwin, 2006), despite concerns over the negative impact of the "spaghetti (noodle) bowl" phenomenon.

Our study points to a different assessment. Despite some elements of emulation in the early stage, the major trigger of FTA proliferation in recent times has been competitive pressure, and all three aspects of competition—economic, political, and legal—result in regional fragmentation or even disintegration. A clear sign of contradiction between FTAs and regional cooperation projects in the Pacific Rim is the number of cross-regional trade arrangements. Table 12.3 makes it clear that FTAs are spread throughout the world, and cross-regional FTAs such as Mexico–EU and South Korea–United States are frequent (Solís and Katada, 2007a). Especially for small countries, there are as many or more FTA partners from outside the region as from within.

A source of interest in cross-regional agreements is economic competition, particularly for small countries, which leads governments to seek FTAs with countries that have large markets and are a source of investment irrespective of their geographic location. For example, Stallings (Chapter 6) argues that an active FTA promoter like Chile is viewed by its neighbors as an agent that undermines regional integration, as it signs many FTAs irrespective of the partners' location. Likewise, Singapore and Korea have signed FTAs with countries far and near, large and small. This is a way for these countries to become FTA hubs in their respective regions, which not only strengthens their economies, but also enhances their economic and political leverage over intraregional FTA negotiations.

Political competition, especially among major powers, also undermines regional integration. When the United States extended its bilateral FTA network into Asia, this reinforced the tendency toward a hub-and-spokes system between the United States and its allies in that region. Moreover, major power rivalry between Japan and China has prevented the emergence of coherent regional trade arrangements in East Asia. The chapters on these two countries make it clear that this rivalry accelerated the spread of FTAs in the region, but such dynamics have had negative consequences when it comes to regional coherence and convergence. Even ASEAN, which currently constitutes the core of East Asian

Table 12.3   Geographic coverage of FTAs (as of March 2009)

	Immediate neighbor	Within the "region"†	Cross-region
The United States	Canada (1988/1994*) Mexico (1994)	Chile (2004) CAFTA–DR‡ (2006) Dominican Republic (2006) Costa Rica (2009) Peru (2009)	Israel (1985) Jordan (2001) Singapore (2004) Australia (2005) Bahrain (2006) Oman (2006) Morocco (2006) Korea (signed 2007)
Chile	Bolivia (1993) Peru (1998/2009)	Mexico (1992/1999) Venezuela (1993) Colombia (1994) Ecuador (1994) Mercosur (1996) Canada (1997) Costa Rica (2002) El Salvador (2002) United States (2004)	EU (2003) EFTA (2004) Korea (2004) China (2006) P-4¶ (2006) India (2007) Japan (2007)
Mexico	United States (1994) Guatemala (2001)	Chile (1992/1999) Canada (1994) G-3§ (1995) Bolivia (1995) Costa Rica (1995) Uruguay (1998) Nicaragua (1998) Honduras (2001) El Salvador (2001)	EU (2000/EU 15+12 2004) Israel (2000) EFTA (2000) Japan (2005)
Singapore		Japan (2002) Korea (2006)	New Zealand (2001) Australia (2003) EFTA (2003) United States (2004) Jordan (2005) India (2005) Panama (2006) P-4¶ (2006) Peru (signed 2008)
ASEAN		China (2005) Korea (2007) Japan (2008)	Australia/ New Zealand (signed 2008)
South Korea	Singapore (2006) ASEAN (2007)		Chile (2004) EFTA (2006) United States (signed 2007)

(continued)

Table 12.3 (Continued)

	Immediate neighbor	Within the "region"[†]	Cross-region
Japan		Singapore (2002) Malaysia (2006) Thailand (2007) Philippines (2008) Indonesia (2008) ASEAN (2008) Brunei (2008) Vietnam (2008)	Mexico (2005) Chile (2007) Switzerland (signed 2009)
China	Macao (2004) Hong Kong (2004)	ASEAN (2005)	Chile (2006) Pakistan (2007) New Zealand (2008) Peru (signed 2008)

* Years are those when the agreements came into force, unless otherwise specified.
† Region defined according to the World Bank categorization.
‡ CAFTA-DR includes El Salvador, Guatemala, Honduras, and Nicaragua.
¶ P-4 is short for Pacific-4 that includes Singapore, New Zealand, Chile, and Brunei.
§ G-3 includes Mexico, Colombia, and Venezuela.
Source: FTA tables from country chapters (Tables 5.2, 6.1, 7.1, 8.1, 8.2, 9.1, 10.1, and 11.1), WTO RTA data (http://www.wto.org/english/tratop_e/region_e/a_z_e.xls, downloaded October 2008).

regionalism, has had difficulty in managing broader regional cooperation in the face of the Japan–China rivalry. The proliferation of "ASEAN+1" FTAs, discussed by Terada (Chapter 8), illustrates the challenge of establishing regional cohesion when different types of FTAs are promoted by major powers. In such a context, ASEAN has no leverage over or interest in the consolidation of those arrangements into a broader and more coherent regional trade arrangement.[4] In the Western Hemisphere, the US strategy of "competitive liberalization" and the introduction of "new" issues in the WTO Doha Round have created two groups of countries: the "can do" countries that support the American agenda and an anti-American bloc that insists on the traditional trade issues. In addition, events in the early 2000s, from the Argentine financial crisis to the Iraq War, created a wedge in the region leading to the failure of the FTAA.

Finally, some aspects of legal competition undermine regional integration. The emergence of multiple and incompatible rules and different modalities of FTAs establishes path-dependence under which coherent rules and standards have a difficult time emerging. The NAFTA standard promoted by the United States (along with Mexico and Chile) has created a rival to the pre-existing shallower regional integration modality in Latin America. This standard has also been incorporated as a negotiation model among some of the East Asian countries that have FTAs with these countries, particularly

Singapore and Korea. In East Asia, Nakagawa argues that Japan champions its own emphasis on trade facilitation, its unique competition policy, and ways to restrict certain antidumping procedures. Those approaches are often supported by East Asian countries that face the similar trade constraints vis-à-vis the United States and Europe. The Japanese government seeks to capitalize those efforts to demonstrate its trade leadership in the region.

In summary, coherent regional integration is by no means a logical or natural consequence of FTA proliferation in the Pacific Rim, and it is misleading to assume, at least in the medium term, that bilateral FTAs will lead to regionalism. Some countries such as Mexico, Korea, and China have experienced a period of emulation, when their governments looked to first movers of FTAs. As we explained earlier, emulation can lead to common trade policies within a region, and thus improved possibilities for integration projects. All the countries in our study, however, became active FTA adopters when competitive pressures set in. Because those competitive pressures come in different forms, from economic to political to legal, and because small and large countries are influenced by different forms of FTAs, these pressures create multiple layers of challenges to coherent regional integration projects. These range from contradictory preferences ("noodle bowl") to cross-regional partners to rivalry in political and legal contexts.

Conclusions

FTAs have become a popular policy instrument for many countries in the last two decades. Despite their ambiguous payoffs and the possible domestic costs of adjustment, FTAs proliferated dramatically in the Pacific Rim. Our study found that it is the spread of FTAs and the competitive pressures engendered that make many countries hasten to follow suit. In short, once competition sets in, it is costly to remain outside of the rapidly spreading FTA networks.

Nonetheless, countries entered into the FTA boom in different ways. On the one hand, the countries that adopted FTAs early, as first movers, were able to opt for agreements that satisfied their domestic and foreign policy needs. The United States, for example, engaged in its earliest FTA for security purposes, while Chile and Singapore pursued both economic and diplomatic interests. On the other hand, those that adopted FTA policies later had some models to emulate. But as the number of FTAs began to increase, competitive pressures mounted, and all the countries in our study reacted to them by rapidly engaging in more and more FTAs. Economic pressures were especially important for small countries such as Singapore, Chile, Korea, and Mexico, as they aggressively sought to expand their preferential market access in large countries to counter current or future competitors. Large countries, by contrast, were not only responding to economic competition, but their FTAs were also driven by political competition. Furthermore, the large countries used FTAs to set and spread the rules and standards of trade.

These recent FTAs triggered by competitive pressures have an unexpectedly negative impact on regional integration projects on both sides of the Pacific. While market-seeking motives among the small countries created unruly networks of FTAs crisscrossing regions, political rivalry among the large countries undermined the unity in the region through diplomatic as well as rule-setting competition. Together, these two dynamics will prevent the consolidation of coherent regional projects in either East Asia or Latin America anytime soon.

Notes

1. Many economists caution that FTAs are the second (or third) best policy option; see, for example, Bhagwati et al. (1998).
2. APEC was established in 1989 as a trade liberalization and facilitation forum under the initiative of Australia and Japan. The forum, which includes the annual heads-of-state summit, expanded its membership in the mid-1990s to 21 members including all of the countries in our study. APEC has emphasized voluntary unilateral liberalization efforts on the part of members, particularly in the context of the Bogor declaration in 1994. The EVSL negotiation took place in 1997 to promote market liberalization of selected sectors. The attempt failed due to Japan's opposition to the inclusion of forestry and fisheries in the package (Krauss, 2003).
3. It is important to note, however, that this bottom-up pressure does not always succeed in moving governments to act. A very telling example comes from Japan. Even though China is the country with which Japanese businesses would most like to establish an FTA, there is no sign of the government moving to launch such an effort. This result is because bottom-up pressure can be both in favor of an FTA (by big business) and in opposition (by the agricultural sector) (see Chapter 10).
4. Each major power promotes regional trade arrangements that would enhance its own position. Thus, China prefers an ASEAN+3 agreement, which would only include China, South Korea, and Japan plus ASEAN. Japan prefers an ASEAN+6, which would add Australia, New Zealand, and India to tip the weight of power in Japan's favor. Moreover, resentful and fearful of being excluded, the United States has been keen on reinvigorating APEC as it proposed the Free Trade Area of the Asia Pacific (FTAAP) in the fall of 2006.

Bibliography

Abbott, F. M. (2001) "NAFTA and the Legalization of World Politics: A Case Study," in J. Goldstein, M. Kahler, R. O. Keohane, & A. M. Slaughter (eds) *Legalization and World Politics* (Cambridge: The MIT Press), pp. 135–63.

Abbott, F. M., R. O. Keohane, A. Moravcsik, A.-M. Slaughter, & D. Snydal (2001) "The Concept of Legalization," in J. Goldstein, M. Kahler, R. O. Keohane, & A. M. Slaughter (eds) *Legalization and World Politics* (Cambridge: The MIT Press), pp. 17–35.

Acharya, A. (2000) *The Quest for Identity: International Relations of Southeast Asia* (Singapore: Oxford University Press).

—— (2007) "Made in America? Agency and Power in Asian Regionalism," *Journal of East Asian Studies*, Vol. 7, No. 3, pp. 371–8.

Acharya, A. & S. S. Tan (2005) "Betwixt Balance and Community: America, ASEAN, and the Security of Southeast Asia," *International Relations of the Asia-Pacific*, Vol. 6, No. 1, pp. 37–59.

Aggarwal, V. K. (2006) "Bilateral Trade Agreement in the Asia-Pacific," in V. K. Aggarwal & S. Urata (eds) *Bilateral Trade Agreements in Asia-Pacific: Origins, Evolution, and Implications* (New York and London: Routledge), pp. 3–26.

Aggarwal, V. K. & M. G. Koo (2005) "Beyond Network Power? The Dynamics of Formal Economic Integration in Northeast Asia," *The Pacific Review*, Vol. 18, No. 2, pp. 189–216.

—— (2006) "The Evolution and Implications of Bilateral Trade Agreements in the Asia-Pacific," in V. K. Aggarwal & S. Urata (eds) *Bilateral Trade Agreements in Asia-Pacific: Origins, Evolution, and Implications* (New York and London: Routledge), pp. 279–99.

—— (2007) "Northeast Asia's Economic and Security Regionalism: Withering or Blossoming?" in G. Shin & D. C. Sneider (eds) *Cross Currents: Regionalism and Nationalism in Northeast Asia* (Washington, DC: Brookings Institution Press), pp. 43–76.

—— (2009) "Economic and Security Institution Building in Northeast Asia: An Analytical Overview," in V. Aggarwal & M. G. Koo (eds) *Northeast Asian Regionalism: Ripe for Integration?* (New York: Springer), pp. 1–36.

Aggarwal, V. K. & S. Urata (eds) (2006) *Bilateral Trade Agreements in the Asia-Pacific: Origins, Evolution, and Implications* (New York and London: Routledge).

Ahn, D. (2007) "Emerging Diversity in Trade Remedy Systems: The Case of East Asian FTAs," in Tamio Nakamura (ed.) *The Dynamics of East Asian Regionalism in Comparative Perspective*, ISS Research Series No. 24. (Tokyo: Institute of Social Science, University of Tokyo), pp. 211–21.

Ai, H. (2006) "Jingji quanqiuhua diertiao daolu: Zhongguo FTA zhanlue" [The Second Way of Economic Globalization: China's FTA Strategy], *Guangdong Shenji* [*Guangdong Auditing*], No. 2, pp. 4–9.

Alter, K. J. (2001) "The European Union's Legal System and Domestic Policy: Spillover or Backlash?" in J. Goldstein, M. Kahler, R. O. Keohane, & A. M. Slaughter (eds) *Legalization and World Politics* (Cambridge: The MIT Press), pp. 105–34.

Amsden, A. (1989) *Asia's Next Giant: South Korea and Late Industrialization* (New York: Oxford University Press).

Ando, M. & S. Urata (2007) "The Impacts of East Asia FTA: A CGE Model Simulation Study," *Journal of International Economic Studies*, Vol. 11, No. 2, pp. 3–75.

Aninat, A. & M. Botto (2005) "The Influence of Locally Produced Research on Trade Policy Making: The Case of Chile," paper prepared for Global Development Network project on "Bridging Research and Policy" (Washington, DC: GDN).

Aninat, C., J. Londregan, P. Navia, & J. Vial (2004) "Political Institutions, Policymaking Processes, and Policy Outcomes in Chile," unpublished paper (Washington, DC: Inter-American Development Bank).

Antkiewicz, A. & J. Whalley (2005) "China's New Regional Trade Agreements," *The World Economy*, Vol. 28, No. 10, pp. 1539–57.

Arase, D. (1995) *Buying Power: The Political Economy of Japan's Foreign Aid* (Boulder: Lynne Rienner).

Armitage, R. L. & J. S. Nye (2007) *The US–Japan Alliance: Getting Asia Right through 2020* (Washington, DC: Center for Strategic and International Studies).

ASEAN–China Expert Group on Economic Cooperation (2001) *Forging Closer ASEAN–China Economic Relations in the 21st Century*, October, http://www.aseansec.org/newdata/asean_chi.pdf, accessed on October 20, 2007.

Azuma, S. (ed.) (2007) *FTA-no Seijikeizai Gaku [Political Economy of FTA]* (Tokyo: IDE-JETRO), p. 258.

Baier, S. L. & J. H. Bergstrand (2004) "Economic Determinants of Free Trade Agreements," *Journal of International Economics*, Vol. 64, pp. 29–63.

—————— (2007) "Do Free Trade Agreements Actually Increase Members' International Trade?" *Journal of International Economics*, Vol. 71, pp. 72–95.

Balassa, B. (1961) *The Theory of Economic Integration* (London: Richard D. Irwin).

Baldwin, R. E. (1995) "A Domino Theory of Regionalism," in R. E. Baldwin, P. Haaparanta & J. Kiander (eds) *Expanding Membership of the European Union* (Cambridge: Cambridge University Press), pp. 25–48.

—————— (1997) "The Causes of Regionalism," *The World Economy*, pp. 865–88.

—————— (2006) "Multilateralising Regionalism: Spaghetti Bowls as Building Blocs on the Path to Global Free Trade," *The World Economy*, pp. 1451–518.

—————— (2007) "Managing the Noodle Bowl: The Fragility of East Asian Regionalism," *Working Paper Series on Regional Economic Integration, No.7*, (Tokyo: Asian Development Bank).

Baldwin, R. E. & A. J. Venables (1995) "Regional Economic Integration," in G. M. Grossman & K. Rogoff (eds) *Handbook of International Economics 3* (Elsevier: Amsterdam, The Netherlands), pp. 1597–644.

Bank of Korea (2001) "Comparative Analysis and Prospects of South Korea–China–Japan Trade Relationships," *Policy Report* (Seoul: The Bank of Korea) (in Korean).

Bergsten, C. F. (2007) "China and Economic Integration in East Asia: Implications for the United States," *Policy Briefs in International Economics, No.PB07-3.* (Washington, DC: Peter G. Peterson Institute for International Economics), http://www.iie.com/publications/pb/pb07-3.pdf.

Bhagwati, J. (1992) "Regionalism versus Multilateralism," *The World Economy*, Vol. 15, No. 5, pp. 535–55.

—————— (2008) *Termites in the Trading System: How Preferential Agreements Undermine Free Trade* (New York: Oxford University Press).

Bhagwati, J. (1995) "U.S. Trade Policy: The Infatuation with Free Trade Areas," in J. Bhagwati & A. O. Krueger (eds) *The Dangerous Drift to Preferential Trade Agreements* (Washington, DC: American Enterprise Institute), pp. 1–18.

Bhagwati, J., D. Greenaway, & A. Panagariya (1998) "Trading Preferentially: Theory and Policy," *Economic Journal*, Vol. 108, pp. 1128–48.

Bhuyan, R. (2007) "India–China FTA talks soon," *The Business Standard* (India), 30 October, http://www.bilaterals.org/article.php3?id_article=10134, accessed on May 24, 2008.

Bi, Y. (2005) "WTO kuangjia xia shijie FTA de fazhan yu Zhongguo de maoyi zhanlue tiaozheng" [The Development of FTA within the Framework of WTO and Strategic Adjustments of China's Trade], *Yatai Jingji [Asia-Pacific Economic Review]*, No. 3, pp. 15–17.

Bisley, N. (2004) "Asia-Pacific Regionalism and Preferential Trade Agreements: the Australian Case," *International Relations of the Asia-Pacific*, Vol. 14, pp. 239–64.

——— (2008) "The Japan–Australia Security Declaration and the Changing Regional Security Setting: Wheels, Webs and Beyond?" *Australian Journal of International Affairs*, Vol. 62, No. 1, pp. 38–52.

Blanco Mendoza, H. (1994) *Las Negociaciones Comerciales de México con el Mundo* (México: Fondo de Cultura Económica).

Bowles, P. (2002) "Asia's Post-Crisis Regionalism: Bringing the State Back in, Keeping the (United) States Out," *Review of International Political Economy*, Vol. 9, No. 2, pp. 244–70.

Brailovsky, V. (1989) "Las Implicaciones Macroeconómicas de Pagar: La Política Económica ante la 'Crisis' de la Deuda en México, 1982–1988," in C. Bazdrech, N. Bucay, S. Loaeza, & N. Lustig (eds) *México: Auge, Crisis y Ajuste* (México: Fondo de Cultura Económica), pp. 105–27.

Braun, D. & F. Gilardi (2006) "Taking 'Galton's Problem' Seriously: Towards a Theory of Policy Diffusion," *Journal of Theoretical Politics*, Vol. 18, No. 3, pp. 298–322.

Bravo Aguilera, L. (1989a) "La Política Comercial de México y el Acuerdo General sobre Aranceles Aduaneros y Comercio," in B. Torres & P. Falk (eds) *La Adhesión de México al GATT: Repercusiones Internas e Impacto sobre las Relaciones México-Estados Unidos* (México: El Colegio de México), pp. 25–61.

——— (1989b) "La Política de Comercio Exterior de México y su Presencia en las Relaciones Comerciales con Estados Unidos," in W. Glade & C. Luiselli (eds) *La Economía de la Interdependencia: México y Estados Unidos* (Mexico: Fondo de Cultura Económica), pp. 125–56.

Breslin, S. (2007) *China and the Global Political Economy* (Basingstoke: Palgrave Macmillan).

Bridges, B. (1993) *Japan and Korea in the 1990s: From Antagonism to Adjustment* (Bookfield: Edward Elgar).

Brink, G. & T. Kobayashi (2007) "South Africa," in J. Nakagawa (ed.) *Anti-Dumping Laws and Practices of the New Users* (London: Cameron), pp. 203–45.

Brown, D. K., A. V. Deardorff, & R. M. Stern (1996) "Computational Analysis of the Economic Effects of an East Asian Preferential Trading Bloc," *Journal of the Japanese and International Economies*, Vol. 10, pp. 37–70.

Bull, B. (2008) "Policy Networks and Business Participation in Free Trade Negotiations in Chile," *Journal of Latin American Studies*, Vol. 40, No. 2, pp. 195–224.

Butelmann, A. & P. Meller (eds) (1992) *Estrategia Comercial Chilena para la Década del 90* (Santiago: CIEPLAN).

Cabezas, M. (2003) "Tratado de Libre Comercio entre Chile y Estados Unidos: Revisión de Estudios que Cuantifican su Impacto," *Working Paper 239* (Santiago: Central Bank of Chile).

Cai, K. G. (2003) "The ASEAN–China Free Trade Agreement and East Asian Regional Grouping," *Contemporary Southeast Asia*, Vol. 25, No. 3, pp. 387–404.

Cai, P. (2005) "Yatai ziyou maoyiqu dui APEC jizhihua jincheng de yingxiang" [The Impact of FTA of Asia Pacific on the Institutionalization of APEC], *Shijie Jingji Yanjiu [World Economy Study]*, Vol. 2, pp. 9–13, 38.

Calder, K. & M. Ye (2004) "Regionalism and Critical Junctures: Explaining the "Organization Gap' in Northeast Asia," *Journal of East Asian Studies*, Vol. 4, No. 2, pp. 191–226.

Cameron, M. A. & B. W. Tomlin (2000) *The Making of NAFTA: How the Deal Was Done* (Ithaca: Cornell University Press).

Capling, A. (2008) "Preferential Trade Agreements as Instruments of Foreign Policy: An Australia–Japan Free Trade Agreement and Its Implications for the Asia Pacific Region," *Pacific Review*, Vol. 21, No. 1, pp. 27–43.

Caryl, C. (2007) "It's not about Money," *Newsweek International*, June 4.

Casar, M. A. (1984) "PRONAFICE: Industriales y Gobierno en una Estrategia Compartida," *Política Mexicana*, Vol. 1 (July–August).

—— (1989) "Empresarios y Estado en el Gobierno de Miguel de la Madrid: En Busca de un Nuevo Acuerdo," in C. Bazdrech, N. Bucay, S. Loaeza, & N. Lustig (eds) *México: Auge, Crisis y Ajuste* (México: Fondo de Cultura Económica), pp. 290–312.

Cha, A. E. (2009) "Taiwan, China Negotiating a Landmark Free-Trade Agreement," Washington Post, 21 February.

Chan, M. (2005) "US Trade Strategy of Competitive Liberalization," *Tamkang Journal of International Affairs*, http://www2.tku.edu.tw/~ti/Journal/8-3/831.pdf.

Chase, K. (2005) *Trading Blocs: States, Firms and Regions in the World Economy* (Ann Arbor: University of Michigan Press).

Chen, H. (2005) "Chile warm to FTA," *China Daily*, 28 May, http://www.bilaterals.org/article.php3?id_article=1973, accessed on September 25, 2007.

Cheng, H. (2006) "Asian Economic Cooperation in the New Millennium: China's Economic Presence (Book review)," *China Review International*, Vol. 1, No. 1, pp. 284–89.

Cheong, I. (1999) "Korea–Chile FTA: Economic Effects and Implications," *Journal of International Economic Studies*, Vol. 2, No. 4.

—— (2001) "The Economic Effects of a Korea–Japan FTA and Policy Implications," *KIEP Policy Paper 01-04* (Seoul: Korea Institute for International Economic Policy, KIEP).

—— (2005) "Economic Assessment of Korea–Japan FTA," in C. Y. Ahn et al. (eds) *Korea–Japan FTA: Toward a Model Case for East Asian Economic Integration* (Seoul: KIEP), pp. 123–57.

Cheong, I. & J. Cho (2006) "Market Access in FTAs: Assessment Based on Rules of Origin and Agricultural Trade Liberalization," *RIETI Discussion Paper Series, 07-E-016*, http://www.rieti.go.jp/en/publications/summary/07030022.html, accessed on October 11, 2007.

Cheong, I. & K. Lee (2000) *Korea–Chile FTA: Background, Economic Effect, and Policy Implications* (Seoul: KIEP).

Chilean Directorate of International Economic Affairs, Ministry of Foreign Affairs, www.direcon.cl.

Chilean Export Promotion Agency, www.prochile.cl.

Chilean Foreign Investment Committee, www.foreigninvestment.cl.

"China, India to Advance Feasibility Research on Regional Trade Arrangement" (May 30, 2007) *People's Daily Online*, http://www.bilaterals.org/article.php3?id_article=8492, accessed on September 25, 2007.

"China–Pakistan FTA to Promote Bilateral Trade" (2006) *Industry Update*, 16 December.

Christensen, T. J. (2006) "Fostering Stability or Creating a Monster: The Rise of China and US Policy toward East Asia," *International Security*, Vol. 31, No. 1, pp. 81–126.

Chu, S. (2006) "China's Approach to the Free-Trade Area," paper for the Foreign Policy Research Institute. http://www.fpri.org/pubs/20061102.chu.chinafreetradearea.pdf, accessed on October 3, 2007.

Chung, H. (2003) "The Korea–Chile FTA: Significance and Implications," *East Asian Review*, Vol. 15, No. 1, pp. 71–86.

Cohn, T. (2007) "The Doha Round: Problems, Challenges, Prospects," in I. Studer & C. Wise (eds) *Requiem or Revival? The Promise of North American Integration* (Washington, DC: Brookings Institution Press), pp. 147–65.

Colvin, J. (2004) "The Costs of Competitive Liberalization," http://www.americanprogress.org/issues/2004/11/b255995.html, accessed on November 1, 2007.

Cooper, W. (2005) "The U.S.–Australia Free Trade Agreement: Provisions and Implications— Congressional Research Service Report for Congress," http://www.nationalaglawcenter.org/assets/crs/RL32375.pdf, accessed on May 1, 2008.

Cox, G. & M. McCubbins (2001) "Institutional Dimensions of Economic Policy Outcomes," in S. Haggard & M. McCubbins (eds) *Presidents, Parliaments and Policy* (New York: Cambridge University Press), pp. 21–63.

Cypher, J. M. (1994) "Mexico's Export Promotion Policy: Un Nuevo Patrón de Acumulación?" in P. Ganster, A. G. Espinoza, & A. Grunstein (eds) *Changes in U.S.–Mexican Economic Relations: Beyond the Border* (Mexico: Universidad Autónoma Metropolitana, PROFMEX, and ANUIES), pp. 2229–50.

de Castro, I. (2002) "Politics: New Pacts May Give China Key Role in Southeast Asia," *Global Information Network* (New York).

Del Castillo, G. (1980) "The Generalized System of Preferences and Mexican–U.S. Relations," paper prepared for the *Latin American Studies Association* (Bloomington, Indiana).

——— (1991a) "El Tratado de Libre Comercio y las Empresas Manufactureras Mexicanas," *Comercio Exterior*, Vol. 41, No. 7, pp. 682–88.

——— (1991b) "Institutional Concerns and Mechanisms from Tripartite Free Trade Negotiations in North America," in S. J. Randall, H. Konrad, & S. Silverman (eds) *North America Without Borders? Integrating Canada, the United States, and Mexico* (Calgary: University of Calgary Press), pp. 41–54.

De la Madrid, M. (1985) *Las Razones y las Obras. Crónica de Sexenio. Tercer Año.* (Mexico: Fondo de Cultura Económica).

——— (1986) *Las Razones y las Obras. Crónica de Sexenio. Cuarto Año.* (Mexico: Fondo de Cultura Económica).

——— (1987) *Las Razones y las Obras. Crónica de Sexenio. Quinto Año.* (Mexico: Fondo de Cultura Económica).

——— (1988) *Las Razones y las Obras. Crónica de Sexenio. Sexto Año.* (Mexico: Fondo de Cultura Económica).

deLisle, J. (2006) "Free Trade Areas: Legal Aspects and the Politics of US, PRC and Taiwan Participation," paper for the Foreign Policy Research Institute, http://www.fpri.org/pubs/20061110.asia.delisle.freetradeareasusprctaiwan.html, accessed on October 3, 2007.

De Mateo, F. (1980) "Contribución a la Polémica sobre el GATT," *Comercio Exterior*, Vol. 30, No. 2, pp. 111–17.

——— (1986) "Del ¡NO! al ¡SI! Historia de un Matrimonio por Conveniencia (México frente al GATT)," in G. del Castillo (ed.) *Mexico en el GATT: Ventajas y Desventajas* (México: El Colegio de la Frontera Norte).

——— (1988) "La Política Comercial de México y el GATT," *El Trimestre Económico*, Vol. 217, pp. 175–216.

Dent, C. M. (2003) "Networking the Region? The Emergence and Impact of Asia-Pacific Bilateral Free Trade Agreement Projects," *The Pacific Review*, Vol. 16, No. 1, pp. 1–28.

——— (2006a) "The New Economic Bilateralism in Southeast Asia: Region-Convergent or Region-Divergent?" *International Relations of the Asia-Pacific*, Vol. 6, pp. 88–111.

——— (2006b) *New Free Trade Agreements in the Asia-Pacific* (New York: Palgrave Macmillan).

———— (2007) "Full Circle? Ideas and Ordeals of Creating a Free Trade Area of the Asia-Pacific," *Pacific Review*, Vol. 20, No. 4, pp. 447–74.

Department of Foreign Affairs and Trade, Australian Government (2008) "Australia–China Free Trade Agreement Negotiations," http://www.dfat.gov.au/geo/china/fta/, accessed on May 14, 2008.

DeRosa, D. A. (2004) "US Free Trade Agreements with ASEAN," in J. J. Schott (ed.) *Free Trade Agreements: US Strategies and Priorities* (Washington, DC: Institute for International Economics), pp. 117–71.

Destler, I. M. (2005) *American Trade Politics.* (Washington, DC: Institute for International Economics).

———— (2007) "US Trade Politics during the Uruguay Round," in I. Studer & C. Wise (eds) *Requiem or Revival? The Promise of North American Integration* (Washington, DC: Brookings Institution Press), pp. 166–85.

Development Research Center of the State Council (2005) "Zhongguo jingji zengzhang de qianjing yu zhanlue [China's Economic Growth Prospects and Strategies]," http://www.gzass.gd.cn/content/skwc/wc20050401_10.htm, accessed on October 3, 2007.

Devlin, R. & P. Giordano (2004) "The Old and New Regionalism: Benefits, Costs, and Implications for the FTAA," in A. Estevadeordal, D. Rodrik, A. Taylor, & A. Velasco (eds) *Integrating the Americas: FTAA and Beyond* (Cambridge: Harvard University Press), pp. 143–88.

DIRECON (2006) "Acuerdo Estratégico Transpacífico de Asociación Económica: Chile, Nueva Zelandia, Singapur, Brunei Darussalam," http://cms.chileinfo.com/documentos/p4.pdf.

Dobbin, F., B. Simmons, & G. Garrett (2007) "The Global Diffusion of Public Policies: Social Construction, Coercion, Competition or Learning?" *Annual Review of Sociology*, Vol. 33, pp. 449–72.

Dreyer, T. (2006) "Sino-Japanese Rivalry and Its Implications for Developing Nations," *Asian Survey*, Vol. 46, No. 4, pp. 538–57.

Duval, Y. (2006) "Cost and Benefits of Implementing Trade Facilitation Measures under Negotiations at the WTO: an Exploratory Survey," *Asia-Pacific Research and Training Network on Trade Working Paper Series, No.3* (Bangkok: UNESCAP, Asia-Pacific Research and Training Network on Trade).

ECLAC (2003) "Latin America and the Caribbean in the World Economy, 2001–2002," *Briefing Paper* (New York: United Nations Publications), http://www.cepal.org/publicaciones/Comercio/9/LCG2189PI/lcg2189i.pdf, accessed on November 10, 2007.

———— (2007) "Latin America and the Caribbean in the World Economy, 2006: 2007 Trends," *Briefing Paper* (New York: United Nations Publications), http://www.eclac.org/cgi-bin/getProd.asp?xml=/publicaciones/xml/8/29528/P29528.xml&xsl=/comercio/tpl-i/p9f.xsl&base=/tpl-i/top-bottom.xslt, accessed on November 15, 2007.

Edmonds, C. & V. Jean-Pierre (2002) *The Role of Preferential Trading Arrangements in Asia* (Manila: Asia Development Bank).

Either, W. (1988) *Modern International Economics*, 2nd edn. (New York: Norton).

Elkins, Z., A. T. Guzman, & B. A. Simmons (2006) "Competing for Capital: The Diffusion of Bilateral Investment Treaties, 1960–2000," *International Organization*, Vol. 60, No. 3, pp. 811–46.

Elkins, Z. & B. A. Simmons (2005) "On Waves, Clusters and Diffusion: A Conceptual Framework," *Annals of the American Academy of Political and Social Science*, Vol. 598, pp. 33–51.

Endoh, M. (2005) *Chiiki boueki kyotei no keizai bunseki* [*Economic Analysis of Regional Trade Agreements*] (Tokyo: University of Tokyo Press).

Erb, G. (1989) "U.S.-Mexican Trade and Investment Agreements," hearing on Bilateral Trade Agreements by the Subcommittee of International Trade, Committee on Finance, US Senate, March 13, 1989.

Estevadeordal, A., D. Rodrik, A. M. Taylor, & A. Velasco (eds) (2004) *Integrating the Americas: FTAA and Beyond* (Cambridge, MA: David Rockefeller Center Series on Latin American Studies, Harvard University).

Ethier, W. J. (1998) "The New Regionalism," *The Economic Journal*, Vol. 108, pp. 1149–61.

Evans, P. (1995) *Embedded Autonomy: States and Industrial Transformation* (Princeton: Princeton University Press).

Evenett, S. J. & M. Meier (2008) "An Interim Assessment of the U.S. Trade Policy of 'Competitive Liberalization'," *The World Economy*, Vol. 31, No. 1, pp. 31–66.

Fairbrother, M. (2007) "Making Neoliberalism Possible: The State's Organization of Business Support for NAFTA in Mexico," *Politics and Society*, Vol. 35, No. 2, pp. 265–300.

Faust, J. (2004) "Latin America, Chile and East Asia: Policy Networks and Successful Diversification," *Journal of Latin American Studies*, Vol. 36, pp. 743–70.

Fauver, R. C. & D. T. Stewart (2003) "US–Japan Comprehensive Economic Partnership Agreement: Cementing a Geostrategic Economic Partnership," *SAIS Review*, Vol. 23, No. 2, pp. 23–39.

Feinberg, R. E. (2002) "Regionalism and Domestic Politics: U.S.–Latin American Trade Policy in the Bush Era," *Latin American Politics and Society*, Vol. 44, No. 4, pp. 127–51.

—— (2003) "The Political Economy of United States' Free Trade Agreements," *The World Economy*, Vol. 26, No. 7, pp. 1019–40.

—— (2005) "US' Bilateral and Regional Free Trade Arrangements in the Asia-Pacific," in V. K. Aggarwal & S. Urata (eds), *Bilateral Trade Arrangements in the Asia-Pacific: Origins, Evolution, and Implications* (London/New York: Routledge), pp. 95–115.

Fischer, C. (2007) "Chile, Japan Sign Free Trade Agreement," *Chile News*, 27 March, http://www.chileangovernment.gov.cl/index.php?option=com_content&task=view&id=1480&Itemid=1.

Flores-Quiroga, A. (1998) *Proteccionismo versus Librecambio: La Economía Política de la Protección Comercial en México, 1970–1994* (México: Fondo de Cultura Económica).

—— (2001) "El Tratado de Libre Comercio México-Triángulo del Norte," *Revista Mexicana de Política Exterior*, Vol. 63, pp. 65–90.

Foxley, A., R. Pizarro, E. Santos, & S. Sáez (1993) "Debate sobre la Política de Comercio Internacional de Chile," *Cono Sur*, Vol. XII, No. 4, pp. 1–21.

Frankel, J. A., E. Stein, & S. Wei (1997) *Regional Trading Blocs in the World Trading System* (Washington, DC: Institute for International Economics).

Friedberg, A. L. (1992/93) "Ripe for Rivalry: Prospects for Peace in a Multipolar Asia," *International Security*, Vol. 18, No. 3, pp. 5–33.

Frieden, J. A. (1991) "Invested Interests: The Politics of National Economic Policies in a World of Global Finance," *International Organization*, Vol. 45, No. 4, pp. 425–51.

Frieden, J. A. & R. Rogowski (1996) "The Impact of the International Economy on National Policies: An Analytical Overview," in R. O. Keohane & H. V. Milner (eds) *Internationalization and Domestic Politics* (Cambridge: Cambridge University Press), pp. 25–47.

Frohmann, A. (2005) "Political and Institutional Context of Trade Policy in Chile," unpublished paper (Santiago: Ministry of Foreign Affairs).

Fukao, K., H. Ishido, & K. Ito (2003) "Vertical Intra-Industry Trade and Foreign Direct Investment in East Asia," *RIETI Discussion Paper Series 03-E-01* (Japan: Research Institute of Economy, Trade and Industry).

Fukui, H. (1978) "The GATT Tokyo Round: The Bureaucratic Politics of Multilateral Diplomacy," in M. Blaker (ed.) *The Politics of Trade. US and Japanese Policymaking for the GATT Negotiations* (New York: The East Asia Institute), pp. 75–169.

Garrett, G., F. Dobbin & B. A. Simmons (2008) "Conclusion," in B. A. Simmons, F. Dobbin & G. Garrett (eds) *The Global Diffusion of Markets and Democracy* (New York: Cambridge University Press).

Gill, B. (2007) *Rising Star: China's New Security Diplomacy* (Washington, DC: Brookings Institution Press).

Gilpin, R. (1987) *The Political Economy of International Relations* (Princeton: Princeton University Press).

Glaser, B. S. & P. C. Saunders (2002) "Chinese Civil Foreign Policy Research Institutes: Evolving Roles and Increasing Influence," *The China Quarterly*, Vol. 171, pp. 597–616.

Goh, C. T. (2001) "Interview," *Nikkei Business*, January.

—— (2002a) "Comment," the Signing Ceremony of the Japan–Singapore Economic Agreement for a New Age Partnership, 13 January.

—— (2002b) "Deepening Regional Integration and Cooperation," keynote speech delivered at the East Asia Economic Summit, 8 October.

Goh, E. (2007/08) "Great Powers and Hierarchical Order in Southeast Asia: Analyzing Regional Security Strategies," *International Security*, Vol. 32, No. 3, pp. 113–57.

Gowa, J. (1994) *Allies, Adversaries, and International Trade* (Princeton: Princeton University Press).

Graham, E. (2000) *Fighting the Wrong Enemy: Antiglobal Activists and Multinational Enterprises* (Washington, DC: Institute for International Economics).

Gray, V. (1994) "Competition, Emulation, and Policy Innovation," in L. Dodd & C. Jillson (eds) *New Perspectives on American Politics* (Washington, DC: CQ Press), pp. 230–48.

Grieco, J. M. (1996) "State Interests and Institutional Rule Trajectories: A Neorealist Interpretation of the Maastricht Treaty and European Economic and Monetary Union," *Security Studies*, Vol. 5, No. 3, pp. 261–305.

Grossman, G. M. & E. Helpman (1995) "The Politics of Free-Trade Agreements," *The American Economic Review*, Vol. 85, No. 4, pp. 667–90.

Gruber, L. (2000) *Ruling the World: Power Politics and the Rise of Supranational Institutions* (Princeton: Princeton University Press).

Haas, E. (1964) *Beyond the Nation-State* (Stanford: Stanford University Press).

Haggard, S. & R. R. Kaufman (1995) *The Political Economy of Democratic Transition* (Princeton: Princeton University Press).

Hall, P. A. (1993) "Policy Paradigms, Social Learning, and the State: The Case of Economic Policymaking in Britain," *Comparative Politics*, Vol. 25, No. 3, pp. 275–96.

Han, Y., G. Yu, L. Wang, X. Tang, G. Li, W. Liao, H. Bian, Q. Guo, & D. Hou (2005) *Quanqiuhua yu Zhongguo Da Zhanlue* [*Globalization and China's Grand Strategy*], Zhongguo Shehui Kexue Chubanshe (China: Social Sciences Press).

Harrison, G., T. Rutherford, & D. Tarr (1997) "Trade Policy Options for Chile: A Quantitative Evaluation," *Policy Research Paper 1783* (Washington, DC: World Bank).

—— (2003) "Chile's Regional Arrangements: The Importance of Market Access and Lowering the Tariff to Six Per Cent," *Working Paper No. 238* (Santiago: Central Bank of Chile).

Hatakeyama, N. (2002) "Short History of Japan's Movement to FTAs (Part 1)," *Journal of Japanese Trade & Industry*, (November/December), pp. 24–5.

———— (2003) "Short History of Japan's Movement to FTAs (Part 4)," (November) *Journal of Japanese Trade and Industry*.

———— (2006) "Why a Community Rather than an FTA?" http://www.jef.or.jp/en_act/ act_article_topics.asp?cd=56&num=10, accessed on October 19, 2007.

Hatch, W. & K. Yamamura (1996) *Asia in Japan's Embrace: Building a Regional Production Alliance* (Cambridge: Cambridge University Press).

He, X. & H. Hu (2006) "Zhongguo zai quyu maoyi hezuo zhong de zuoyong jiqi zhan-lue yitu" [China's Role and Strategic Motivations in Regional Trade Cooperation], *Zhujiang Jingji* [*South China Review*], No. 11, pp. 2–8.

Hearing Before the Subcommittee on Trade of the Committee on Ways and Means on Implementation of U.S. Bilateral Free Trade Agreements with Chile and Singapore (2003) U.S. House of Representatives, 108th Congress First Session, June 10, 2003, Serial No. 108–24 in http://frwebgate.access.gpo.gov/cgi-bin/getdoc.cgi?dbname=108_ house_hearings&docid=f:91677.pdf, accessed on May 19, 2008.

Heginbotham, E. & R. J. Samuels (2002) "Japan's Dual Hedge," *Foreign Affairs*, Vol. 81, No. 5, pp. 110–21.

Heredia, B. (1994) "Making Economic Reform Politically Viable: The Mexican Experience," in W. C. Smith, C. H. Acuña, & E. A. Gamarra (eds) *Democracy, Markets, and Structural Reform in Latin America: Argentina, Bolivia, Brazil, Chile, and Mexico* (Miami, FL: North–South Center, University of Miami and Transaction Publishers), pp. 265–95.

Hernández Cervantes, H. (1980) "El Futuro del Comercio entre México y Estados Unidos," *Comercio Exterior*, Vol. 30, No. 100 (Oct.), pp. 1128–30.

Higashi, A. (2004) "*Nitchuukan—higashi ajia boueki kouzou no henka to inpakuto* [Changes and Impact of the Japan–China–South Korea East Asia Trade Framework]," (NEXT-ING, Mitsubishi Research Institute), Vol. 5, No. 4, pp. 20–1.

Higgott, R. (2004) "US Foreign Policy and the 'Securitization' of Economic Globalization," *International Politics*, Vol. 41, pp. 147–75.

———— (2007) "The Theory and Practice of Regionalism in East Asia: Peter Katzenstein's Value Added," *Journal of East Asian Studies*, Vol. 7, No. 3, pp. 378–87.

Higgott, R. & R. Stubbs (1995) "Competing Conceptions of Economic Regionalism: APEC Versus EAEC in the Asia Pacific," *Review of International Political Economy*, Vol. 2, No. 3, pp. 516–35.

Hirschman, A. O. (1980) *National Power and the Structure of Foreign Trade* (Berkeley: University of California Press).

Hoadley, S. (2007) "Southeast Asian Cross-Regional FTAs: Origins, Motives and Aims," *Pacific Affairs*, Vol. 80, No. 2, pp. 303–25.

Hoadley, S. & J. Yang. (2007) "China's Cross-Regional FTA Initiatives: Towards Comprehensive National Power," *Pacific Affairs*, Vol. 80, No. 2, pp. 327–48.

Hornbeck, J. F. (2003) "The U.S.–Chile Free Trade Agreement: Economic and Trade Policy Issues," *Congressional Research Report for Congress* (Washington, DC: CRS), http://assets.opencrs.com/rrts/RL31144_20030910.pdf.

Hsueh, R. (2006) "Who Rules the International Economy: Taiwan's Daunting Attempts at Bilateralism," in V. K. Aggarwal & S. Urata (eds), *Bilateral Trade Agreements in the Asia-Pacific: Origins, Evolution, and Implications* (London: Routledge), pp. 160–83.

Huang, J., Z. Heqin, & B. Shihong (2008) "Cong zhanlue gaodu renshi he shenhua yu Bajisitan de quanmian hezuo [Understanding and Deepening the Comprehensive Cooperation with Pakistan from a Strategic Perspective]," *Yatai Jingji* [*Asia-Pacific Economic Review*], No. 2, pp. 64–7.

Hufbauer, G. C. (2008) "Interactions between Regional and Global Trade Agreements," in J. A. McKinney & H. S. Gardner (eds) *Economic Integration in the Americas* (London and New York: Routledge), pp. 213–26.

Huffbauer, G. & J. J. Schott (2005) *NAFTA Revisited: Achievements and Challenges* (Washington, DC: Institute for International Economics).

Ibarra-Yuenz, A. (2003) "Spaghetti Regionalism or Strategic Foreign Trade: Some Evidence for Mexico," *Journal of Development Economics*, Vol. 72, pp. 567–84.

Ikenberry, J. (1990) "The International Spread of Privatization Policies: Inducements, Learning, and Policy Bandwagoning," in E. Suleiman & J. Waterburt (eds) *The Political Economy of Public Sector Reform and Privatizations* (Boulder: Westview Press), pp. 88–110.

Intellectual Property Strategy Headquarters (Government of Japan) (2006) *Comprehensive Strategy for International Standardization* (Tokyo: Intellectual Property Strategy Headquarters), http://www.kantei.go.jp/jp/singi/titeki2/keikaku2006_e.pdf.

International Enterprise (IE) Singapore (2007) *Annual Report 2006–2007* (Singapore: International Enterprise Singapore).

International Monetary Fund (1991) *Direction of Trade Statistics Yearbook, 1991* (Washington, DC: IMF).

Japan External Trade Organization (JETRO) (2003) *Current Status of AFTA and Corporate Responses* (Tokyo: Japan External Trade Organization).

—— (2006) "FY 2005 Survey of Japanese Firms International Operations," http://www.jetro.go.jp/en/stats/survey/pdf/2006_04_biz.pdf, accessed on August 13, 2007.

—— (2007) *FTA Guidebook 2007* (Tokyo: Japan External Trade Organization).

Japan Pacific Economic Cooperation Conference (2002) "An Assessment of Impediments to Foreign Direct Investment in APEC Member Economies, Tokyo."

Jiang, J. (2007) "Ziyou maoyiqu de fazhan taishi jiqi duice [The Development Trend of FTAs and China's Policy]," *Duiwai Jingmao [Practice in Foreign Economic Relations and Trade]*, No. 2, pp. 19–21.

Johnston, A. I. (2004) "Beijing's Security Behavior in the Asia-Pacific: Is China a Dissatisfied Power?" in J. J. Suh, P. J. Katzenstein, & A. Carlson (eds) *Rethinking Security in East Asia: Identity, Power, and Efficiency* (Stanford: Stanford University Press), pp. 34–96.

"Joint Study for Enhancing Economic Relations between Japan and Australia including the Feasibility of Pros and Cons of a Free Trade Agreement" (2006), http://www.mofa.go.jp/region/asia-paci/australia/joint0612.pdf, accessed on October 22, 2007.

Jones, C. A. (2006) "Foundations of Competition Policy in the EU and USA: Conflict, Convergence and Beyond," in H. Ullrich (ed.) *The Evolution of European Competition Law: Whose Regulation, Which Competition?* (Cheltenham, UK and Northampton, MA: Edward Elgar), pp. 17–37.

Kahler, M. (2001) "Legalization as Strategy: The Asia-Pacific Case," in J. Goldstein, M. Kahler, R. O. Keohane, & A. M. Slaughter (eds) *Legalization and World Politics* (Cambridge: The MIT Press), pp. 165–87.

Kajita, A. (2004) "The Influence on Japanese Companies by East Asian FTAs, and an Overview of East Asian Countries' Tariff Rates," *Working Paper Series 03/04, No. 5* (Tokyo, Japan: IDE APEC Study Center).

Kang, D. C. (2007) *China Rising: Peace, Power, and Order in East Asia* (New York: Columbia University Press).

Katada, S. (2007) "Old Visions and New Actors in Foreign Aid Politics: Explaining Changes in Japanese ODA Policy to China," in K. Warren & D. Leheny (eds) *Inescapable Transnationalism: Japan, Foreign Aid, and the Search for Global Solutions* (book manuscript under review).

Kate, T. A., R. B. Wallace, A. Waarts & M. D. Ramirez de Wallace (1979) *La Política de Protección en el Desarrollo Económico de México* (Mexico: Fondo de Cultura Económica).

Katzenstein, P. J. (2006) "East Asia-Beyond Japan," in P. J. Katzenstein & T. Shiraishi (eds) *Beyond Japan: The Dynamics of East Asian Regionalism* (Ithaca: Cornell University Press), pp. 1–33.

Katzenstein, P. J. & T. Shiraishi (eds) (2006) *Beyond Japan: The Dynamics of East Asian Regionalism* (Ithaca: Cornell University Press).

Kawai, M. (2005) "East Asian Economic Regionalism: Progress and Challenges," *Journal of Asian Economics*, Vol. 16, pp. 29–55.

Kawai, M. & G. Wignaraja (2007) "ASEAN+3 or ASEAN+6: Which Way Forward?" Paper presented at the Conference on Multilateralisng Regionalism. Sponsored and organized by WTO—HEI, co-organized by the Centre for Economic Policy Research (CEPR) in Geneva, Switzerland (September 10–12, 2007), http://www.wto.org/english/tratop_e/region_e/con_sep07_e/kawai_wignaraja_e.pdf.

Kawai, M. & S. Urata (1998) "Are Trade and Direct Investment Substitutes of Complements? An Empirical Analysis of Japanese Manufacturing Industries," in H. Lee & D. Roland-Holst (eds) *Economic Development and Cooperation in the Pacific Basin: Trade, Investment and Environmental Issues* (Cambridge, UK: Cambridge University Press), pp. 251–93.

——— (2004) "Trade and Foreign Direct Investment in East Asia," in G. de Brouwer & M. Kawai *Exchange Rate Regimes and East Asia* (London: RoutledgeCurzon), pp. 15–102.

Kawashima, F. (2006) "Chiiki Tōgō ni okeru Dumping Bōshi Sochi no Tekiyō ni kansuru Kiritsu—Ōdanteki Hikaku wo Tsūjita Kiritsu Dōnyū no Jōken ni kansuru Kōsatsu [Regulation of the application of anti-dumping under regional integration: Analysis of the conditions for introducing regulation based on cross-issue comparison]," *RIETI Discussion Paper Series 06-J-053* (Tokyo: Research Institute of Economy, Trade and Industry, RIETI).

Keidanren (1999) "Report on the Possible Effects of a Japan–Mexico Free Trade Agreement on Japanese Industry," http://www.keidanren.or.jp/english/policy/pol099.html, accessed on August 6, 2007.

——— (2000) "Urgent Call for Active Promotion of Free Trade Agreements. Toward a New Dimension in Trade Policy," http://www.keidanren.or.jp/english/policy/2000/033/proposal.html, accessed on July 25, 2007.

——— (2002) "Toward the Creation of International Investment Rules and Improvement of the Japanese Investment Environment," http://www.keidanren.or.jp/english/policy/2002/042/proposal.html, accessed on January 17, 2007.

——— (2003) "Urgent Call for the Opening of Negotiations toward Japan–Thailand Economic Partnership (JTEP) Agreement," http://www.keidanren.or.jp/english/policy/2003/042.html, accessed on July 23, 2007.

——— (2006) "Call for the Start of Joint Study for a Japan–U.S. Economic Partnership Agreement," http://www.keidanren.or.jp/english/policy/2006/082.html, accessed on January 17, 2007.

——— (2007) "Call for the Start of Joint Study for a Japan–EU Economic Partnership Agreement," http://www.keidanren.or.jp/english/policy/2007/050.html, accessed on July 12, 2007.

Kemp, M. & H. Wan (1995) "An Elementary Proposition Concerning the Formation of Customs Unions," in M. Kemp (ed.) *The Gains from Trade and the Gains from Aid: Essays in International Trade Theory* (New York and London: Routledge).

Kennan, J. & R. Riezman (1990) "Optimum Tariff Equilibrium with Customs Unions," *Canadian Journal of Economics*, Vol. 90, No. 1, pp. 70–83.

Kim, Y. (2007) "Korea cautious on free trade talks with China," *Korea Times*, 15 April.

Koo, M. G. (2006) "From Multilateralism to Bilateralism? A Shift in South Korea's Trade Strategy," in V. K. Aggarwal & S. Urata (eds), *Bilateral Trade Agreements in the Asia-Pacific: Origins, Evolution, and Implications* (New York and London: Routledge), pp. 140–59.

—— (2008) "The Economics–Security Nexus in East Asia," a paper presented at the 2008 Annual Meeting of the American Political Science Association (Boston, August 28–August 31).

Korea Trade-Investment Promotion Agency (KOTRA) (2007) *Coping with South Korea's Falling Market Share in the US and Utilizing the Korea–US FTA* (Seoul: KOTRA).

Krasner, S. (1976) "State Power and the Structure of International Trade," *World Politics*, Vol. 28, pp. 317–47.

Krauss, E. (2000) "Japan, the Emergence of Multilateralism in Asia," *The Pacific Review*, Vol. 12, No. 3, pp. 473–94.

—— (2003) "The US, Japan, and Trade Liberalization: From Bilateralism, to Regional Multilateralism, to Regionalism+," *The Pacific Review*, Vol. 16, No. 3, pp. 307–29.

—— (2004) "The United States and Japan in APEC's EVSL Negotiation: Regional Multilateralism and Trade," in E. Krauss & T. J. Pempel (eds) *Beyond Bilateralism: US–Japan Relations in the New Asia-Pacific* (Stanford: Stanford University Press), pp. 272–95.

Krauss, E. & M. Naoi. *The Domestic Politics of Japan's Regional Foreign Economic Policies* (manuscript).

Krugman, P. (1991) "Is Bilateralism Bad?" in E. Helpman & A. Razin (eds) *International Trade and Trade Policy* (Cambridge: MIT Press), pp. 9–23.

Kwan, C. H. (2004) "China's Rise Pressures ASEAN to Make Industrial Adjustments—Industrial Upgrading or Deindustrialization" (Tokyo: Research Institute of Economy, Trade and Industry), http://www.rieti.go.jp/en/china/04012601.html

Kwei, E. S. (2006) "Chinese Trade Bilateralism: Politics Still in Command," in V. K. Aggarwal & S. Urata (eds), *Bilateral Trade Agreements in the Asia-Pacific: Origins, Evolution, and Implications* (New York and London: Routledge), pp. 117–39.

Lampton, D. M. (2001) "China's Foreign and National Security Policy-Making Process: Is It Changing, and Does It Matter?" in D. M. Lampton (ed.) *The Making of Chinese Foreign and Security Policy in the Era of Reform, 1978–(2000)* (Stanford: Stanford University Press), pp. 1–36.

Lardy, N. R. (2002) *Integrating China into the Global Economy* (Washington, DC: Brookings Institution Press).

Lawrence, R. Z. (1996) *Regionalism, Multilateralism, and Deeper Integration* (Washington, DC: Brookings Institution Press).

Lee, K. Y. (2007) "Contests for Influence in Asia-Pacific Region," *Forbes*, Vol. 179, No. 13, p. 25.

Lee, R. (2003) "China views FTA with ASEAN a top priority," *The Straits Times*, 6 March.

Lee, S. (2006) "The Political Economy of the Korea–US FTA: The Korean Government's FTA Strategy Revisited," paper presented at the Spring 2006 convention of the Association of Korean Political and Diplomatic History (in Korean).

Leifer, M. (2000) *Singapore's Foreign Policy: Coping with Vulnerability* (New York and London: Routledge).

Lemke, D. (1997) "The Continuation of History: Power Transition Theory and the End of the Cold War," *Journal of Peace Research*, Vol. 34, No. 1, pp. 23–36.

Lengyel, M. & D. Tussie (2006) "The Global Governance of Trade: A Trilemma," *Latin American Trade Network Working Paper No.55*, July, http://www.latn.org.ar/archivos/documentacion/PAPER_DOC55_WP_Lengyel,%20Tussie_The%20Global%

20Governance%20of%20trade%20a%20trilemma.pdf, accessed on November 15, 2007.

Li, F. & J. He (2007) "Meiguo ziyou maoyi xieding zhanlue ji Zhongguo de yingdui cuoshi [US FTA Strategy and China's Response]," *Xian Caijing Xueyuan Xuebao* [*Journal of Xi'an University of Finance and Economics*], Vol. 20, No. 3, pp. 66–70.

Lim, H. (2003) "Singapore's Perception of ASEAN–Japan Comprehensive Economic Partnership," in I. Yamazawa & D. Hiratsuka (eds) *Towards ASEAN–Japan Comprehensive Economic Partnership* (Tokyo: Institute of Developing Economies), pp. 15–39.

Lincoln, E. (2004) *East Asian Economic Regionalism* (Washington, DC: The Brookings Institution).

Liu, C. (2005) "Shijie shuangbian ziyou maoyi fazhan de yuanyin tedian yu woguo de duice [The Causes and Characteristics of the Development of Bilateral Trade Liberalization in the World and China's Policy]," *Sijie Jingji Yanjiu* [*World Economy Study*], No. 4, pp. 4–10.

Liu, C. & Z. Gong (2007) "Zhongguo canyu shuangbian FTAs jincheng jiqi yu APEC de zhengce xietiao [China's Participation in Bilateral FTAs and its Policy Co-ordination between FTAs and APEC]," *Yatai Jingji* [*Asia-Pacific Economic Review*], No. 2, pp. 17–20.

Liu, W. & W. Jiang (2005) "Free trade deal with Chile in the pipeline," *China Daily*, 16 August, http://www.bilaterals.org/article.php3?id_article=2496, accessed on September 25, 2007.

López Portillo, J. (1988) *Mis Tiempo* (Mexico: Fernández Editores).

Luna, M., R. Tirado, & F. Valdéz (1986) "Businessmen and Politics in Mexico," in S. Maxfield & R. Anzaldúa (eds) *Government and Private Sector in Contemporary Mexico* (San Diego, CA: Center for U.S.–Mexican Studies, University of California, San Diego).

Lustig, N. (1992) *Mexico: The Remaking of an Economy* (Washington, DC: Brookings Institution).

Lyman, D. (1989) "Astucia Diplomática: Política Estadounidense para un Pacto de Subsidios Bilateral y la Entrade de México al GATT (1980, 1985)," in B. Torres & P. Falk (eds) *La Adhesión de México al GATT: Repercusiones Internas e Impacto sobre las Relaciones México-Estados Unidos* (México: El Colegio de México).

Ma, Y. (2004) "Yuanchandi guize de 'huise' quyu yu qianzai bilei [The 'Grey' Area of Rules of Origin and Potential Barriers]," *Tongji yu Juece* [*Statistics and Decision*], Vol. 6, pp. 46–7.

MacIntyre, A. (2001) "Institutions and Investors: The Politics of Economic Crisis in Southeast Asia," *International Organization*, Vol. 55, No. 1, pp. 81–122.

Manger, M. (2005) "Competition and Bilateralism in Trade Policy: The Case of Japan's Free Trade Agreements," *Review of International Political Economy*, Vol. 12, No. 5, pp. 804–28.

——— (2009) *Investing in Protection: The Politics of Preferential Trade Agreements between North and South* (Cambridge: Cambridge University Press).

Mansfield, E. D. & E. Reinhardt (2003) "Multilateral Determinants of Regionalism: The Effects of GATT/WTO on the Formation of Preferential Trading Arrangements," *International Organization*, Vol. 57, No. 4, pp. 829–62.

Mansfield, E. & H. Milner (1999) "The New Wave of Regionalism," *International Organization*, Vol. 53, No. 3, pp. 589–627.

Mansfield, E., H. Milner, & J. C. Pevehouse (2004) *Vetoing Cooperation: The Impact of Veto Players on International Trade Agreements* (unpublished manuscript).

Markheim, D. (2008) "Free Trade Agreements Promoting Prosperity in 2008," 2 May, http://www.heritage.org/research/tradeandforeignaid/bg2132.cfm#_ftn10, accessed on May 12, 2008.

Mastanduno, M. (2003) "Incomplete Hegemony: The United States and Security Order in Asia," in M. Alagappa (ed.) *Asian Security Order: Instrumental and Normative Features* (Stanford: Stanford University Press), pp. 141–66.

Mattli, W. (1999) *The Logic of Regional Integration. Europe and Beyond* (Cambridge: Cambridge University Press).

McLachlan, C., L. Shore, & M. Weiniger (2007) *International Investment Arbitration Substantive Principles* (Oxford: Oxford University Press).

McNamara, K. (1999) "Consensus and Constraints: Ideas and Capital Mobility in European Monetary Integration," *Journal of Common Market Studies*, Vol. 37, No. 3, pp. 455–76.

Mearsheimer, J. J. (2006) "China's Unpeaceful Rise," *Current History*, Vol. 105, No. 690, pp. 160–2.

Medeiros, E. S. (2005/06) "Strategic Hedging and the Future of Asia-Pacific Stability," *Washington Quarterly*, Vol. 29, No. 1, pp. 145–67.

Medeiros, E. S. & M. Taylor Fravel (2003) "China's New Diplomacy," *Foreign Affairs*, Vol. 82, No. 6 (November/December), pp. 22–35.

Meseguer, C. (2004) "What Role for Learning? The Diffusion of Privatization in OECD and Latin American Countries," *Journal of Public Politics*, Vol. 24, pp. 299–325.

Mesquita Moriera, M. & J. Blyde (2006) "Chile's Integration Strategy: Is There Room for Improvement?" *IADB-INTAL-ITD Working Paper No. 21* (Washington, DC: IADB).

Messerlin, P. A. & J. Zarrouk (2000) "Trade Facilitation: Technical Regulations and Customs Procedures," *The World Economy*, Vol. 23, No. 4, pp. 574–93.

Mexico–U.S. Business Committee (MUSBC) (1987) *Report of the Advisory Group on Capital Development for Mexico* (Washington, DC: Mexico–U.S. Business Committee).

———— (1989a) "Testimony of Guy F. Erb. Hearing on Bilateral Trade Agreements by the Subcommittee on International Trade, Committee of Finance, U.S. Senate," March 13, 1989 (Washington, DC: U.S. Council of the Mexico–U.S. Business Committee).

———— (1989b) *Options for Liberalizing U.S.–Mexico Trade and Investment* (Washington, DC: U.S. Council of the Mexico–U.S. Business Committee).

Milner, H. (1997) "Industries, Governments, and Regional Trade Blocs," in E. D. Mansfield & H. V. Milner (eds) *The Political Economy of Regionalism* (New York, NY: Columbia University Press), pp. 77–106.

Ministry of Economy Trade and Industry (METI), Japan (2000a) *White Paper on International Trade 2000*. Tokyo: METI. http://www.meti.go.jp/english/report/index.html, accessed on October 1, 2008.

———— (2000b) "The Economic Foundations of Japanese Trade Policy: Promoting a Multilayered Trade Policy," http://www.meti.go.jp/english/report/data/g00W021e.pdf, accessed on October 11, 2007.

———— (2006) *2006 Report on the WTO Inconsistency of Trade Policies by Major Trading Partners* (Tokyo: Tsūshō Sangyō Chōsakai).

———— (2007) *Tsūshou Hakusho 2007* [*White Paper on International Economy and Trade 2007*] (Tokyo: METI).

Ministry of Finance and Economy of Korea (MOFE) (2005) *Economic Bulletin*, Vol. 27, No. 11, 22 November.

Ministry of Foreign Affairs and Trade of Korea (MOFAT) (2004) *Rules and Procedures on the Special Law to Support Farmers and Fishermen affected by FTAs*, http://www.fta.go.kr/pds/data/200407224131655.pdf, accessed on May 3, 2008.

———— (2006) *Key Initiatives of Year 2006* (Seoul: MOFAT).

266   Bibliography

Ministry of Foreign Affairs, China (2005) *Hu Jintao Delivers an Important Speech at the UN Summit*, 16 September, http://www.fmprc.gov.cn/eng/wjdt/zyjh/t212614.htm, accessed on August 12, 2007.

Ministry of Foreign Affairs (MOFA), Japan (2000) *Areas Covered by Agreement Between Japan and the Republic of Singapore for a New-Age Economic Partnership (JSEPA)*.

Ministry of Trade and Industry, Singapore (2004) *Agreement between Japan and the Republic of Singapore for a New-Age Economic Partnership: Media Info-Kit*.

Mo, J. (1999) "The Politics of Economic Reform," in *The Politics of the Economic Crisis in Asia: Consensus and Controversies* (Washington, DC: Carnegie Endowment for International Peace, CEIP).

Mo, J. & C. Moon (2003) "Business–Government Relations under Kim Dae-jung," in S. Haggard, W. Lim, & E. Kim (eds) *Economic Crisis and Corporate Restructuring in Korea: Reforming the Chaebol* (New York: Cambridge University Press), pp. 127–49.

Mochizuki, M. M. (2007) "Japan's Shifting Strategy toward the Rise of China," *Journal of Strategic Studies*, Vol. 30, pp. 739–76.

Montero, D. (2007) "China, Pakistan team up on energy," *The Christian Science Monitor*, 13 April.

Moon, C. (2005) "Community-Building in Northeast Asia: A South Korean Perspective," presented at conference *Northeast Asia's New Institutional Architecture and Community-Building in a Post-9/11 World* (Berkeley: Berkeley APEC Study Center, University of California at Berkeley).

Morales, I. (2006) "Contested Regionalisms in the Americas: The American and Brazilian Approaches—Convergence or Dissent?" in T. Nakamura (ed.) *The Dynamics of East Asian Regionalism in Comparative Perspective* (Tokyo: Institute of Social Science, University of Tokyo), pp. 67–80.

Moravcsik, A. (1991) "Negotiating the Single European Act: National Interests and Conventional Statecraft in the European Community," *International Organization*, Vol. 45, No. 1, pp. 19–56.

——— (1993) "Preferences and Power in the European Community: A Liberal Intergovernmental Approach," *Journal of Common Market Studies*, Vol. 31, pp. 18–85.

Mulgan, A. (2005) "Where Tradition Meets Change: Japan's Agricultural Politics in Transition," *The Journal of Japanese Studies*, Vol. 31, No. 2, pp. 261–98.

Munakata, N. (2001) "Evolution of Japan's Policy Toward Economic Integration," *2001CNAPS Working Paper*, December (Washington DC, Brookings Institution).

——— (2006a) *Transforming East Asia: The Evolution of Regional Economic Integration* (Washington, DC: Brookings Institution Press).

——— (2006b) "Has Politics Caught up with Markets? In Search of East Asian Economic Regionalism," in P. J. Katzenstein & T. Shiraishi (eds) *Beyond Japan: The Dynamics of East Asian Regionalism* (Ithaca: Cornell University Press), pp. 130–57.

Muramatsu, M. & E. Krauss (1987) "The Conservative Policy Line and the Development of Patterned Pluralism," in K. Yamamura & Y. Yasuba (eds) *The Political Economy of Japan* (Stanford: Stanford University Press), pp. 516–54.

Nakahata, T. (2005) "Nichiboku EPA to Nihon Kigyô [The Japan–Mexico EPA and Japanese firms]," in *JETRO, Shinkôkoku no taigai keizai senryaku (FTA nado) to nihon kigyô [The Economic Strategy (including FTAs) of Emerging Countries and Japanese Firms]* (Tokyo: JETRO), pp. 302–22.

Nakagawa, J. (2004a) "Keizai Kisei no Kokusaiteki Chôwa VIII Kyôsô Hô no Kokusaiteki Chôwa (1) [International harmonization of economic regulation, VIII International harmonization of competition law (1)]," *Bôeki to Kanzei [Trade and Tariffs]*, Vol. 52, No. 6, pp. 46–54.

―――― (2004b) "Keizai Kisei no Kokusaiteki Chōwa VIII Kyōsō Hō no Kokusaiteki Chōwa (2) [International harmonization of economic regulation, VIII International harmonization of competition law (2)]," *Bōeki to Kanzei [Trade and Tariffs]*, Vol. 52, No. 7, pp. 27–41.

―――― (2006) "Taigai keizai seisaku: Nichibei kōzō kyōgi kara Higashi Ajia Kyōdōtai he [External economic policy: From Structural Impediments Initiative to East Asian Community]," in Institute of Social Science, University of Tokyo (ed.), *"Ushinawareta 10-nen" wo koete, II. Koizumi kaikaku heno jidai [Beyond the "Lost decade": An era toward Koizumi reform]* (Tokyo: University of Tokyo Press), pp. 313–40.

―――― (2007) "No More Negotiated Deals?: Settlement of Trade and Investment Disputes in East Asia," *Journal of International Economic Law*, Vol. 10, No. 4, pp. 837–67.

Nam, Y., Y. Nam, J. Lee, M. Ji, & I. Cheong (2004) "Economic Effects of Korea–China FTA and the Main Issues," *KIEP Policy Analysis 04-03* (Seoul: KIEP).

National Bureau of Statistics of China (1998–2007) *China Statistical Yearbook*.

Newmayer, E. & L. Spess (2005) "Do Bilateral Investment Treaties Increase Foreign Direct Investment to Developing Countries?" *World Development*, Vol. 33, No. 10, pp. 1567–85.

Ng, F. & A. Yeats (2003) "Major Trade Trends in East Asia: What are their Implications for Regional Cooperation and Growth?" *Policy Research Working Paper* 3084 (Washington, DC, USA: The World Bank).

Nogués, J. (1986) "Nota sobre los Casos de Aranceles Compensatorios de Estados Unidos en contra de México," *Estudios Mexicanos*, Vol. 1, No. 2, pp. 337–55.

Nowak-Lehmann, F., D. Herzer, & S. Vollmer (2005) "The Free Trade Agreement between Chile and the EU: Its Potential Impact on Chile's Export Industry," *Discussion Paper* 125 (Gottingen, Germany: Ibero-American Institute for Economic Research, Georg-August-Universitat).

"NW: East Asia FRA Crucial, Execs Say" (2004) *Nikkei Report*, 29 March.

Ogita, T. (2003) "Japan as a Late-Coming FTA Holder: Trade Policy Change for Asian Orientation?" in J. Okamoto (ed.) *Wither Free Trade Agreements? Proliferation, Evaluation, and Multilateralization* (Japan: Institute of Developing Economies), pp. 216–51.

Oike, A. (2007) "Higashi Ajia-wo Butai-tosuru Kakkoku-no Kobo [Struggles over FTAs among Major States in East Asia]" *Boueki to Kanzei [Trade and Tariffs]*, September, pp. 10–40.

Oliveira, G. (2007) "What Went Wrong? Brazil, the United States and the FTAA," in I. Studer & C. Wise (eds) *Requiem or Revival? The Promise of North American Integration* (Washington, DC: The Brookings Institution Press), pp. 124–46.

Ong, E. C. (2003) "Anchor East Asian Free Trade in ASEAN," *Washington Quarterly*, Vol. 26, No. 2, pp. 57–72.

Ono, K. (2007) "The Australia–Japan FTA Negotiations: What Do They Really Mean?" *Japan Focus*, 24 July, http://www.bilaterals.org/article.php3?id_article=9758, accessed on October 18, 2007.

Organization for Economic Cooperation and Development (OECD) (2003) *OECD Economy Survey: Korea* (Paris: OECD).

Organization of American States, *Foreign Trade Information System*, www.sice.oas.org.

Oyane, S. (2003) "The International Political Economy of FTA Proliferation," in *Whither Free Trade Agreements?: Proliferation, Evaluation, Multilateralization*, J. Okamoto (ed.). Tokyo: Institute of Developing Economies.

"Pak–China FTA" (2006) *Business Recorder*, December 29.

"Pakistan: China displays growing interest in Pakistan" (2007) *Asia Money*, June 12.

Pandey, S. (2005) "EC versus United States: Zeroing or No Zeroing—The Biggest Antidumping Issue," February 11, 2005, http://ssrn.com/abstract=860084.

Pang, E. (2007) "Embedding Security into Free Trade: The Case of the United States–Singapore Free Trade Agreement," *Contemporary Southeast Asia*, Vol. 29, No. 1, pp. 1–32.

Pangestu, M. & S. Gooptu (2004) "New Regionalism: Options for China and East Asia," in H. Kharas & K. Krumm (eds) *East Asia Integrates* (Washington, DC: The World Bank), pp. 79–99.

Park, S. & M. G. Koo (2007) "Forming a Cross-Regional Partnership: The South Korea–Chile FTA and Its Implications," Pacific Affairs, Vol. 80, No. 2, pp. 259–78.

Pastor, M. (1998) "Pesos, Policies, and Predictions: Why the Crisis, Why the Surprise, and Why the Recovery?" in C. Wise (ed.) *The Post-NAFTA Political Economy: Mexico and the Western Hemisphere* (University Park, PA: Pennsylvania State University Press), pp. 119–47.

Pastor, M. & C. Wise (1994) "The Origins and Sustainability of Mexico's Free-Trade Policy," *International Organization*, Vol. 36, No. 2, pp. 195–231.

Pastor, R. A. & J. Castañeda (1988) *Limits to Friendship: The United States and Mexico* (New York: Knopf).

Pekkanen, S. (2008) *Japan's Aggressive Legalism: Law and Foreign Trade Politics Beyond the WTO* (Stanford: Stanford University Press).

Pekkanen, S., M. Solís, & S. N. Katada (2007) "Trading Gains for Control: International Trade Forums and Japanese Foreign Economic Policy," *International Studies Quarterly*, Vol. 51, No. 4, pp. 945–70.

Pempel, T. J., (ed.) (2005) *Remapping East Asia: The Construction of a Region* (Ithaca: Cornell University Press).

Pempel, T. J. & S. Urata (2006) "Japan: a New Move toward Bilateral Trade Agreements," in V. K. Aggarwal & S.Urata (eds) *Bilateral Trade Agreements in the Asia-Pacific* (New York and London: Routledge), pp. 75–94.

Peñaloza Webb, T. (1985) "La Adhesión de México al GATT," *Comercio Exterior*, Vol. 35, No. 12, pp. 1160–8.

Peng Er, L. (2001) "Japan's Diplomatic Initiatives in Southeast Asia," in S. J. Maswood (ed.) *Japan and East Asian Regionalism* (New York and London: Routledge), pp. 118–31.

Perroni, C. & J. Whalley (2000) "The New Regionalism: Trade Liberalization or Insurance?" *Canadian Journal of Economics*, Vol. 33, No. 1, pp. 1–24.

Phillips, N. (2008) "The Politics of Trade and the Limits to U.S. Power in the Americas," in D. Sanchez-Ancochea & K. Shadlen (eds) *The Political Economy of Hemispheric Integration* (London: Palgrave Macmillan), pp. 147–69.

Pitofsky, R. (1999) "Competition Policy in a Global Economy—Today and Tomorrow," *Journal of International Economic Law*, Vol. 2, No. 3, pp. 403–11.

Porras, J. I. (2003) "la Estrategia Chilena de Acuerdos Comerciales: un Análisis Político," *Working Paper 36, Division of Trade and Integration, UN Economic Commission for Latin America and the Caribbean* (Santiago: ECLAC).

Press-Barnathan, G. (2003) *Organizing the World: The United States and Regional Cooperation in Asia and Europe* (New York and London: Routledge).

"President Roh Says Seoul's FTA with Beijing Inevitable" (May 23, 2007) *Chosun Ilbo*.

Presidential Committee on Northeast Asian Cooperation (2004) *Toward a Peaceful and Prosperous Northeast Asia* (Seoul: the Government of Republic of Korea).

Preusse, H. G. (2004) "The Future of MERCOSUR," in G. Boyd, A. Rugman, & S. Weintraub (eds) *Free Trade in the Americas* (North Hampton: Edward Elgar), pp. 127–52.

Purcell, J. F. (1982) "Trade Conflicts and U.S.–Mexico Relations," *Working Papers in U.S.–Mexican Studies*, Program in U.S.–Mexican Studies (San Diego: UCSD).

Pyo, H. K. (1999) "The Financial Crisis in Korea and Its Aftermath: A Political-Economic Perspective," a paper presented to the Center for International Political Economy and the Paul H. Nitze School of Advanced International Studies (Washington, DC: The Johns Hopkins University).

Qiu, D. (2005) "Zhongguo-Dongmeng ziyou maoyiqu: Zhongguo heping jueqi de diyuan jingjixue sikao [China–ASEAN Free Trade Area: Geo-economic analysis of China's peaceful rise]," *Dangdai Yatai [Contemporary Asia-Pacific]*, No. 1, pp. 8–13.

Rajan, R., R. Sen, & R. Siregar (2001) *Singapore and Free Trade Agreements: Economic Relations with Japan and the United States* (Singapore: Institute of Southeast Asian Studies).

Ramasamy, B. & M. Yeung. (2007) "Malaysia—Trade Policy Review (2006)," *The World Economy*, Vol. 30, No. 8, pp. 1193–208.

Rao, G. (2005) "Guoji falu zhixu yu Zhongguo de heping fazhan [International Legal Order and China's Peaceful Development]," *Waijiao Pinglun [Foreign Affairs Review]*, No. 6, pp. 48–54.

Ravenhill, J. (2000) "APEC Adrift: Implications for Economic Regionalism in Asia and the Pacific," *The Pacific Review*, Vol. 13, No. 2, pp. 319–33.

——— (2001) *APEC and the Construction of Pacific Rim Regionalism* (Cambridge: Cambridge University Press).

——— (2005) "The Political Economy of the New Asia-Pacific Bilateralism: Benign, Banal, or Simply Bad?" in V. Aggarwal & S. Urata (eds) *Bilateral Trade Agreements in Asia-Pacific: Origins, Evolution, and Implications* (New York and London: Routledge), pp. 27–49.

——— (2008) "Preferential Trade Agreements and the Future of Australian Trade Policy," *Australian Journal of International Affairs*, Vol. 62, No. 2, pp. 121–8.

Riezman, R. (1985) "Customs Unions and the Core," *Journal of International Economics*, Vol. 19, No. 3-4, pp. 355–65.

Rodrik, D. (2007) *One Economics, Many Recipes: Globalization, Institutions, and Economic Growth* (Princeton, NJ: Princeton University Press).

Rogowski, R. (1989) *Commerce and Coalitions* (Princeton: Princeton University Press).

Ros, J. (1987) "Mexico from Oil Boom to the Debt Crisis: An Analysis of Policy Response to External Shocks," in R. Thorp & L. Whitehead (eds) *Latin American Debt and the Adjustment Crisis* (Pittsburg: University of Pittsburgh Press), pp. 68–116.

——— (1994) "On the Political Economy of Market and State Reform in Mexico," in W. C. Smith, C. H. Acuña, & E. A. Gamarra (eds) *Democracy, Markets, and Structural Reform in Latin America: Argentina, Bolivia, Brazil, Chile, and Mexico* (Miami: North–South Center, University of Miami and Transaction Publishers), pp. 297–323.

Rosales, O. (2003) "Chile–U.S. Free Trade Agreement: Lessons and Best Practices," paper presented to the American Chamber of Commerce (Washington, DC).

Rosales, O. & M. Kuwayama (2007) "Latin America Meets China and India: Prospects and Challenges for Trade and Investment," *CEPAL Review*, Vol. 93, pp. 81–103.

Ross, R. S. (2006) "Balance of Power Politics and the Rise of China: Accommodation and Balancing in East Asia," *Security Studies*, Vol. 15, No. 3, pp. 355–95.

Rozman, G. (2004) *Northeast Asia's Stunted Regionalism: Bilateral Distrust in the Shadow of Globalization* (Cambridge: Cambridge University Press).

——— (2006) "South Korean–Japanese Relations as a Factor in Stunted Regionalism," a paper presented at conference "Northeast Asia's Economic and Security Regionalism: Old Constraints and New Prospects," (Los Angeles, USA: Center for International Studies, University of Southern California).

Saavedra-Rivano, N. (1993) "Chile and Japan: Opening Doors through Trade," in B. Stallings & G. Székely (eds) *Japan, the United States, and Latin America: Toward a Trilateral Relationship in the Western Hemisphere* (Baltimore: Johns Hopkins University Press), pp. 191–209.

Sáez, S. (2005a) "Chile," in IDB/INTAL *Talleres de Formulación de Políticas Comerciales Nacionales* (Buenos Aires: INTAL).

——— (2005b) "Implementing Trade Policy in Latin America: The Cases of Chile and Mexico," *Working Paper 54, Division of Trade and Integration, UN Economic Commission for Latin America and the Caribbean* (Santiago: ECLAC).

Sáez, S., J. Salazar, & R. Vicuña (1995) "Antecedentes y Resultados de la Estrategia Comercial del Gobierno Alywin," *Colección de Estudios Cieplan*, Vol. 41, pp. 41–66.

Sáez, S. & J. G. Valdés (1999) "Chile and its 'Lateral' Trade Policy," *CEPAL Review*, Vol. 67, pp. 854–99.

Salacuse, J. W. & N. P. Sullivan (2005) "Do BIT's Really Work?: An Evaluation of Bilateral Investment Treaties and Their Grand Bargain," *Harvard International Law Journal*, Vol. 46, No. 1, pp. 67–130.

Salinas de Gortari, C. (2002) *México: El Difícil Paso a la Modernidad* (México: Planeta).

Sally, R. (2004) *Southeast Asia in WTO: Southeast Asia Background Series No. 5* (Singapore: Institute of Southeast Asian Studies).

——— (2006) "Free Trade Agreements and the Prospects of Regional Integration in East Asia," *Asian Economic Policy Review*, Vol. 1, No. 2, pp. 306–21.

——— (2007) "Thai Trade Policy: From Non-discriminatory Liberalization to FTAs," *The World Economy*, Vol. 30, No. 10, pp. 1594–620.

Samsung Economic Research Institute (SERI) (2001) *Three Years after IMF Bailout* (Seoul: SERI).

Sato, Y. (2007) "Indonesia," in S. Azuma (ed.) *FTA-no Seijikeizai Gaku [Political Economy of FTA]* (Tokyo: IDE-JETRO), pp. 165–98.

Schott, J. J. (2000) *The WTO after Seattle* (Washington, DC: The Institute for International Economics).

——— (2001) *Prospects for Free Trade in the Americas* (Washington, DC: The Institute for International Economics).

——— (2004a) "Assessing US FTA Policy," in J. J. Schott (ed.) *Free Trade Agreements: US Strategies and Priorities* (Washington, DC: Institute for International Economics), pp. 359–81.

——— (ed.) (2004b) *Free Trade Agreements: US Strategies and Priorities* (Washington, DC: Institute for International Economics).

——— (2006) "Free Trade Agreements and US Trade Policy: A Comparative Analysis of US Initiatives in Latin America, the Asia-Pacific, and the Middle East and North Africa," *The International Trade Journal*, Vol. XX, No. 9, pp. 95–138.

——— (2007) "Trade Negotiations among NAFTA Partners: The Future of North American Economic Integration," in I. Studer & C. Wise (eds) *Requiem or Revival? The Promise of North American Integration* (Washington, DC: Brookings Institution Press), pp. 76–88.

Schott, J. J. & I. Choi (2001) *Free Trade between Korea and the United States?* (Washington, DC: Institute for International Economics).

Schuschny, A., J. Durán, & C. de Miguel (2007) "Política Comercial de Chile y los TLC con Asia: Evaluación de los Efectos de los TLC con Japón y China," paper presented at 10th Annual Conference on Global Economic Analysis at Purdue University, http://www.gtap.agecon.purdue.edu/resources/res_display.asp?RecordID=2354

Scollay, R. & J. P. Gilbert (2001) *New Regional Trading Arrangements in the Asia Pacific? Institute for International Economics*, (Washington, DC: Institute for International Economics).

Secretaria Comercio y Formento Industirial (SECOFI) Mexico (1980) "Concesiones Recibidas por México en el GATT," *Comercio Exterior*, Vol. 30, p. 2.
―― (1985) *Programa de Fomento Integral a las Exportaciones*, (mimeo).
―― (1988) *Apertura Comercial y Modernización Industrial*. México: Cuadernos de Renovación Nacional-Fondo de Cultura Económica.
Secretaría de Hacienda y Crédito Público (SHCP) (1988) *Deuda Externa. Cuadernos de Renovación Nacional* (Mexico: FCE).
Secretaría de Hacienda y Crédito Público (SHCP) & Banco de México (1985), "Carta de Intención al FMI," *Comercio Exterior*, Vol. 4, pp. 414–18.
Sekizawa, Y. (2008) "Nihon no FTA Seisaku: Sono Seiji Katei no Bunseki," [Japan's FTA Policy: An Analysis of its Political Process], *ISS Research Series, No. 26* (Tokyo: University of Tokyo Institute of Social Science).
Senado de la República (1986) *Consulta sobre el GATT* (Mexico: Talleres Gráficos de la Nación).
Severino, R. C. (2006) *Southeast Asia in Search of ASEAN Community* (Singapore: Institute of Southeast Asian Studies).
―― (2007) *Southeast Asia in Search of an ASEAN Community: Insights from the Former ASEAN Secretary-General* (Singapore: Institute of Southeast Asian Studies).
Shambaugh, D. (2002) "China's International Relations Think Tanks: Evolving Structure and Process," *China Quarterly*, Vol. 171, pp. 575–96.
Shiino, K. (2005) "Indo-no FTA: Senryaku-to Kozo Kaikaku [India's FTA: Its Strategy and Structural Reform]," in UFJ Research Institute (ed.) *Minami Ajia Kakkoku-no Saimu Shoukan Noryoku-to Wagakuni-no Shien* [Repayment Capacity in South Asian Countries and Japan's Assistant] (Tokyo: UFJ Research Institute), pp. 48–60.
Silva, V. (2001) "Estrategia y Agenda Comercial Chilena en los Años Noventa," *Working Paper 11, Division of Trade and Integration, UN Economic Commission for Latin America and the Caribbean* (Santiago: ECLAC).
―― (2004) "Chile: A Multi-track Market Access Strategy," in M. Lengyel & V. Ventura-Dias (eds) *Trade Policy Reforms in Latin America: Multilateral Rules and Domestic Institutions* (London: Palgrave Macmillan), pp. 27–46.
Simmons, B. A., F. Dobbin, & G. Garrett (2006) "Introduction: The International Diffusion of Liberalism," *International Organization*, Vol. 60, pp. 781–810.
Singh, H. (2006) "Stronger Through Alliance," *Malaysian Business*, Vol. 1 January, p. 14.
Soesastro, H. (2004) "Towards a U.S.–Indonesia Free Trade Agreement," *CSIS Working Paper Series*, No.85 (Jakarta: Centre for Strategic and International Studies).
―― (2006) "Regional Integration in East Asia: Achievements and Future Prospects," *Asian Economic Policy Review*, Vol. 1, No. 2, pp. 215–34.
Soeya, Y. (2004) "Japan in East Asia: Changes in the 1990s and New Regional Strategy," *RIETI Discussion Paper Series*, 04-E-013 (Tokyo: RIETI).
Sohn, C. (2001) "Korea's FTA Developments: Experiences and Perspectives with Chile, Japan, and the US," paper presented at conference "Regional Trading Arrangements: Stocktake and Next Steps" (Bangkok: Trade Policy Forum).
Sohn, C. & J. Yoon (2001) "Does the Gravity Model Fit Korea's Trade Patterns?" *KIEP Working Paper 01-01* (Seoul: KIEP).
Solís, M. (2003) "Japan's New Regionalism: The Politics of Free Trade Talks with Mexico," *Journal of East Asian Studies*, Vol. 3, pp. 377–404.
―― (2006) "How Japan's economic class views China and the future of Asian Regionalism," *Internet Research Report* (Japan Institute of International Affairs), http://www2.jiia.or.jp/en/pdf/polcy_report/pr20060712.pdf.

—— (Forthcoming) "Can FTAs Deliver Market Liberalization in Japan? A study of Domestic Political Determinants," *Review of International Political Economy*.

Solís, M. & S. N. Katada (2007a) "Understanding East Asian Cross-Regionalism: An Analytical Framework," *Pacific Affairs*, Vol. 80, No. 2, pp. 229–58.

—— (2007b) "The Japan–Mexico FTA: A Cross-Regional Step in the Path towards Asian Regionalism," *Pacific Affairs*, Vol. 80, pp. 279–302.

Solís, M. & S. Urata (2007) "Japan's New Foreign Economic Policy: A Shift toward a Strategic and Activist Model?" *Asian Economic Policy Review*, Vol. 2, pp. 227–45.

Song, Z. (2007) "MeiHan FTA yingxiang Zhongguo" [The Impact of US–South Korea FTA on China], *Shijie Zhishi* [*World Affairs*], No. 9, pp. 38–9.

"South Korea: US Buyers Keen to Source more Apparel, Textiles" (2007) *just-style.com*, 17 April.

Stallings, B. (2009) "Regional Integration in Latin America: Lessons for East Asia," in T. Nakamura (ed.) *East Asian Regionalism from Legal Perspective: Current Features and a Vision for the Future* (New York and London: Routledge), pp. 59–79.

Stefoni, C. & C. Fuentes (1998) "Chile and Mercosur: How Far Do We Want Integration to Go?" *Discussion Paper 25, Management of Social Transformations Project* (Paris: UNESCO).

Stoler, A. (2004) "Australia–US Free Trade: Benefits and Costs of an Agreement," in J. Schott (ed.) *Free Trade Agreements: US Strategies and Priorities* (Washington, DC: Institute for International Economics), pp. 95–116.

—— (2006) "Regionalism v. Multilateralism: A View from the Asia-Pacific," paper presented at CEPAL-BID-OBREAL Regional Integration Seminar, Santiago, Chile.

Story, D. (1986) *Industry, the State, and Public Policy in Mexico* (Austin: University of Texas Press).

Strang, D. (1991) "Adding Social Structure to Diffusion Models: An Event History Framework," *Sociological Methods and Research*, Vol. 19, No. 3, pp. 324–53.

Stubbs, R. (2002) "ASEAN Plus Three: Emerging East Asian Regionalism?" *Asian Survey*, Vol. 42, No. 3, pp. 440–55.

Swaine, M. D. & Kamphausen, R. D. (2005) "Military Modernization in Taiwan," in A. J. Tellis and M. Wills (eds) in *Strategic Asia 2005–06: Military Modernization in an Era of Uncertainty* (Seattle: National Bureau of Asian Research), pp. 387–422.

Swank, D. (2006) "Tax policy in an Era of Internationalization: Explaining the Spread of Neoliberalism," *International Organization*, Vol. 60, pp. 847–82.

"Taiwan's Ma Seeks FTA with China" (July 3, 2007) *Daily Times*, Pakistan.

Takamine, T. (2002) "Domestic Determinants of Japan's China Aid Policy: The Changing Balance of Foreign Policymaking Power," *Japanese Studies*, Vol. 22, No. 2, pp. 191–206.

Tanner, M. S. (2002) "Changing Windows on a Changing China: The Evolving 'Think Tank' System and the Case of the Public Security Sector," *China Quarterly*, Vol. 171, pp. 559–74.

Ten Kate, A. (1992a) "Trade Liberalization and Economic Stabilization in Mexico: Lessons of Experience," *World Development*, Vol. 20, pp. 659–72.

—— (1992b) "El Ajuste Estructural de México. Dos Historias Diferentes," *Pensamiento Iberoamericano*, Vol. 21, pp. 57–78.

Ten Kate, A. & F. de Mateo (1989a) "Apertura Comercial y Estructura de la Protección en México: Estimaciones Cuantitativas de los Ochenta," *Comercio Exterior*, Vol. 39, No. 4, pp. 312–29.

—— (1989b) "Apertura Comercial y Estructura de la Protección en México: Un Análisis de la Relación entre Ambas," *Comercio Exterior*, Vol. 39, No. 6, pp. 497–511.

Terada, T. (2003) "Constructing an East Asian Concept and Growing Regional Identity: From EAEC to ASEAN+3," *The Pacific Review*, Vol. 16, No. 2, pp. 251–77.

—— (2005) "The Japan–Australia Partnership in the Era of the East Asian Community: Can they Advance Together?" *Australia–Japan Research Centre, Pacific Economic Paper no. 352*, http://www.waseda.jp/asianstudies/en/news/ias/02.html, accessed on October 7, 2007.

—— (2006a) "Forming an East Asian Community: A site for Japan–China Power Struggles," *Japanese Studies*, Vol. 26, No. 1, pp. 5–17.

—— (2006b) "The Making of Asian's First Bilateral FTA: Origins and Regional Implications of the Japan–Singapore Economic Partnership Agreement," *Australia–Japan Research Centre, Pacific Economic Paper no. 354*, http://www.waseda.jp/asianstudies/news/ias/doc/JSEPA-Terada_pep354.pdf, accessed on October 10, 2007.

Thacker, S. C. (2000) *Big Business, the State, and Free Trade: Constructing Coalitions in Mexico* (New York: Cambridge University Press).

Torres, B., & P. Falk (1989) *La Adhesión de México al GATT* (México: El Colegio de México).

Tow, W. T. (2005) "Sino-American Relations and the 'Australian Factor': Inflated Expectations or Discriminate Engagement?" *Australian Journal of International Affairs*, Vol. 59, No. 4, pp. 451–67.

Trade Policy Bureau, METI (2006). *2006 Report on the WTO Inconsistency of Trade Policies by Major Trading Partners.* (Tokyo: Tsūshō Sangyō Chōsakai).

Tsebelis, G. (1995) "Decision Making in Political Systems: Veto Players in Presidentialism, Parliamentarism, Multicameralism, and Multipartyism," *British Journal of Political Science*, Vol. 25, No. 3, pp. 289–325.

—— (1999) "Veto Players and Law Production in Parliamentary Democracies: An Empirical Analysis," *The American Political Science Review*, Vol. 93, No. 3, pp. 591–609.

Tussie, D. & M. Lengyel (2006) *The Global Governance of Trade: A Trilemma*, http://www.latn.org.ar/archivos/documentacion/PAPER_DOC55_WP_Lengyel,%20Tussie_The%20Global%20Governance%20of%20trade%20a%20trilemma.pdf, accessed on November 28, 2007.

Tussie, D. & C. Quiliconi (2005) "The Current Trade Context," *Occasional Paper 2005/24*, Human Development Report Office.

Twomey, C. (2000) "Japan, a 'Circumscribed Balancer': Building on Defensive Realism to Make Predictions about East Asian Security," *Security Studies*, Vol. 9, No. 4, pp. 167–205.

UNCTAD (2000) *Bilateral Investment Treaties 1959–(1999)* (New York and Geneva: United Nations), http://www.unctad.org/en/docs/poiteiiad2.en.pdf.

United States General Accounting Office (GAO) (2004) *International Trade: Intensifying Free Trade Negotiating Agenda Calls for Better Allocation of Staff and Resources* (Washington, DC: GAO).

United States Trade Representative (USTR) (2002) "Free Trade with Singapore: America's First Free Trade Agreement in Asia," *USTR Fact Sheets*, http://www.ustr.gov/Document_Library/Fact_Sheets/2002/Free_Trade_with_Singapore_America's_First_Free_Trade_Agreement_in_Asia.html, accessed on March 25, 2008.

—— (2003a) "USTR Notifies Congress of Intent to Initiate Free Trade Talks with the Dominican Republic," *Press Release*, August 2003.

—— (2003b) "USTR Notifies Congress of Intent to Initiate Free Trade Talks with Bahrain," *Press Release*. http://www.ustr.gov/Document_Library/Press_Releases/2003/August/USTR_Notifies_Congress_of_Intent_to_Initiate_Free_Trade_Talks_with_Bahrain.html?ht, accessed on April 28, 2008.

—— (2006) *2006 National Trade Estimate Report on Foreign Trade Barriers* (Washington, DC: USTR).

—— (2007a) "NAFTA Facts," *NAFTA Policy Brief*, October 2007, http://www. ustr.gov/assets/Trade_Agreements/Regional/NAFTA/Fact_Sheets/asset_upload_ file366_13495.pdf, accessed on May 11, 2008.

—— (2007b) "CAFTA–DR Facts," *CAFTA Policy Brief*, July 2007, http://www. ustr.gov/assets/Trade_Agreements/Regional/CAFTA/Briefing_Book/asset_upload_ file601_13191.pdf, accessed on May 8, 2008.

Urata, S. (2001) "Emergence of an FDI–Trade Nexus and Economic Growth in East Asia," in J. Stiglitz & S. Yusuf (eds) *Rethinking the East Asian Miracle* (New York: Oxford University Press), pp. 409–59.

—— (2005a) "East Asia's Multi-Layered Development Process: The Trade–FDI Nexus," in K. Fukasaku, M. Kawai, M. G. Plummer, & A. Trzeciak-Duval (eds) *Policy Coherence Towards East Asia: Development Challenges for OECD Countries* (Paris: OECD), pp. 347–410.

—— (2005b) "Free Trade Agreements: A Catalyst for Japan's Economic Revitalization," in T. Ito, H. Patrick, & D. E. Weinstein (eds) *Reviving Japan's Economy* (Boston: MIT Press), pp. 377–410.

—— (2006) "The Changing Patterns of International Trade in East Asia," prepared for the "East Asia Project" of the World Bank (Washington, DC: World Bank).

Urata, S., C. S. Yue, & F. Kimura (eds) (2006) *Multinationals and Economic Growth in East Asia: Foreign Direct Investment, Corporate Strategies, and National Economic Development* (London and New York: Routledge).

U.S. Senate Finance Committee (2003) Hearing on the "Implementation of US Bilateral Free Trade Agreement with Singapore and Chile," 108th Congress, First Session, June 17, 2003, S. HRG, pp. 108–333.

U.S. House of Representatives, Committee on Ways and Means. Hearing on the "Implementation of U.S. Bilateral Free Trade Agreements with Chile and Singapore," 108th Congress. First Session: June 10, 2003 (U.S. Governments Printing Office), Serial No. 108–24.

Vatikiotis, M. & M. Hiebert (2003) "China's Tight Embrace," *Far Eastern Economic Review*, Vol. 166, No. 28, pp. 28–30.

Vega Cánovas, G. (1983) "Las Exportaciones Mexicanas y el Neoproteccionismo Norteamericano," in L. Meyer (ed.) *México-Estados Unidos, 1982* (México: El Colegio de México), pp. 33–58.

—— (ed.) (1991) *México ante el Libre Comercio con América del Norte* (México: El Colegio de México-Universidad Tecnológica de México).

Vieth, W. (2005) "Bush Wins Approval of Trade Pact: Contentious House Vote to Ratify CAFTA is Seen as More of a Political than Economic Victory," *Los Angeles Times*, 28 July, A.1.

Villarreal, R. (1989) *El Desequilibrio Externo en la Industrialización de México: Un Enfoque Estructuralista* (Mexico: El Colegio de México).

Viner, J. (1950) *The Customs Union Issue* (New York and London: Carnegie Endowment for International Peace and Stevens & Sons Ltd.).

Wan, M (2003) "Economic Interdependence and Economic Cooperation: Mitigating Conflict and Transforming Security Order in Asia," in M. Alagappa (ed.), *Asian Security Order: Instrumental and Normative Features*, pp. 280–310.

—— (2006) *Sino-Japanese Relations* (Stanford: Stanford University Press).

Wang, Y. (2005) "'Dongya Gongtongti': diqu yu guojia de guandian ['East Asia Community': Views of Regions and Countries]," Waijiao Pinglun [Foreign Affairs Review], Vol. 83, pp. 19–29.

Watanabe, Y. (2004) "Japan's FTA Strategy and the Japan–Mexico EPA," *Gaiko Forum*, English Edition, Vol. 4, No. 2, pp. 54–63.

Weintraub, S. (1984) *Free Trade between Mexico and the United States?* (Washington, DC: The Brookings Institution).

——— (1989) *Mexico Frente al Acuerdo de Libre Comercio Canada-Estados Unidos* (Mexico: Editorial Diana).

——— (1990) *A Marriage of Convenience: Relations between Mexico and the United States* (New York: Oxford University Press).

——— (2004) "Lessons from the Chile Singapore Free Trade Agreement," in J. Schott (ed.) *Free Trade Agreements: US Strategies and Priorities* (Washington, DC: Institute for International Economics), pp. 79–92.

Wesley, M. (2008) "The Strategic Effects of Preferential Trade Agreements," *Australian Journal of International Affairs*, June 2008, Vol. 62, No. 2, pp. 214–28.

White, H. (2005) "The Limits to Optimism: Australia and the Rise of China," *Australian Journal of International Affairs*, Vol. 59, No. 4, pp. 469–80.

Wijers-Hasegawa, Y. (2006) "METI's Asia-Oceania FTA Pitch Surprises, But Is Predictable: Seizing the Initiative Before It's Too Late," *Japan Times*, 18 April.

Wils, Wouter P. J. (2005). "Is Criminalization of EU Competition Law the Answer?" *World Competition: Law and Economics Review*, Vol. 28, No. 2, pp. 117–59.

Wilhelmy, M. (2005) "Chile, Latin America, and the Asia-Pacific Region," *Revista de Ciencia Política*, Vol. 25, No. 2, pp. 190–7.

Wilson, J. S., C. L. Mann, & T. Otsuki (2003) "Trade Facilitation and Economic Development," *World Bank Policy Research Working Paper No.2988* (Washington, DC: World Bank).

Winters, L. A. (1991) *International Economics*, 4th edn (London: Harper-Collins).

Wise, C. (1998) "Introduction: NAFTA, Mexico, and the Western Hemisphere," in C. Wise (ed.) *The Post-NAFTA Political Economy: Mexico and the Western Hemisphere* (University Park: Pennsylvania State University Press), pp. 1–40.

——— (2007) "No Turning Back: Trade Integration and the New Development Mandate," in I. Studer & C. Wise (eds) *Requiem or Revival? The Promise of North American Integration* (Washington, DC: Brookings Institution Press), pp. 1–23.

——— (2008) "The U.S. Competitive Liberalization Strategy: Canada's Policy Options," in J. Daudelin & D. Schwanen (eds) *Canada among Nations: What Room to Maneuver* (Montreal and Kingston: McGill-Queen's University Press), pp. 225–47.

Wise, C. & C. Quiliconi (2007) "China's Surge in Latin American Markets: Policy Challenges and Responses," *Politics and Policy*, Vol. 35, No. 3, pp. 410–38.

Wong, J. & S. Chan (2003) "China–ASEAN Free Trade Agreement: Shaping Future Economic Relations," *Asian Survey*, Vol. 43, No. 3 (May/June), pp. 507–26.

Woo-Cumings, M. (1999) "Introduction: Chalmers Johnson and the Politics of Nationalism and Development," in M. Woo-Cumings (ed.) *The Developmental State* (Ithaca: Cornell University Press), pp. 1–31.

World Bank (1993) *The East Asian Miracle: Economic Growth and Public Policy* (Oxford: Oxford University Press).

——— (2000a) *East Asia: Recovery and Beyond* (Washington, DC: World Bank).

——— (2000b) *Trade Blocs* (New York: Oxford University Press).

——— (2005) *Global Economic Prospects* (Washington, DC: World Bank).

World Trade Organization (2007) "Anti-dumping Initiations: Reporting Member vs Exporting Country, From: 1 January 1995 to 31 December 2006," http://www.wto.org/english/tratop_e/adp_e/adp_stattab3_e.xls, accessed on September 15, 2007.

Wu, X. (2007) "Meiguo yu Dongya yitihua [The United States and the Integration of East Asia]," *Guoji Wenti Yanjiu [International Studies]*, Vol. 5, pp. 47–52.

Xinhua (2006) "China, Chile Put Free Trade Agreement into Effect," October 1. http://www.bilaterals.org/article.php3?id_article=6120, accessed on July 12, 2008.

Yang, J. (2003) "Sino-Japanese Relations: Implications for Southeast Asia," *Contemporary Southeast Asia*, Vol. 25, No. 2, pp. 306–27.

Yang, Z. (2004) "FTAA: Chongji Zhongguo [FTAA: Impacts on China]," *Shijie Zhishi [World Affairs]*, No. 6, pp. 48–50.

Ye, M. (2007) "Security Institutions in Northeast Asia: Multilateral Responses to Structural Changes," in V. K. Aggarwal & M. G. Koo (eds) *Asia's New Institutional Architecture: Evolving Structures for Managing Trade, Financial, and Security Relations* (New York: Springer), pp. 121–49.

Yeo, G. (2002) "Building an ASEAN Economic Community," speech delivered at the AFTA Symposium, Jakarta, Indonesia, 31 January.

Yeo, L.H. (2006) "Japan, ASEAN, and the Construction of an East Asian Community," *Contemporary Southeast Asia*, Vol. 28, No. 2, pp. 259–75.

Yonan, A. (2004) "Asia Economy Watch: Japan, China, South Korea Mull Trade Pact," *Dow Jones International News*, 30 January.

Yoshimatsu, H. (2005) "Japan's Keidanren and Free Trade Agreements: Societal Interests and Trade Policy," *Asian Survey*, Vol. 45, No. 2, pp. 258–78.

Yu, X. (2006) "DongYa diqu ziyou maoyi xieding jincheng zhong de RiZhong jingzheng [China–Japan Competition in the Process of Reaching FTAs in East Asia]," *Xiandai Riben Jingji [Contemporary Economy of Japan]*, No. 4, pp. 17–22.

Zabludovsky, J. (1989) *Trade Liberalization and Macroeconomic Adjustment in Mexico, 1983–1988*, (Mexico: The Secretaria to Promote Commerce and Industry in Mexico [SECOFI]).

—— (1994) "Las Negociaciones del Tratado de Libre Comercio de Norte América," in *Testimonios sobre el* TLC (México: Grupo Editorial Miguel Angel Porrúa).

—— (2005) "Escenarios de la Integración Hemisférica: Implicaciones para México," in A. Ortega et al. (eds) *Hacia la Profundización de la Integración Económica de México* (México: Ibergop-México, ITAM, and Editorial Porrúa), pp. 99–109.

Zabludovsky, J. & L. S. Gómez (2007) "Beyond the FTAA: Perspectives for Hemispheric Integration," in I. Studer & C. Wise (eds) *Requiem or Revival? The Promise of North American Integration* (Washington, DC: The Brookings Institution Press), pp. 91–107.

Zeng, R. (2007) "Ta Zhili tiaoban tingjin Lamei dalu [Chile, a Springboard to Jump into Latin America]," *Zhongwai Wanju Zhizhao [Toy Industry]*, No. 6, pp. 12–13.

Zhang, A. (2006) "China's FTA wenti [China's FTA Question]," *Zhongguo Haiguan [China Custom]*, No. 9, p. 7.

Zhang, F. (2004) "Lun goujian Zhongguo de FTA zhanlue [On the Construction of China's FTA Strategy]," *Kaifang Daobao [China Opening Herald]*, No. 5, pp. 74–7.

Zhang, J. (2004) "Chile rolls out red carpet for Chinese mining firms," *China Daily*, 28 May, http://www.bilaterals.org/article.php3?id_article=186, accessed on September 25, 2007.

—— (2007) "China's FTA Arrangement with Other Countries and Its Prospects," in KPSA (Korean Political Science Association) International Conference on "The Rise of Asia and Its Future" (Seoul, Korea).

Zhang, Y. (2003) "The ASEAN Partnership with China and Japan," in *ASEAN–Japan Cooperation: A Foundation for East Asian Community* (Tokyo: Japan Center for International Exchange), pp. 223–34.

—— (2005) "Future Perspective on EAFTA and China's Strategy," RIETI BBL Seminar, 24 October, http://www.rieti.go.jp/en/events/bbl/05102401.html.

Zhang, Y., R. Huang (eds) (2004) *2004 Zhongguo Guoji Diwei Baogao* [*China's International Status Report 2004*] (Beijing: Renmin Chubanshe [People's Publishing House]).

——— (2003) *2003 Zhongguo Guoji Diwei Baogao* [*China's International Status Report 2003*] (Shanghai: Shanghai Yuandong Chubanshe [Shanghai Far East Publishers]).

Zhang, Z. (2004) "FTA: Dongya huzuo de xin langcao [FTA: A New Wave of Cooperation in Northeast Asia]," *Dongnanya* [*Southeast Asia*], Vol. 3, pp. 1–6.

Zheng, X. (2002) "Quanqiu xin yilun shuangbian ziyou maoyi tanxi [An Analysis of A New Round of Global Bilateral Free Trade]," *Duiwai Jingmao Wushi* [*World Economy & Trade*], No. 11, pp. 30–4.

——— (2003) "Shuangbian ziyou maoyi: Xin shiji Zhongguo waimao zhengce xin xuanze [Bilateral Free Trade: China's new choice of foreign trade in the new century]," *Jingmao Luntan* [*Forum of Economy and Trade*], Vol. 1, pp. 4–8.

Zoellick, R. (2001) "American Trade Leadership: What Is At Stake?" Remarks made at a speech at the Institute for International Economics, 24 September (Washington, DC).

——— (2003) "Our Credo: Free Trade and Competition," *Wall Street Journal*, 10 July, http://www.usembassy.at/en/policy/zoellick.htm.

Index

Page numbers in *italics* indicate pages containing figures or tables